The Complete Critical Assembly

The Collected *White Dwarf* (and *GM*, and *GMI*) SF Review Columns

David Langford

Other Books by David Langford

Fiction

An Account of a Meeting with Denizens of Another World, 1871
The Dragonhiker's Guide to Battlefield Covenant at Dune's Edge: Odyssey Two (collection)
Earthdoom! (with John Grant)
Guts (with John Grant)
Irrational Numbers (collection)
The Leaky Establishment
A Novacon Garland (collection)
The Space Eater

Nonfiction

A Cosmic Cornucopia (with Josh Kirby)
Critical Assembly
Critical Assembly II
Facts and Fallacies (with Chris Morgan)
Let's Hear It for the Deaf Man
The Necronomicon (with George Hay, Robert Turner and Colin Wilson)
Pieces of Langford
Platen Stories
The Science in Science Fiction (with Peter Nicholls and Brian Stableford)
The Silence of the Langford
The TransAtlantic Hearing Aid
The Third Millennium (with Brian Stableford)
The Unseen University Challenge
War in 2080: The Future of Military Technology

As Editor

The Encyclopedia of Fantasy (with John Clute, John Grant and others)
Maps: The Uncollected Stories of John Sladek (forthcoming)
Wrath of the Fanglord

The Complete Critical Assembly

The Collected *White Dwarf* (and *GM*, and *GMI*) SF Review Columns

David Langford

Cosmos Books

THE COMPLETE CRITICAL ASSEMBLY

Published by:

Cosmos Books, an imprint of Wildside Press
PO Box 301, Holicong, PA 18928-0301
www.wildsidepress.com

Columns 1 to 50 were published by Ansible Information as *Critical Assembly*, 1987; reset and expanded 1992; reissued with corrections 1994. Columns 51 to 101 were published by Ansible Information as *Critical Assembly II*, 1992; reissued with corrections 1994. The two volumes are merged in this edition.

ISBN: 1-58715-330-0

Contents

Introduction: Close to Critical

I'm still not certain how I came to sweat through years of monthly *Critical Mass* science fiction review columns in British games magazines, but the effort seems to have permanently warped a number of young minds. To this day, people keep introducing themselves with 'I remember your column from when *White Dwarf* used to be good.' Back then, sf fans would say cautiously nice things about the column while dissociating themselves from anything so uncool as the surrounding games material: 'Well, I just *thumb through it* at the newsagent's ...' All right, cheapskates, this is the street-credible edition. With notes for students, too, just like *The Waste Land*!

The worst problem of regular reviewing is that of the endless prairie. On one hand, the fiftieth adequately written fantasy trilogy about the unlikely defeat of a Dark Lord may not be hugely inferior to the first or fifteenth, but sheer monotony will have ground down the reviewer to a state of 'Oh no, not again.' On the other hand, the tiniest hummock of quality seems mountainous after the dreary plainlands, and can be greeted with more ecstasy than it merits: examples will, alas, follow. I have nothing to add about the almost godlike act of reviewing, since every time a bright thought or unsafe generalization struck me, it usually turned up in the current column. Instead, I can reveal that the very first of the columns from *White Dwarf 39* is numbered 1, and so on, allowing mathematically-minded readers to work out the *Dwarf* issue number in which each appeared by adding 38 (until this system breaks down at column 69). Next, I will teach you how to suck eggs.

A certain number of token role-playing references were dutifully inserted. For someone who never plays the games, I seem to be good at self-serving camouflage. (Watch for occasional mendacious use of game applicability to push favoured books, and guilty dragging-in of game references when the editors wanted more 'relevance'.) A tiny glossary appears at the end of the text. The aberrant column 70 resulted from a broad editorial hint that material other than book reviews could be included from time to time; what was really wanted was scabrous gossip about the games scene, but I didn't know any. Some gossip about sf people crept in, though....

The 1987 *Critical Assembly* was hastily photocopied from the original and error-raddled *Dwarf* typesetting, with an introduction, endnotes and index added by me. A posh, reset version appeared in 1992 to match the companion volume *Critical Assembly II* (1992, comprising columns 51-101), and I've revised the text slightly here and there. Blatant afterthoughts are indicated in square brackets: [I have now thought better of the previous sentence, which should be ignored]. For the sake of completeness, brief mentions of paperback reissues have been left intact. Anyone who kept the original magazines may find that an occasional paragraph seems to have migrated to an earlier column, having been cut by cruel subeditors for space reasons and later stuck back in by me for laziness reasons.

My epigraph for the whole lot was stolen at colossal expense from E. Nesbit's *The Treasure Seekers*:

'If what we have written brings happiness to any sad heart we shall not have laboured in vain. But we want the money too.'

Now read on....

1 In the Beginning

My story is that since sf and fantasy games are so often based on sf and fantasy books – occasionally even with proper acknowledgement – it's only logical that *White Dwarf* should feature this page. The first essential for anyone wishing a better grounding in sf is of course to rush out now and buy the superb hard-sf novel *The Space Eater* by David Langford (Arrow £1.75) and, approximately one-third as superb, the indispensable reference work *The Science in Science Fiction* by Nicholls, Stableford and Langford (Michael Joseph £10.95), which ... *[Enough of this – Ed.]*

Sorry about that. Let's begin by surveying some landmarks of recent sf. One which genuinely would be useful if your knowledge of the sf/fantasy field is shaky is Neil Barron's *Anatomy of Wonder: a Historical Survey and Critical Guide to the Best of SF* (Bowker £15, £21.50 hardback). At this price, most people will prefer to borrow a library copy. The book records hundreds of 'major' sf works from antiquity to 1980, with useful plot summaries (game-players take note) and idiosyncratic recommendations for building up a collection of fine sf. A unique reference book, shortlisted for the 1982 Hugo award, non-fiction category.

Somewhere in the desolate wastes of Outer Mongolia, or Watford, there may still be one person unsure of what 'Hugo Winner' on a book's jacket actually means. It *can* mean that the 97-year-old author of this rotten book once won the award for a short story published decades ago in a year of little competition. The Hugos aren't infallible, being voted by members of the World SF Convention (usually held in America – can it be coincidence that non-American work is rarely even shortlisted?) and subject to strange whims. Authors get awards for writing an sf novel for the first time in fifteen years, for being the convention's guest of honour, for dying just before voting time. Good books can win Hugos, and quite often do, but don't rely on it.

[The whirligig of time brings in his revenges. Now in 2001 there are eighteen of those little rocket-ships on my mantelpiece, and when new fans complain about the boring old sods who win Hugos without publishing anything worthwhile in the current year, they are quite often looking sidelong at me.]

Several 1982 books look likely to reach the 1983 Hugo shortlist; most have yet to be published in paperback over here. Looking at them, it seems that dinosaurs of the sf field are stirring everywhere. Arthur C. Clarke's *2010: Odyssey Two* (Granada £7.95) is of course a sequel to *2001* – to the film, where the spaceship

Discovery reaches Jupiter only, rather than the book, where it continues on the long, long haul to Saturn. Since the strength of *2001*'s mystical ending came from the teasing unanswerability of the question 'what happens next?', it's depressingly anticlimactic when Clarke now tells what happens next. And though some interesting things happen, smoothly described, there's a certain familiarity when the book halts on the brink of another and less interesting question.

Foundation's Edge by Isaac Asimov (recently published by Granada at £7.95) is yet another sequel, this time to the noted - and also quite entertaining - Foundation trilogy. At 200,000 words, the sequel seems longer than the entire original series; endless pages of grey dialogue about the fate of the galaxy add up to a vast and soggy morass of boredom, so the trilogy is weakened and not strengthened by the addition. For example, the original books' goal of peaceful Galactic Empire is now rejected, presumably because of its fascist implications ... which is all very Politically Correct but converts the first three books to pointless chronicles of misguided effort. Remarkably, *Edge* is a US bestseller.

Robert Heinlein's *Friday* (NEL £7.95) was also enthusiastically greeted, largely because it came as such a relief after his unreadably awful *'The Number of the Beast'*. *Friday* has a good future background, where all-powerful corporate states along the lines of IBM think nothing of nuking pockets of undue sales resistance; lots to annoy even the least committed feminist (being gang-raped is fine, thinks heroine Friday, if only the current guy doesn't have bad breath - and later on she shacks up with one of the nicer rapists. *Really?*); and a rambling plotline with all the thrust of overcooked spaghetti.

Three more possibles for the Hugo shortlist-of-five are William Kotzwinkle's hugely selling *E.T.* novelization (the film looks a cert for the dramatic presentation Hugo, though I prefer the daft computer games of *Tron*), Frank Herbert's *The White Plague* (fiendish scientist revenges himself on IRA murderers by inventing a plague which kills women and only women, so notoriously the predominant sex in the IRA); and, believe it or not, the pulp epic *Battlefield Earth* by L. Ron Hubbard of Scientology fame. While rumours of Hubbard's death circulate, the 'Church' of Scientology is promoting the book in America with far greater enthusiasm than its publishers, and there are fears that Scientologists may even join the 1983 World Convention - to be held in Baltimore - in huge numbers in order to vote L. Ron a Hugo.... Take these awards with a pinch of salt, friends.

The first worthwhile sf to arrive in 1983 is John Sladek's *Roderick at Random* (Granada £1.95), sequel to his *Roderick: the Education of a Young Machine.* These blackly funny books are the newest variant of Voltaire's *Candide*, with Roderick the intelligent but very confused robot trying to work out just what's so special and different about being human. With good reason, since Sladek's satire is merciless, hilariously demonstrating how humans prefer not to think for themselves but are programmed by newspapers, TV, tranquillizers, food fads or batty cults, becoming much more predictable and less rational than poor Roderick the machine. Sad, but not far from being true. Read this one.

Further off the sf trail, GMs who like to boggle players with obscure lore and puzzles will find lots in John Grant's *A Book of Numbers* (Ashgrove Press £6.95). 'This is *not* a book for mathematicians; it is a book of numerically arranged information.' (Indeed Grant is a lousy mathematician, as he shows when trying to work out probabilities for a dice-game under *26*, or speculating wonkily about *pi*.) So you find the legend of the Seven Sleepers of Ephesus amid twelve pages of entries for mystical *7*; under *90* is Theodore Sturgeon's famous law '90% of *everything* is rubbish'; the *159* entry records the 159 awful sf/fantasy titles hacked out in thirteen years by notorious Robert Lionel Fanthorpe; and so on. Enormous fun for bedside browsing.

March 1983

2 Covenant Revisited

Bulking hugely on my desk is the latest doorstop blockbuster from Stephen Donaldson, *White Gold Wielder* (Collins 509pp £8.95), the sixth book of **The Chronicles of Thomas Covenant the Unbeliever** and possibly - as the third was supposed to be - the last. That's nearly 3,000 pages of unremitting Covenant now.

I have mixed feelings about these books. As anti-heroic fantasy they're remote descendants of Michael Moorcock's **Elric** saga ... but while Elric does all the routine fantasy-hero things with just that extra doomed Byronic twist into guilt or betrayal, Covenant is utterly riddled with guilt, self-doubt and sheer disbelief in the fantasy world that needs him. In the first trilogy this left him powerful but ineffectual, as if forced to play a high-level character in a role-playing game he couldn't take seriously. The second trilogy sees him *too* powerful to be effective, as if playing a game which he now regards seriously but in which the merest twitch of his littlest finger is liable to smash the world, trample the playing board and burn the pieces.

All the books involve long, long Quests, sometimes featuring nice creations (the effective though detachable Sandhold and Sandgorgons of *The One Tree*; the ice-monsters in this book) but mainly serving to delay the final confrontation with arch-baddie Lord Foul, in which Donaldson juggles with power, rejection, sacrifice, apotheosis and defeat. Here as before the coin of defeat is glibly turned over to reveal a mixed victory for the good guys - a little too glibly, perhaps. In essence, the hitherto unmentioned Rule 42 provides that if invincible Lord Foul should win he automatically loses.

Donaldson's convoluted approach to fantasy is in fact original and welcome, though Covenant's endless tortured dilemmas can pall. A further annoyance is the diction, clumsily erudite as ever. *Hurled like a jerid ... he made his preterite way ... argute with concentration ... beneficent mansuetude ... analystic refulgence ...* argh! If only some editor had cleaned out this nonsense and trimmed the book to liftable size.

By contrast, Ian Watson's new sf novel *Chekhov's Journey* (Goliancz 183pp £7.95) is a straightforward, stripped-down work which does its stuff in minimal space. Not that the fiendishly clever Watson can be called straightforward. We begin with playwright Anton Chekhov's real-life 1890 journey across Siberia; this Chekhov, though, is a simulated personality induced by 'hypnotic reincarnation' in an actor from the 1990 Soviet film unit producing their documentary *Chekhov's Journey*. But simulated-Chekhov strays from his script into an investigation of the mysterious 1888 Tunguska explosion, causing concern in 1990 owing to the fact that the Tunguska event didn't happen until 1908. The hypnotic subject is thus urged 'forward' in time, only for him to convey that he's now Captain Anton Astrov aboard the doomed Soviet timeship plunging back from 2090 on collision course with Siberia in 1908....

There are clever twists in this neatly-executed story, which is as 'conventional' a reality-bending yarn as Watson has written. Lacking the vaulting ambition of his *God's World* or the sheer outrageousness of the recent *Deathhunter*, it's good entertainment with some philosophical bite.

Run to the Stars by Michael Scott Rohan (Arrow 295pp £1.95) is a first novel in the best tradition of 'hard' sf. A convincingly run-down and bureaucratic Earth is failing to meet the challenge of space, despite interesting hardware like the Infall space-drive (another version of sf's Amazing Doubletalk Drive, here a limited form of gravity control which is wisely not described in detail), anti-matter-powered probes and a very nifty relativistic weapon which some years ago I shamelessly plagiarized in my own *War in 2080: the Future of Military Technology*. The problem is for the tough hero to outwit a corrupt Earth government, save at least one world, escape on a colony ship to somewhere fresh and unexploited, and get the girl. Rohan avoids the usual pitfall of having his hero do too much single-handed or achieve all these objectives while smelling of roses; scraps salvaged from defeat are more convincing than easy victory. Though slow-moving to begin with, and relying on a truly boggling coincidence at its climax, this is a superior sf adventure from an author I know well (bias declared) and whom I hate for getting a fan letter from Ursula Le Guin on his first published story.

Sometimes review copies arrive all the way from America – books which may never be printed here. Starblaze Editions, for example, do a nice-looking line of large-format ('trade') paperbacks which you can find in sf/fantasy specialist bookshops.

Myth Directions by Robert Asprin (Starblaze 169pp $5.95) is the third in a series of light, humorous fantasies featuring a semi-skilled young magician who's apprenticed to a 'demon' from the world Perv (who is therefore called a Pervert, a gag which amuses the author greatly and frequently). There's remarkably little successful humour in sf and apparently even less in fantasy; the classic example is L. Sprague de Camp's and Fletcher Pratt's **Incomplete Enchanter** series. Even this frequently sacrifices humour to plot needs or fantasy conventions, in well-justified fear that too much slapstick may spoil readers' belief in the book's imagined world.

Alas, Asprin isn't as good a writer as de Camp or Pratt, and his previous effort *Myth Conceptions* was frequently pretty dire, with overdone anachronistic humour spoiling the effect exactly as suggested above. A fantasy 'inn' is described in painful detail which shows it to be identical to a modern fast-food place, etc. But this time the humour is milder and better-judged, though it can still be hard to take the sheer cretinousness required from every character in order to make the plot work. (To make people simultaneously believable and as thick as this needs the talents of a P.G. Wodehouse, and P.G. Wodehouse is dead.) It's a harmless and quite likeable little book, an undemanding fantasy romp: Asprin does seem to be improving.

Since we're in *White Dwarf* you may be curious about games possibilities. An Asprin-based RPG would resemble many other simple fantasy games - there's one already, based on his and others' **Thieves' World** series - though the element of humour is especially difficult to translate into game form. Rohan's book would be fun as the basis of a 'realistic' interstellar war game, with relativistic weapons of appalling power creeping for years between their targets thanks to the limiting speed of light, while bureaucratic double-dealers confuse the issue with complex cover-ups. The *Chekhov's Journey* game would presumably feature players each trying to tip the balance of reality in a preferred direction, with the devastating Tunguska explosion happening in 1908, in 1888, or - your objective if you're playing Captain Astrov - not at all! And in a Thomas Covenant game the players (if they could be persuaded to believe in the thing) would stagger on from defeat to glorious defeat, amassing huge scores for Agony, Remorse, Bitterness, Humilation and Dictionary-Swallowing, until one of them reaches the stage of Utter Downfall ... which by Donaldson's Rule 42 generally indicates victory.

April 1983

3 The SF Awards

The time for science fiction awards is staggering round again. The British SF Association award is for stuff first published here in 1982, and the novel finalists are *Helliconia Spring* by Brian Aldiss (Cape), *No Enemy But Time* by Michael Bishop (Gollancz), *Little, Big* by John Crowley (Gollancz), *The Divine Invasion* by Philip K. Dick (Corgi) and *The Sword of the Lictor* (Sidgwick & Jackson; Arrow). All are damn fine books; my first-place vote went to the intricate and lovely fantasy *Little, Big* if anyone's interested. Incidentally, those wanting information on the BSFA and its magazines need only write to [updated December 2000: Paul Billinger, 1 Long Row Close, Everdon, Daventry, Northants, NN11 3BE, England; billinger@enterprise.net], enclosing a stamped addressed envelope.

The current Nebula awards will be given for work first published in the USA during 1982, the voters being the SF Writers of America - filthy professionals who've published lots and paid lots of membership fees. Finalists: *Helliconia Spring*, *Foundation's Edge* by Isaac Asimov (Granada), *No Enemy But Time*, *The Transmigration of Timothy Archer* by Philip K. Dick (Gollancz), *Friday* by Robert Heinlein (NEL) and *The Sword of the Lictor*. The Asimov and Heinlein aren't such fine books; the Dick is excellent but not sf or fantasy; my UK-chauvinist vote went to Aldiss, who's just delivered the sequel *Helliconia Summer* for publication in - you guessed it - autumn.

Just now the fattest book to hand is Frank Herbert's *The White Plague* (Gollancz 445pp £8.95), a remarkably effective version of that good old sf theme the world-ravaging epidemic. Scientist O'Neill's family is killed in an IRA outrage; illogically he vows to do to the murderers what they did to him, and take away their wives. Being a molecular biologist working in genetic engineering, he's the first sf super-villain to be credibly capable of doing the dirty deed. Chemicals and processes are relatively cheap (Herbert argues powerfully) once the genetic know-how is loose in the world; in no time he's brewed in the bathtub a fiendish disease which is 100% fatal to women, *only* women. Loosed in Ireland, the infection is out of control over half the world before anyone quite believes what's going on.

There's plenty of edge-of-the-seat suspense and good thumping melodrama in the race to crack the gene structure of the plague while a few women are still left alive. Herbert leaps about from character to character, giving dozens of viewpoints on disaster, like a horrific kaleidoscope. And O'Neill the 'Madman' wanders the remnants of Ireland, still no crude baddie but a near-sympathetic schizoid whose mind has blotted out the memory of his crimes – while Herbert gravely and compassionately tries to tackle the old issue of Irish fanaticism, as mirrored in O'Neill. So far, so good.

When the book's over, though, there are pangs of doubt. Until then the crackling tension almost stops you noticing there's only *one female viewpoint* in that cast of thousands; the relief when the plague is licked fails to cover a lack of credibility as this scatterbrain cheerfully accepts that from now on she and the other 0.01% of surviving women are going to be multi-husbanded baby factories and bye-bye to silly old ideas like feminism. There's even a suggestion that, because O'Neill's genetic breakthroughs have turned out to be the key to immortality and a perfect complexion, the White Plague was really, on the whole, a pretty good thing. Oh *dear.*

Man and the Planets by Duncan Lunan (Ashgrove Press 306pp £9.50) is the non-fiction book for sf game players who want credible scenarios. It analyses the Solar System's resources planet by planet, plugging the benefits of space exploration and human expansion to the planets and beyond. Want the figures on why it might be worth heading for Mercury (the enormous energy flux from the Sun implies free power for future industry there) or Jupiter (helium-3 'mined' from its atmosphere is a likely fuel for starships)? Lunan's enthusiasm is infectious, his research exhaustive; he's utterly committed to the Dream of Space and has no time for the many equally learned people who fear that the expense of truly opening up this 'high frontier' would wreck our world economy long before producing tangible benefits. Read it and decide for yourself.

A few American books to look for in the import shops ... *Aurelia* by R.A. Lafferty (Starblaze 185pp $5.95) has what sounds like a simple story, hardly a story at all: fourteen-year-old Aurelia is from a world which routinely sends out schoolkids to do a class project in World Government by ruling an unknown planet for a while. She lands on Earth (or is it?), causes huge controversy, goes on a three-day walkabout making convoluted speeches, and comes to a much-prophesied sticky end. Only this is Lafferty, pushing 70 but still a bizarre and original author who's an acquired taste, and the book bulges with jokes and philosophical bits (hard, sometimes, to spot which is which), tall tales and weird people: horned men, sinister yo-yos, doppelgangers, miracles, the extra prime number between five and seven, and a worm with a gun. Indescribable. I loved the parts I could understand.

People who like *Star Trek* immensely will no doubt enjoy Bjo Trimble's book of anecdotes and trivia, *On the Good Ship Enterprise* (Starblaze 286pp $5.95). It's *uncensored* and *unauthorized*, the cover boasts, but you could have fooled me. Certainly there are discreet references to Kirk/Spocking (which is what naughty-minded fans imagine the Captain and First Officer getting up to while off duty) and how that irrepressible Harlan Ellison says flagrant, uncensored things like – and I quote – '@#$%¢&**' ... but the book froths with too much uncritical enthusiasm and too many exclamation marks for comfortable reading.

Finally, let me strongly recommend one newish American author Rudy Rucker. If you're lucky you may find a remaindered Virgin Books edition of his

White Light; if not, grab the imported Ace paperback of this remarkable mathematical sf novel. It does the sort of things with infinite set theory that *Through the Looking-Glass* did with chess. Another weird Rucker book is *Software* (Ace 212pp $2.25), about what it might be like to *become* a robot operated by the software of your own personality program, which program is running on a computer disguised for excellent plot reasons as a Mr Frostee ice-cream van following 'your' 'body' around – leading to such deadpan dialogue as, '"I think you should kill him and eat his brain," Mr Frostee said quickly. "That's not the answer to *every* problem in interpersonal relations," Cobb said....' Lastly, Rucker is a real-life mathematician specializing in infinity and has published a non-fiction work whose knobbly ideas and boggling paradoxes should stimulate the more numerate GMs into devising wicked new riddles and traps. The title is *Infinity and the Mind* (Harvester Press 342pp £12.95), a must for anyone who has enjoyed Douglas Hofstadter's *Gödel, Escher, Bach* or the works of Martin Gardner.

Speaking of Gardner reminds me to plug his *Science Good, Bad and Bogus*, just out in paperback from Oxford University Press at £4.95 – putting the boot into numerous pseudoscientists, the great spoon-bending nonsense, and much more.

I have room for a spare sentence here: being interested in feedback, I'd appreciate letters c/o *White Dwarf* about the content of this page. Would you like to see more or less on books/awards/fiction/non-fiction/rude gossip about easily embarrassed sf authors? Let me know. Requests for 'less Langford' or 'very much less Langford' may not be treated with entire sympathy.

Next month, the BSFA and Nebula award winners! Oh, the nerve-racking suspense, I can hardly wait (he said, falling asleep over the typewriter).

May 1983

4 Hugos and Horrors

Once again it's those very special thirteen months of the year, the award season: our sf/fantasy field presents so many awards that it seems extraordinary that any book should escape. The British SF Association award for best novel of 1982 went to Brian Aldiss's *Helliconia Spring*, about which I've previously said nice things. It's the first book of a colossal trilogy covering thousands of years on the planet Helliconia; the paperback is out from Granada in June and volume two, *Helliconia Summer*, from Cape in the autumn. Meanwhile the SF Writers of America have voted Michael Bishop's *No Enemy But Time* (Gollancz) the Nebula novel award. Bishop is a fine writer who improves with each book and this time-travel story is his best yet, say numerous critics who unlike me have been able to get hold of review copies and read the thing. Gnash, gnash.

Next comes the shortlist for the Hugo award, thought of by publishers as the important one. According to the voters (members of the coming World SF Convention), 1982's best novels were Asimov's *Foundation's Edge*, Cherryh's *The Pride of Chanur*, Clarke's *2010*, Heinlein's *Friday*, Kingsbury's *Courtship Rite* and Wolfe's *The Sword of the Lictor*. It would be base and evil to suggest that three of these are by authors who seem past their sell-by date, whose inferior work gets nominations largely on the basis of past successes ... and anyway I suggested that a couple of issues ago. More later about the others. Meanwhile, you can't help noticing that the books thought best by Brits and American sf professionals aren't even shortlisted for the Hugo. Indeed, no British items at all appear on the various Hugo shortlists, apart from some obscure hack called Langford in the category 'best fan writer'. [He said, with becoming immodesty.]

Onward. To dismiss all children's titles as immature and 'just for kids' is to be in danger of missing many good books. *The Gruesome Book* (Piccolo £1.00) is edited by Ramsey Campbell, who complains that junior ghost-story collections are too tame. 'I want those kids trembling with dread and lying awake sweating all night,' he said, or words to that effect, and the book's nine stories should achieve approximately this. [Actually he said 'I want to scare the shit out of the little bastards,' but *Dwarf* liked to pretend it was a family magazine.] Seven are loathsome oldies, classics of grue; two are nasty but new, one by the editor and one by Modesty Forbids. The blurb explains that the book ends with 'the ultimate horror of "The Graveyard Rats"!' (by Henry Kuttner), so presumably even the blurb writer couldn't summon the courage to read the story which follows Kuttner's.

The Borribles by Michael de Larrabeiti (Piccolo 286pp £1.50 - *why* are children's books always so cheap?) was published in hardback some years ago, in 1976. It and its sequel *The Borribles Go For Broke* did well in the USA, but editorial cowardice or something precluded a British paperback until this year. Borribles, you see, are souped-up juvenile delinquents with pointy ears - street kids who never grow up but go in for much luxurious squalor, foul language and gratuitous violence. After far too many sanitized plastic 'children' whose alleged naughtiness never gets beyond the apple-pie-bed and banana-skin level, it's refreshing to read about these likeable toughs murdering their way across London and even coming to sticky ends themselves. The Famous Five would have been reduced in no time to bloody rags.

The Borribles is a kind of fantasy quest epic, with a trained gang of Borrible assassins trekking from Battersea to 'Rumbledom' (Wimbledon) on a nefarious errand. Descriptions of places like the Thames at Wandsworth make the desolation before the Black Gate of Mordor sound quite cosy and homelike. The aim is to slaughter the leaders of the Rumbles, vile and vicious heavies like huge rats who live on Wimbledon Common, are armed with murderous spiked sticks, and have this tewwible pwobwem of speech impediments, not to mention names like Vulgarian and Orococco. Yes, quite. I don't know what the Americans made of all this, but I gather that Wombles fans were unamused by scenes of wholesale carnage in which countless Rumbles have their stuffing or worse knocked out, and your reviewer failed to contain his chortles.

The book isn't merely rowdy anarchy. The Borribles' underground society is nicely imagined, and the heroisms, treacheries and callousness follow logically from the way Borribles are. Without going all preachy, the author makes it clear that this kind of fun adventure is liable to get you killed: half the main characters are nastily betrayed and die futilely. As well as considerable imaginative flair, *The Borribles* has the ring of truth. Expect a game version any day.

Back in the good old universe of 'hard' sf, we have Stanislaw Lem's *More Tales of Pirx the Pilot* (Secker & Warburg 220pp £7.95). Robots run amok, spaceships shudder and clank, computers go neurotic: it's old-fashioned stuff with a modern twist, since underneath the creaking apparatus of lasers and fusion drives Lem is often thinking hard about people's relations with machine intelligence. The perfect thinking machine is never perfect because it's been built by fallible us. 'A robot that can match man mentally and not be capable of lying or cheating is a fantasy.' So much for Asimov's Three Laws of Robotics!

Another American book worthy of your refined attention is *Nifft the Lean* by Michael Shea (DAW 304pp $2.95 - see your friendly import bookshop). Shea's previous book *A Quest for Simbilis* was remarkable as an authorized continuation of Jack Vance's *The Eyes of the Overworld* (second in the **Dying Earth** sequence), written in an almost perfect pastiche of Vance's gorgeously ornate style. Traces of Vance are still visible here in the adventures of master-thief Nifft, but Shea has developed a personal line in ghoulish inventiveness which makes his cosmos lurid and unforgettable.

There are four stories of Nifft. One is an adequate fantasy caper about an ingenious theft; another rehashes the old theme of the Ancient Slumbering

Doom Which Comes To The Sinful City, and (despite interesting twiddly bits) lumbers on like a Vance short injected with too many anabolic steroids. The remaining two are why you should buy the book: both deal splendidly with trips to hell. First comes a gruesome journey to the 'Place of the Raging Dead', featuring a great deal of the sort of thing H.P. Lovecraft used to call unspeakable, unnameable and indescribable; Shea speaks, names and describes each shuddering detail, and tells a good story. The book's heart of darkness is the other hell-trip, 'The Fishing of the Demon-Sea', a 125-page mini-novel wherein Nifft unwillingly descends to one of several diabolic subworlds in a hopeless attempt to retrieve some snotty kid who conjured a demon and suffered the usual fate of those who mispronounce spells. In this garish hell the damned suffer grotesque transformations and torments, described with vast relish and elaboration; the visceral quality of Shea's unpleasantness never flags, and the gaudy landscapes will infect your dreams. I enjoyed this one a lot.

A word about sf conventions. The 34th British Easter Convention was held in Glasgow this year, guests of honour being James White (best known for his **Sector General** books of medical sf), Marion Zimmer Bradley of **Darkover** fame, and US fan Avedon Carol – famous as the only female Armenian sf fan to have been bitten in the ankle by Jim Morrison. As Toastmaster, your reviewer was able to shower hideous insults and burnt toast on them all. The 1984 convention is being combined with the biennial European sf event ('Eurocon') and will be held in Brighton over the Easter weekend. Its guests include Isaac Asimov [but see below] and Christopher Priest (don't neglect to buy his tortuous *The Affirmation* – Arena 213pp £2.50 – if you haven't already).

Next month I'll be writing scathing killer reviews of all the gamebooks by Ian Livingstone and Steve Jackson now infesting our shops. *[Oh no you won't – Ed.]*

June 1983

5 Zapping Uri Geller

There's a popular theory that anyone dabbling in sf/fantasy must have a shaky hold on reality. As an sf fan who reads about mighty spacecraft trundling through the void, I find that journalists therefore expect me to believe devoutly that every other light in the sky must be a flying saucer packed with alien pranksters who from time to time land and contact picked eccentrics in remote parts of the woods, while carefully avoiding centres of civilization. Fantasy gamers in America suffer from the fearful Moral Majority, like Mary Whitehouse with huge brass knobs on, which assume that because D&D features simulated plastic gods and demons, its players are therefore satanic devil-worshippers who ought to be sprinkled with holy water and burnt. No doubt readers of detective stories constantly commit untraceable murders with blunt instruments in locked rooms, while devotees of the Mills and Boon romances rush off to eternal bliss with a different One Perfect Spouse each week until hunted down by Scotland Yard's crack Bigamy Division.

In fact sf fans these days seem less gullible than the general public. Dear old Erich von Däniken made a fortune from such theories as that the primitive, cave-dwelling Ancient Egyptians could never, without extraterrestrial aid, have hauled those stone blocks to build the pyramids – they *had no rope to drag the stones with*. For some reason he neglects to mention the several miles of Ancient Egyptian rope displayed in museums around the world. Stuffed with misrepresentation and outright lies, von Däniken's books became bestsellers. Meanwhile, the sf fans remained sceptical, and many sf authors were among those who exposed the absurdities of such books in works which did *not* become bestsellers. Publishing common sense seems to be almost a hopeless cause.

For review I have two aggressive books on the common-sense side. Don't hold your breath for their appearance as mass-market paperbacks or bestsellers! These, along with Martin Gardner's *Fad and Fallacies*, John Sladek's *The New Apocrypha*, Ronald Story's *The Space Gods Revealed* and others, are for those interested in hearing the other, sceptical side of today's all too devalued tales of miracles. Both are by James 'The Amazing' Randi, a professional magician whose hackles rise when conjurers of lesser ability – Uri Geller, for example – carve a swathe through the credulous by claiming their sleight of hand to be the result of Real Psychic Powers. Even physicists tend to be fooled: all their training is with laboratory instruments and specimens which don't deceive and misdirect you as is routine for conjurors. As Gardner likes to say, 'Rats and electrons don't lie; "psychics" do.'

In *The Truth About Uri Geller* (Prometheus 234pp £6.95, 1982 revision of 1975 exposé) Randi puts the boot into charismatic Uri. His scorn is withering and exhilarating; even if you think he leans too far towards blind scepticism (I don't), it's impressive and damning that Randi himself can duplicate any and all of Geller's paltry tricks without needing to claim astral powers - while Geller's awesome abilities mysteriously desert him when Randi or other professional magicians happen to be watching. Even a video camera interferes somehow with the psychic vibes and can force poor Uri to fake the powers which according to his fans are genuine on all occasions when no one catches him pulling a fast one. Yes, and I operate my typewriter by direct telekinetic flux whenever nobody's looking.

Flim-Flam! (Prometheus 342pp £7.45, with enthusiastic introduction from Isaac Asimov) carries the battle into other camps: the cardboard fairies that fooled poor Conan Doyle, the Bermuda Triangle myth and its fraudulent statistics, UFOs, transcendental meditation, von Däniken again (with a gorgeous quote from the Master about how amazing it was that primitive folk were able to carve accurate human skeletons *when X-rays weren't discovered until 1895!*), Geller again, biorhythms, the Filipino 'healers' who by sleight of hand remove chicken-liver 'tumours' from their luckless patients' bodies, spoonbending in general, spiritualism, Scientology, and more. Always he thrusts under your nose the parts of the story which believers' books omit. Even if inclined towards the loony, I mean the uncritical viewpoint, you should consult these books for the devil's advocate arguments. They are important. In a world where an ounce of sensationalism sells better than a ton of rationality any day, they are very important.

The British distributor of both books will happily deal by mail order and can be contacted at Prometheus Books, 10 Crescent View, Loughton, Essex, IG10 4PZ.

Speaking of sensationalism, would you believe a quiet, well-written and understated book about an insidious alien psychic vampire? Christopher Evans's *The Insider* (Granada 237pp £1.50) is accurately billed as chilling rather than terrifying, loathsome or liable to put you off your breakfast for a fortnight. The apparent scenario: Blair is an aging author, his commonplace body concealing an alien mind which moved in to erase the real Blair 51 years before. Blair/alien is reclusive and morose, shunning human contact. Then the old body dies and the mind parasite switches to Marsh, an outgoing family man. Though well equipped to play the part - he/it has access to all the expunged Marsh's memories - this rather likeable mentality can't take the stresses of human relations. Marriage and other links begin to disintegrate as a near-future Britain slides downhill into repressive intolerance and National Frontery.

All this is well enough done, but Evans now extends it into the realm of works like Priest's *The Affirmation* as assumptions and realities prove to be built on quicksand. Suppose, the false March wonders, that he's the real Marsh, only sufferingly from mental disturbances which have produced these exotic memories of other lives? Suppose ... More chilling than any number of lurching, blood-spattered vampires, the low-key tensions and domestic concealments make you feel that this lurking mind – always play-acting for fear of exposing its real nature to an unsympathetic world – could almost be your own. Isn't this play-acting what we all do? The ending is sad but satisfying; *The Insider* is recommended.

Remember Alfred Bester's gaudy, junky, unforgettable sf classics *The Demolished Man* and *Tiger! Tiger!* (alias *The Stars My Destination*)? His latest novel *The Deceivers* (Pan 255pp £1.95) is here in paperback, two years after its US publication as 'the true successor to *Tiger! Tiger!*' [Pan didn't quite seem to grasp this and billed it as 'his most important new novel since *The Demolished Man*, expunging *Tiger! Tiger!* from history.] Indeed, much of the new book's fun, games and adventure in the 27th century seems a conscientious attempt to recreate the earlier success: here again are elements like a circus as a cover operation for derring-do, Oriental masterspies and much background on Oriental superstition, magic fuels defying thermodynamics, economic war between the inner planets and outer satellites, even typewriter doodles – which in *The Deceivers* achieve great silliness when a computer video display seven *centuries* hence is limited to crude asterisk-patterns by way of graphics. Science never was Bester's strong point, and here we also have a 1,500 million volt electric fence (to keep that lot from discharging straight to earth it must have been a *damn well insulated* electric fence), human/alien interfertility, crystallized helium and other unlikely wonders.

The strong points are Bester's colourful imagination and general wildness: a Maori Mafia hunting mutant boars in vacuum; a pattern-sensitive hero (see his earlier story 'The Pi Man') who in one clever set-piece follows a trail from twelve lords a-leaping in a street pageant, all the way along to the goal of a partridge in a pear tree; a shapeshifting alien heroine; kidnapping, battle, torture and gaudy adventure. Against this, the actual characters never reach those peaks of sheer obsessiveness which powered the early novels ... they're dilettantes, they're twee, and there's even a narrator who removes all possible suspense by tipping you off in advance about the happy ending. Some of the extended dialogue sequences even read like Heinlein's recent excesses – than which there is no lower blow a reviewer can strike.

The Deceivers is mildly good fun, more so than Bester's other 'late' novels *The Computer Connection* (alias *Extro*) and *Golem*^{100}, but still substandard for this author. However, no defect of Bester's could possibly deserve the horrible, grubby and irrelevant cover Pan have slapped on it, perhaps with a view to discouraging sales.

Puzzle for alert readers: why, in the same week that it was on the UK paperback bestseller list, was Julian May's *The Nonborn King* (Pan £1.95) extensively displayed in my local remainder shop at £1.30? Answers on a postcard to Pan, please, not to me.

July 1983

6 Wolfe at the Door

For reasons known best to itself the Book Marketing Council is having a big sf promotion this October. You may remember the Best of Young British Authors splurge earlier this year: this was estimated to have sold several hundred thousand books by relatively unknown authors whose careers got a much-needed boost. I predict that the sf promotion will *not* sell similar numbers of extra sf books, since in a fit of what looks like cowardice the selection panel has picked far too many classics and high sellers which have already reached their market saturation level. I'm disappointed.

The books: *Helliconia Spring* (Aldiss), the **Foundation** trilogy (Asimov), *The Drowned World* (Ballard), *Timescape* (Benford), *No Enemy But Time* (Bishop), *Downbelow Station* (Cherryh), *2001* and *2010* (Clarke), *White Gold Wielder* (Donaldson), *The Stainless Steel Rat for President* (Harrison), *Dune* (Herbert), *Brave New World* (Huxley), *The Crystal Singer*, (McCaffrey), **Dancers at the End of Time** (Moorcock), *The Mote in God's Eye* (Niven/Pournelle), *Nineteen Eighty-Four* (Orwell), *Majipoor Chronicles* (Silverberg), *The Citadel of the Autarch* (Wolfe), *The War of the Worlds* (Wells) and *The Day of the Triffids* (Wyndham).

Spies tell me that the oldies had to be included to make up the package, because there just wasn't enough contemporary sf in print which the publishers were prepared to back (at a cost of a few hundred quid per book) for the promotion. The selection panel was thus forced to pretend that a 'historical' theme had been planned all along. The number of British authors is still shameful for a British campaign: seven, and three of them dead. Some authors are unrepresented because their publishers don't belong to the Book Marketing Council (and would thus have been charged an extra 50% for BMC publicity) or are just plain mean. Where are Britain's Bob Shaw, Ian Watson, Christopher Priest, Robert Holdstock, John Brunner, Richard Cowper, Garry Kilworth ...? You may well ask.

One of the bright spots is that Gene Wolfe's **Book of the New Sun** tetralogy will get more attention. The final book *The Citadel of the Autarch* was recently published by Sidgwick & Jackson (317pp £8.95) and will appear as an Arrow paperback in – what a coincidence – October. Wolfe himself will be visiting Britain around then, and appearing as guest of honour at the hastily scheduled Fantasycon VIII in Birmingham. More of this later.

At last I've been able to read the whole of **The Book of the New Sun** in sequence, and the experience is much to be recommended. The first three books (all published in S&J hardback and Arrow paperback) are *The Shadow of the Torturer*, *The Claw of the Conciliator* and *The Sword of the Lictor*. The four together are the best thing in extreme far-future 'science fantasy' since Jack Vance's *The Dying Earth*.

In synopsis the story seems quite a simple and rambling one. Severian is an apprentice and then a journeyman in the Order of Seekers for Truth and Penitence, better known as the guild of torturers. Guild headquarters is one of the ancient towers comprising the Citadel of the Autarch of the Commonwealth ... and the unimaginable remoteness of the story's future comes slowly into focus as you realize that this tower has bulkheads, round windows and a long-disused propulsion chamber; that an ancient painting in the Autarch's Library shows a knight with a golden visor standing in a stony desert, Earth shining blue in the sky behind him; that in this time of a dying sun the sky is always dark blue and stars are visible at noon; that the operating principle of the most hallowed of all the guild's torture machines is so nearly forgotten that the nearest word anyone can manage is 'lightning'.

Severian is a torturer. A lesser writer would instantly equip him with a twentieth-century liberal conscience: not Wolfe. When through half-unwilling emotional involvement Severian eases the death of a 'client' he very properly feels himself a traitor to his guild and meekly accepts exile, paying his way en route by 'practising the mystery of his craft' (hiring out as public executioner). There are strange encounters, fights, giants, subhumans, robots, alien 'cacogens', monstrous pursuing beasts, a 'magic' gem (the Claw), interstellar travel via mirrors, an invisible palace and a flying cathedral, a war in which things called lances and spears are high-tech energy weapons – and a curious fate which from the beginning is guiding Severian towards the throne of the Autarch.

From that summary it could of course be terrible. Instead it's marvellously good: finely written, with a feel for language which Stephen Donaldson would do well to study. Unlike Donaldson's, Wolfe's obscure words lurk unobtrusively until they seem both familiar and – thanks to their careful planting in context – meaningful. The real Wolfean obscurities are displayed out in the open, nothing up his sleeve: occasionally he describes an event with piercing clarity yet deliberately leaves you uncertain of what happened. But read the books in sequence and with the attention they deserve, and almost all becomes plain. The first two in particular feature highly enigmatic events towards their ends, light being cast on each mystery if you carry straight on into the next volume.

Perhaps **The Book of the New Sun** isn't perfect. Some of the final revelations about the New Sun itself are less earth-shattering than one might hope, and a few minor points (*who* was Severian's mother?) stay annoyingly elusive to the very end. But its style, wit, inventiveness and fresh atmosphere set it far above today's endless output of mediocre fantasy novels – or rather, sf novels, for virtually every fantasy trope in this tetralogy has an sf rationale behind it.... It'll do until perfection comes along.

After which, I've not much room left. Diana Wynne Jones's *The Magicians of Caprona* (Beaver 191pp £1.25) can be found on 'children's' paperback shelves ...

though not her best book (try *The Spellcoats*), this shows how Jones can work in a genre without getting bogged down in all its old clichés. Set in the same parallel-world-where-magic-works as her deservedly popular *Charmed Life*, this one features pleasantly dotty goings-on in an Italian city-state whose principal magician families are busily playing Montagues and Capulets to considerable comic effect, while a diabolical and thoroughly hissable villain is at work behind the scenes. Great fun.

Two issues ago I mentioned that Isaac Asimov had promised to come to Britain as guest of our 1984 national sf convention. It seems he has now decided that his time would be far more profitably spent writing another novel, and the search for a new guest is under way. [Roger Zelazny obliged.] *The Sun Shines Bright* (Avon/Discus 242pp $2.95) is not a novel but yet another collection, the fifteenth, of Asimov's slightly too regular columns from *Fantasy and Science Fiction*. Each essay presents some interesting insight or viewpoint, usually scientific; many, alas, are padded and smothered with great wads of facts, statistics and numbers in general, the result being relatively dull. When Big Ike descended to several fascinating pages listing the largest cities in *(a)* the world and *(b)* the United States which start with each letter of the alphabet from A to Z, I found my eyelids beginning to droop. For Asimov completists, and insomniacs.

Books received which I haven't had time to read properly: *The Prometheus Man* by Ray Faraday Nelson (Starblaze 233pp $5.95) was runner-up for the first Philip K. Dick memorial award (the winner was Rudy Rucker's *Software*, recommended in column 3), and Dick himself had earlier commented 'Mind bending ... this is what real science fiction is all about' – though you can't believe *every* plug printed on the back of a book. *Hello America* by J.G. Ballard (Granada 236pp £1.50) is the first paperback appearance of this 1981 novel by our own home-grown Master, and is considerably more accessible than the experimental works like *The Atrocity Exhibition* which seemed to put so many readers off Ballard. *The Citadel of Steve Jackson* and *The Forest of Ian Livingstone* are [more references to the 'fighting fantasy gamebooks' of Games Workshop's founders – forget it].

August 1983

7 Downbelow Expectations

Since I began writing these columns the Earth has lumbered halfway around its orbit, an estimated 5,271,009 Langfordian brain cells have succumbed to the effects of alcohol and bad sf, and about the same number of pins have been stuck into Langford-shaped wax images by lovers of Stephen R. Donaldson. Yet still I continue, with all the stamina and endurance of a kamikaze pilot. What keeps me going against such odds? All together now: '*The money!*'

About Donaldson. Because I made snide comments on the great man's lapses into awful, turgid prose, several fans wish to lure me into a dark alley and belt me over the head with the complete **Chronicles of Thomas Covenant** (how they get the necessary lifting equipment into the dark alley is their problem). Because I've also said that Donaldson has flashes of peculiar power and originality, I've additionally been denounced as a member of that vile cult the Illiterati - by other fans unshakable in their devout belief that our Stephen is the worst fantasy writer of all time. I can't win.

So rather than review the rare 'unpublished' Donaldson poem now on my desk (cut from *White Gold Wielder* and published in an Australian sf fanzine edited by Jack Herman), I'll simply exercise the reviewer's privilege of quoting a bit. It's called 'Scroll the Appalling' -

Upon a time he fought a war
With whales beached upon the shore,
For which he has been slightly sung.
His losses there were rather dear:
One ship, two longboats and a spear.
But Scroll could not be reached by fear,
For which he has been wryly sung.
Dead fishes could not him affright:
He flailed at whales all the night.
And when the tide bore them away,
'How bravely we have won today!'
He said -
For which he has been sung.

Wasn't that nice? Move over Shakespeare, Milton, McGonagall....

Downbelow Station by C.J. Cherryh (DAW 432pp $2.75, Methuen 432pp £1.95) was last year's Hugo winner. Other finalists were John Crowley's *Little, Big* (Gollancz; Methuen release imminent as I write), whose range, subtlety and density make it for my money one of the best fantasies I've ever read, and Gene Wolfe's *The Claw of the Conciliator*, covered last column. Having triumphed over this opposition and also over Julian May's hugely hyped *The Many-Coloured Land*, Cherryh's novel ought to be great stuff.

Instead it's traditional stuff. Adequately but unexcitingly written, massive and fragmented but not really complex in the manner of Crowley or Wolfe, *Downbelow Station* is old-fashioned 'hard' sf about a long and wearisome power struggle which for the most part is numbingly realistic: messy compromises, forced decisions, lies and betrayal, no room for heroics.

In summary: *Earth Company* colonized the stars but *Union*, a vaguely communistic colonial alliance, rebelled, causing Earth to build the retributive *Fleet*, now independent renegades; conflict between these and interstellar traders or *Merchanters* focuses on would-be neutral *Downbelow Station*, orbiting planet *Downbelow*, home of the mildly interesting but dispensable alien *hisa*. On this station the *Konstantins* are in charge, the *Lukases* rebellious, and *Q* is a vast quarantine zone of rioting refugees from Fleet/Union strife. *Now read on....*

The trouble with this multi-multi-sided struggle (and I haven't mentioned the splits and double agents) is that just as one's getting interested in the diplomacy of *X*, the action cuts to *Y* in the middle of a riot; no sooner does imminent death have *Y* by the short and curlies than we're hurried off to eavesdrop on the sabotage plans of *Z*. It's possible to make this kind of stuff compulsive reading, but Cherryh doesn't succeed all the time: for all the book's length, this jerky cross-cutting allows only a few characters to develop and come alive.

Without actively disliking the book, I found it much easier to put down (and to forget to pick up again) than much previous Cherryh. She doesn't seem as involved with her writing as she should be; her former drive and visual detail are lacking. Here's the opening sentence of her *The Faded Sun: Kesrith*. 'It was a game, *shon'ai*, the passing-game, Kel-style, in the dim round hall of the Kel, the middle tower of the house - black-robed men and a black-robed woman, a circle of ten.' It catches the mind; and the *shon'ai* game is a vital symbol running through all the story; and halfway down the next page we're sucked into the plot.

In contrast, here's the opening sentence of *Downbelow Station*: 'The stars, like all man's other ventures, were an obvious impracticality, as rash and improbable an ambition as the first venture of man onto Earth's own great oceans, or into the air, or into space.' Abstract, vague, windy. Eight pages of this, no more plausible than other future-history synopses, before the narrative proper; many more pages again until the plot is properly rolling on its long course to an ultimate conclusion strangely resembling the twist endings to each segment of Asimov's *Foundation*. In short, Cherryh can do better than this - though others have done it far worse.

Recently I've read three enjoyable books which definitely exude that special aura of sf/fantasy, without actually *being* sf or fantasy outright. Try them:

• *Freddy's Book* (Abacus £2.50) by the late John Gardner - the chap who wrote *Grendel*, not the dire thriller writer - is a fantasy novel within a realistic frame, letting the author *(a)* make ironic connections between the story-within-a-story and its supposed author the 'real' Freddy Agaard, a young man distorted into a giant by glandular imbalance; *(b)* sneak a fantasy allegory through under the very noses of suspicious lit-crit academics. The inner fantasy is rather good, and oddly reminiscent of some of R.A. Lafferty's eccentric work, in particular *The Flame is Green*.

• *If On a Winter's Night a Traveller* by Italo Calvino (Picador £2.50) is a splendidly batty book about books. The hero is you, the reader. The first chapter opens, 'You are about to begin reading Italo Calvino's new novel *If on a winter's night a traveller*' ... and after revealing that your copy of the book is unfortunately defective, the story goes on to chronicle your efforts to locate the missing Chapter Two in a spreading maze of fascinatingly varied first chapters and elusive authors. Offbeat and fun – a highly enjoyable literary joke. You get the girl in the end, by the way.

• Finally, *The Rebel Angels* by Robertson Davies (King Penguin £2.95) looks at first glance like the traditional novel of university life but is crammed with the fantastic. Witchcraft, forgotten secret arts, erudition, mysticism, a semi-mad scientist called Ozias Froats seeking the answer to life, the universe and everything in carefully gathered and dissected human, er, faeces. Not for the squeamish, it features a murder whose inventive nastiness makes the destruction of whole shiploads of people in *Downbelow Station* seem pale and insignificant.

[This opened Davies's **Cornish Trilogy** of loosely connected novels. The other two are also nifty books, haunted by angels and unquiet spirits: *What's Bred in the Bone* and *The Lyre of Orpheus*.]

There's even something for games addicts in all these books. *Downbelow Station* could be translated chapter by chapter into the sf universe of the *Traveller* game; without being 'gameable' in that sense, each of the other three contains bizarre and novel stuff to inspire off-trail thoughts and fiendish notions. If you read only conventional sf/fantasy you'll have only conventional sf/fantasy ideas; take time out to patrol the borders and explore the fringes of the conventional, and who knows?

Aaaaargh. I can write no more. I have set down this brief account of my final hours; but now *it* is scrabbling awfully at the door. Eldritch, loathsome, partly rugose and partly squamous, *it* shambles towards me, noxious, unspeakable, indescribable, that hellish spawn of the Ancient Old Ones, the *deadline!*

September 1983

8 From Gentle to Gorey

What I'd like to pick up in one of these dungeon games is a Ring of Unfailing Literary Judgement, enabling me merely to lay one hand on a book's cover before writing the usual flawless and perceptive review. As it is, each month I'm strapped down in the torture chambers far beneath the Dark Tower of *White Dwarf*, my eyes are cruelly wired open as seen in *A Clockwork Orange*, and page by remorseless page the evilly grinning editors force me to read the latest accumulation of books. Luckily there are compensations.

Here's one. *Golden Witchbreed* by Mary Gentle (Gollancz 479pp £8.95) is the sf debut of a young British author who Gollancz plainly think will go far: not everyone gets such a nicely produced book and jacket. [At that time and from that publisher, hardly anyone.] But don't read the blurb, which crudely reveals points Gentle prefers to keep up her auctorial sleeve until page 100.

Despite two pages of characters' names at the front and twenty of maps and appendices at the back, this isn't the usual fantasy quest epic. Christie, the narrator, is Earth's envoy to the planet Orthe and spends most of the book among the disconcertingly human-like natives. Their social and political structure have been carefully worked out; there's a suitable snarl of intrigue in a bewildering complication of factions, with the power-play mirrored illuminatingly in the native game *ochmir*, a vague relation of reversi (alias Othello) which sounds quite playable. [I've since been told that it isn't.]

But this isn't a high-tension political thriller; it's a low-key - indeed, a gentle - account of Christie's submersion in Orthean culture, with generous helpings of the sort of telling detail that makes a world real. Orthe feels real. Its surprises aren't brain-warping science-fictional bogglements, but creep up on you in a slow and cumulative way as again and again Orthe lulls Christie into thinking she understands more than she does - until its alienness breaks out anew in unexpected switches of sexuality, priorities or ethics. And because the secrets of Orthe aren't given a colossal build-up as riddles of the universe, the revelations don't (as in lesser sf) fall flat.

Golden Witchbreed is not for readers who demand slam-bang action and exploding suns. Its leisurely opening will irritate some; Gentle is almost arrogant in her refusal to do anything quick and obvious by way of narrative hook. Eventually, though, you wish the book were longer. The author writes with enviable calmness and assurance, and has produced a remarkably classy novel.

From the sublime to ... well, let's not be snide. The **Nighthunter** horror series by Robert P. Faulcon is published by Arrow, three volumes to date: *The Stalking* (199pp £1.50), *The Talisman* (200pp, £1.50), *The Ghost Dance* (192pp £1.60). After collecting his royalties Faulcon vanishes into a telephone box to emerge in his unsecret identity of famous Robert P. Holdstock, that promising sf author also known to the review police as film novelizer Robert P. Black, **Berserker** series author Chris P. Carlsen, and doubtless others yet to be disclosed.

Because Holdstock chose not to write these under his own name, I expected hack rubbish; and *The Stalking* is indeed a bit routine, with major atrocities or supernatural outbreaks appearing with clockwork regularity every nine or ten pages, people's gorges constantly rising at foetid stenches, and a peak of fine writing when someone's head 'suddenly began to peel, the flesh tearing away from the bone in ragged strips, like a pink banana.' Oo-er. But already Holdstock is getting involved despite himself, and there's much inventive material on psychic defences which makes Dennis Wheatley's pentacles look like the threadbare stuff they are. Book two is better, with old Norse nasties deployed to useful effect, plus original twists; book three seems better again, using American Indian dark forces this time around (it also features a body count well into three figures after several enthusiastic orgies of blood and guts).

The continuing plot? Oh, the hero's family is abducted by evil cultists in book one, and he spends the rest of the series in none-too-close pursuit. Horror fans could do worse than these books. The third has a cross-reference to *Necromancer*, published under the Holdstock name, which is a superior example of the genre.

Staying Alive: A Writer's Guide by Norman Spinrad (Donning Company, 162pp, $5.95) isn't a textbook on writing sf/fantasy, nor is it likely to help writers stay alive, but it provides appropriately gloomy insights into the workings of the industry. Read it as a horror anthology. It reveals incredibly sleazy details of the economic forces behind sf publishing, making you wonder how you could ever have been so naive as to think a good book will automatically sell well or even at all. Spinrad's strong on punchy facts, but writes with remarkable sloppiness considering he's a professional *and* current leader of the SF Writers of America. In his *Bug Jack Barron* one used to wait cringing for the next, far too frequent, appearance of the phrase 'the nitty-gritty' which constantly hit one between the eyes like a sockful of porridge. Here he seems unable to stop saying, again and again, 'the bottom line' or calling publishing bosses 'mavens'. Part of the trouble is that despite being nominally on the other side, he's fallen in love with the tough-guy jargon of publishing's big money and big hype with all its horrid incantatory value. Another is that the book is assembled from columns dashed off for an sf fanzine; Spinrad adds some new material but has explicitly chosen not to revise and smooth the old stuff. Illuminating, but a pain to read.

Tanith Lee is, intermittently, a fine fantasy author; her work is better known in the USA than in her native Britain, though Hamlyn – recently bought up by Hutchinson/Arrow – produced her very atmospheric *Night's Master* and *Death's Master* in 1981-2. *Red as Blood* (DAW 208pp $2.50) is a collection of nine retold fairytales, for the most part very nicely written in Lee's favourite perverse vein of fantasy. The new Pied Piper tries to wean a village from its ill-considered worship of rats, but still proves unsafe to know; a long-suffering Queen works to exorcise the evil power of her stepdaughter Bianca, or Snow White to you and me; Ashella alias Cinderella is another chilly witch-girl who perverts the Prince's ball into the Masque of the Red Death.... Fun – but read too many of them at a sitting and the inversions begin to seem repetitious, while Lee's sf 'Beauty and the Beast' founders altogether in a morass of creaky pseudoscience. Her full-length novel *Sung in Shadow* (DAW 349pp $3.50) performs the same kind of imaginative reshuffling on *Romeo and Juliet*, set in an alternate Renaissance Italy with added ingredients of real alchemy and witchcraft. Knowing the play makes for extra enjoyment, not to mention a surprise or two.

Two columns ago I mentioned J.G. Ballard's *Hello America* (Granada 236pp £1.50). As I suspected, this is the Ballard novel for those who think they don't like Ballard: set in an America being rediscovered after its collapse, it's full of marvellous images, from New York choked with golden sand to Los Angeles in a rain-forest. It even satirizes Ballard's own surreal vision of the American Dream – I mean, a platoon of 44 robot US Presidents charging into combat! – and ends with absurd optimism. Very enjoyable.

Something completely different ... Methuen have produced Edward Lear's nonsense poems *The Jumblies* and *The Dong with a Luminous Nose* in one volume (88pp £2.50), with drawings by the strange and macabre Edward Gorey. W.H. Auden, with particular reference to Lear's best poem 'The Dong', once noted that he was the only poet to have been visibly influenced by Poe – so grab this one, fantasy fans. Meanwhile Gorey is something of a cult-figure for his elaborate pen-drawings, often resembling Victorian etchings – usually surreal, enigmatic, sadistic or all three. His works, when available at all over here, are usually absurdly expensive ... this paperback is a bargain. Hey, Methuen, how about affordable editions of eldritch Gorey books like *The Vinegar Works* or the fat collection *Amphigorey*?

[Such is my influence that Penguin rushed to produce a British edition of *Amphigorey*. In 1991.]

To readers who answered last issue's questionnaire and managed to feign enthusiasm for the book reviews, this column says: thank you, thank you both. To those who demands that Langford be cast without further ado into a radioactive furnace, this column says: ha ha, this page has included subliminal messages tuned to your warped psyche, programming you with a deep compulsion to lose any future games you may play. Rush me a fiver for the antidote.

October 1983

9 After the Battle

None of this month's books have much to do with battles or their aftermath, actually; my brain just feels a bit that way, having reached the culmination of long toil with the delivery of a novel called *The Leaky Establishment* to Frederick Muller Ltd. Maybe next spring I'll be allowed to review this merry tale of domestic nuclear weaponry ('Triffic' – Mrs Langford).

Meanwhile books and events have been piling up. At the 41st World SF Convention in Baltimore, USA, I lost another Hugo, *Blade Runner* beat out *E.T.* as best dramatic presentation, and the novel Hugo went to the Isaac Asimov novel which supersedes Valium, *Foundation's Edge*. The two-years-in-advance site selection voting gave Australia the 1985 Worldcon, and already plots are being hatched for a British one in 1987.

Asimov on Science Fiction (Granada 334pp £7.95) is non-fiction from Dr A., who should have much wisdom to impart. Unfortunately, although he remarks 'I don't like to explain anything briefly,' the 55 essays here (eked out with the usual apparatus of forewords and afterwords) are mostly brief bits of journalism or monthly editorial comments from *Isaac Asimov's SF Magazine* (*IASFM* for short), too short to say much of weight about anything.

Good features here include clarity, lucidity, sensible if deeply unsurprising advice to young sf authors, and condemnation of the horrid term 'sci-fi'. Not so good: Asimov's pose as lovable egomaniac can grow tedious, with his own stories forever referred to as examples of excellence in this or that area of sf, with ceaseless flaunting of his fame, achievements and awards, with crass hints that the SF Writers of America should give him their Grand Master trophy. [Eventually they did.] As well as this he's a shaky critic: he maligns *Nineteen Eighty-Four* on the incredible ground that George Orwell didn't do a good job of predicting the real 1980s. Is there *any* other sf expert who failed to twig that *Nineteen Eighty-Four* isn't prediction but a cautionary tale and political parable for the year when it was written, 1948?

If you enjoy Asimov's good-humoured essay style, and don't mind bittiness and repetition, this is an interesting collection to dip into.

Also from *IASFM* we have Martin Gardner's *SF Puzzle Tales* (Penguin 148pp £2.95): the 'tales' are nothing but thin and joky camouflage for the puzzles, which as always with Gardner are brain-stretching and apt to teach a little painless Higher Mathematics. Many are actually familiar from Gardner's former books, but he's added new twists to fool smart-alecs; often a puzzle's solution leads to a variant puzzle, and another – there are three sets of answers! A minor irritant: because of where these appeared, great ingenuity is misapplied to work in Asimov's name wherever possible. 'By Asimov!' people swear, giving me a severe pain in my asimov. On page 123, tiring of all this, Gardner contrives to associate Asimov's name with the word 'fat'. Fancy that.

One thing Asimov-as-critic doesn't like is the largely British 'New Wave' sf associated with *New Worlds* magazine in and after the 60s: all sex and violence, he complains. Brian Aldiss thought differently, writing in 1969: 'In twenty years time ... collectors will be fighting for tatty old issues, to read every precious word we wrote. Other firms will reprint it and make a bomb.' Here in 1983 we have *New Worlds: an Anthology* edited by Michael Moorcock (Flamingo 512pp £3.50), with a smart abstract cover and the disreputable term 'sf' hidden decorously away at the back. And indeed the 30 stories, poems and articles are a consciously 'literary' and Moorcockian selection, including some very good things indeed but relatively little that I (and less that Asimov) would call sf. Ballard is represented by one of his most impenetrable pieces, Sladek by his least Sladekian story, Barrington Bayley by the one tale whose larding of Burroughs pastiche (William, not Edgar Rice) swamps his usual exhilarating metaphysics. It's an immensely valuable book for fans, no fewer than 131 pages being devoted to a complete index of all 216 issues of *NW* (and *New Worlds Quarterly*). But the magazine's range was better displayed in the eight out-of-print Panther *Best SF from New Worlds* anthologies.

Three quibbles: it would have been graceful to reveal that the 'James Colvin' appearing frequently in the index was a magazine house name most often used by Moorcock himself, to add a footnote to Bayley's 'The Four-Colour Problem' mentioning that the mathematical enigma of the story was cracked (in the real world) in 1976, and to name among the 'successors' to *NW* the only magazine doing comparable work today – Britain's very own *Interzone*. [True enough at the time; other and smaller small-press magazines now abound, some as obscure and fey as *NW* at its avant-garde worst.]

Onward.... Piers Anthony's *Juxtaposition* (Granada 415pp £1.95) completes the trilogy begun with *Split Infinity* and *Blue Adept*, an uneasy mix of fantasy, sf and Anthony's favourite hobby-horse of obsessive game-playing. Most annoying is the sheer thickness of his characters, who spend ages having the plot explained to them or explaining it to others. A favourite moment comes in *Blue Adept*, whose hero enters the forbidden cave to fight the invincible dragon who has slain all previous applicants. The moment of truth looms; the hero smites his brow in sudden realization and says, approximately, 'Dear me, I forgot to bring my sword.' (Since you insist on knowing ... yes, yes, he wins anyway.) *Juxtaposition* is more, much more, very much more of the same stuff from the previous two, and sometimes I thought it would never end, as in a final stroke of miscalculation Anthony allows his twin worlds of magic and technology to merge in a prolonged tussle – goblins, golems, robots, tanks, power winches, unicorns, plastic explosive, magicians, cannon and an Ultimate Spell Book generated by computer – which bores on into wearisome farce.

A pleasant little novel by way of relief: *Tea with the Black Dragon* by R.A. MacAvoy (Bantam/Corgi 166pp £1.50), which is only *just* fantasy, one of the characters being a retired Imperial Chinese dragon manifesting as an abnormally strong old man. The eccentric blend of mythology, Zen, prophecy, gentleness and computer crime is engaging. This is a new writer who should be watched. A rare thing [well, it was then], the computer jargon is correct; no doubt we can blame the printers for 'CPM' where it should be 'CP/M'.

Everyone has read T.H. White's *The Once and Future King* - if not, why not?. A collection of his fine short stories, including several fantasies, is out in paperback: *The Maharajah* (Futura 210pp $2.50). This includes the noted 'The Troll', whose frivolous and understated telling achieves a curiously scary effect, nearly as soul-chillingly dreadful as a *White Dwarf* rejection slip.

[Historical note: I later learned that this collection is lifted from White's 1935 *Gone to Ground*, where survivors of an sf holocaust tell each other stories. *The Maharajah* consists of all the book's more or less fantastic tales, ripped out of context and (says John Clute) reduced in effectiveness by this.]

Paladin, another disguise for the sinister Granadoids who appear to be taking over this column, are doing a series of 'paranormal' books under the auspices of the Society for Psychic Research. *Beyond the Body* by Dr Susan Blackmore (271pp £2.50 - gosh, I was on TV with her once, Granada of course) is a sensible and hard-headed look at out-of-the-body experiences. Blackmore decides that almost certainly OOBEs are subjective, abnormal physio/psychological states ... raising fascinating questions about persistent similarities between the experiences, even when reported from remote and obscure tribes. Could they be a consequence of the 'wiring' of our brains? [Specifically, of our visual system ... this is the trend of Blackmore's later work.] Also included is much analysis of case histories and the theories of odd lots like Theosophists. Perhaps the availability of so much information might inspire D&D players to have another try with the astral/ethereal rules, which never seem too popular - no doubt because it's irritating when Tharg the fifth-level Theosophist drifts astrally off to have fun while everyone else has to guard his vacated body from being skewered by gnolls.

Arthur C. Clarke's *Tales of Ten Worlds* (Pan 205pp £1.75) and *Profiles of the Future* (Pan 255pp £1.95) have been reissued for the umpteenth time. The first is a story collection including some classics, the second a somewhat inadequate update of this stimulating work of futurology first published in 1962. You ought to have them both and probably already do.

If I've timed this right the next big sf convention will be Novacon 13 at the Royal Angus Hotel, Birmingham, 4-6 November. *White Dwarf* readers are invited to challenge me at the bar with the words, 'You are Dave Langford and I claim my right to be permitted to buy you a pint.' [This transparent ploy was treated with the apathy it deserved.]

November 1983

10 Spock in Manacles!

Eye-catching headlines are hard to come by; space forbids such glories as the *News of the World* classic NUDIST WELFARE MAN'S MODEL WIFE FELL FOR THE CHINESE HYPNOTIST FROM THE CO-OP BACON FACTORY. Can this month's heading have any basis in reality? Read on....

The Complete Book of SF and Fantasy Lists by Maxim Jakubowski and Malcolm Edwards (Granada 350pp £2.95) may call up memories of Mike Ashley's 1982 *Illustrated Book of SF Lists* (Virgin 190pp £2.95). Actually I'm told the Jakubowski/Edwards book was in fact the first to be conceived; bad feeling between evil Virgin and their erstwhile employee Jakubowski led to Virgin's commissioning Ashley to rush out a pre-emptive book of lists in about 45 nanoseconds.

In general the Jakubowski/Edwards tome is very much better value, fatter, witter, more exhaustive - for example, its inevitable lists of Best SF Stories include not only award winners but hundreds shortlisted for awards or selected for best-of-the-year anthologies. It's more imaginative: rather than too many lists of So-and-So's Favourite Stories we have Aldiss on cities, Watson on fan letters, Sladek on very silly Unexplained Mysteries, and lists covering sf porn, clichés, coffee, plagiarisms, parodies, editorial boobs, lawsuits, unreadables....

Of course, despite a couple of lists from D. Langford, the book has shortcomings. It isn't, the editors admit, complete: they have enough material for another whole volume, while mean old Granada cut a good deal of stuff that appears in the American edition (34 pages longer). It is unusable for reference because there is no contents list, nor - a failing shared with the Virgin book - any kind of index. I don't know whether I'm criticizing the authors or publishers when I complain that the proofreading's almost as sloppy as in the Virgin rush-job (I'm tired of being told about several hundred misprints in the paperback of one of my own books, Sphere having simply not bothered to send proofs for correction). Heinlein's 'By His Bootstraps' becomes 'By His Footsteps', Fanthorpe's awful *March of the Robots* becomes *Coming of the Robots*, Clark Ashton Smith's 'Zothique' is spelt 'Zoothique' throughout, John Myers Myers is printed as Roy Myers Myers and Simak's *They Walked Like Men* appears as Russell's *Three To Conquer*, a perfectly accurate snippet about 'Doc' Smith on page 213 is repeated on page 215 ... I could go on and on. Buy the book anyway, especially pages 73 and 216.

Here is an unusual first novel, *Pzyche* by Amanda Hemingway (NEL 235pp £2.50) - a most peculiar mixture. It's well and wittily written, and I relished such lines as 'Like all major villains, he liked to discuss the meaning of life, particularly after dinner. It went well with the digestifs.' But the story lurches between serious psychological study of heroine/antiheroine Pzyche Corazin (living with her loony father in a castle on a dead world, yet another mouldy *Tempest/Forbidden Planet* scenario) and an incredible old rattletrap plot out of 1940s *Planet Stories*, complete with hissable baddies hot-foot after precious and subtly named 'Mammonite' crystals, *deus ex machina* volcanic eruptions saving the good guys at a critical moment, a race against time to escape the exploding planet....

Hemingway clearly has talent but seems to regard sf as an amusing playground where one needn't work one's talent too hard. ('My next novel will be a serious work of contemporary fiction,' she keeps telling the world.) A pity: *Pzyche* is fun for all its wild unevenness and I'd like to see this author try sf at full stretch.

The same goes for Robert Silverberg, whose finest novels appeared in one amazing spurt from the 1967 *Thorns* to the 1972 *Dying Inside* and *The Book of Skulls*, and whose recent work is smoothly readable yet oddly hollow. *Majipoor Chronicles* (Pan 317 £1.95) is a pendant to the novel *Lord Valentine's Castle*: ten stories set in the same oversized world of Majipoor and spanning 9,000 years of its colourful history. Pleasant and highly competent, they never quite engage the emotions they should. One reason may be the framing device linking the book, with a lad of Valentine's time spying on history by illicit replaying of bygone folks' 'memory records'. Because of this, we know in each story that the current hero(ine) must survive to deposit their life's memories in the House of Records - a subtle deflater of tension. (Yes, this can be said of any first-person narrative, but such narration has counterbalancing advantages of immediacy and empathy. The *Chronicles* are all told in the third person.) There's interesting background material here for those who liked *Lord Valentine's Castle* and did not share Ian Watson's socialist wrath at this being 'sf about the Divine Right of Kings'.

New Arrivals, Old Encounters by Brian Aldiss (Granada 240pp £1.95) comprises twelve stories from Britain's premier sf stylist, variously profound, funny, silly and bizarre. 'The Impossible Puppet Show', a cycle of unplayable nonsense plays, is hilariously opaque in the manner of Ring Lardner. *No Enemy But Time* (Sphere 397pp £2.25) is Michael Bishop's Nebula-winner, here in paperback at last, a highly successful tale of time travel via dreams to a beautifully described Africa of protohumans. *A Secret History of Time to Come* by Robie Macauley (Corgi 219pp £1.95) shows the advantages and disadvantages of writing post-holocaust sf from a viewpoint outside the sf field: the freshness of touch works well during impressionistic scenes of black insurrection and white genocide destroying the USA, but despite striking images the bulk of the book is routine - capture and escape from wicked Suth'n slavers and so on. **Dancers at the End of Time** (Granada 663pp £2.50) is excellent value, bringing together Michael Moorcock's bizarrely witty and pseudo-decadent Jherek Carnelian (not, ahem, to be confused with Jerry Cornelius) novels *An Alien Heat*, *The Hollow Lands* and *The End of All Songs*. *The Citadel of the Autarch* (Arrow 317pp £1.95) is the fourth volume of Gene Wolfe's epoch-making **Book of the New Sun**, mentioned so often in this column that I merely note the paperback's existence.

The *Star Trek* phenomenon continues with *Star Trek III: The Search for Spock*, now being directed by Leonard Nimoy himself – perhaps because, as my mole R.I. Barycz suggests, he once did hordes of 'In Search Of ...' TV shows looking for Yeti, Nessies, Bigfeet, you name it, *and never found any of them*. To hand is William Rotsler's *Star Trek: Short Stories* (Sparrow 159pp £1.25), set after the first Trek film with Kirk as admiral and a few back references to the movie's events. Rotsler plays dead safe with brief tales leaning heavily on Trek stereotypes: Kirk agonizes all over the place but decides right, Spock is logical, McCoy wry, Uhura sexy, Chekov dim, Scotty's engines canna take the strain. The deadly piffle plague ravages the *Enterprise* but succumbs when taken with, quite literally, a pinch of salt; similar well-worn sf tropes abound. Very much for younger fans.

That column title? Many Trek addicts write their own stories: there's a whole subgenre known as K/S or KirkSpocking, wherein the Captain and First Officer melt into one another's arms and so on. (A 'K/S' fanzine sold for £105 at a recent convention. Jokes about which other bits of Spock are pointed have been endemic since the series began.) *Spock in Manacles* (Pits Press 44pp) is a send-up of all this, a bit wordy for effective parody but not without its moments, if your sense of wonder can withstand Kirk's eyes being forever described as 'gold-flecked orbs' while some portion of Spock, presumably his saluting finger, is invariably a 'jade column'. Those of a nervous disposition should steer well clear. Personally I suspect the authoress, Lotta Bottle, of being an ingeniously plausible pseudonym....

[This fan-fictional trend became generalized as 'slash', named for the stroke or slash in the original K/S, and covering a vast range of stories about throbbing romance between unlikely, usually same-sex couples from written or media sf and fantasy. For example, 'Pooh/Eeyore slash', which I hope I'm only making up but which someone out there has quite probably written.]

December 1983

11 Seasonal Spirit

Christmas looms as I write, filling your reviewer with jolly benevolence towards all this month's books. (Things might have been different had Collins not neglected to send me a copy of Donaldson's *Gilden-Fire: or, Bits The Editor Wisely Cut From My First Draft.*) Even our rival™ magazine [*Imagine*] is feeling festive: entering a low pub for purposes of research I found their Pete Tamlyn® heroically playtesting TSR's new game *Legless.* Exhausted by savage hand-to-mouth combat with a fifteen-dice Irish whiskey, he confided that more than once he'd tried to praise *Critical Mass* as the best bit of *White Dwarf*, only for all such comments to be hacked from his column by chainsaw-wielding editors. A likely story.

The most hyped fantasy this winter is Michael Ende's *The Neverending Story* (Allen Lane 396pp £8.95 – rising to £9.95 on 1 January!). It's a best-seller in umpteen countries; a $30-million-budget film is in production; I approached it with fear and trembling.

This one, like some of Jorge Luis Borges's shorts, is *about* fantasy as well as *being* fantasy. Juvenile hero Bastian (whose real-world bits of the book are printed in red) pinches a copy of *The Neverending Story* and reads the fantasy tale within (printed in green), which opens rather clumsily but picks up interest as it emerges that the red and green texts aren't independent. The book obviously affects Bastian (and us), Bastian affects the book, and the fantasy quest epic of the green passages is a search for Bastian himself as the human needed to give life to this fantasy (to begin with, by reading it) and indeed to add to it as author.

All this tricksiness is perhaps a bit too clever for its own good, but interest picks up in the second half ... by which time Bastian himself has fallen into the green text and is acting out the role of all-potent demiurge. Things begin to go subtly and then less subtly wrong as he uses up his imaginative resources tinkering with the inner fantasy world. Yes – this is a splendid allegory about creativity, about the balance between fantasy and reality, about writing and reading, catching the mind in its mirror-mazes.

Sometimes the writing is clumsy (I don't go a bomb on names like 'Cheesiewheezies', but this may be the fault of the translator Ralph Manheim), overwhimsical, and muddles symbols from too many sources. And despite plush production the artwork is grotty, while the promised 'shimmering cop-per-coloured silk' binding looks like plain red cloth to me. A good buy, though, unless you suffer from red/green colour blindness.

My all-time favourite fantasy author is James Branch Cabell (1879-1958), whose *The Silver Stallion* is now out from Unicorn (272pp £2.50). Loosely connected to Cabell's *Figures of Earth* (233pp £2.50) and *Jurgen* (forthcoming), *The Silver Stallion* stands up well on its own: moving, erudite and very, very witty. Here are the improbable fates of seven of the nine barons ('these genial murderers') who sustained the rule of the allegedly great but very clay-footed Dom Manuel, dealt with in *Figures of Earth*. Hordes of fantasy clichés are massacred with deadly irony. When young Queen Morvyth sends her princely lovers on quests to win her hand, Baron Gonfal suavely injures himself and spends the years of successive quests recuperating in the Queen's court, and bedroom. Baron Miramon's three wishes nearly cause the farcical end of the universe and the coming of the awful 'day upon which every god must shave with a razor that is hired'. Baron Ninzian is secretly a demon sent to work ruin on Earth, but has married, gone native and finds himself wholly unready to deal with a vicious thug of a saint who likes blasting people with apoplexy and holy fire. Baron Donander's ascent from glorious death to Paradise goes awry when he's collected by the Valkyrie sent for his heathen opponent: mistakenly wafted to Valhalla, he marries into the nobility and reluctantly, though a sort of Christian, becomes a Norse god.

This and *Jurgen* are by far the best introductions to the quirky Cabell multiverse, which sprawls over eighteen volumes, including essays, verse, twentieth-century novels, short stories and plays. For the curious: the two left-over barons meet their dooms in allegorical tales tucked away in the moderately rare essay collection *Straws and Prayer-Books*.

I've been asked for more anthology reviews. [By whom, I can no longer remember.] A hideous disaster happened to the anthology market after over-saturation in the 70s; many publishers now say automatically, 'Anthologies don't sell.' But here is volume one of Maxim Jakubowski's *Lands of Never* (Unicorn 167p £2.50), comprising stories by Silverberg, Chant, Aldiss, Evans, Watson, Carter (Angela, *not* Lin), Tem, Grant, Ballard and Horwood. One or two items seem a bit incongruous in a collection labelled as fantasy - such as Ballard's cosmological 'Report on an Unidentified Space Station' - but it's a fine collection. For sf fans there's Terry Carr's excellent *Best SF of the Year 12* (Gollancz 350pp £9.95): Silverberg, Sterling, Russ, Gibson (whose 'Burning Chrome' has been called 'what *Tron* should have been like'), Pohl, Johnson, Le Guin, Disch, Benford, Willis, Niemand, Kress, McAllister. Carr has much better taste in sf than the Hugo voters, I tell you.

John Sladek's *Tik-Tok* (Gollancz 184pp £7.95) is a murderously funny romp through yet another Sladekian satirical future. A nuclear-powered *land* aircraft carrier equal in area to the state of Delaware, requiring 135 million tyres and a change every 100 yards ... a crooked fast-food chain selling foetal armadillos as Szechuan duck ... a bizarrely afflicted invalid ('Later she developed an allergy to oxygen, which gave her many doctors some considerable difficulty') who ends up safe from all allergens, in orbit, until she develops her allergy to space....

Against this demented background, the smarmy ex-domestic robot Tik-Tok rises to fame. In Sladek's previous *Roderick*, nice robot Roderick is cruelly treated by our weird world and suffers no end. But Tik-Tok isn't nice, his 'asimov circuits' have failed, he's murderous, wicked and bad – and so naturally he does very well, leaving a trail of bodies en route to becoming the first robot candidate for US Vice-President. 'I shouldn't be laughing at this,' I kept telling myself as I rolled around the floor in hysterics.

A touch of humour also helps Barrington Bayley in *The Zen Gun* (DAW 159pp $2.50). Bayley has brilliant short story ideas, but many of his novels are leaden, with clichéd Galactic Empires and space-operatic doings obscuring the philosophical fireworks. *The Zen Gun* has a Galactic Empire all right, but an incredibly silly one, since the pure blood of humanity has run a bit thin and posts are manned by robots – legally declared non-sentient, and hence their sulking union's work-to-rule during most space battles – and IQ-enhanced pigs who politely take over the reins of Empire when too exasperated by human inefficiency. The deadpan humour blends with loony physics (rationalizing the old crank theory 'Gravity is not really a pull but a push'), the fabric of space coming apart, and the zen gun itself ... which is the most powerful weapon ever, designed to make centralized interstellar empires impossible, and is pocket-sized, carved from wood.

His Master's Voice by Stanislaw Lem (Secker and Warburg 199pp £7.95) is deadly serious. This is one of Lem's ferociously intellectual works like (bits of) *Solaris*, which leave ordinary mortals limp and overawed. His mathematician narrator records the failure or success of the HMV Project set up to analyse neutrino signals from Out There Somewhere: the *feel* of intense research is well handled, the rival theories all make sense, and the book is thoroughly gripping despite minimal action. Decoding a tiny fragment of the Message leads to the synthesis of a remarkable new substance, 'Frog Eggs', leading to the question of whether this *is* part of the intended 'meaning' or just a crude error (as though we'd tried to run a symphony as a computer program or vice-versa). Lem offers a sheaf of cosmic answers, none final, some truly mind-blowing ... but it isn't easy reading.

The Meaning of Liff by Douglas Adams and John Lloyd (Pan 191pp £1.95) isn't another Hitcher book (though one is on the way, entitled *So Long, and Thanks for All the Fish*): unlike the last, it's very funny. *Liff* evolved from a parlour game in which you decide what a place-name *ought to* mean, as in Paul Jennings's 1964 essay containing such explanations as that Bodmin is a unit of work equal to one-sixtieth of a man-hour. Picking a few Adams/Lloyd examples of particular interest to *White Dwarf* readers, Massachusetts are defined as those items or particles which people are searching for when they look into their hankies after blowing their noses ... Skegness is malleable nose excreta ... Peebles are small, carefully rolled pellets of skegness ... and so on.

I'm really looking forward to the face-to-face game version. Enjoy your Christmas dinners, everyone.

January 1984

12 The Golden Years Return

Fifty issues of *White Dwarf* ... good grief. Things have changed since I first contributed, to issue two in 1977, when the text was laboriously impressed in cuneiform on tablets of damp clay, when the latest role-playing game was noughts and crosses, when the editors hired out their (then) young and unblemished bodies to raise the cost of postage, when Marcus Rowland was but a crazed gleam in some mad scientist's eye, when the proffraedding was m$_o$re wurse thAn¶ it are now!

The golden years have returned in Brian Aldiss's *Helliconia Summer* (Cape 398pp £8.50), successor to the award-winning *Helliconia Spring* and a pretty good book in its own right. The background of this trilogy – book three yet to come – is a merciless translation into celestial mechanics of the historical cycles in Shelley's poem 'Hellas':

> *The world's great age begins anew,*
> *The golden years return,*
> *The earth doth like a snake renew*
> *Her winter weeds outworn....*

This vision becomes nightmare when Shelley sees that as the wheel turns on, Golden Ages give way inexorably to iron and leaden ones. In the Aldiss trilogy we know the world of Helliconia is trapped in the cycle of the Great Year as its feeble sun Batalix moves to or from the much hotter Freyr, in a 2592-year ellipse where midwinter lasts five centuries and midsummer sets the equator on fire.

We've had the fine *Helliconia Spring*, a book with flaws but great virtues. Now midsummer approaches, the primitive city-founders of book one are now disputed myths, the chilly phagors (among recent sf's best aliens) who rule the winter have been subdued and enslaved, traders grow rich dealing in ice, and there are glimpses of a scientific Renaissance. The story is wide-ranging, with kings, queens, generals, priests, proto-scientists, common folk, phagors and not-quite-humans scheming in their different ways. It has a grand complexity which should be a lesson to planners of game campaigns.

Nifty writing, unforgettable images: and hanging over it all, the doomy awareness of Helliconia-watchers in the orbiting Earth Station Avernus, who know and remind us that all this differs only in detail from the summer of the last Great Year. The stench of burning grows through the book, with volcanoes and brush-fires and only 83 local years to the hell of midsummer ... after which, the long slide back into the dark. Can some shreds of civilization survive? I'll be biting my toenails in frustration until *Helliconia Winter.*

From an imaginary Renaissance we move to the final glories of the real one in *The Notebook of Gismondo Cavalletti* by R.M. Lamming (Cape 248pp £7.95). Set in historical Florence and told through the multiply flawed Gismondo's notes, it's not a fantasy despite numerous bizarre inventions (this being the time of da Vinci and a million imitative gadgeteers) and the dustjacket's patched-up lizard with a horn, three sets of winged, feathers and eyed flanks. I merely mention that Lamming writes beautifully, that she gives an object lesson in how to evoke period flavour without dusty fake-archaic speech, and that famous Christopher Priest, reading a partial draft of *Notebook* at the Milford SF Writers' Conference, moaned: 'Posterity is going to know me as a minor acquaintance of the celebrated R.M. Lamming.' Don't miss.

Oddly enough, the next four books disgorged by my ever-unreliable piling system are also not strict sf or fantasy. It's a plot of those publishers, I tell you, to ruin my credibility as an sf reviewer by inflicting this stuff on me, to – *[Quick, Watson, the needle! - Ed.]*

When Voiha Wakes by Joy Chant (Unicorn 168p £2.95) is marketed as fantasy but is in fact a magic-free tale which could have been set almost as well in the past of our own world as of Chant's. It competently reworks the familiar – and usually satirical, but not here – inversion of society whereby women wear trousers and run things while skirted and powdered men practise or are expected to practise coquetry, and aren't allowed to learn to read. 'Naturally his untaught mind could have neither the breadth nor the firmness of a woman's.' Naturally. So one member of the supposedly second-class sex wants to be a musician, shock horror; a way is found but this means grief for a partner who can't abandon job responsibilities. Arrange the sexes exactly as you like: it stays a relatively mundane story. Caused me no pain.

Zomba Books are producing multi-novel omnibuses, often by sf writers straying into the crime genre. The Fredric Brown collection (Black Box 569pp £8.95 hc £5.95 pb) comprises *Night of the Jabberwock*, *The Screaming Mimi*, *Knock 3-1-2* and *The Fabulous Clipjoint*. Brown was a master of the short sf shocker; these late-40s novels show he was even better at thrillers, which some fans tend not to read on principle. Good value – and for lovers of Lewis Carroll the first novel is crammed with Carrollian esoterica, including a distinct suggestion that the Jabberwock itself is abroad and up to no good.

In Search of Nikola Tesla by David Peat (Ashgrove Press 143pp £3.95) is offbeat non-fiction whose facts and speculations could fuel a *Traveller* or *Call of Cthulhu* game campaign that played with the fringes of physics – bizarre alternative technology, electronics plus Arcane Forces. Tesla pioneered high-voltage AC power transmission (opposed by the prejudiced Edison), invented the AC induction motor and could actually have shared a 1912 Nobel Prize with Edison if he hadn't refused ... a fact I didn't find in this book. Lately he's been weirdly credited with a perfect broadcast-power system, his unfulfilled ambition, and lots more things like lasers and energy beams. Peat approaches his

Tesla researches autobiographically and can be quite insufferable: 'This task was the culmination of my own scientific ventures. I felt that I was ideally suited to meet such an adversary as Nikola Tesla.' Sifting through the maze of Tesla's later, loony patents and the modern cultists who overvalue them, he charts a fascinating voyage through the self-deceptions and genuine achievements of the great man and others. I could have used a great deal less information about Peat ('The following morning was one of those when I took my time getting dressed') and more about Tesla, but it's a genuinely interesting read.

The Hamlyn Book of Horror and SF Movie Lists by Roy Pickard (Hamlyn 223pp £1.95) is another mass of pleasant trivia, better produced than those mentioned in column 10 but less my cup of tea – I'm no movie fan. Good if you want to read about scenes cut from famous films, or forty movie versions of *Dracula*, or King Kong's inside leg measurement ... not exhaustive, but wide-ranging stuff.

Back to real sf. *The Lazarus Effect* by Frank Herbert and Bill Ransom (Gollancz 381pp £8.95) is a continuation of the authors' fairly awful *The Jesus Incident* (1979, itself a belated sequel to Herbert's distinctly minor *Destination: Void* (1966). It's enjoyable Good Average sf, neither unputdownable nor unpickupable, featuring political and biological machinations on the water world Pandora where mutant Islanders in their floating cities (full of revolting, smelly organic technology) are in semi-conflict with clean-limbed Mermen who inhabit hygienic undersea domes. Each side is split into multiple factions; there's lots of manoeuvring and struggle, including the gory scuttling of a city. A vast, egregious *deus ex machina* emerges gradually from the deeps to wind up the plot. Not top-class Herbert (dunno about Ransom), but far better than its predecessor.

If you're sick of horror/fantasy anthologies full of the same old stories, I can recommend Alberto Manguel's *Black Water* (Picador 967pp £4.95), a fat collection of 72 pieces from writers variously well-known (for horror, fantasy, mainstream or sf), little-known, and appearing in English translation for the first time. Refreshingly different: despite a few duds you can't complain at only ½p a page.

This seems to have been the twelfth *Critical Mass* column. Er ... Happy Birthday?

February 1984

13 Awful Secrets

You know that most unbalanced of all role-playing games, *Freelance Author*? The players pretend to be able to write, and by strategic use of characteristics like Doubletalk and Flattery they coax the implacable foes, known as Publishers, into parting with magical faery gold. Random perils are always waiting to strike as hapless participants make their way through the untamed literary wilderness, perils like Alcohol Shortage, Writers' Block and Mastercard.

The game's unbalanced because the dark forces of Publishing have altogether too much power (designers please take note and correct in the next edition). Ironclad contracts are signed in blood, the Author trembling lest the Publisher escape from the pentacle and rend him limb from limb ... and what if the contract is broken? Should the Author misbehave, he's instantly dragged to hell by swarms of demonically cackling lawyers. Should the Publisher ignore the contractual terms, as he often does, it's still the Author who suffers through being paid late or never. (Or, most especially, being remaindered about two years before the first date on which the contract permits this.) Oh, the awful secrets I could tell you.

Brian Aldiss sends a note on his *SF Quiz* (Weidenfeld & Nicolson 128pp £2.95): 'It has gone on to cassette, and is so published by Acornsoft, as a Grandmaster Quiz entitled, briefly, *Brian Aldiss Science Fiction Quiz For The BBC Microcomputer And Acorn Electron*. Two cassettes, leaflet, lavish packaging.... Just think – this miserable bit of hackwork is currently earning me more than **Helliconia**.' (See the previous column.) The book comprises thirty quizzes of eight to ten questions: amusing, diverse, good value and sort-of-educational, but hardly major Aldiss. Earning more than **Helliconia** ... I think I'll lie down for a bit.

But no appalling fact should surprise us in sf. Could you imagine a publisher acquiring a six-book series, publishing two, printing *but not distributing* two more (they were remaindered without bookshop appearance), putting out the penultimate book four years later in 1984, and allegedly planning not to publish the last at all? The series is Brian Stableford's **Daedalus Mission** sextet from Hamlyn, taken over by Arrow during that long gap: *The Florians, Critical Threshold, Wildeblood's Empire, City of the Sun, Balance of Power* and *The Paradox of the Sets*. They're readable, low-key, unpretentious sf containing meaty ideas – Stableford is a former biologist who now teaches sociology. [He writes full-time these days.] Unfortunately the characters are low-key too, and even a bit flat, not up to the standard of his earlier **Hooded Swan** series (Pan); and the writing is merely functional. The just-published *Balance of Power* is one of the series' better books, with the starship *Daedalus* contacting its fifth lost human colony to find the struggling natives left standing – technological also-rans – by the native aliens' unaccountable Industrial Revolution. As usual, drab hero Alexis Alexander flies round the universe lecturing people on biology and sociology ... but interestingly.

An awful secret you'll have guessed is that the sf world is terribly inbred. Even this despised reviewer is on speaking terms with Messrs Aldiss and Stableford, plus about 50% of authors reviewed in past columns, and their publishers too. The Old Boy Network is blatantly visible when it comes to *Habitation One* by Frederick Dunstan, a product of my old Oxford college. Will my words of praise not be deeply suspect?

This book is a wondrous cornucopia of things for young writers to avoid. There's a plonking prologue written unsuccessfully in the present tense; a pulp-style description of the remarkably silly edifice 'Habitation One', so obsessed with details (I particularly like 'filamentary stanchions') that it quite fails to convey a picture of the thing; flatulent outbursts of adjectives ('amazing, symmetrical, fantastically balanced' ... 'enormous – incredible – incomprehensible' ... 'superb, colossal, brilliant'); much awkwardness about the narrative point of view; a stupid, disorienting change of tense during the first conversation, which starts 'he listens attentively to his friend's ... exposition' and ends 'answered Settle firmly'; and loveliest of all, in only the third speech, two hallmarks of truly rotten sf – off-putting polysyllables and a lecture in which A tells B things *which B already knows* because the author can think of no more realistic way to convey background data to readers. 'You know that we – that I – founded the Scribaceous and Anagnostic Society some years ago because ...' etc, etc. All this in the first eight pages! Later comes the even more traditional seven-page lecture wherein A recites the entire historical background and, oddly enough, nobody yawns.

Despite lumpish prose and wooden characters (who are motivated by either unfathomable caprice or arbitrary monomania), the book does liven up a bit as Dunstan injects gratuitous nastiness. His total body-count approaches three figures, not counting sundry mutilations – you'll enjoy the scene where a young Romeo and Juliet find true love as he helps her try on her first wooden leg. (Her problem arises from another character's liking for practical jokes in the form of exploding shoes that blow your feet off.) With relish but no great skill our author has people maimed, tortured, murdered, driven mad, executed, spattered across wide tracts of land after falling from a great height ... Even death is no escape, and one lady who's already had parts of her (from breast to toes) sliced off by an axe, followed by multiple fractures and public execution, is dragged back on-stage for faintly anticlimactic scenes of necrophilia and cannibalism. The major climax is hilarious. Hurled skyward and pulverized from the waist down by an immense steam-catapult, one public hero nevertheless retains consciousness through his flight, successfully shoots an arrow into the madman who (for reasons never all that clearly explained) is dangling from a rope high up, fields the small nuclear device with which said madman planned to destroy the entire plot, and arcs onward, nuke in hand, to glorious immolation somewhere over the edge of the world. I forgot to mention that earlier on he was tortured by having his moustache ripped off with hydraulic jacks.

Dunstan does try to save this final nonsense by a cringingly sententious epilogue which ascribes the unlikely happy ending to divine intervention. Personally I don't see why God should carry the can for the ineptitudes of F. Dunstan. A real running sore of a book, this.

Who knows what evil lurks in the hearts of Zomba Books? Specifically, who would imagine that a novel about honest-to-God vampires would be concealed in a 'thriller' omnibus comprising Marc Behm's *The Eye of the Beholder, The Queen of the Night* and *The Ice Maiden*? (Black Box 462pp £4.95 pb £7.95 hc.) The latter is certainly a thriller, in that sexy vampire Cora works in a casino - by night, of course - and the light-hearted story is about her embarkation on a life, or unlife, of crime. The other two are powerful 'straight' novels, most unlike your average thriller (*Eye* is a classic). I merely mention *The Ice Maiden* for those of you who are Undead fans and morbidly dote on vampires, publishers, editors.... *[Watch it - Ed.]*

Lastly, *The Steps of the Sun* by Walter Tevis of *The Man Who Fell To Earth* fame (Gollancz 251pp £7.95). Well written and characterized, this has an old-fashioned sf feel despite up-to-date lack of inhibitions. Multi-billionaire Ben Belson flies illegally starwards, seeking new fuel to rejuvenate decaying Earth. Though all past expeditions failed, he swiftly discovers whole mountains of 'safe uranium', only radioactive when magnetized (howls of scorn from physicists), which is exactly what Earth needs, *and* a miracle pain-killer without any side-effects whatever (derisive catcalls from biologists) which is just what his crippled daughter needs. This nonsense over, the main story is enjoyable, with Earth unkeen on Belson's goodies and Belson himself on the run. A typical Tevis sf frisson: 'The Pope wrinkled his wise old Japanese eyes in pain' ... yes, nice touch, but most sf authors would sense the need to present it more subtly.

The truly triffic *Micromania: the Whole Truth about Home Computers* by Charles Platt and yours truly (Gollancz 185pp £7.95) should be out this month, ripping the lid off Awful Secrets of home computers and revealing sordid facts the nice optimistic books never tell you. I won't review this supremely marvellous work since that would be Advertising, shock horror.

March 1984

14 Machines and Magic

You start wondering if you've been reviewing too long when, brushing the cobwebs from your dim spectacled eyes and fumbling with arthritic fingers through the latest books, you find paperback editions of stuff you covered in hardback while still the fire of youth was in your veins....

In other words, here is Asimov's *Foundation's Edge* Granada 432pp £1.95), reviewed here last year. My complaint was that Asimov's famous fluency and egotism had run away with the book. He's done a nice enough job of recapturing the old rough-hewn style of the **Foundation** trilogy, but these 432 pages contain barely more plot - and on the whole less action - than each forty-page episode of *Foundation* itself. And even then, most of the real revelations are being saved for another sequel! To quote Kenneth Tynan: 'The trouble with reviewing commodities like this is that you know in advance that, for all the effect it will have, you might as well fill your column with a relief map of Death Valley.' No die-hard sf enthusiast will want to miss this book; Asimov and Granada will make lots of money from it, and because they are lovable I wish them well, but ...

Piers Anthony also prolongs his series without mercy. *Dragon on a Pedestal* (Del Rey 306pp $2.95), to be distributed or reprinted by Futura here) is the seventh **Xanth** fantasy ... my austere litcrit friends will gasp in horror when I confess to mildly enjoying the first couple. Despite a predilection for very didactic explanations and very stupid protagonists, Anthony can be engagingly breezy and inventive, titivating each tired old quest plot with new varieties of 'magic'. Unfortunately he's now invented so many magical talents, creatures and objects that Xanth is getting too full for comfort - high-powered characters have to be put out of action for the sake of the plot, as in old *Justice League of America* comics where the inconveniently tough Superman tended to be away fighting a swarm of meteors or something of the sort, while everyone else ganged up on the evil but doomed Thargs.

Dragon is annoying for its re-use of old plot devices like the dread 'wiggles' (flying woodworm from book one), forget-spells (book three), goblin/harpy wars (ditto), dragons (*passim*) and 'spell-reversal wood' (book two), the last item suggesting a deplorably obvious solution to the current book's problem of someone being regressed to babyhood by a Fountain of Youth jag. (See what I mean about Xanth being cluttered?) Instead, Anthony cops out by arbitrarily introducing a person whose useful magic talent is: increasing people's age. Groan. Egalitarians will be delighted to find this book extending Xanthian civil rights - previously granted to centaurs, ogres, nightmares, and eventually women - to a token zombie. Token, because the zombie in question is a fairly fresh one who hardly smells at all. Will book eight introduce Gay Lib, I wonder?

Much more enjoyable was Fred Saberhagen's *Empire of the East* (Futura 558pp £2.95), not merely thanks to my delighted laughter at the Larry Niven cover quote, 'Better than *Lord of the Rings*.' Well, there's no law against preferring a pleasantly rattletrap science-fantasy mix of magic and machines to books which say upsetting things about the moral effects of power. *Empire* first appeared here in three volumes from Tandem (1973-4) but has been revised 'substantially' by what looks like some trimming of superfluous adjectives here and there.

In this far future, magic works, the appalling East lords it over the nice West ('More original than *Lord of the Rings*, too!'), and the Free Folk use white magic plus dug-up technology to topple fine melodramatic baddies like the Satrap Ekuman, Som the Dead and the Demons Zapranoth and Orcus. I liked the climaxes of the three volumes, with Ekuman being wasted by a purely human use of logic yet in accordance with an earlier prophecy which we're left to recall *without* a nudge-nudge from Saberhagen (lesson for Piers Anthony there); with deathproof Som getting it in the neck in properly logical-unexpected manner (ditto); with vile Demon Orcus discovering his true nature as a former atomic fireball, milliseconds before 'victory'. Swashbuckling fun, routine plot, boldly unsubtle characters, clever technology-based magic, and my only real quibble is that according to book three's revelations, the atomic dreadnought unearthed in book one ought not to have worked.

Contrast Vonda McIntyre's new book. *Superluminal* (Gollancz 298pp £8.95) has much that *Empire* lacks - nifty writing, real characters, believable 'villains' who are decent people acting for the best, moments of genuine, moving joy and tragedy. Alas, while able to take Saberhagen's science-fantasy on its own light-hearted terms, I couldn't suspend disbelief in McIntyre's sf plot devices. Firstly, the pilots of superluminal (meaning faster-than-light, not better-than-Valium) spacecraft must swap their hearts for mechanical pumps to withstand the stresses ... a good macabre notion, but these 'stresses' are unconvincingly vague, supposedly to do with biorhythms and relativity, making little sense. Secondly, de-hearted pilots, with their supreme powers of bodily control, go all woozy when near - and especially when in bed with - ordinary people. Why? It's glossed over with some piffle about out-of-phase biorhythms; I suppose we're lucky it wasn't conflicting astrological signs.

If you can swallow this lot, the book moves well, with lovers parted by the difficulty above. leading to lost-in-hyperspace melodrama for the hero and heroine (both proving incredibly special, super-powered, telepathic ...) and a satisfying climax. After this the plot runs gently down for seventy pages, typing up loose ends and leaving the original couple Together In Spirit Alone - 'I have been faithful to thee, Cynara, in my fashion.' Minor characters are well handled, especially the sexy, undersea-adapted secondary heroine who is the book's best creation, and in whose arms ... ah, you're ahead of me. A pleasant and gentle book which could have been in the major league with just a touch more sf plausibility.

Robertson Davies's *High Spirits* (Penguin 198pp £2.50) isn't plausible either, but doesn't need to be. It's a variable-quality but most enjoyable collection of donnish, tongue-in-cheek ghost stories ... like a comic M.R. James. The eighteen tales are set in the Canadian college of which Davies was Master and include hilarious set-pieces (though one cavil is that some college in-jokes remain and should have been edited out). The ghost exorcised by Ph.D *viva-voce* (that is, by degrees); a horde of irate ex-saints defrocked in Pope John Paul VI's purge; the 'Ugly Spectre of Sexism'; the biophysicist Victor Frank Einstein who by unhallowed acts builds a monstrous new college cat. He: 'Cursed be the day, abhorred devil, in which you first saw the light!' Cat: 'You mean you don't love your own dear little Pussikins best....' Buy this one.

But avoid Jack Chalker's *The Return of Nathan Brazil* (Penguin 289pp £1.95). This is the fourth **Well World** book. The first was a mildly interesting pulp space opera; the second and third were more of the same, laced with Chalker's distasteful relish for making his puppet characters suffer degrading changes of bodily form; *Return* consists of long-winded efforts to set up the background for the final *Twilight at the Well of Souls*, in which the universe appears likely to get blown up ... but alas, probably reconstituted. Personally I can do without an sf universe in which cardboard spokesmen really do say, no kidding, 'We're tearing a hole in the fabric of space-time! ... Sustained nullification on a huge scale might be beyond nature's ability to counteract!' Yes, it's back to the bad old days of sf, without even E.E. Smith's boyish enthusiasm to make the nonsense palatable. Can Penguin's long-standing reputation for good taste in sf survive this brutal assault?

A Better Mantrap by Bob Shaw (Granada 239pp £1.50) is a nine-story sf collection featuring excellent tales of suspense/horror ('Conversion'), hilarity ('The Kingdom of O'Ryan', 'The Cottage of Eternity') and mystery (the long 'Frost Animals', a locked-room gem with the clues stone cold at the wrong end of an 18-year relativistic timelag) plus lesser stuff. Shaw's always a good entertainer. [Later he mentioned to me that the collection had originally been carefully balanced between serious and humorous tales ... but 'as usual' the publishers insisted in cutting thousands of words and cocked all that up.] *Easy Travel to Other Planets* is Ted Mooney's much-praised borderline fantasy - telepathic sex with dolphins, etc - which shamefully I haven't yet found time to read. Complaints about this vile dereliction may be personally delivered to me, accompanied by the traditional pint of beer, at the Easter SF Convention - Seacon '84 at the Brighton Metropole Hotel.

April 1984

15 Bonfire of Dragons

Instead of the usual opening jokes about editors' piles, writers' dlysexia and publishers' dangerously swollen and hypertrophied bank accounts ... a few words on a fearful threat to civilization.

This month, May, there's an interesting test case in the Old Bailey, Our wonderful police have decided the Obscene Publications Act can, by judicious interpretation of its words 'to deprave and corrupt', be used to suppress non-obscene literature - specifically, information on drugs. The supposed motive of fighting addiction may seem lofty, but the means (censorship, book-burning) are incredibly dangerous to freedom.

You think it won't affect your favourite reading? The unwritten rule which seems to be the current police criterion for prosecution us, 'thou shalt not go into any detail about drugs in any book'. Thus, among the many titles now impounded are well-known items like Hunter Thompson's *Fear and Loathing in Las Vegas* and Tom Wolfe's *The Electric Kool-Aid Acid Test.* The implications of each are fairly *anti*-drug (who can read *Fear and Loathing* without thinking 'this is the state my brain could be in if I carried on like Thompson'?), but as Bernard Shaw pointed out in 1899, censors work by rules and prejudices rather than actual intelligence. Further confiscated works could include Philip K. Dick's sf novels, such as *A Scanner Darkly* or *The Three Stigmata of Palmer Eldritch*; reams of sf featuring such routine predictions as legalized pot; the **Lensman** books (yes!); and *White Dwarf.* Preposterous? Look back at the reality-bending potions described over the years in 'Treasure Chest' [a *Dwarf* department which suggested new magical devices and gimmicks for fantasy games], and imagine™ how they might seem to a sufficiently nasty-minded censor. Think of the Moral Majority loons who truly believe that D&D depraves and corrupts, and could prosecute its 'pushers' under the Obscene Publications Act if the legal precedent is set. Me, I've sent a couple of quid to the defence fund in that test case.

[I lacked space to go on about the special evil of selective prosecution. The Thompson and Wolfe books in fact remained on sale in 'respectable' outlets like W.H. Smith. Meanwhile, grubby little 'alternative' bookshops could (and can) be given a very hard time by impounding even their more innocuous stock, a useful expedient when the law makes it difficult to lock up the owners for their actual major crimes of Suspected Approval of Cannabis, Overt Support for Homosexuals, Lefty Politics and Wrong Attitude To H.M. Police.]

No doubt the DPP will be after Anne McCaffrey's latest dragonsequel, *Moreta: Dragonlady of Pern* (Severn House 410pp £8.95; Corgi 410pp £3.95), which has lots about drugs since it concerns a 'flu pandemic ravaging the now over-familiar world of Pern. This plague is countered by alternative-technology vaccinations which the *Critical Mass* biology consultant, Brian Stableford, assures me would rapidly replace the 'flu with an epidemic of serum hepatitis. The plot thus centres logically on Pern's fumbling paramedics; perhaps realizing that her fans wouldn't stand for this, McCaffrey inserts extraordinary plot contortions to keep the beloved dragons as stage centre. Example: despite extensive metalworking and glassblowing industries, Pernfolk use hollow thorns for hypodermics, which for some arcane reason can't possibly be sterilized and re-used ... so when supplies run low the heroine, Moreta, must save the day by dragon-powered time travel to the next hollow thorn harvest.

All the usual gimmicks recur - dragon telepathy, teleportation and time travel, excessive dragon cuteness, sugary scenes of 'Impression' in which boy/girl meets dragon, and a range of stock McCaffrey characters all too familiar from previous books (for all that *Moreta* is set nine centuries earlier). The time travel is surely a mistake. It's wholly absurd that such a useful talent, which in this book young dragonriders are apt to stumble on by accident, could be forgotten in the next few centuries, as it must be for its dramatic (re)discovery in the enjoyable *Dragonflight* of 1968 - while unlimited time-travel makes nonsense of the supposed tragedy of Moreta's final heroism, which consists of ... a race against time. Oh, dear.

Much better - and for me, a pleasant surprise - is Isaac Asimov's *The Robots of Dawn* (Granada 419pp £8.95), the successor to his previous sf/detective novels *The Caves of Steel* and *The Naked Sun*. A considerable improvement on the terminally flatulent *Foundation's Edge*, it recaptures the feel of those two robotic puzzles which most critics regard as Asimov's best books. Again detective Elijah Baley is called to solve an off-planet murder, or quasi-murder since here the victim is an advanced robot whose programming could only have been coaxed into the fatal crash by one man, as even the one man admits - while maintaining his innocence.

It's a cerebral book, with the intellectual pattern of the crime unravelling bit by bit in a reasonably interesting display of pacing and plotting, while the high point of physical excitement merely consists of Baley getting caught out in the rain (quite an effective scene thanks to his raging agoraphobia). The setting is Aurora, the colony planet referred to in former books as having a fully integrated robot/human society, and Asimov relishes inventing and throwing in details which illuminate the culture. To pick an unsubtle example, sex is very free-and-easy on Aurora (indeed Baley gets laid for the first time in any of the books), so the word 'jealousy' appears only in risqué historical romances where it's spelt 'j -'! As for whodunnit ... clues are planted with John Dickson Carr-style misdirection to ensure you don't recognize them as clues, and the double climax satisfies. The butler - no, no, my lips are sealed.

Of course there are flaws. Randall Jarrell once *defined* the novel as being 'a prose work of some length that has something wrong with it'. Though less flabby than *Edge*, *Dawn* is indeed overweight - do we need to follow Baley in remorseless detail to the last shake and wiggle each time he visits the toilet? And the people he questions are forever revealing their deepest secrets in the flattest possible prose. Again, in a traditional and irritating ploy for spinning out mysteries, Baley keeps Seeing It All just as he's dropping off each night, only to Forget It All by morning ... though Asimov does provide, perhaps for the first time in crime fiction, an outrageous justification of the cliché.

Two good books packaged for younger readers: Diana Wynne Jones's *The Homeward Bounders* (Magnet 224pp £1.50) and Michael de Larrabeiti's *The Borribles Go For Broke*. The Jones novel is expansive science-fantasy, with repulsive war-gamers using numberless universes as their playing boards; the story's told by a Victorian-born boy who stepped into the wrong hex at the wrong moment, to be treated as an annoying random factor and discarded from the game. Forbidden to 'enter play', meaning to live any normal life, he travels endlessly between the worlds like the Wandering Jew or Flying Dutchman ... both of whom actually appear, as does Prometheus. Few writers can bring off this kind of thing though all too many of them try; Jones seems to handle it effortlessly. She has the trick of conviction and empathy, of larding the narrative with humour and excitement where appropriate in order to heighten the desolation and horror elsewhere. A powerful little book.

The second novel of London's super-delinquents the Borribles is also successfully funny-appalling, winning sympathy by its convincing pose of total real-life honesty. Without being specially foul-mouthed, de Larrabeiti's writing reeks with sordid relish, as witness his pongy meths-drinker ('Ben spat, and a solid oyster of gob spun once in the air'), the richly aromatic sewer scenes, the lovable horse which deposits an immense turd on hygienic Inspector Sussworth of the police Special Borrible Group. Sussworth and his minion Sergeant Hanks are brilliantly awful grotesques, like Dickens characters; with their ghastly dedication they'd burn any number of ideologically unsound books, especially this one. Meanwhile the main story is about bloody internecine strife between Borribles, and amounts to a mini-epic. Fine stuff.

The Big Wheel by William Rollo (NEL 283pp £2.25) is impressively researched near-future sf, full of high-tech, high-jargon strife in orbit as the sands run out for Earth and US/USSR orbital stations fight over the corpse. Stripped-down characters and general unremittingness make it an exhausting read, but not bad at all.... *The Science in SF* ed. Peter Nicholls (Mermaid 208pp £7.95), a multi-authored, multi-illustrated reference book already plugged here, will never be any cheaper than this softcover edition – essential, despite a few lapses, for *Traveller* players.... *The Robert Sheckley Omnibus* (Penguin 392pp £2.50), a welcome reissue, is a good introduction to one of sf's wittiest and most anarchic authors.... *Terrahawks* (Sparrow 121pp £1.25) seems to be a juvenile novelization of a TV series whose name escapes me.... Frank Herbert's *Heretics of Dune* (Gollancz), Russell Hoban's *Pilgermann* (Picador) and L. Ron Hubbard's *Battlefield Earth* (Quadrant) came late and will be dealt with next issue, if I survive reading their combined 1,443 pages. No flowers by request.

May 1984

16 Brain Death

Tensely the specialists hovered around the hospital bed. 'Absolute quiet, please. Absolute quiet for Mr Langford.' Outside, vast crowds of both the *Critical Mass* fans waited trembling for the latest sickbed news. A Harley Street expert adjusted a real-ale dripfeed into the inert body's haggard arm, whispering, 'God, what happened to him? Did he fall off Everest? Wrestle a rhino? Get breathed on by Gary Gygax™?'

'Worse than that, Doctor. He read the whole of L. Ron Hubbard's *Battlefield Earth* in just two days.'

'The ... *fool*. The poor, brave fool.'

I'm on the mend now, but must admit this trauma has left me briefly incapable of looking a big fat book in the eye. Thus, although *Heretics of Dune* by Frank Herbert (Gollancz 384pp £8.95) fills this month's Tasteful Cover spot [the magazine page used to sport badly reproduced book jackets], there's no actual review ... besides which, I made my excuses and left after *Children of Dune*. Doubtless *Heretics* is just as wonderful as *God-Emperor of Dune*; further reports may follow when I've convalesced, but don't hold your breath.

Battlefield Earth (Quadrant 819pp £8.95) should be popular indeed among the teeming crowds who disagree with all Langford reviews: I loathed it. Although most sf fans expected it to be bad, I'd faintly hoped for a fast-paced novel of trashy action-adventure, the sort of thing Hubbard used to be able to knock off with some panache before he gave up fiction to write Holy Books. But no. The plot: young chap liberates Earth from vile 'Psychlo' oppressors circa 3000AD, wiping out the entire Psychlo race in such style as to leave mere Hitlers and Pol Pots greenly envious, and ends up owning the galaxy. This, adequate for a 1930s pulp novelette, is distended to 819 pages by merciless use of short one-sentence paragraphs, banal repetition, flatulent speechifying and other devices from when authors were paid by the line.

One particular irritation is Hubbard's introduction, which tries to rewrite history and establish him as a dominant figure of 'Golden Age' sf. Wrong. Why do you think he's been out of print since then?

[Those were the days! But I don't deny that L. Ron was prolific and even popular in his time. So were many other authors now deservedly forgotten. *You* remember David H. Keller, Otis Adelbert Kline, Eando Binder, Vargo Statten, Volsted Gridban, Austin Hall, Homer Eon Flint, Captain S.P. Meek ...?]

L. Ron further explains that this book is *real* sf, with plausible science, no fantasy rubbish. Examples of this vaunted plausibility follow:

• Coming as they do from another galaxy, Psychlos have a different periodic table of the elements.

• Their world's entire atmosphere explodes on contact with uranium (spot the coming plot device).

• Their 'instantaneous conceptual knowledge transmitter', designed for their own alien brains, happens to work on humans too. (Yes, and my VCR will play 78s.)

• They build really tough armour plate. 'Here was a mark where a atomic bomb had hit it.'

• Someone dissects a Psychlo and looks at the bits with an old-fashioned optical microscope. 'Their structure isn't cellular. Viral! Yes. Viral!' In mere paragraphs this someone, though limited to home-workbench technology, has completely mapped the Psychlo nervous system using a multimeter and a couple of test prods. ('I have found the nerve that relays walk commands ...')

• A planet-busting atom bomb explodes! Pause. A second bomb, *which was sitting right next to the first* and just got reduced to plasma, explodes. Pause. A third, a fourth ...

• A moon is reduced to its constituent electrons and nuclei, which float there and show absolutely no urge to recombine. What about gravity and electrostatic forces? As a nod to the latter, the remains have a vast electric charge which zaps anything nearby with lightning bolts.

• Hubbard electrolysis: molecules flow along a solid metal wire. Extract bullets from wounds by electricity!

• Having five talons on one hand and eight on the other, Psychlos use base-11 arithmetic, which we're told is inherently almost impossibly difficult, while decimal is the best and easiest in the universe no matter how many fingers you have. 'Whenever they discover it on some planet they engrave the discoverer's name among the heroes.'

From this, *Battlefield* may sound almost worth looking at for its sheer laughable badness. No. It's dreadful and tedious beyond endurance. In fact it's *[Editor's note: for legal reasons we are substituting a less actionable ending to this sentence]* not as good as *Foundation's Edge.*

A Theatre of Timesmiths by Garry Kilworth (Gollancz 185ppp £7.95), his fifth novel, is a stab at the always interesting sf 'puzzle environment' situation. A bleakly atmospheric city is made a prison by surrounding ice-walls, and the half-senile computer which runs the central heating is close to failure. Why is the situation like this; how can our heroes survive? This kind of book demands a stream of small revelations en route to the big ones; Kilworth handles this rather well, concluding with a sideways leap into metaphysics which might have taken me entirely by surprise if I hadn't read too much Ian Watson in my misspent youth. Overall: effectively and colourfully written.

M. John Harrison's *In Viriconium* (Unicorn 126pp £2.25) also stars an afflicted city. Here the affliction itself is metaphysical, a *fin-de-siècle* languor like the (literary if not real-life) effects of TB. Viriconium is a carefully anachronistic melange of cities, beautifully described, exquisitely sleazy. Phrase after phrase evokes the *Yellow Book* atmosphere ... a sinister dwarf has 'a massive signet ring which he treated nightly in powdered sulphur to preserve its tarnish'. Even the city's gods are trying out low life, inventing Lovecraftian horrors like 'donkey jackets, wellington boots and small white plastic trays covered in congealed food.' while the plague zone grows. Oblique and enigmatic, but ace stuff.

From the sublime to Brentford ... Robert Rankin's *East of Ealing* (Pan 192pp £1.95) concludes a loose trilogy begun with *The Antipope* and *The Brentford Triangle*. It features perpetual motion, robots, time travel, Merlin, Sherlock Holmes and a microchip Antichrist plotting to stamp the Number of the Beast in bar-code form on every British hand. [Bar-codes are a particular focus of dippy fundamentalist dread, owing to the verse in *Revelations* that goes, '... no man might buy or sell, save that he had the mark, or the name of the beast, or the number of his name.' Similarly, the villainous organization of the book is called Lateinos & Romiith, two contrived words used centuries ago in a numerological 'proof' that the Roman Catholic Church was the real Beast 666. Rankin knows a lot about this kind of thing.] This profusion of plot devices does take the book rather too far over the top, but it's huge fun. Its best feature is still the very funny dialogue of heroes Pooley and Omally, and I laughed like a drain at some of their appalled discoveries ... that Eden was in Brentford, Babylon in Chiswick and the Virgin Mary's birthplace in Penge.

The best book this month is *Pilgermann* by Russell Hoban (Picador 240pp £2.95). Like *In Viriconium*, this uses anachronism effectively: the time is 1096-99, during the incredible atrocities of the First Crusade, but our eunuch-hero Pilgermann ('pilgrim') has since his death spread through all space/time in a kind of standing wave and speaks to us in the clear tones of the twentieth century. There's a lesson here for fantasy creators; Dante achieved his power with plain but heightened contemporary speech, and Hoban manages terrific effects by mixing Jewish/Turkish metaphysics with today's cabalistic esoterica of waves, particles and mathematical infinity. If you have the imaginative power to start with, you don't need fake-archaic diction to transport readers very far away from here and now. *Pilgermann* is part historical novel, part fantasy (Pilgermann converses at length with dead characters, Christ and Death himself), part theological, wholly recommended.

The Descent of Anansi by Larry Niven and Steve Barnes (Orbit 278pp £1.95) is a quick, slick read, a technothriller about a near-future attempt at a space shuttle hijack. The familiar plot gimmick (cf. *Ringworld* and earlier hard sf stories in *Analog* magazine) is a super-strong, super-thin cable which is 'one atom thick' (blurb), 'almost as thin as spider silk' (p146) and 'eight-tenths of a millimetre thick' (p15): you tell me. Fast-moving, predictable, inoffensive, forgettable.

Frederik Pohl's *Starburst* (NEL 217pp £1.75) is also familiar – an inflation of his short 'The Gold at the Starbow's End', with its crew of doomed astronauts forced by their plight to Think Laterally, revolutionize science, become superfolk, build planets, etc. This worked well at novelette length when Pohl just hinted at the details of their strange apotheosis ... but the more you hear about it the less likely it sounds, and the book becomes a prolonged anticlimax. A smooth read still, but the original sharp little story is diluted to insipidity.

[For example, in both versions one character is killed on the voyage and hangs around as a ghost. His offstage presence was an effective teaser in the short version: had the evolving travellers computer-simulated him, or what? In the novel, his arbitrary survival as a 'soliton wave' who can also make himself both visible and solid is utterly out of sequence in the travellers' development and never makes any sense at all.]

Pavane by Keith Roberts (Gollancz 279pp £8.95) is a collectors' must – the first complete British edition of this sf classic, with the formerly missing segment 'The White Boat'. A glowing patchwork novel of the alternate world where the Spanish Armada won.... A few centuries earlier, James Blish's finest book *Doctor Mirabilis* (Arrow 318pp £1.95) reconstructs the life of the suspected sorcerer and genuine proto-scientist Roger Bacon.

Also: Stuart Gordon's *Fire in the Abyss* (Arrow 322pp £1.95), a competent melodrama with an Elizabethan knight hauled forward in time by rotten US experiments, and *Someone's Watching* by Andrew Neiderman (Arrow 326pp £1.95) – yet again 'something stalks the young lovers in the empty building' and need I say more? Finally, Malcolm Bradbury's *Rates of Exchange* (Arena 310pp £2.95) may not be sf despite being set in an imaginary Eastern European country where the State has rather feebly tried to impose language reforms, but what the hell: it's interesting and witty, has plenty of good jokes as well as some awful old ones, and helped me recover from a stupor induced by the truly appalling *Battlefield Earth*.

June 1984

17 Solitaire Games

The mighty *Critical Mass* computers have analysed a representative sample of three readers' letters, to reveal the three questions most often asked: • 'Why did you review grotty old A but not the infinitely wonderful B?' Probably because B wasn't sent for review. • 'Why review hardbacks which no one can afford?' Because the publishers (whom we must always humour) send them, and haven't you parsimonious lot heard of public libraries? • 'Why a column on bleeding books in a games magazine?' Er, because I blackmail the editors ... and because countless games have their roots in fiction. So this page covers the Raw Material. (Fritz Leiber's son reports that in the D&D 'source book' *Gods and Monsters*, only Greek mythology takes up more space than Lankhmar. Strangely enough, Leiber never seemed to get rich from this.)

You want games? Martin Gardner's *Wheels, Life and Other Mathematical Amusements* (W.H.Freeman 261pp £13.95) comprises 22 revised and extended 'Mathematical Games' columns from *Scientific American*. From halma, nim and chess to esoteric new games like Slither, this is a goldmine of tricky ideas for tricky players. Would you like to number four six-sided dice so that *whichever* one a sucker chooses, you can pick another that gives you a two-to-one chance of rolling higher than your victim? Try 4,4,4,4,0,0; 3,3,3,3,3,3; 2,2,2,2,6,6; 1,1,1,5,5,5. Two times out of three, each will beat the next ... *and* the last will beat the first. If you really wanted to deceive, you would of course wickedly hide the pattern by using larger and more varied numbers.

Nearly non-fictional is *The Planiverse* by A.K. Dewdney (Picador 272pp £2.95), which builds on geometrical fantasies like Edwin A. Abbott's 1884 *Flatland* to invent Arde, a literally two-dimensional world with a quite convincing physics and ecology. Arde has no north or south: the available directions are east, west, up and down, which should usefully simplify Adventure games. The Arde building trade has a hard time of it since any nail driven anywhere through a 2-D plank automatically separates it into two; but balloons are easy since an airtight loop of string will enclose a volume - that is, an area - of 2-D gas. Dewdney even devises a workable flat steam-engine. This amusing book will be inspiring 2-D game scenarios any second now.

[I should have added that *The Planiverse* is pretty horribly written - pure pulp. That ole mathematics got me in its spell again. It is however only consistent that all the characters should be flat.]

Two 'mainstream' novels this month deal with the ultimate fantasy game of solipsism ... the one played inside your head. You are warned that both contain naughty bits to offend younger readers' parents and repressed *Imagine*™ editors.

John Fowles's *Mantissa* (Granada 190pp £1.95) is staged within the brain of a thinly disguised Fowles in no-holes-barred confrontation with his version of the muse Erato, once in charge of love poetry but now stuck with the ghastly responsibility of inspiring the Modern Novel. Although crammed with allegory about what creativity or inspiration actually *is*, this book is wonderfully and unexpectedly funny. An in-joke or so too many, perhaps, but all major novelists should allow themselves an occasional frolic.

[Or maybe not – a book dealer has been reported to me as saying, 'The bottom really dropped out of the John Fowles first edition market when he published *Mantissa*.' Oh.]

Similarly, Alasdair Gray's *1982, Janine* (Cape 347pp £8.95) happens inside the head of 'an aging, divorced, alcoholic supervisor of security installations who is tippling in the bedroom of a small Scottish hotel. Though full of depressing memories and propaganda for the Conservative Party it is mainly a sado-masochistic fetishistic fantasy'. [Gray writes his own blurbs as well as masterfully designing the entire appearance of each book.] Sounds unpromising to say the least ... but it's very witty and powerful, with the hero continually losing control over the rude fantasies he's trying to enjoy. 'I have only once had enough self-control, enough insomnia to shepherd all my fantasies up to one point and it brought on a very bad attack of hay fever.' God and several sf themes make guest appearances, and there's a chapter of the most boggling typography since early Alfred Bester. This one knocked me flat and I'm still gasping. A gentler introduction to Gray is the author-illustrated *Unlikely Stories, Mostly* (Penguin 276pp £4.95), an uneven but fine collection of fantasies and parables – mostly. The best closing lines are affixed to a Tower of Babel reinterpretation: 'For two thousand years this construction gave employment to mankind and a purpose to history. But there was a sky. We reached it. Everyone knows what happened after that.'

Graham Dunstan Martin's *The Soul Master* (Unwin 292pp £9.95) is nearly a fine fantasy novel, with some goodish writing and a nifty central idea. Arch-baddie Kosmion absorbs other men, building an army of puppet extensions of himself. But his own flaws are multiplied with his body, and the Kosmion-army's perception of the world has fatal gaps ... quite literally. I admired the ingenuity but less so the writing: portentousness, out-of-place reminders of the author's presence ('How shall I put it?' he wonders in print, breaking the narrative spell) and overuse of Significant Understatement. Flawed, but definitely worth your attention – and far better than Unwin's other offering, *Frost* by Robin W. Bailey (Unicorn 209pp £2.95), an utterly routine and derivative fantasy. 'This is Demonfang, and it is well named, for a warning comes with it; do not draw it idly from its silver sheath; once removed the dagger must taste blood,' etc, etc.

Stephen R. Donaldson has at last put aside his bizarre dictionary for a seven-story collection, *Daughter of Regals* (Collins 349pp £8.95). The long title story is by far the best, a Melodrama of Monarchs, Mages, Regals, Sceptres, Creatures and Capital Letters. Its interesting system of magic – sorry, Magic – goes thus: only certain rare mythic Creatures and Elements are Real and thus Magic, with common Magery operating by invoking images of these Realities. High-class magic is limited to the Regals, shapeshifting human/Creatures.

The story concerns Chrysalis, the plain but at least not leprous daughter of the late Phoenix-Regal, surrounded by intrigue on the evening of her hoped but unlikely Ascension to Regal status. The subplots are too neatly Symmetrical and the denouement (visible some 40 pages in advance) slightly Fudged, but it's a Good Rattling Yarn. Other stories here are less interesting: one about a chap in a *1984*-ish world turning into a unicorn is, in the *author's* words, simple-minded; another falls into the trap of fake archaism – 'Mayhap all unknowing I ate the mushroom of madness', etc. It's a patchy collection, whose strong points are the title story and the last, 'Ser Visal's Tale', more gory melodrama with witches and an Inquisition, related with ghoulish relish. Donaldson's sf ventures are less successful. Wait for the paperback.

The Book of the River by Ian Watson (Gollancz 208pp £7.95) is a surprise. From the most fiendishly intellectual sf author in Britain comes a story which is straightforward, colourful, light-hearted ... and the first volume of a trilogy. Heroine Yaleen is one of the riverwomen plying up and down the eastern shore of an immense river which splits the world in two, and can't be crossed owing to the sinister, gelatinous 'Black Current' running its full length. The current allows only women to sail the river: it is in fact the vast 'worm of the world', tail in the river-source mountains and head far out at sea, collecting souls by way of rehearsal for being God. Yaleen develops an exceedingly odd relationship with this Worm. 'Outside, the world was in chaos. A giant tadpole wanted to make love to me, or something. And the roof was falling on my head. In such a moment, what could save a girl but a sense of humour?' Not exactly major Watson, but good-humoured and enormously readable. Next, *The Book of the Stars.*

Mute (NEL 441pp £2.50) is another of Piers Anthony's sprawling space operas, in which Knot, a mutant who makes people forget things, joins sexy galactic agent Finesse and numerous psychic fauna – including crabs, weasels and, so help me, fleas – to combat the possibly evil Lobos who want to take over the mighty Galactic Coordination Computer. Parts are exciting; parts are risible; Anthony's tortuously fair conclusion may surprise trad space-opera fans (what, the bad guys had a point after all?). His heart's in the right place, I suppose, but he isn't half verbose, didactic and condescending. This is at any rate better than his current fantasies.

Also: *Greybeard* by Brian Aldiss (Granada 272pp £1.95) is a minor classic of universal sterility now reissued with a lovely cover showing ruined Oxford. *The Weird of the White Wolf* and *The Bane of the Black Sword* (Granada £1.95; 155pp and 171pp) add further terrors to the Curse of the Completist Collector, being revisions of Moorcock sword-and-sorcery potboilers to form volumes three and five in the definitive saga of Elric, proud possessor of the unhealthiest complexion in fantasy.

Award news! This column's hot tip John Sladek won the BSFA novel award for his *Tik-Tok* (Gollancz), and a special European SF Award went to *The Science in Science Fiction* by Langford, Nicholls and Stableford (Michael Joseph/Mermaid) – whoopee! I am too modest to tell you about my two Hugo nominations this year....

July 1984

18 From the Sickbed

I type this half-dead from the foulest cold I can remember. Have friends of L. Ron Hubbard blown subtle virus-dust through my letter-box? Could the Home Secretary be using KGB methods as reproof for my hideous insinuations about Ministry of Defence life, in that wonderful novel *The Leaky Establishment* (Frederick Muller 197pp £8.95, buy one for every room in the house)? Or is it a *White Dwarf* editorial purge, like the recent one at *Imagine*™ which clobbered the erstwhile column of Pete Tamlyn[RIP]? Undaunted your hero sniffles onward, thanks to a Philtre of Untiring Verbosity provided by the mage Glenfiddich....

The fattest book this month, despite hefty competition, is Donald Kingsbury's *Geta* (Granada 512pp £2.50), printed in the USA as *Courtship Rite* and shortlisted for the Hugo. This is about the first novel I've read which actually lives up to a blurb about the 'mighty *Dune* tradition'. Geta is an even harsher planet than Arrakis/Dune, with practically all native life deadly poisonous: human colonists live on a menu of eight imported plants eked out with ritual cannibalism (baby paté, anyone?). Their murderous ethos allows killing, culling and breeding for meat, but war is unthinkable because you never, never kill more than you can eat.

The labyrinthine plot begins with a twisted Getan courtship. Three brother/husbands ordered by their clan to make their third marriage (the 'ideal' family unit is six) to a heretical thinker choose to be awkward sods about it, and therefore pay court via the Death Rite which is the society's harshest test of *kalothi* or general fitness-to-survive. The repercussions eventually change Geta's whole weird and variegated culture. Convincing biology and sociology make a remarkably successful novel, even if the 'poison planet' aspect is watered down later in the story for reasons of plot convenience ... but venturers into the untamed interior of *Geta* should take a ball of string. Kingsbury shoves you in at the deep end and holds you under, to flounder for several chapters in complex Getan nomenclature, society and ways of thought. On the whole it's well worth the trouble.

Jack Vance in *Lyonesse I: Suldrun's Garden* (Granada 436pp £2.95) offers more apparent complexity – screeds of names, glossaries and genealogy of his pre-Arthurian fantasy era. But as he observes, you can skip much of that: the story, though many-stranded, is smooth and straightforward. Kings, queens and mages wrangle over lands which have long since dropped into the sea; fairies replace abandoned kids with changelings; various folk go questing after this, that and the other. By comparison with most epic fantasy on the market, Vance's effortless prose and colourful descriptions seem outstanding; compared with his own richness and wit in (say) the **Dying Earth** sequence, *Lyonesse* falls a bit flat. Though it has its moments (the visit to the magic land Irery, cameo appearances of some fine rogues and picaroons, a spell reminiscent of the Total Perspective Vortex in *Hitch-Hiker*, and more), these are diluted by merely adequate passages, as though Vance needs to hoard his strength for this marathon. An amusing epilogue foreshadows sequels: 'Who nets the turbot who swallowed the green pearl? Who proudly wears the pearl in her locket and is compelled to curious excesses of conduct?' Next year, same time, same channel....

Valentine Pontifex by Robert Silverberg (Gollancz 347pp £9.95) follows *Lord Valentine's Castle* and *Majipoor Chronicles*. Like *Lyonesse* it slips down very easily and falls short mainly by contrast with certain earlier work of the author. In this one, the sinister Metamorphs are spreading ecological nasties to drive humans from their native world of Majipoor; bossman Lord Valentine is on a ceremonial progress which runs into one appalling discovery after another; his protegé Hissune is being schemed against by jealous lordlings; awesome 'sea-dragons' are aiding the Metamorph plot ... rousing stuff, eh? Somehow, though, the baddies crumble much too easily, as when the whole Metamorph threat turns out to collapse with the (virtually *deus ex machina*) liquidation of one person, or when the opposition to Hissune is so quickly won over by his niceness that not one rude word is said about Valentine's possible motives in elevating this good-looking commoner lad to the peerage (nudge, nudge, wink, wink).

It's still a rattling good read, and one very tense plot thread remains - the reluctance of Valentine to make way for fresh blood (that is, Hissune) and let himself be booted upstairs as Pontifex, a title which for reasons of state means you have to live in a hole in the ground. What will his lordship's ultimate, cosmic decision be? Readers will remain in an agony of suspense unless they've cheated by reading the book's title.

Not many surprises, then, but if you liked the previous two you won't be disappointed.

Lies, Inc. by Philip K. Dick (Gollancz 199pp £7.95) is one I rather expected to find disappointing. In a sense it's Dick's last novel, revised shortly before his death in 1982; much of it, however, appeared in 1964/6 as that not very inspiring story *The Unteleported Man*. Despite my misgivings, the huge chunk of new material (roughly, pages 74-173) and some sneaky revisions have flipped the novel inside out. Routine political double-dealing gives way to nightmare 'paraworlds', and the almost unchanged ending corkscrews back into this central delirium. The new plot elements include some echoes of Dick's disquieting 1967 short 'Faith of our Fathers' in *Dangerous Visions*, and of that enigmatic, prophetic Book in his *Galactic Pot-Healer* (1969). Maybe it's my own current feverish state, but I'm not sure that *Lies, Inc.*'s maze of nightmares does in fact make sense in objective plot terms: it's a strangely hallucinatory experience, though, far more striking than the original *Unteleported Man*. Must re-read this one when I feel more intelligent.

Another mild surprise was Sydney J. van Scyoc's *Darkchild* (Penguin 249pp £1.95), which despite a depressingly routine cover and blurb is pleasant science fantasy. On one hand we get mental powers so potent and mysterious that they may as well be called sorcery; on the other, 'Darkchild' is a programmed clone being used as an organic surveillance device. His progress towards humanity counterpoints the heroine's path to 'sunwielding' powers: after the happy ending comes an epilogue with, again, that heady scent of coming sequels. *Darkchild* succeeds through evocative writing and precise 'information feed', that unobtrusive trickle of data which keeps satisfying your curiosity and at the same time stimulating it with fresh questions concerning the way things are. It makes a welcome change from all those Penguin 'fighting fantasy gamebooks' by people whose names momentarily escape me.

Kurt Vonnegut's *Deadeye Dick* (Granada 224pp £1.95) makes it as near-sf by including the neutron-bombing of a US city, but is chiefly a straight tragicomedy of power, responsibility and the awful things we do to each other. The Vonnegut idiom of brief, flip, casual paragraphs lets him sneak through some shrewd blows from beneath his lighthearted camouflage, but though often effective and moving this technique can ring hollow. Vonnegut knows a neutron bomb doesn't really 'kill people and leave houses untouched' – in fact he admits as much in the introduction – but he still can't resist using the facile statement and image in his plot. He must know, too, that electric chairs are notorious for *not* killing people painlessly 'in a microsecond' ... yet he'd still rather be cool and laid-back than honest, it seems. Read the book, but warily.

Also enjoyed: three collections of shorts, Richard Cowper's *The Tithonian Factor* (6 stories, Gollancz 150pp £7.95), R.A. Lafferty's *Through Elegant Eyes* (15 stories, Corroboree Press 238pp; about £15 from importers) and *Thieves' World* ed. Robert Asprin. The first two are very characteristic of their authors, though not perhaps as good as some previous collections. The third is a patchy multi-author anthology with the common **Sanctuary** setting many readers will know through the tie-in games: it's adequate but wildly uneven.

Who are the best sf authors? Wolfe, Aldiss, Priest, Dick. Who are the worst? Asimov, Heinlein, Brunner, Hubbard, Fanthorpe. The most pretentious? Brunner, Watson, Delany, Ellison, Donaldson. The most sexist? Heinlein, Norman, Cooper, Joanna Russ (oo-er), Pournelle. The most obnoxious ... I have been earnestly asked not even to think of naming names under this heading. Such were the results of an sf fan poll at the enjoyable sf convention 'Tynecon II: the Mexicon' in May.

August 1984

19 The Hard Line

Apologies this month to all denizens of fantasy, to dragons, elves, hobbits, tebbits, nameless tentacular abominations frothing in primal slime from Kadath in the Cold Waste, and Lew Pulsipher. Fantasy books receive short shrift this time around because, maddened perhaps by sunspots, the ever-loving publishers have neglected to send any. Instead it's spaceships, computers, black holes and hard sf all the way. (30,000 fantasy games addicts fling down the magazine with vile oaths.) Four of the batch have vaguely common themes of interstellar conflict, cosmic events and such ... plus sidelights on presenting background data (about which creators of games always worry) and on ethics and morality (about which hardly anyone worries enough).

First comes Frederik Pohl's *Heechee Rendezvous* (Gollancz 311pp £8.95), sequel to the excellent *Gateway* and its follow-up *Beyond the Blue Event Horizon*. Pohl likes to think big, as with his devilish alien 'Assassins' who have reversed the expansion of our entire universe and are now waiting - in a black hole, where else? - for its collapse and a new Big Bang in which they plan to have a say. I must say I rather balk at black holes being mere convenient suspended-animation chambers.... The fairly benevolent Heechee, whose mysterious abandoned artifacts drove the previous books' plots, come on-stage at last, while the familiar not-quite-hero Robinette Broadhead finally gets apotheosed. What convinces is the way that life's tiresomeness carries on in the face of miracles: Pohl's spacecraft are plausibly smelly, while the Heechee technology that gives you the stars is equally helpful to terrorists. *Rendezvous*'s complex narrative is ingeniously presented as a computerized documentary, with inset information boxes and some showy to-and-fro scene-shifting by the omniscient AI narrator. The ending's less than perfect, with some problems ignored rather than confronted, but *Heechee Rendezvous* completes a worthy trilogy. [It become a tetralogy with the 1987 *Annals of the Heechee*: see column 60.]

Lost Dorsai by Gordon R. Dickson (Sphere 152pp £1.95) got its Hugo award - not Nebula as claimed on the cover - in the short 'novella' category and is padded out here with two shorts. Why are these extras not mentioned in the blurb? Because, dear readers, surveys show you're 30-50% less eager to buy a short story collection than an apparent novel, however thin. The 100-page title story is a pleasant addition to the **Dorsai** series, skilfully setting up a preposterous situation (five people versus an army!) and making it almost reasonable by sketching in the motives of honour, obligation and machismo leading up to this tableau. Background problems: those who've not read earlier Dorsai tales will be confused by portentous early references to them, while those who do know the books will spot the chronology (before the novel *Soldier, Ask Not*) and deduce which characters *must* survive. From the surprisingly satisfactory resolution, which turns the enemies' machismo judo-style against them, I suspect Dickson has been reading Kipling again.

What James P. Hogan has evidently been reading is Eric Frank Russell. His *Voyage from Yesteryear* (Penguin 377pp £2.50) is Russell's 'And Then There Were None' (that is, the long final section of *The Great Explosion*) writ large, minus the wisecracks but with much authoritative physics thrown in. A heavily militarized Earth space-ark arrives to assume control of the Chiron colony out Centaurus way, only to find there's no government, no visible military force, no medium of exchange, no handle for Terran politicians at all. Russell's pompous Earthlings, like the British Empire confronted with Gandhi, were insufficiently ruthless to cope with across-the-board passive resistance. Hogan's are very much nastier, and here the rather plodding story picks up interest, with the anarchic colonists also proving not as guileless as they seem. Background is presented in stodgy lectures; most readers will skip the one on physics occupying most of chapter 24. Solid and quite worthy stuff, but practically devoid of characterization.

Last of the four: E.E. 'Doc' Smith rises from the grave with *Subspace Encounter* (Granada 239pp £1.50) – a genuine unpublished Smith novel rather than the pathetic imitations by people called Stephen Goldin and Dave Kyle. This is a sequel to *Subspace Explorers*, which mercifully I have not read, and features lots of zappy action, grotty slang ('In sync to the skillionth of a whillionth of a nanosecond!'), superpowered folk who whiz round several universes psionically nobbling evil-doers, and tin-eared overwriting. 'Stark' and 'starkly' remain favourite words, as in 'the theretofore starkly unknowable environment of a zeta field'. OK, one doesn't read Smith for literary graces, but this one is far inferior to the equally awfully written **Lensman** books because our hyperbrained Earthlings have it all too easy. Lensman Kim Kinnison used to suffer for his victories (e.g. erethism, amputation, terrible hangovers, infection with hideous alien fungi) ... this lot get theirs on a plate.

I promised to pass some remarks on morality, but am hiding them down here since Games Workshop don't really approve of these things. Doc Smith's ethics are heartily Neanderthal as ever: basically there are *baddies* who are *evil*, so decent folk just have to *grit their teeth* and *wipe out* the whole goddamn *race*. Page 140: 'Genocide is supposed to be reprehensible. But ...' Hogan is disturbing in the opposite sense: his Chironians have a near-perfect society and ethos thanks to their nice, rich upbringing – it's hard to swallow this bland dismissal of what I'd call chronic human perversity and a theologian would identify as Original Sin. Dickson breaks new ground, for him, with the plight of a trained Dorsai warrior who's psychologically unable to kill. It's quite a study in plot construction, the way that in spite of this our lad becomes a brave martyr, preserves total honour and machismo, saves the world, etc. (Dickson's solutions are notorious for working only in the author's carefully devised settings.) Lastly, Pohl gets frightfully American or even Californian about sharing and communication, with characters forever being analysed by others or by themselves to trace the root cause of each mental quirk. Even the unspeakable and unknowable Assassins, the book's ending implies, will be good buddies once we've learned to Understand them. [Which is just how it turned out.]

All right, games people, what moral bias goes into *your* scenarios and role-playing? If you think there isn't one, it's probably just that you haven't recognized it.

Less heavy, yet serious beneath a hysterically funny surface, is John Sladek's 18-story collection *The Lunatics of Terra* (Gollancz 192pp £7.95). In Sladek's world-view it's only logical that a visiting alien is soon eclipsed as a TV attraction by a far more interesting mass murderer, or that cyborgization should be neither nightmarish nor utopian but just a status symbol. ('Except for her foot and her fingerprints, all of her visible parts had been replaced with improvements made of metal, high-quality plastics and mahogany.') He's especially good on pseudoscience, getting right inside the viewpoint of a paranoid 'independent thinker' in the tragicomic 'An Explanation for the Disappearance of the Moon'. Topnotch stuff.

New discovery of the month: Hilbert Schenck's *A Rose for Armageddon* (Sphere 190pp £1.75), a first novel by the latest writer to have grasped that a weird name is the key to sf success. In his convincing and intellectually exciting narrative, a computerized soft science called 'morphology' is tested on the microcosm of a little island with a long inhabited history, and goes on to predict the end of the world. But there is an anomaly; the island also holds the key to something special; history is not purposeless; and the mystical turn of the final pages is a surprise and a delight after Schenck's underplayed but escalating evocations of doom. I don't believe a word of it after page 166, but recommend it just the same.

At the bottom of the heap is another reprint of the late great Philip K. Dick's *Time Out Of Joint* (Penguin 187pp £1.95), which develops along marvellously paranoid lines as the protagonist Ragle Gumm - name misspelt as always by Penguin in the blurb - learns that his familiar world is a fake set up to fool him alone. Later explanations may not be wholly satisfying, but there are classic moments ... as when reality blows one of several successive fuses and a soft-drink stand disintegrates before Gumm's eyes, leaving behind only a bit of paper with the words SOFT-DRINK STAND. Just as I am now fading from view, leaving only a slip of paper saying *That's enough reviews - Ed.*

September 1984

20 Into the Jungle

'The reviewing of novels is the white man's grave of journalism,' wrote Cyril Connolly in 1929; 'it corresponds, in letters, to building bridges in some impossible tropical climate. The work is gruelling, unhealthy and ill-paid, and for each scant clearing made wearily among the springing vegetation the jungle overnight encroaches twice as far.' Correct in every detail; and, wearily taking up my blunted machete, here I go again.

Gregory Benford's *Across the Sea of Suns* (Macdonald 399pp £8.95) is a fat, impressive demonstration that one can do ultra-'hard' sf with every rivet placed just so, and still write well. It helps if like Benford you're a professor of physics. This sequel to *In the Ocean of Night* features extraterrestrial and machine intelligence, grittily credible star-travel, and a powerful sense of inhospitable alienness; the intelligent machines all over the galaxy don't *want* evolved organic life messing up the place. Benford fans will recognize the invaded-Earth scenes as his praised 1981 story 'Swarmer, Skimmer', itself a prolongation of the 1972 'And the Sea Like Mirrors' ... a thrifty author, this. One nitpick: the occasional passages of condensed description/dialogue, with no paragraph breaks, make very heavy going.

Benford's *Against Infinity* (NEL 251pp £1.75) is also hard sf, a sort of *Moby Dick* set amid the terraforming of rustic Ganymede, where colonists with Hispanic names and sub-Faulkner/Hemingway speech patterns hunt the roaming, tunnelling 'Aleph'. This is an almost inconceivably alien quasi-machine, ever-changing, carefully not described in too much detail ('alabaster in parts and in others oozing an amber, watery light') – highly effective. I was less keen on the Faulkner/Hemingway plebs on Ganymede ... like Asimov's point-for-point translation of the Roman into the Galactic Empire, it doesn't quite ring true. A good, thoughtful novel all the same.

[A letter I had from Greg Benford seems worth quoting here: 'I suspect that the entire subtext (as we intellectuals say) of reference to US lit traditions, the deliberate Southern storytelling voice that opens and concludes the book, the whole theme of southern concerns etc – all will be lost on UK audience. In latest *Locus* I noted Chinese rug dealer reviewer was totally "bewildered" by last third of book, even after [the editor] relayed word to him that reading some Faulkner might be helpful. On the other hand we must remember that sf is a nawthern intell-lecsul imperialism phenomenon anyway.' Malcolm Edwards, who bought *Against Infinity* for Gollancz here, confessed that the 'subtext' was certainly lost on *him*.]

A very good one: *Mythago Wood* by Robert Holdstock (Gollancz 252pp £8.95), opening with his award-winning short of the same name (whose electrifying Freudian punchline marks the first place where one should go and lie down for a bit). This will be remembered as a 'breakthrough' book, with Holdstock's special creepy evocativeness finally operating at full length. His mythagos - elemental myth-images born from racial memory and human desire in ancient woodlands - are earthy and real, refreshingly new to fantasy. No standard props of dragons and unicorns ... Holdstock is working with red-hot archetypes of English and Celtic myth, as his hero follows a dream into the entire legendary universe hidden in three square miles of primary woodland, to find his own personal story becoming the stuff of legend. Powerful, impressive and magical, it deserves all manner of awards.

Unicorn have released another horde of fantasies, two of them classic. *Jurgen* by James Branch Cabell (288pp £2.95) has long been high on my Ten Best Fantasy Novels list, tracing the witty, ironic and sometimes moving adventures of Jurgen the pawnbroker through history, myth, countless love-affairs and much wicked symbolism (which got the book suppressed in 1920!) - don't miss. *Monkey* by Wu Ch'eng-en is very much older, dating back to 16th-century China, and is even more broadly comic in its juggling with folklore. Those were the days when Chinese civilization really was civilized ... while the Spanish Inquisition showed European intolerance at its worst, this classic was far more sensibly cocking a snook at every god in several pantheons. Recommended.

The newer Unicorns: *Beyond Lands of Never* ed. Maxim Jakubowski (166pp £2.50) collects 'high fantasy' from T. Lee, J. Gaskell, R. Chilson, G. Kilworth, J.A. Salmonson, P. Ableman, R. Pollack, the editor himself, R. Holdstock and me. Like its predecessor it's a patchy collection with fine things in it - like Lee's stylish perversion of the old Maiden, Dragon and Hero story. *The Castle of Dark* (180pp £2.95) is Tanith Lee alone, telling a simple and quick-moving story of the vampire persuasion, possibly aimed at younger readers: doomed maiden trapped in cursed castle must be rescued by magical harpist. Fluid writing and effortless atmosphere; overall, quite a success. (But why is there a 'but' in the page-one sentence 'She was slight, but not tall'? 'Burly but not tall' would make rather more sense.) Geraldine Harris's *The Children of the Wind* (196pp £2.50) is book two of a tetralogy. Unicorn neglected to send book one, but on the evidence of this one Harris is reasonably - though not wildly - inventive, and puts real effort into making her characters humanly flawed and changeable. The book's better than its blurb, in fact, whose stuff about questing for seven keys of seven sorcerers recalls famous critic Nick Lowe's bitter remarks about reliance on 'plot coupons': you know, fantasy heroes have to collect the full set before they can send off to the author for the ending.

[The Nick Lowe critical terminology of plot tokens and plot coupons is so useful and I've quoted it so often that certain persons (this means *you*, Bruce Sterling!) now keep incorrectly ascribing it to me. Let justice be done.]

Bob Shaw's *Fire Pattern* (Gollancz 190pp £7.95) opens with typical smooth compulsiveness: people are spontaneously bursting into flames, the reporter hero is enmeshed in the mystery and his own problems (including of course the problem of reporting something so scientifically disreputable), you can't put it down. All this then twists into a Shaw Tall Tale, with psi powers and outrageous pseudoscience explaining the auto-combustions; loses impetus with the arrival of some not quite convincing extraterrestrials; and finally shifts to one man's odd, bleak choice between nuclear holocaust and the loss of humanity's free will. Overall, a good read but – in its implications and its appearance from witty Bob Shaw – a slightly depressing one.

Nancy Springer's *The White Hart* is 'in a class with Donaldson's **Chronicles of Thomas Covenant**,' quoth Marion Zimmer Bradley, but I tried not to let this prejudice me against it. Frankly, it seems pretty awful and derivative, pieced together from bits of other fantasies: the life-giving Cauldron from the *Mabinogion*, Elves and their Sea-Longing wholesale from Tolkien & Co, the (here far too easily intimidated) Dragon on its Pile of Cursed Gold from just about everywhere, the invincible Magic Sword (plot coupon) ditto, the Faceless Arch-Baddie from Tolkien, Donaldson and Terry Brooks, etc, etc. The style, alas, doesn't transcend the fifth-hand material, being full of dusty rhetoric like 'But it was not for cowardice that Ellid was called daughter to Pryce Dacaerin.' (Conceivably, one wonders, it was because she was his daughter?) I also liked 'The stranger lifted a thick green limb for Ellid to creep beneath.' (No, he's not a randy Hulk; after the double-take you remember the trees mentioned a couple of sentences back.) And more, and worse, and two sequels coming.

[Nancy Springer has since written much better stuff, and cheerfully agreed with much of the above. But, she added mutinously, *The White Hart* sold awfully well – so take that, Langford!]

In *Twilight at the Well of Souls* (Penguin 304pp £2.50) Jack Chalker brings his five-book space opera to a merciful end. Despite making the blowing-up of the whole universe a quite startlingly dull affair, this is a better read than the previous three. Isaac Asimov's *The Winds of Change* (Granada 300pp £1.95) collects 21 mostly new stories, though the best one is 31 years old. Several are overblown puns deserving of euthanasia rather than reprinting. Thankfully there are a few good items, but it's almost tragic that the title story – whose subject Asimov considers vitally important, and he's right – should be ruined by such ham-handed telling. Piers Anthony's *Thousandstar* (Granada 320pp £1.95) is an independent spinoff from the forest-annihilating **Cluster** series, without all the godawful astrological longueurs ... a pleasant space opera, albeit a bit long and a bit prone to tell you the Moral of each and every event on the assumption that you're too thick to see it yourself. The lead character is an alien blob whose method of reproduction is so disgusting, it even disgusts him. Gosh.

And two reissues. *The Golden Barge* (NEL 189pp £2.50) is a nice packaging of Michael Moorcock's first novel, a Peake-style allegorical fantasy about an Angry Young Quest Hero, which reads rather well. *The Space Merchants* by Frederik Pohl – who's just written a sequel to it; see column 32 – and Cyril Kornbluth is the classic sf 'comic inferno' satire on advertising, still fine fun despite coming into the world in the same remote year as your aging reviewer. How does that Connolly quotation continue, now? 'A novel-reviewer is too old at thirty; early retirement is inevitable ... and their later writings all exhibit a bitter and splenetic brilliance whose secret is only learnt in the ravages on the liver made by their terrible school.' H'mm. Mine's a pint.

[Cyril Connolly's 'Ninety Years of Novel-Reviewing' can be found in his 1945 *The Condemned Playground: Essays 1927-1944*. Highly recommended.]

October 1984

21 SF Stars!

Imagine a reference work which makes this column unnecessary, a Michelin Guide to SF, unerringly fingering the five-star books and authors. David Wingrove tries it in *The Science Fiction Sourcebook* (Longman 320pp £8.95), grading more than 2500 books by 800 authors and awarding up to five stars in each of four categories: Readability, Characterization, Idea Content and Literary Merit. There's also lots of useful - especially to newer readers - material on sf subgenres, writing, criticism, magazines and publishing. So far, so good.

The trouble lies in those star ratings. Readers may inspect by appointment my list of 90-odd sf notables who don't get top marks in *any* category for *any* of their works ... including Amis, Blish, Brunner, Burgess, Chesterton, Disch, Forster, Hoban, Kipling, Leiber, Niven, Poe, Priest, Pynchon, Rushdie, Spinrad, Stevenson, Sturgeon, van Vogt, Verne, Vidal, Voltaire and Wyndham. But five stars for readability are given to my own *The Space Eater* (Arrow £1.75), which is nice but doesn't convince me that I'm more readable than *all* those people. Five stars for characterization go to pulpsmith Jack Chalker, putting him ahead of Angela Carter, Frank Herbert and D.M. Thomas as well as everyone above. Five for literary merit are awarded to competent, uninspired Charles Sheffield, decreeing him a better writer than Aldiss, Dick, Huxley, Lem, Nabokov, Orwell, Mary Shelley, Swift, Twain, Vonnegut and Wells, as well as ...

This is a game with no ending. The *Sourcebook* is huge fun for browsing in, raising your eyebrows at, and violently disagreeing with. Just don't trust those stars!

[My full-length review, with the famous List of Failed Authors, had just appeared in *Vector 122* (1984).]

Harry Harrison's *West of Eden* (Granada 578pp £8.95) is shorter than that page count suggests - the typeface is so huge, I had to read it at arm's length. Inspired by those inaccurate stories of Primitive Man battling the long-extinct Dinosaurs, Harrison's alternate world has somehow evolved intelligent saurian life to the east and ordinary humankind to the west of the Atlantic. When the thunder lizards reach the New World, there's an inevitable clash. Impressively researched (Harrison subcontracted his biology and linguistics to experts), *West of Eden* offers one of those fascinating backgrounds you find only in sf: the culture of the saurian 'Yilanè' and their advanced biotechnology.

The story is slowish and simple enough: a boy is captured by Yilanè, learns their ways (including a spot of kinky lizard sex), escapes, and duly masterminds the human counterblow. This is all remarkably stodgy, and the climactic stroke against the Yilanè has a pulp-sf crumminess which slips back thirty years in credibility. Nevertheless the density of background detail makes this, not a Great book, but the best (the only?) serious Harrison for some while. There are nice illustrations, rather like sf versions of Thomas Bewick's vignettes.

'Background material' is also the term for the latest Tolkien exhumation, *The Book of Lost Tales II* (Unwin 385pp £12.50), comprising some of the very first drafts of the *Silmarillion* myths. Completists will lust after this high-class production, especially the bits omitted in later drafts. I have mixed feelings, myself: though Tolkien's major work gained depth from this lifelong background mythology, I'm uncertain that it's *all* worth publishing and annotating with such ghastly solemnity. Would Tolkien himself, with his marvellous ear for names, have wanted the world to know that back in callow 1917 he perpetrated things like an elf called Tinfang Warble?

[Or indeed that in the first draft of *The Lord of the Rings*, Frodo was called Bingo.]

The Integral Trees (Macdonald 240pp £8.95) is Larry Niven's latest hard-sf romp, much more fun than the weary *Ringworld Engineers*. As usual the action comprises a guided tour of a vast astronomical feature: the Smoke Ring, a doughnut-shaped zone of breathable atmosphere thirty times the size - the *volume* - of the Earth, stabilized by a bizarrely unlikely configuration of sun, neutron star and gas-giant planet, 10^{14} cubic kilometres of free-fall ecology.... 'Trees' up to 100km in length float in orbit, tidal forces producing pseudo-gravity for human colonies at each end (quibble: no visible reason for such monster trees to evolve). Delightfully ingenious stuff, as far as the background goes. There may have been a plot in there somewhere, and even some characters, but Niven travelogues rather tend to skimp such details.

Neuromancer (Gollancz 252pp £8.95) is William Gibson's tensely awaited first novel: violence and computer crime in the high-tech, high-squalor, drug-ravaged future briefly seen in his short stories like 'Burning Chrome'. Gibson crackles with creative energy, hammering your forebrain with ideas, colour, future slang and (the time-tested Ian Fleming technique) brand names. Aided by a female assassin and a dead man coded into ROM, our computer-jockey hero ends up riding a Chinese killer-virus program through *Tron*-style cyberspace against the dreaded walls of ice (Intrusion Countermeasures Electronics) surrounding a monstrous artificial intelligence. I spent the whole time on the edge of my seat and got cramp as a result. Gibson's pace is almost too frenetic, so unremitting that the reader never gets a rest and can't see the plot for the dazzle. Otherwise: nice one.

Something completely different is Thomas Disch's *The Businessman: A Tale of Terror* (Cape 292pp £8.95), the best 'horror' novel I've read in years and also the funniest. Beautifully tongue-in-cheek passages and scenes of wild farce make the murders, transformations, resurrections and demonic possessions all the nastier. When the villain flees a condign haunting with all sphincters loosened, he collapses trembling on the toilet and is at once taken from beneath by a ghoulish severed hand - which clamps tight on to a tender part of him, refusing to let go until he's crawled to the phone and confessed his crimes: I was laughing and hunching up nervously at the same time. Like that hand, Disch keeps coming at you from unexpected angles and tweaking tender places. You never know whether it'll be the adrenals or the funny-bone. Highly recommended.

Raven of Destiny by Peter Tremayne (Methuen 286pp £8.95) looks anachronistic - a pal of Cuchullain's travelling from Ireland to fight at Thermopylae and sack Delhi - but proves to be based on the Celtic invasion of Greece in 279BC, of which I'd never heard. Score one to Tremayne for painstaking accuracy and innovative use of history. The rest is more familiar, too familiar. His writing is competent; the plot moves in a haze of doomy prophecy as hero Bran stubbornly does all the wrong things. He lacks the stature to be a true Tragic Hero: ungenerous and not over-bright - fancy falling for drugged victuals *twice* - he performs lots of the usual fantasy-hero Deeds without ever being *interesting* enough to follow to the foretold climax. Oh, the book isn't particularly awful, just sort of ... routine.

Billed as fantasy but in fact sf, *The Fishers of Darksea* by Roger Eldridge (Unicorn 214pp £2.95) is a powerful, mystical tale set on the remote, icy and volcanic island Darksea. Everything is shown uncompromisingly though a native Fisher's eyes and mind; finding (what later proves to be) a radiophone on the foreshore, he sees an odd, squared-off sea creature with a hard shell and a long feeler. This is a nice example of a consistent and well-imagined 'alien' society.

Help! Space runs low. *The Birth of the People's Republic of Antarctica* by John Calvin Batchelor (Granada 388pp £3.50) is wild, wonderful, weird and epic, only sf to the extent implied in the title. Clifford Simak's *Special Deliverance* (Methuen 218pp £1.95): minor but pleasant sf pastoral, marred by dependence on a 'puzzle' which any D&D novice would solve in minutes. *Bluesong* by Sydney J. van Scyoc (Penguin 261pp £1.95) is the expected sequel to *Darkchild* - reviewed in column 18 - and is equally nicely written but has less impact if you've read book one. *The Omicron Invasion* (Granada 205pp £1.75) carries E.E. Smith's name but is by Stephen Goldin - the ninth in the posthumous **Family D'Alembert** cash-ins on Smith's popularity. Read it at your peril. T.J. Bass's *Half-Past Human* (Methuen 279pp £1.95) prefaces his more successful *The Godwhale*: a quirky adventure of devolving humanity in a future of 'Hive' dwellings. *Elvis - The Novel* by Robert Graham and Keith Baty (Granada 254pp £2.50) *is*, believe it or not, sf of a sort - in which Presley survives to this day, makes a guest appearance with the Clash and lives 'the life he should have led'. Music is a blank area to tone-deaf Langford; as Wittgenstein liked to put it, 'Wovon man nicht sprechen kann, darüber muss man schweigen,' meaning roughly 'Bye-bye until next month, everyone.'

November 1984

22 Luxury Goods

The Moral Majority was right. Fantasy role-playing games have corrupted my very soul, and shortly I shall be offering up unhallowed prayers to terrible gods in hope of an obscene material reward. Or, translating into English, I'm preparing a list of what I want for Christmas. A *Charm Editor* spell-scroll, of course ... +5 Enchanted Word Processor ... Goblet of Perpetual Real Ale (especially that) ... Helm of Infallible Hangover Prevention ...

Foremost on many sf readers' lists will be *The Glamour* (Cape 303pp £8.50), the first novel in years from Christopher Priest. Like his *The Affirmation*, this book bears out Brian Aldiss's remark that sf can be at its best when in the process of turning into something else. Like *The Affirmation* it's written with a cool lucidity shot with hints of unease, luring you towards shocking and fantastic revaluations of the story so far. The earlier book is vaguely related to the sf theme of parallel worlds; *The Glamour* relates in the same skewed way to H.G. Wells's *The Invisible Man* - with a nod to G.K. Chesterton's even more relevant short story of the same name.

What is invisibility? Aha. Something you don't notice is, for the time being, invisible. Hypnosis can block you from noticing, or from admitting to yourself that you notice, a person in the same room. Invisible things also lurk in the interstices of memory, invisible because they've been edited out - forgotten. Priest's hero is a cameraman, accustomed to editing; he is also an amnesiac. Behind successive veils of forgetfulness, quasi-blindness and 'glamour' is a cleverly worked-out sf rationale, but this too is not to be trusted. *The Glamour* needs to be read, not described, in all its strange detail. Hypnotic, tricky, uneasy and full of double meaning, it demands to be reread the moment you've finished.

A present for the affluent film-fan: Phil Hardy's *Aurum Film Encyclopaedia Volume 2: Science Fiction* (Aurum Press 400pp £17.95 - volume one dealt with Westerns and volume three will cover Horror). The price is high but justified: this is a huge-format, quality production with over 450 photographs, some in colour, built to survive the heavy use it'll get from sf fans and professionals. More than 1200 sf films are covered, from one-minute fantasies of the 1890s to the major releases of 1983. The listings give title, studio, running time, and names of directors, producers, screenwriters, effects people and lead actors. Best of all, there's a crisp critical essay on each movie. These mini-articles are unfailingly intelligent and provocative; they don't just describe but analyse. I can only admire a book which makes the illuminating point that, though utterly worthless and dire, the 1956 *Plan 9 from Outer Space* is still a revealing mirror of 1950s American phobias.

Laid out chronologically, the *Encyclopaedia* provides a quick picture of sf filmic activity at any given time. The index lists movies alphabetically, cross-referenced to the appropriate year. Its most serious omission is a 'people index'; this lack makes it impossible to check through a given director's productions, or trace the career of one actor or effects expert. Slapped wrists there ... otherwise it's a top-class work for both browsing and reference.

George Allen and Unwin offer three suave Xmas gifts with snazzy colour pictures. The inevitable *1985 Tolkien Calendar* (16pp £3.95) features twelve large, painstaking and often grim paintings by the Swedish artist Inger Edelfeldt. A large-format, lavishly produced reissue of Tolkien's *The Hobbit* (290pp £11.95) has more than 50 full pages painted by Michael Hague. And Alan Lee's *Castles* (192pp £12.95) ranges through almost every aspect of the castle in history, myth and fantasy; the clear narrative text by David Day is suitable for readers of any age, and the book's almost impossible to open without finding one or more of Lee's ethereal drawings and paintings.

As you'd expect from Unwin, famous proprietors of Tolkien, all three have high production standards. On the whole I liked Hague's illustrations best: their muted stained-glass or ancient-tapestry look suits a classic tale of long ago and far away – though like many before him, Hague doesn't quite succeed with Gandalf. *Castles* is constrained by subject matter: a castle is a castle, and despite Lee's evident skill – especially at far-off vistas – there are only so many changes to be rung. (Is it a joke that an almost identical delicate pink is used for Ariosto's Castle of Earthly Paradise and for Barad-Dûr?) But the Gormenghast picture is almost worth the price of admission all by itself. Edelfeldt has the hardest task, with yet another *Calendar*; she's undeniably good, yet her stiff figures and the hard-edged, near-photographic quality of most of these paintings seemed rather discordant. Nevertheless she makes a good stab at the near-impossible task of painting Gollum.

Garry Kilworth's sf shorts are something special, with concentrated colour and impact: thirteen are collected in *The Songbirds of Pain* (Gollancz 187pp £8.95). Themes? Ordinary things – pain, religion, death, immortality, yearnings for impossible ideals. They're sf/fantasy, though, with mind transfers, alien places, ETs waging war with philosophical weapons, time travel and, outrageously, the quest for a new primary colour. Amid Kilworth's exotic settings, the 'ordinary' and 'fantastic' aspects fuse in a blaze of style. Try it.

Collectors and libraries will seize on the **SF Alternatives** series from John Goodchild – solid hardback editions of those thumbed, disintegrating classics. Alfred Bester's *Tiger! Tiger!* (249pp £8.95), soon to be 30 years old, has long deserved a new British hardback. The compulsive, pyrotechnic tale of obsession and revenge needs no introduction. Read it, read it! A somewhat less obvious choice is John Crowley's *Beasts* (184pp £8.95), a strange story of genetically engineered man/beast hybrids who are greater than the sums of their genes. This one's a bit young for canonization (1976), but it's a pretty good book. Quibbles for series editor David Wingrove: *Tiger! Tiger!* follows the Penguin typesetting with two bits of fancy typography indicated but missing on page 231, while the author's dedication and epigraph are omitted from *Beasts*. Tch-tch.

[The *Tiger! Tiger!* anomaly goes back through earlier Panther editions to the 1956 British first from Sidgwick and Jackson. It took me years to learn that the 1957 US version, titled *The Stars My Destination*, has a slightly different text – the book's most famous line is 'Vorga, I kill you filthy' rather than the British editions' familiar 'kill you deadly'.]

A timely reprint for the grim 1980s is H.G. Wells's *The Croquet Player* from 1936 (Ian Henry 82pp £5.25). Its evocation of a Nameless Evil haunting English marshland is better than anything Lovecraft could contrive ... but the horror relates to prehistoric savageries of our remote ancestors, a haunting (as in *The Glamour*) from deep inside our own minds. As civilization totters, the blood-spattered caveman begins to re-emerge. Read this, remember what happened soon after its publication, look around you today, and allow yourself a small shudder.

Savoy Dreams: the Secret Life of Savoy Books (Savoy 260pp £7.95) is a monument to another worrying facet of 1980s Britain. Savoy, interesting Manchester-based publishers, were stamped on again and again for publishing and selling allegedly rude things. They tried to play safe by asking the police what was regarded as OK to sell. No, went the reply, we're not going to tell you: *first* you try selling things and *then* we decide whether to do you for it.... *Dreams* is a Savoy retrospective, for completists, worriers about liberty and fans of the old avant-garde *New Worlds*, with bits by Burroughs, Moorcock, M. John Harrison; with articles on being persecuted, reviews, extracts, clippings and graphics which I thoroughly disliked. Fascinating. Very 1960s.

Mick Farren's *Protectorate* (NEL 252pp £1.95) is far-future sf – decaying Earth under alien rule – which shows deep and well-researched knowledge of decadence. The story of rebellious forces is over-long and more or less irrelevant to the black ending. A competent novel. *Tales from the Vulgar Unicorn* ed. Robert Asprin (Penguin 223pp £1.95) is the second **Sanctuary** fantasy anthology – it must be good, there's a story from A.E. van Vogt which actually makes sense! *The History of the Runestaff* (Granada 573pp £2.95) packs the four Dorian Hawkmoon novels in one almost liftable volume, a reminder of how fluently Moorcock could churn out heroic fantasy even when asleep. See hardback coverage in columns 2 and 9 for the now paperbacked *Chekhov's Journey* by Ian Watson (Granada 176pp £1.95) – enjoyable, ingenious sf albeit minor Watson – and *Asimov on SF* (Granada 384pp £2.50), so-so non-fiction with some interesting bits.

Help ... a whole column gone and I haven't been unforgivably rude to anyone. I must slip off to re-re-read Hugh Kingsmill's *Anthology of Invective and Abuse*.

December 1984

23 After 1984

By this issue, ominous 1984 will have ended without a world-destroying nuclear holocaust or brutal government suppression of *White Dwarf*: I can predict these rash things because if I'm wrong you won't get to read them. Either way, Happy New Year.

Robert Heinlein strikes again with *Job: a Comedy of Justice* (NEL 368pp £8.95), a rather peculiar theological satire which – as did his last one, *Friday* – shines by comparison with the awful *Number of the Beast* without equalling his best work. Like Job in the Bible, the hero is mucked around no end by Higher Powers; like Jurgen in Cabell's *Jurgen: a Comedy of Justice*, he goes to hell, heaven and beyond, finally meeting the real ruler of the universe, Koshchei.

The writing is sprightly and the book slips down easily enough. Deficiencies? First, the hero is rather an uninteresting fellow: I never worked out why the far more competent and sensible heroine was so keen on this wimp. (There's not nearly enough of the best character, Satan, latest of Heinlein's wisecracking knowalls.) Secondly, the hero's torments merely consist of washing dishes to survive in a series of grubby parallel worlds through which God, like a vindictive gamesmaster, is shuttling him – all a bit monotonous. Thirdly, the irreverent treatment of the Day of Judgment, Heaven and Hell – though fairly amusing – falls far below Cabell's. When blasphemy stops being witty and shocking it tends to become pointless, like dingy graffiti scrawled on church walls. I didn't *dislike* this one, but ... wait for the paperback, eh?

Daybreak on a Different Mountain (Unwin 246pp £8.95) is the first novel from Colin Greenland, internationally celebrated as an editor of *Interzone*. This fantasy has its own odd flavour, full of leisurely metaphysical reflection and sudden narrative jumps; try to skim a slowish bit and you lose the thread altogether.

Two unlikely allies, a sceptical fighter and a semi-mystical poet, leave their sealed and ennui-ridden city (vaguely reminiscent of Harrison's Viriconium) on a dubious quest. There's virtually no hacking and slashing: the people met en route aren't hostile, just revealingly different. Even the magical elements are low-key and ambiguous (is the climactic moment on the sacred mountain 'real'?), and the conclusion – when the heroes return to redeem their city – suggests that sceptic and mystic are both right. I found this one unusually well-written, but short on narrative energy.

Completely different and bubbling over with bizarre ideas, Ian Watson's *The Book of the Stars* (Gollancz 208pp £8.95) is second in the *Book of the River* trilogy – see column 17. It's fine tongue-in-cheek fun, coming close to farce as lovable heroine Yaleen dies temporarily, only to be resurrected by her world's dotty trainee god the Worm, to spy on the even dottier electronic Godmind responsible for Earth's colonization of the galaxy. The Godmind's master plan for the universe is bizarrely silly even for Watson, but what can you expect from a near-deity whose hobby is growing roses on the Moon?

All Watson's books are crammed with ideas to boggle sf readers who have seen it all, but this latest trilogy presents them in uniquely digestible form. I hope he finishes work soon on number three, *The Book of Being*.

No doubt there'll be – if there isn't already – a *Dune* game in the wake of the film. Save your money: you'll have far more fun fitting the world of *Dune* into your favourite sf RPG with the aid of Willis McNelly's *The Dune Encyclopaedia* (Corgi 526pp £5.95). This 'work of painstaking scholarship' (says the blurb – I'd call it pseudo-scholarship myself) tells you infinitely more than you wanted to know about Frank Herbert's universe. The production is quite impressive, though real or faked photos instead of line-drawings would have added greatly to the 'encyclopaedia' look. Whether it's of interest to mere readers is debatable, but game-players and trivia hounds will be fascinated. On its way: *The Helliconia Encyclopaedia*, covering Brian Aldiss's now almost famous world. Is this a new trend? I hope not.

[Later I actually saw what purported to be the completed typescript of *The Helliconia Encyclopaedia*, but this never made it into print.]

Terry Carr's *Best SF of the Year 13* (Gollancz 378pp £4.95 trade pb, £9.95 hc) is really his choice of the best sf of the year 1983 – editors always have difficulty with numbers. The featured authors are Frederik Pohl, Ian Watson, Connie Willis, Greg Bear (the Nebula winner), Robert Silverberg, Cherry Wilder, Richard Cowper, Jack Dann, John Sladek (with a 1976 story: editors always have difficulty ...) and Michael Bishop. Most stories were shortlisted for major awards. No duds: Carr's good taste can be trusted. Worth a look.

John Brunner's *The Sheep Look Up* has been reissued (Arrow 461pp £2.50): his gloomiest novel, one long massive downer bulging with dire warnings to us all. Its unremitting eco-despair is at its 'cheeriest' when at the end, Europeans can smell all North America burning. The word is Schadenfreude – look it up.

Normally I view computer games with aloof, aristocratic disdain (even if I am writing this on a new word processor). However, I couldn't resist begging a copy of *The Stainless Steel Rat Saves The World* (Mosaic £9.95, with the 158pp Sphere novel thrown in), based of course on Harry Harrison's lighthearted story. The game is a text adventure with snappy graphic decorations; I borrowed two sf/Adventure buffs and watched in awe as they swiftly solved the first challenge (basically, you have to do the obvious thing *quickly* or get zapped). Now comes the embarrassing part.

The second scene halted my trusty suckers. They complained bitterly that the wretched program wouldn't let them go anywhere or do anything interesting. They sat admiring its incredibly slow response time, frustrated by the effort to find a command which didn't give 'Try another object/action' or 'You can't do that, Jim/Slippery Jim/James/diGriz/Rat' ... Eventually the test crew went home, cursing the name of Shards Software (the programmers) and muttering things like 'Harry Harrison should sue.' Perhaps this experience is not typical. More in our next.

By the way, if any Siberian hermit out there hasn't yet read Umberto Eco's *The Name of the Rose* (Picador £2.95), go and do so at once. The chapters about mapping the mysterious library/maze are quite the most D&D-like stuff ever to appear in a 'respectable' novel: and it's a fine novel too.

It's only 1985, but Brian Stableford and I have just finished writing *The Third Millennium: A History of the World AD 2000-3000*. Now pay attention. When this is published by Sidgwick & Jackson later in the year, you will all go to your local bookshops and – *[Do not adjust your magazine. There is a fault in Dave Langford, as usual. Normal service will be resumed next month – Ed.]*

January 1985

24 Sequels Anonymous

Sometimes the strain becomes too much for ashen-faced, trembling sf authors. The terrible *craving* seizes them; only the strongest try to resist, and stumble sweating to phone the 24-hour hotline. 'Sequels Anonymous? For God's sake talk me out of this - my will-power's gone, I can feel a sixth *Dune* book coming over me ...' Alas, the SA counsellors are rarely persuasive enough - and the trouble with sequelholism is that it damages not only the writers' brains but the readers'.

There are sequels and sequels, as shown by the first three books now moving down the conveyor belt towards *Critical Mass*'s rotating knives. Douglas Adams is the gravest case, with *So Long, and Thanks for All the Fish* (Pan 191pp £6.95) - 'fourth book in the **Hitch-Hiker** trilogy.'

They say Adams finds it increasingly hard to write Hitcher books; you can see why. Book one was a small miracle, frothy jokes balancing pessimism in a tightrope-dance that needed no actual plot. Book two: similar but diluted. Book three had a plot, showing Adams to be hopeless at plots. Book four, even at a skimpy 45,000 words, is full of padding. 'It's guff. It doesn't advance the action.' (p.131). A few good jokes and clever ideas, a shaggy-dog punchline as God's Final Message To His Creation is revealed - and that's it. Sequelholism has drained Adams of the high-speed inventiveness which made him famous. No doubt he'll agree with me all the way to the bank.

Anne McCaffrey has unexpectedly published a sequel to what even rabid fans agree is her worst book, *Dinosaur Planet* (1978). Billed as part one of a trilogy, this novel was quite devoid of interest and passed straight into merciful oblivion. *The Survivors: Dinosaur Planet II* (Orbit 283pp £1.95) wraps up the story without visible need for a third volume, but remains half-hearted and dull.

What's the problem? This is 'straight' sf adventure and McCaffrey never seems *interested* in it, as she is in her romantic sf/fantasies with their dragons and singers. The writing's slipshod and the science dodgy. Portentous questions about murky plot points (what happened to the missing spaceship, etc) are repeated *ad nauseam* - they not only lack narrative interest but prove to have singularly banal answers. I'd spent most of the book hoping against hope that the question of why this planet has Earth-type dinosaurs was *not* going to be answered with traditional guff about ancient aliens who like zoos....

Our third 'sequel' is the best. The Adams novel should probably have stayed unwritten, and the McCaffrey boiled down with its predecessor into one tight story; but I like a preplanned, episodic fantasy series when it's done right, as in Geraldine Harris's *The Dead Kingdom* (Unicorn 182pp £2.50) - book three of her **Seven Citadels** tetralogy. Several issues ago I emitted lukewarm praise for book two, *Children of the Wind*, only to be told by One Who Knew that this was the weakest of the four. Pausing to acquire book one, *Prince of the Godborn*, I zipped through the lot ... yes, this is good stuff. Book three has quirky humour, high-fantasy passages almost on a par with Le Guin, and some heartening surprises. It's refreshing for any jaded reviewer or reader when characters fail to act stereotyped, fail to do what one yawningly assumes they must.

Harris's other secret is simple: evidently she planned the four books as a whole rather than writing blindly into the unknown or tacking extensions on to a self-contained novel. To all sequelholics I say, go thou and do likewise.

Your reviewer is also a sucker for hard-sf novels tackling the complexities of how science is really done. Under this rubric the *Critical Mass* seal of approval goes to Paul Preuss's *Broken Symmetries* (Penguin 335pp £2.95). In a near-future Hawaii, scientific and political infighting surround the ultra-powerful US/Japanese TERAC accelerator and its production of 'I-particles' ... stable quarks with awesome potential. Jaw-breaking jargon is kept to a couple of pages. Manipulation is the name of the game, both political and personal: Preuss will scare you rigid with his convincing picture of mostly well-meaning people and bureaucrats colliding, like particles in TERAC, and chain-reacting towards disaster.

Broken Symmetries has its flaws - like a spy-novel cliché or three - but it's an impressive and unnerving performance. In the tradition of Greg Benford's *Timescape*, if not at all up to that book's weight.

I'm not sure what John Grant's *The Truth about the Flaming Ghoulies* (Muller 224pp £8.95) is in the tradition of ... but since it's inexplicably dedicated to my wife and myself, you'll understand the possibility of bribery and corruption. The Flaming Ghoulies are a chart-topping group of the late 1980s, who establish the book as sf and incidentally cause mild alarm when a final performance features their detonation in a multimegaton blast which razes Chicago. The writing of the Ghoulies' official history is turned over to a crack geomorphologist (because, in case you were going to ask, he knows all about rock), who traces their career through a maze of extremely silly letters and clippings making up the book.

Inevitably the ultimate revelation is a shaggy-dog joke, but there are plenty of laughs en route. Particularly implausible is Grant's libellous future slang ... to pick printable examples, 1988 people don't say 'he threw up' but 'he heseltined everywhere'; they refer not to rude diseases but to 'some exotic variety of the reagan.' Is the author trying to tell us something?

[Langford to Grant: 'Knowing you, I'm amazed you didn't use the word "thatcher" for some particularly revolting activity.' Grant to Langford: 'I intended to, but just couldn't think of one revolting enough to merit that name.']

The Frozen City (Unwin 231pp £8.95) comes from new authors David Arscott and David J. Marl. It's a curious and interesting book, accessible to younger readers but using the fantasy city as a frame for political allegory. The city's 'frozen' under a brutal regime; movement is restricted by mazelike streets; art and beauty are exiled to a secret, buried city which is a literal underground; the young hero is beset with problems of honesty vs practical politics (sometimes too didactically expressed); the final revelation of the regime's leadership has a philosophical brutality echoing Orwell's famous line 'The object of power is power.'

Not particularly new or astonishing in itself, this gains freshness and force from the allegorical presentation. A modest success. Fantasy's so hidebound that it's still a novelty for authors to suggest that even a benign dictatorship or monarchy may *not* be a good thing.

Hello? Sequels Anonymous? I've this terrible urge to continue my comments on the Shards *Stainless Steel Rat Saves the World* adventure (Mosaic, for CBM64, £9.95) ... argh, too late to stop. Seems my investigators last issue failed to be sufficiently obvious and simple-minded. Having passed the game's initial barrier, they say it gets slightly better - but recommend Harry Harrison's original books, especially the first, as being a whole lot more fun. Ned Ludd lives!

Next month - can enslaved Langford resist another sequel to the endless *Critical Mass* series? Will the SA hotline be able to talk me out of my vicious habit? I doubt it somehow.

February 1985

25 The Dead Time

Midwinter sees the reviewing business at its lowest ebb (and likewise, after too many Xmas and New Year's parties, the reviewer). Publishers huddle in their cosy offices rather than brave the wintry chill to post out books for review. Or they go completely bananas like Granada, deluging me with Len Deighton thrillers and autobiographies of loony clairvoyants. I don't know whether Allen & Unwin intended a veiled hint when they sent (with a covering slip promising a copy of *Shields of Trell* by Jenny Summerville, £4.95) a paperback called *First Aid in Mental Health*. Perhaps it's meant as useful background reading for *Call of Cthulhu* players?

In this month's scant handful of books, one stands out because it's the biggest – a paperback as tall as *White Dwarf* and of course much fatter. This is Peter Nicholls's *Fantastic Cinema* (Ebury Press 224pp £6.95), a serious but not at all pompous look at the history and highlights of sf/fantasy films. The coverage slops over into horror and the surreal, so Nicholls discusses major items omitted from the far more theoretically comprehensive Aurum encyclopaedia reviewed in column 22.

Despite the natural, human instinct to be rude to Peter Nicholls (the things I could tell you about the writing of *The Science in Science Fiction*!), I must say this is one of the few worthy books on sf films. Too many are cheap exploitation or publicity jobs, all pictures and lame plot rehashes. Nicholls is eclectic and witty; he passes the important test of being interesting to read even when discussing films one has never seen and will probably never see; he also scores well on the infallible *Critical Mass* scale, by frequently agreeing with D. Langford. 'Puerile ... riddled with bad science ... the sociology is fatuous' – anyone praising *Silent Running* in these terms is OK by me.

A specially interesting chapter called 'Key Directors and Producers since 1968' assesses the careers of Altman, Broccoli, Carpenter, Cohen, Cronenberg, De Laurentiis, De Palma, Kubrick, Lucas, Python (I said eclectic!), Romero, Scott and Spielberg. In short: good stuff, with plenty of stills as well as text.

Incurable addicts of fantasy trilogies may possibly have drooled over *The War of Powers* by Robert Vardeman and Victor Milan (NEL 457pp £2.95), a whopping one-volume package which appeared as three books in the USA. 1985 sees the three-in-one 'sequel' subtitled *Part II: Istu Awakened* (NEL 511pp £2.95) – finishing the maddeningly incomplete story of volume one, published last February with no indication that important bits of plot were missing. Not that it matters much.

How shall I put it? The authors keep their narrative moving, they crack the occasional joke, they're refreshingly uninhibited (I lost count of the sex scenes, but will just mention the one in which a multiply endowed lizard-man pleasures the heroine twice simultaneously). But after six books I felt as though I'd spent a week listening to Muzak while eating nothing but monosodium glutamate flavoured crisps. *The War of Powers* is 968 pages of junk food for the mind, and it doesn't half give you indigestion.

Besides which, you find yourself gifted with an eerie ability to predict the plot far in advance. Gosh, the hero and heroine are going to meet after long separation – looks like their interim lovers will have to be killed off. Yep, there they go, both of them. Gosh, two major villains are written off in book four after falling from great heights, yet *no one saw them land*: can it be ...? Yep, here they are again in book five. Connoisseurs of hackwork will enjoy the random variations in magic ability with the needs of the plot: one moment it's 'Alas, my powers are weak so far from my home city,' but shortly afterwards (when said powers have done something totally unprecedented) the word is 'My powers have grown with practice' ... There is also the Destiny Stone, a wondrous amulet which, like red kryptonite in Superman comics, exists solely to account for ludicrous improbabilities and reversals of fortune.

People who like routine sword-and-sorcery, with a heart-warming killing or orgasm (sometimes both) every few pages, will no doubt love this book. These two books. These six books....

For something offbeat and unexpected you can rely on Diana Wynne Jones, who's often underrated because she appears on the 'children's' shelves. Her *Archer's Goon* (Methuen 241pp £6.95) is a complicated and funny extravaganza set in an ordinary English town secretly run by seven eccentric demigods. It's the freshness of approach which makes it succeed, with streetwise magic which curses your electric supply, conjures up traffic jams or bugs the drainpipes. One of the seven lives in the vault of the local bank and is mad on gadgetry; another wields dread power over the sewers; one lives in the past and one in the future (some lively time paradoxes here); all are deeply interested in the 2000 words of worthless prose the young hero's father regularly writes to avoid paying taxes (no, he doesn't do *Critical Mass*). After this, things begin to get complicated. Though one dodgy moral question goes unanswered, the ending is splendidly silly; Jones has written better books, but her inventiveness is a constant reminder that there's life in fantasy if you know where to look.

A quick mention for those who ask about Harlan Ellison: the essay collection *Sleepless Nights in the Procrustean Bed* (Borgo Press 192pp $7.95, import shops only) is the latest from an author who has yet again 'given up sf'. His scathing attack on video games, included here, provoked squawks of anguish from Atari themselves. As ever, over the top is where Ellison begins.

The Conglomeroid Cocktail Party by Robert Silverberg (Gollancz 284pp £8.95) is, at last, a collection of new stories – Silverberg used to have the depressing habit of assembling early, inferior work with introductions tolerantly pointing out how naive but promising the stories were. These sixteen were written in the 80s, and are very polished indeed: suave, cosmopolitan, exotic. Sometimes, too, a bit routine in their use of well-worn sf elements; Silverberg's effects rely not on new twists but on atmosphere and irony. It's a good collection ... though his 1967-76 novels remain his best work.

Speaking of atmosphere, of course I went to see *Dune*, which to look at was magnificent. Luckily I'd read the book and was able to supply the missing chunks of plot lost when a rumoured four-hour version was cut to a shade over two hours for release. We will not dwell on the giggles of the preview audience at the line 'Your water will mingle with ours,' or for that matter the remark addressed to Baron Harkonnen by his personal physician, 'It is an honour to prick your boils, my lord.' The visual impact of that scene was ... excuse me, I think I'd better nip off to the bathroom till next month.

March 1985

26 No More Niceness?

Often I get letters from my enormous readership (a phrase I'll have to stop using if, like the other half of the Langford fan club, he goes on a diet). Typical comments: 'You are the greatest literary genius the world has known, can you lend me a fiver?' 'Why won't you review my wonderful Penguin Fighting Fantasy Gamebooks, you bastard?' 'Why don't you just throw yourself down a forty foot canvas tube lined with fish-hooks?' The latest letter, though, contains a hideous accusation – that this column has become *too nice*. Argh ... anything but *that*!

The appalling truth is that publishers have rumbled me. No longer do they send Stephen Donaldson epics neatly trussed for the slaughter, or Asimov novels so flatulent that you daren't squeeze them in public: I even hear I've been blacklisted and won't receive my coveted freebie copies of L. Ron Hubbard's 12-volume follow-up to *Battlefield Earth*. Instead, some fiendish publishers have hit on the idea of offering good stuff.

Such as Terry Pratchett's *The Colour of Magic* (Corgi 238pp £1.75). I enjoyed his earlier *Strata*, an essential companion to the *Ringworld* RPG since it comprehensively takes the piss out of Niven's **Known Space** sequence. The new book tackles fantasy, titivating its loony plot with pokes at Fritz Leiber, D&D, numerous myths, Robert E. Howard, H.P. Lovecraft, Anne McCaffrey (Mr Pratchett, how could you be so cruel? 'I didn't know dragons could be seen through ...'), Jack Vance and many more – including Larry Niven, with magical science as manically inventive as anything in Douglas Adams.

On a flat world supported by four elephants who in turn stand on a mighty turtle plodding through the void, Rincewind the failed magician moves on as daft a 'quest' as the annals of fantasy have known – watched by dice-throwing gods on their mountain home, 'Dunmanifestin'. It's one of those horrible, antisocial books which impel the reader to buttonhole friends and quote bits at them. My ceiling is covered with brown spots from when I tried to read Pratchett's jokes and drink beer at the same time. Only native sadism makes me recommend this disgraceful work.

Next comes another novel of cruel parody, mercilessly lampooning A.E. van Vogt's excesses of incoherence and incomprehensibility. *Null-A Three* (Sphere 215pp £1.95) is by A.E. van – oops! Not (intentionally) a parody, this is a sequel to *World of Null-A* (1948) and *Players/Pawns of Null-A* (1956). *World* in particular is a classic example of a frenetic, lunatic plot which works on some obscure level without ever actually making sense: van Vogt's weird writing technique encourages free-association plotting, with his mandatory New Idea or Plot Twist *every 800 words.* Unfortunately *Null-A Three* doesn't work on any level. Another clone of superpowered yet thickwitted Gilbert Gosseyn pops up in a far galaxy (gosh!) peopled by humans (wow!) led by a boy-emperor of awesome powers (cor!) locked in an immense death struggle with aliens (blimey!): and those are just the sensible bits from the opening chapters.

Soon Gosseyn is teleporting intergalactically every few pages, potentially interesting characters are lost in narrative hiccups, ludicrous pseudoscience sprouts like mildew and is about as palatable, and van Vogt loses track of his own nonsense: on page 197 Gosseyn, able at will to teleport anyone or anything into the next galaxy, and having already done so *ad nauseam*, sees an assassin about to hurl a bomb at him. And: 'He could not take any counter-measure until the act of throwing took place.' Why not? Answer came there none; and it's *all* like this.... The book can only be read as parody or in a spirit (several bottles' worth) of overwhelming nostalgia for the 'Golden Age'.

Frederik Pohl wrote some of the better 1950s sf (usually with Cyril Kornbluth); like van Vogt, he's still at it, but Pohl has visibly matured. *The Years of the City* (Gollancz 334pp £9.95) is an infernally plausible attempt at one of sf's hardest feats - to build a realistic Utopia rooted in the exceedingly mucky soil of today. To add to the challenge, Pohl's chosen site is New York.

Five linked stories offer snapshots from the near future to late next century. 'When New York Hit The Fan' shows the worst, a syndrome of strikes and disasters which help force the introduction of Pohl's first utopian reform: electronic-access democracy via 'universal town meetings'. Story two (the weakest) depicts the inevitable corruption and graft surrounding a project to 'green' slums into communities self-sufficient in energy; story three (the strongest) chronicles similar problems in building 'The Blister', a climate-maintaining dome over the city. The final two are more light-hearted, covering changes in law and custom: I liked the idea of a democratized US Supreme Court, chosen by conscription! There are corny elements, like the traditional whores and crooks with hearts of gold in story one, and things I *can't* believe; but overall it's impressive, with enough 'realistic' bitterness to make us cynics swallow the sugary core of optimism.

A long way from near-future realism: *The Void Captain's Tale* by Norman Spinrad (Granada 256pp £1.95). In the luxurious artificiality of his starship *Dragon Zephyr*, amid the passengers' orgiastic amusements, Void Captain Genro makes huge gestures of cosmic Angst. He has incautiously got to know the ship's (usually shunned) Void Pilot, a woman who, plugged into the Jump circuitry, flings the vessel across space in a timeless instant of orgasm. Like Captain Ahab, Genro becomes obsessed with the unattainable, the 'Great and Only' fulfilment of Jump space; like Ahab, he's led on to disaster.

I feared the book would be disastrous: a mindbogglingly ambitious allegory of the search for transcendence, obsessed with metaphysics and sex, told in a polyglot jargon ('an all-too-necessary foma at the heart of our transtellar weltanschauung'). Incredibly, though, the story succeeds. It's over-long, it bogs down in portentousness, but the chase of the metaphysical white whale still compels. Worth a look, though younger readers may need to protect impressionable parents from the many sex scenes.

It's reissue time. Keith Roberts's *The Furies* (Penguin 220pp £1.95) is a welcome revenant - it's his first novel. A 'typical British disaster tale' of giant wasps ravaging England, it has interesting mystical overtones, is well written, and cuts a little deeper than John Wyndham - because the danger is vivid and breathes in your face, because Roberts's concern for people doesn't allow him to dismiss background megadeaths with a twitch of the stiff upper lip.

Alan Dean Foster's *Bloodhype* (NEL 206pp £1.75) is a reasonably exciting space opera of deathly predictability, with a world-destroying nasty called the Vom (lifted from early van Vogt), numerous cute goodies and alien heavies, and the dreaded drug of the title (*so* totally irrelevant to the plot that one instantly guesses it's there for use on world-destroying nasties). An entirely unnecessary character is included to link this to other Foster novels in the **Humanx** series; if you haven't read *The Tar-Aiym Krang* etc., his presence is baffling.

Michael Moorcock's first novel *The Golden Barge* has been reprinted again (NEL 189pp £2.50), and I have no hesitation in repeating my words in column 20. ('An ... interesting ... read.') I don't want to *think* about what those sods at Games Workshop have just gloatingly sent, *The Dragonlance Chronicles 1*, produced by TSR, based on some interminable AD&D campaign, and apparently written by a committee. Have I really got to ... *[Yes. By next issue, please - Ed.]*

April 1985

27 Spring Fever

Spring publications are now spawning frantically, their gaudy jackets peeping shyly through the rank soil of W.H. Smith's. My heap of review books has put on terrifying spurts of growth, and as it topples to crush me, every title seems in my fear-crazed eyes to be by Frank Herbert....

NEL reissued *Dune* to coincide with the film, followed by uniform editions of *Dune Messiah* (222pp £2.25), *Children of Dune* (380pp,£2.50), *God-Emperor of Dune* (454pp £2.95) and *Heretics of Dune* (508pp £2.95). Not to be outdone, Gollancz offer *Chapter House Dune* (379pp £8.95). I've just read the lot - Guinness Book of Records, please note. *Dune* stands up well despite suety wodges of metaphysics: its mix of simple adventure with complex religion and ecology still appeals. *Messiah* (unusually for sf) effectively tackles the sleazy aftermath of victory; but *Children* seemed chaotic and silly, with Leto's superman transformation pulled rabbit-fashion from the author's hat. *God-Emperor* swung over to the opposite extreme: very controlled, thoughtful, boring, a long book whose sparse action is entirely dictated by omniscient God-Emperor Leto (who's spent a fun 3500 years turning into a sandworm).

Heretics shows Herbert back on form, with power blocs manoeuvring and stabbing one another enthusiastically in the back: ruthless but worthy Reverend Mothers, despicable Tleilaxu with obscene 'tanks' for growing gholas (clones to you and me), megalomaniac Honoured Matres (a new, vicious lot) conditioning mere men into sexual addiction, Ixians perfecting high-tech 'no-rooms' and 'no-ships' invisible to the awesome prophetic power now owned by every third character ... Some of the old excitement returns, with cryptic, subtle conversations as deadly as duels, and some well-timed new revelations. A *deus ex machina* saves the plot as with *Children*, but somewhat less egregiously.

Chapter House Dune is a direct sequel - no millennial gulfs as between *Children*, *God-Emperor* and *Heretics*. Dune itself has been wasted; likewise the worms (all but one), and Tleilaxu (all but one - his irrelevant presence is a minor blemish, a major pointer to Book Seven). It's a straight fight between Reverend Mothers, who have been driven underground, and the now omni-dominant Honoured Matres. The hyper-acute characters are impressive, the resolution thoughtful and humane. Though initially I gave up after *Children*, *Heretics* and *Chapter House* have in some measure Restored My Faith.

Another series I missed is David Eddings's **Belgariad** - didn't get any review copies, did I? Until now: *Enchanter's End Game* (Corgi 372pp £1.95). Spies tell me that despite corny passages and an excessively naive hero, this is a fitting close to an OK series. Couldn't see it myself. Not so OK is *Dragons of Autumn Twilight* by Margaret Weis, Tracy Hickman and a cast of thousands (TSR 447pp £2.25), inspired by an AD&D campaign full of chunks ripped bleeding from Tolkien. The blurb says it: 'The first fantasy novel from the people who know fantasy best - TSR, Inc.' Considering the relationship of games to books, this is a bit like saying 'The first country landscape from the people who know open-cast mining best.' Deadly predictable questing, with stock D&D characters in familiar encounters: nearly as bad as *Valley of the Four Winds....* [A game-related serial in *Dwarf* whose authorship will remain unknown if I have anything to do with it.] Some of the poetry is of McGonagall standard: 'Through his doomed veins the horizon burst,' etc. Couldn't finish this one either.

Three more fantasies offer their tender throats to the reviewer's knife. Tolkien's *Book of Lost Tales 1* (Unwin 297pp £2.95) is paperbacked at last: addicts and scholars will greet it with delight, and probably bought the hardback anyway. I personally am less keen on these rough drafts than on the final, polished *Silmarillion*; casual readers who found even that a bit rarefied will wonder what the fuss is about.

The Bishop's Heir is Katherine Kurtz's latest Deryni book (Century 345pp £2.95), beginning a third trilogy of alternate-Welsh magic, romance and politics. The magic is low-key - pyrotechnics, first aid and occasional long-distance phone calls, barely relevant to the conventional mediaeval intrigue and rebellion. (What poetic force there is centres not on magic but on mundane ecclesiastical ritual.) Overall, this reads like a straight historical novel in plastic fantasy disguise. Brutally inconclusive ending, two sequels to follow.... Interesting but patchy.

Ladyhawke by Joan Vinge is a film novelization in two editions: Piccolo (169pp £1.50) and Pan (photo-cover; probably higher price). A simple story, told with a light touch: irrepressible young thief and drunken monk assist doomed lovers (he turned to a wolf by day, she to a hawk by night) against evil bishop. (Kurtz has whole synods of evil bishops, and TSR featured an evil High Theocrat: should the Archbishop of Canterbury worry about this?) Have fun spotting the obligatory movie clichés - as when someone's running, hotly pursued, down an empty road; stumbles and falls; finds himself staring at mere inches' range at the boots (here hooves) of a previously unnoticed stranger.... But Vinge's clear, witty writing makes up for much.

Interzone: the 1st Anthology (Dent 206pp £3.95) is what it says: a first sampler of fiction from the most exciting and ambitious sf magazine in Britain, or the world. *Interzone* can also make hugely exciting and ambitious mistakes, but they too are vital. About the most powerful of these 13 stories (twelve reprint, one new) was the most hated in a readership poll. If you haven't seen the magazine, buy this - act without thinking - and use the subscription form provided within.

Piers Anthony strikes again: *Refugee* (Granada 333pp £1.95) opens the pentalogy **Bio of a Space Tyrant**. Bio, Anthony explains, stands for biography, biology, biopsy, 'all the ways to study a subject' – watch for small tissue samples sellotaped into future volumes. I wouldn't put it past him: an arguably talented and once sincere author, he *will* overdo things. The hero is Hope Hubris (see what I mean?), doomed to rise through four agonizing sequels to be Tyrant of Jupiter: *Refugee* covers his early trials, consisting of an interplanetary hop during which everything nice is hacked from his life by space pirates. Space pirates have it easy since in this high-tech future airlocks don't lock: the pirate merely hauls alongside and boards his victim for several chapters of cruelly overwritten rape, loot and pillage. So popular is space-piracy that our hero's craft is raped, looted and pillaged no fewer than *eight times* in 333 pages. Crowded place, space. There are exciting bits, but Anthony desperately needs editing: his verbosity stretches scenes which should be quick and brutal into reams of increasingly gratuitous violence, which ultimately put me to sleep.

Philosophy and SF (392pp £11.95, from Prometheus Books, 10 Crescent View, Loughton, Essex, IG10 4PZ) offers 14 stories, one play (Capek's classic *R.U.R.*), two extracts, 30-odd slightly turgid pages of introductory philosophy, and Study Questions: 'What does Borges's story suggest about the nature of truth ... Do you agree?' Too expensive for most; interesting if you contemplate a philosophy course. Can editor and self-confessed philosopher Michael Philips really not spell hermeneutics? He gets it wrong ten times in two pages.

Bob Shaw's *The Peace Machine* (Gollancz 160pp £7.95) revises *Ground Zero Man* (1971), the heart-stopping action-adventure of a man who invents a way to explode every nuclear weapon in the world, and who struggles with the responsibility. Its grim conclusion shows precisely and prophetically – 1971, remember – the flaw in today's plans for 'star wars' energy-beam defences. One bit of science does creak: the 'classical nuclear device with two fissionable masses' was superseded *decades* ago. A minor point. Read this one, and tremble. Just as I tremble at the size of the review-copy stack, and grapple with the awesome responsibility of leaving some till next month.

May 1985

28 The Fantasy Explosion

SF is my true love, what with my degree in physics and former nuclear research job. Fie on fantasy: for me the highest literary values consist of megalomaniac computers, hyperspatial leaps and colliding black holes. Hence the need for Alka-Seltzer when, as this month, the fantasies are consistently better than the sf. Subversive, I call it.

Geoff Ryman's first novel *The Warrior Who Carried Life* (Unwin 173pp £7.95, horrible binding) crackles like an unshielded power line with dangerous energy and originality. The disfigured heroine Cara learns witchery, becoming a man to wreak revenge on the noxious Galu; success fails since the Galu turn defeat to victory through their stomach-turning mystery of the Secret Rose. New ideas keep coming: strange warriors like the Men who have been Baked or Men who Advance like Spiders; the atrocious fate of Cara's family, riddled with actually quite sympathetic worms; a nastily understated Land of the Dead; a Genesis rewrite providing cosmic rationale for the plot; we're barely halfway. For the climax Ryman goes for broke; a sad and gentle coda saves his theme from the common fault of being too big to care about. There are glitches (the appalling poetry of the Secret Rose crashes to earth when clumsily verbalized as 'Humanity was in danger of being replaced'), but Ryman is an author to watch.

Piers Anthony I've watched despairingly, as he hammers ideas into the ground and decks competent prose with archness and cuteness. *On a Pale Horse* (Granada 352pp £2.50) is his best for years, first in the five-book **Incarnations of Immortality**. The five 'incarnations' (Death, Time, Fate, War, Nature) are spiritual Permanent Civil Servants, policing a world theoretically dominated by God and the disloyal Opposition. This volume's hero is a newly appointed Death, learning the ropes ('Yes, Minister') and worrying like other Anthony heroes about the morality of it all. One reason why this book works better than usual is that matters of life and death *deserve* such agonizing – the **Xanth** books often waste it on white lies or table manners. Another is that the mechanics of magic and the afterlife are fresh and inventive, whereas Xanth has been worn smooth. Not great literature or great anything else, but good fun.

R.A. MacAvoy's *Damiano* (Bantam 243pp £1.95) opens a trilogy of gentler, more conventional fantasy (you can tell it's conventional – Anne McCaffrey and André Norton rave about it). Damiano is an unworldly, lute-playing alchemist of Renaissance Italy, on speaking terms with his dog and the archangel Raphael. When war touches his home town, he bumbles on an impossible quest to preserve it in peace, even by dealing with the devil. MacAvoy has a neat touch with small magics and period detail, and writes with charm - which could be a problem for her if, as some reviewers of the sequels have suggested, it slips into saccharine and disneyfication. I do hope not.

A Box of Nothing (Gollancz 128pp £5.95) is eccentricity from Peter Dickinson: a 'junior' novel which is almost an allegory of science - specifically, cosmology. Having acquired a box of 'the original nothing which was there before the universe began', the young protagonist moves to bizarre adventures in a petrified otherworld, an entropy dump. Its most engaging inhabitant is the Burra, a collective organizing principle which animates miscellaneous junk: 'Our first voice came from a dolly and said "Mama" and "Papa". This one came from a video game.' Somewhere in the entropic desert a new universe is gestating, and there's a race to ensure it's the *right kind* of universe.... Amiable and batty.

Quick reissue plug: G.K. Chesterton's *The Ball and the Cross* (Boydell Press 403pp £3.95). Theological fantasy, picaresque adventure; huge fun to read; see where C.S. Lewis pinched bits for the inferior *That Hideous Strength*; buy this or your toes will drop off.

The Seventh Gate by Geraldine Harris (Unicorn 243pp £2.95), concludes her **Seven Citadels** tetralogy. Harris improves throughout: here we get thoughtful word-bandying with one of the genre's rare *intelligent* barbarian chieftains (escaped only by understanding his sole blind spot), rather too much cross-continent trekking, and a double-punch finale which utterly fails to surprise you with the identity of the Saviour our hero's been questing for, but then goes one better - pushing fantasy clichés beyond their limits into a kind of realism. Nifty stuff.

What does sf offer? Reissues and grot, mainly: the best of the grot is in Neil Gaiman's and Kim Newman's lovingly compiled *Ghastly Beyond Belief: The SF and Fantasy Book of Quotations* (Arrow 344pp £2.50). Thrill to golden prose which spatters your enraptured forebrain across the ceiling! Enjoy the greatest lines of the immortal Lionel Fanthorpe - 'What the devil could it be? he asked himself over and over again.... He drew closer, and closer still. Then he recognized the peculiar gleaming object for what it was - a door handle!' Or, as we scientists say in films: 'Mad? I, who have discovered the secret of life! You call me mad?!' This book fills a much needed gap.

'Remember when humans were heroes, androids didn't have social hang-ups and the only good alien was a dead one?' Not *Ghastly Beyond Belief*, but the slogan of Hamlyn's 'Venture SF' series. The proprietors of Birmingham's Andromeda Bookshop have long complained that publishers don't know how to package sf to sell: Andromeda is selecting and presenting these 'the right way', numbered for collectors, with identikit Eddie Jones jackets and an 'action adventure' policy. No.1 is *We All Died at Breakaway Station* by Richard C. Meredith (244pp £1.95); no.2, *Come, Hunt an Earthman* by Philip E. High (176pp £1.75). Both are pretty bloodthirsty - 'She turned on the laser scalpel and slowly lowered it towards his loins' (Meredith, opened at random). High's has the standard High plot of totally downtrodden but gutsy Earthmen resisting omnipotent aliens' machinations and rising to rule the galaxy: at least two

High books handle this theme - such as it is - much better, while his punctuation still hasn't had the copyediting it desperately needs. Not the most promising of starts.

Even a series which opened promisingly, like E.C. Tubb's **Dumarest**, can wear thin after a dozen books. *The Terra Data* (Arrow 172pp £1.95) is number 22, and besides many truly rotten sentences has a plot resembling most of the previous ones. Hero Dumarest, tepidly pursued by the omniscient yet inept Cybers, fights on through unconquerable barriers of padding to obtain the secret whereabouts of lost Earth, only to suffer his 22nd failure. Soporific.

The Fungus by Harry Adam Knight (Star 220pp £1.95) is a horror nasty veneered with scientific rationalization for a dreaded cross between dry rot and athlete's foot, which causes people's favourite parts to suffer spongy outgrowths or fall off - as when a rapist's fungus-riddled organ snaps at the crucial moment. Truly revolting. Even the authors [John Brosnan and Leroy Kettle] are ashamed, and skulk behind a pseudonym.

In brief: Asimov's *The Robots of Dawn* (Granada 477pp £2.50) conceals, beneath layers of flab and theses on the philosophy of toilets, a little sf/detective tale: oh for an editor! Ballard's *Vermilion Sands* (Dent 208pp £2.95): now beautifully packaged, nine stories of the world's weirdest resort and artistic colony - haunting, poetic, more accessible than some Ballard. Frank Herbert's *Destination: Void* (Penguin 219pp £1.95): doomed spacegoers struggle to invent plot-saving artificial intelligence and understand large chunks of cybernetics jargon transcribed from Norbert Wiener's *God & Golem Inc* - tense and gritty, with an all-time corny punchline. *The Survivors* by Marion Zimmer Bradley and Paul Edwin Zimmer (Arrow 238pp £1.95) follows their *Hunters of the Red Moon* - promises of interesting character conflict regularly sabotaged by the appearance of a Ravenous Bugblatter Beast and much consequent swordplay. Banal. (Falls insensible, twitching spasmodically in effort not to think of the just-arrived *Helliconia Winter....*)

June 1985

29 Aldiss at Sunset

Today I plotted an alarming graph. Extrapolating into 1986 or 1987, the sf/fantasy pouring into this column looks like reaching such levels that after I've listed titles, authors and publication details, there will be approximately one (plus or minus 0.61) word left for each actual review. Rather than be reduced to classifying novels on a standard scale ('brilliant', 'OK', 'mediocre', 'unreadable', or 'Hubbard'), I suspect it's time to write longer reviews of fewer books.

I wish I could spend a whole column on Brian Aldiss's *Helliconia Summer* (Granada 576pp £2.50) and, concluding an impressive trilogy, *Helliconia Winter* (Cape 285pp £8.95). *Summer*'s hardback was covered here in 1983: it's the richest and most lyrical of the set, picturing the lush Renaissance which happens every 2600 years or so as civilization recovers from the ruin of planet Helliconia's murderous five-century winter. *Winter* is of course more sombre, with autumn declining into the Great Winter: human society is past its peak, political systems are hardening and freezing with the rest of the world, and the alien phagors who rule the winter are coming into their time of power. But although *Winter* ends with the powerfully gloomy day of Myrkwyr, when sunrise immediately becomes sunset, it's not a depressing book. The hero Luterin's saga is a tense, exciting one which ends in defiant hope; there are lovely inventions too, particularly the Egyptian-flavoured Great Wheel. In the heart of a mountain, the devout haul endlessly on chains to turn the huge stone wheel and, by sympathetic magic, pull Helliconia through its dark winter centuries.

The Aldiss password is 'enantiodromia', the cycle of things turning into their opposites. Winter contains the hope of spring; the murderous phagors carry the plague which humanity needs to survive Helliconia's seasons. In *Winter*, scenes on Earth and the orbiting Avernus Station (sketchy and less successful than the main narrative) offer two escape routes from cyclic history: enlightenment and extinction. All this and a gripping story too, of battle, murder and plague.

Damon Knight offers *The Man in the Tree* (Gollancz 246pp £8.95), a quiet, nostalgic novel about a sort of superman. The hero is a literal giant with an odd superpower seen earlier in Knight's short story 'What Rough Beast?': he can twist probability worlds, duplicating some priceless treasure like, say, *White Dwarf* by borrowing another world's copy. He drifts through life from the 50s to the 80s, pursued by a homicidal loony; appears in such familiar sf settings as carnivals; becomes a low-key messiah in an effort to save the world.... Nicely written, but it provokes nagging questions. Why giantism *and* psychic power when either alone could carry the novel? Why such uninspired use of the hero's special talent, which tends to boil down to routine healings and conjuring? Why, with an intelligent enemy hot on his trail, does he go on public view as a giant in a *carnival*? These are deep waters, Watson.

Deeper and more obscure is the selection policy of Venture SF, whose third choice has been conveyed to me in a tumbril: *Hammer's Slammers* by David Drake (Hamlyn 274pp £1.95). Venture promises only 'novels of action adventure - no short stories, no fantasy, no boredom'. Though *Slammers* is in fact an assembly of short stories, the word 'boredom' never crossed my mind; I favoured 'atrocious' and 'unreadable'. The Slammers are gun-happy mercenaries, 'the toughest regiment that ever killed for a dollar', whose exploits are celebrated in prose so lumpish that often you need to backtrack and puzzle out what Drake is clumsily trying to say. 'The body ballooned under the cyan impact' - cyan being Drake's favourite word. 'Four pongoes were jumpered to Two Star' - pretty pellucid, eh? Such are the lauded military virtues of the Slammers that, fearful that chicken-heartedness will prejudice their future contracts, they nobly disobey their own horrified *employers'* orders to stop slaughtering people and detonating irreplaceable shrines. If you like chainsaw massacres you'll love this.

Unspeakable nasties infest Barbara Hambly's *The Time of the Dark* (Unicorn 284pp £2.50), which opens poorly with an all too familiar 'eldritch unseen horror' - Lovecraftian shoggoths lurking in the basement, squishily poised to destroy civilization. There are other familiar ingredients: the 'true names' magic is very Le Guin, and most Tolkien fans will spot something reminiscent about the wizard Ingold Inglorion. That said, the book perks up when the Dark-threatened fantasy world interacts with ours: having crossed over, the hard-bitten American heroine gets into swordplay while her shiftless male acquaintance studies wizardry, both thus doing better than Inglorion, who on his visit to Earth masters only the ring-pull beer can. Cleverly anti-romantic touches make this a lot more appealing than you might expect from the cover or the chill news that it's volume one of a trilogy. Well above average.

Spellbinder by Stephen Bowkett (Gollancz 120pp £5.95) is a fantasy for 'young adults', whatever that means. The teenage hero has the usual selection of hang-ups; he tries to impress friends with conjuring tricks, only to discover that for him magic actually works. Bowkett's joky, epigrammatic schoolboy repartee is effective - just sufficiently more polished than the real thing to amuse without becoming unbelievable. The other point which gets my thumbs-up is the way in which magic and fantasy do *not* conveniently depart forever from the hero's life the moment he's been taught some cheap moral lesson: here the poor sod has to learn to live with a responsibility which is his for the next sixty years. Right on.

David Harvey, author of *The Song of Middle-Earth* (Unwin 143pp £10.95), won International Mastermind with Tolkien as his special subject: sure enough, he shows a terrifying command of factoids in this, the 5,271,009th book about Middle Earth. The thesis, according to the foreword, is twofold. Firstly, that

Tolkien's work is much more original and less derivative than critics say, and that critical comparisons with past works are to be sternly distrusted. Secondly, that Tolkien was creating a 'Mythology for England', which can be proved by critical comparisons showing how millions of themes from past mythology crop up in Tolkien.... From this dodgy start, Harvey woffles on to recount large chunks of Tolkien, with sporadic mentions of mythic parallels. Alas, his pudding of fact and paraphrase lacks argumentative thrust and doesn't reach any real conclusion. (For criticism that does, try Tom Shippey's excellent *Road To Middle-Earth* – also from Unwin.) This stodge should appeal to hobbits, who you'll remember 'liked to have books filled with things that they already knew, set out fair and square with no contradictions.'

In brief: *Top Fantasy* ed. Josh Pachter (Dent 311pp £9.50) compiles two dozen 'author's choice' stories: most are good, a few are rotten, a couple aren't fantasy. Authors range in fame from Ballard, Bradbury, Disch and Le Guin to obscure authors who presumably wielded some hidden Influence, such as for example that secret master of fantasy Josh Pachter.... Bob Shaw's *Orbitsville Departure* (Granada 192pp £1.95) is a taut, compelling sequel to the nifty *Orbitsville*, which appeals despite my utter inability to believe in all-potent alien 'Ultans' who farm universes.... I have no intention whatever of reading *V: East Coast Crisis* by Howard Weinstein and A.C. Crispin (NEL 305pp £2.50), novelization of a certain TV sequel.... *Storm Season* ed. Robert Asprin (Penguin 220pp £1.95) is more from Thieves' World, the usual mixed bag of fantasy.... *A Pictorial History of SF Films* by David Shipman (Hamlyn 172pp £8.95): lots of stills and erudition, just like all the other recent pictorial histories of sf films.

Keep watching the skies!

July 1985

30 Bicuspid of Doom

Last time I tried it I had a nosebleed; this time, five days of raging toothache (really). A hernia is the usual symptom of trying to lift it. I allude, of course, to that suppurating pustule, that boil on the buttock of literature, *Battlefield Earth* - about whose paperback edition I'm preserving a dignified silence. Isn't that nice of me?

Ian Watson's *The Book of Being* (Gollancz 184pp £8.95) concludes an ambitious, inventive and daft trilogy. Not content with previous deaths, reincarnations and cosmic insights suffered in *Book of the River* and *Book of the Stars*, heroine Yaleen tops the lot by dying more revoltingly than ever before, going mad, watching the universe freak out, and doing a rewrite job on reality. The marathon effort of trilogy-writing is showing: for ages Watson's intellectual gearshift stays in neutral, but crashes into overdrive for the forty pages of Part Three (containing most of the plot). Strangely paced stuff from one of the few sf authors with a truly strange mind.

Robert L. Forward, conversely, is over-straightforward and relates strange physics in a flat, unevocative way. *The Flight of the Dragonfly* (NEL 319pp £2.25) is packed with 'hard' sf notions, Forward being a Top Physicist whose presence makes lesser gravitational astronomers grovel. There's this double planet, whose twin egg-shaped 'lobes' share an atmosphere, and orbit mere kilometres apart, one lobe being land and the other (for excellent reasons) sea, and in the sea are blobby aliens with funny symbols in their names, who divide their time between mathematics and surfing, until Earth's expedition arrives to entangle itself in the tidal and gravitational oddities.... It's a shame that with all this seething behind his marble brow, Forward never puts across the drama and visual excitement of the events he's calculated to the eleventh decimal place. As in so much sf by scientists, the most interesting characters are the computers.

His *Dragon's Egg* (NEL 309pp £2.25) has the same weaknesses but a far more successful and audacious notion: collapsed-matter life and intelligence on the surface of a neutron star, evolving a million times faster than plodding old us, and irresistible if you really like your sf to have Technical Appendices.

Not every such book is labelled in legal, decent, honest and truthful fashion. John Brunner's *Interstellar Empire* (Hamlyn 256pp £1.95) is the fourth 'Venture SF' action-adventure for the young in brain: as such, it's good, rousing, unsophisticated stuff ('A slave with the hot brown skin of a Marzon and the twitching eyes of a man born under a variable star ...') – but the 1976 copyright date is naughty, these being the journeyman space-operas of Brunner in the 1950s. Infinitely more grotty are the **Sojan** (ersatz Conan, or was it ersatz Tarzan?) stories Michael Moorcock started when 15, and which form the bulk of a book wickedly mistitled *Elric at the End of Time* (Granada 208pp £1.95). The amusing semi-spoof title story; one early, inferior Elric tale; nonfictional bits; Moorcock's hilarious but very short self-parody 'The Stone Thing'; and that's your lot.... Gene Wolfe's fine *The Devil in a Forest* (Granada 208pp £1.95) is billed as 'haunting fantasy' but is more a poetic historical novel in Wolfe's unclassifiable manner: good vs evil, rationalism vs superstition, and the outcome deeply ambiguous. Read this.

Octagon (Penguin 272pp £2.50) is more lightweight hard-sf fun, from Fred 'Berserker' Saberhagen. Dating from 1980, it has the musty flavour of an up-to-the-minute book whose minute has passed: in five short years we've got too sophisticated about computers to believe naive visions of kids who gain Total Power by effortlessly guessing Master Passwords (two, in fact, which by sheer chance happen to be the same). That apart, it's a pleasant thriller, with the computer-moderated RPG *Starweb* getting uncomfortable as players are eliminated not by strategy but by assassination. I recommend this technique to Diplomacy addicts. The villain's identity is obvious long before the story reveals it, but it's all quite tense nevertheless. Reissued: Saberhagen's famed *Berserker* killing-machine stories (Penguin 224pp £1.95), with a new, sleazy cover. ROAMING IN SPACE, THE BERSERKERS HAD ONLY ONE IDEA IN MIND ... TO DESTROY! Makes them sound like *White Dwarf* subeditors.

Another fun blurb adorns David Brin's *Sundiver* (Bantam 340pp £1.95): 'A journey into the fires of the sun ... in search of those who made us human.' The Advertising Standards Authority might have preferred 'Several journeys into the fires of the sun ... in search of evidence as to whether the already-discovered inhabitants are or aren't those who made us human.' (I admit it hasn't the same snap.) In *Sundiver*, galactic status is acquired by being a Patron and boosting some inferior species, possibly L. Ron Hubbard fans, to civilized intelligence. Theoretically, this is the way everyone (except the mysterious Original Progenitors – take a bow, von Däniken) got started. In practice, humanity seems strangely unPatronized, and everyone rushes to investigate the solar chromosphere in a whirl of intrigue (human and alien), murder, physics, detection and discovery which admittedly keeps you turning those pages. You will groan at the key plot revelation that one entire alien race has been concealing its incredible super-powers for *scores of millennia*, only for our Earthman hero to deduce them in no time at all. Certain characters' weird actions are performed solely to help Brin's plot: but this *is* a first novel. His second won the Hugo.

Fond of King-style horror, chainsaw massacres, maggoty putrescent hands clawing up from your breakfast cornflakes? Then you, unlike me, will be less keen on Robert Aickman's fine, eerie collection *Night Voices* (Gollancz 185pp £1.95) ... six tales not so much of terror as of unease. Shadows fall obliquely; something is half-seen at the corner of the eye; the telling is quiet and understated, but shivers lurk in the implications. Nothing is ever explained. Those who only giggle at H.P. Lovecraft will find Aickman expert at raising small, persistent goose-pimples.

I like Arthur C. Clarke's nonfiction, and the 31 pieces in *1984: Spring* (Granada 268pp £2.50) include nifty items. While most American hard-sf writers are leaping on Reagan's 'star wars' defence bandwagon (I'll spare you my analysis of why this project is Silly), Clarke puts the boot into it all – as a result of which it's unreliably rumoured that an outraged Heinlein had to be restrained from biffing him. Plenty of good things here: too many, really, as Clarke reprints several speeches which make points in the same words. Where was his editor?

More reissues! One minor classic, George R. Stewart's *Earth Abides* (Black Swan 364pp £3.95) in a well-deserved 'respectable' edition: the post-holocaust novel by which others are judged. Reviewed here in hardback: Geoff Ryman's excellent *Warrior Who Carried Life* (Unicorn 173pp £2.95), compulsory reading; Walter Tevis's *Steps of the Sun* (Corgi 253pp £2.95), well-written and entertaining despite silly science and a self-pitying hero; Robert Silverberg's *Valentine Pontifex* (Pan 367pp £2.50) – if you liked the science-fantasy of *Lord Valentine's Castle* you'll like this paler but literate sequel, but not as much. Also: Jack Vance's skinny but triffic *The Dragon Masters* (Granada 123pp £1.95) and two inferior Heinleins – the racist *Day After Tomorrow* (NEL 141pp £1.95), the icky *Podkayne of Mars* (NEL 157pp £1.95).

Unreadables: *The Sable Moon* by Nancy Springer (Corgi 263pp £1.95), concluding a trilogy whose first volume's prose style made my gonads atrophy, and *V: the Pursuit of Diana* by Allen Wold (NEL 186pp £1.95), about which the less said the better. *[Go on, review it! – Ed.]* Very well, I will speak out, pillaging the uttermost depths of my thesaurus and – *[On second thoughts, don't bother – Ed.]* Let's just say I had more fun in my long afternoon at the dentist's.

August 1985

31 Into the Abyss

As I write I'm staring at the jacket of *The Third Millennium: A History of the World AD 2000-3000* by Brian Stableford and me (Sidgwick & Jackson 224pp £12.95). This sports a hologram – a cunning ploy to make you buy it and take it outdoors, the image being invisible in bookshop lighting. The original hologram showed a nautilus shell, which everybody loved, especially the other two publishers who'd already bagged the same one for *their* books. The hasty replacement shows, for some ungodly reason, two acorns – perhaps conveying our own publishers' opinion that the authors are a pair of nuts. Sunday-supplement photographers have taken surreal pictures of said authors, who drew the line at posing in a tree. We still haven't seen copies of the finished book, only the blurb, memory of which causes us to wake up screaming on alternate nights. Such is the writer's life.

Lucky Robert Silverberg, who, having reached the top via decades of work and millions of words, can write what he wants. This time it's *Gilgamesh the King* (Gollancz 320pp £9.95), a straight historical novel about the 'real' warrior-king Gilgamesh (*floruit* 2500 BC), with nods towards the more mythical *Epic of Gilgamesh*. Long-term readers will remember *Critical Mass*'s review of the Bible, which pointed out that all that Flood stuff had been done in the *Epic* a thousand years previously.... Silverberg's version is laudable, essential reading for Sumerian role-players, but his realistic approach weakens (I think) the theme of immortality. Compare his amazing fantasy *The Book of Skulls*.

An even better historical novel has gone unnoticed, author and publisher being obscure: *The Arabian Nightmare* by Robert Irwin (Dedalus Books – Langford Lodge, St.Judith's Lane, Sawtry, Cambs, PE17 5XE – 253pp £2.95). The setting is Cairo in 1486, nothing else being certain in the labyrinth of dreams sinking into dreams like quicksand. By the time I'd finished my notes were pretty incoherent: 'If Borges and Dick had got together to update *The Arabian Nights* as a horror novel ...' It is a dream without awakening (says the blurb), a flight without escape, a tale without end. It is full of strange erudition and strange loops, is compulsively readable, and will surely be a fantasy classic. I liked it a lot.

Barbara Hambly's *The Walls of Air* (Unicorn 314pp £2.50) continues the somewhat derivative *Time of the Dark*. Again there are literary glitches: I wondered what a 'spatchcocked landscape' might look like, until the dictionary revealed to my delight that 'spatchcock' is also a verb meaning to interpolate words into a story, especially inappropriate ones. And, just as the wizard Ingold Inglorion reeked of Gandalf in book one, so the stench of Saruman's treachery fills book two. Nothing's truly original, though (both Tolkien's and Hambly's betrayals are dramatizations of Nietzsche's warning 'If you gaze into the abyss, the abyss will gaze back into you'), and Hambly is now making much better use of routine materials. Her wizard's character fills out as he reacts to suffering with a singular lack of nobility; the rotten old Bishop with her anti-magic doctrines becomes more sympathetic and may even be in the right; staggering revelations about magic, technology and the enemy Dark are promised for book three. Will Hambly deliver? Fingers crossed.

Keith Roberts delivers novels far too infrequently, but here is *Kiteworld* (Gollancz 288pp £8.85), a cycle of linked stories like *Pavane*. The technological level is higher, with photography, internal combustion and Geiger counters, but the land is similarly Church-dominated. Its man-carrying kites fly at the borders as a hoped defence against legendary 'Demons' which are plainly missiles: kite technology is related in obsessive detail without ever being in the foreground, which is occupied by all too human people having love affairs or crises of faith. The less tolerant of the Churches (which Roberts condemns not openly but by showing you the needless guilt and suffering of innocents) is getting tougher as faith in the kites dwindles: things are clearly falling apart, which doesn't stop two of the episodes being quite funny. Superlative stuff, even if the deus-ex-machina happy ending is a bit jarring.

The ineffable Piers Anthony continues his **Bio of a Space Tyrant** in *Mercenary* (Granada 415pp £2.50), whose foreword contains a hilarious warning that hero Hope Hubris is *ever so much more* cunning and competent than may appear from his inadequate representation in this book! Certainly he doesn't seem a likely candidate for Tyrant of Jupiter, with his habitual air of slack-jawed incomprehension whenever the conversation turns to strategy, protocol, politics or sex. Nevertheless he survives the terrible training course of the Jovian Navy (including compulsory brothel drill, I kid you not) and sets out with a 'Magnificent Seven'-style task force to rid the spaceways of piracy. Parts of this are quite sensible, but are balanced by dottiness like the protracted space-battle which – for reasons known only to God and Piers Anthony – echoes the Mongol invasion of Hungary so faithfully as to neglect the fact that space has three dimensions. Amusing nonsense, but definitely nonsense.

Robert Sheckley's *Dramocles* (NEL 204pp £2.25) is intentionally amusing nonsense, with a loopy plot about King Dramocles of Glorm trying to fulfil his unknown Destiny by obeying mysterious notes he's forgotten having sent himself. In case this fails to remind you of something, there's an extra clue on the cover – a plug from Douglas Adams. Like Adams, Sheckley can do brilliantly funny one-liners, but hasn't lately shone at novel length. *Dramocles* has some hilarious scenes, like the completely irrelevant one in which minor characters try to gain narrative security by establishing a sub-plot of their own; but overall it reads as though Sheckley was desperately making it up as he went along. Pretty good by some standards; insubstantial by Sheckley's own.

There's meatier entertainment in *The Artificial Kid* by Bruce Sterling (Penguin 245pp £2.50), which is crowded with interesting (if implausible) stuff. The

Kid's business is videotaped real-life violence; everyone's fond of improbable dialogue; there's revolution, flight, cloning, returns from the dead, unlikely coincidences, even unlikelier biology, personality swaps, and to cap it all the splendidly daft Chemical Analogue Theory of the body politic. Without being exactly convincing, it's lavishly exuberant in the way sf used to be and literate in the way it wasn't.

For the way things were, see old-timer Edmond Hamilton's reissued *Starwolf* trilogy (Hamlyn 'Venture 05' 456pp £2.50), slam-bang space operas written in 1967-8 but with the authentic 1940s ring, or clunk. 'Who are these crazy people, anyway, who explode worlds as a weapon?' Pulp sf writers, that's who.

In brief: *Top Science Fiction* ed. Josh Pachter (Dent 340pp £2.95) is an fine collection for any sf neophyte, disarming criticism by letting the authors choose their own best stories. I think at least half of them are wrong, but that's just me. Recommended. *The Sentinel* (Granada 299pp £2.95) is a lavish, large-print packaging of 8 familiar Arthur C. Clarke stories plus introductions and a 4-page film outline ('The Songs of Distant Earth'): nice to own, but check the contents against your other Clarke collections before buying.... *The Face of Chaos* ed. Robert Asprin and Lynn Abbey (Penguin 205pp £1.95): yet another outbreak of Thieves' World: people who like books like this will like this book, though personally I think the scenario is looking shopworn.... Terry Brooks's *The Wishsong of Shannara* (Futura 499pp £4.95) concludes the trilogy of an author who, unlike Tolkien and Hambly, can take the most powerfully magical fantasy archetypes and with a single touch of his style transform them into rotting hulks of cardboard. I reeled back in awe as the book slipped from my nerveless fingers. There are secrets of the universe with which reviewers should not meddle: they abandon the effort and go to the pub instead.

September 1985

32 Son of Reprints

Imagine my feelings of embarrassment and eerie power when I study the review puffs on a new paperback, to find that one of the more witless quotations is from me. The unease struck with double force on the arrival of *The Frozen City* (Arscott & Marl, Unicorn 231pp £2.95: 'Curious' - *White Dwarf*): *both* quotes were from a disguised Langford. My next ambition is to publish some review in three places ('This book's lack of literary talent is truly amazing') and appear thrice on the paperback jacket. 'Truly amazing' - *Starlight SF*. 'This ... literary talent' - *Starburst*. 'This book ...' - *White Dwarf*.

Some books feel different the second time round, making me glad I wasn't quoted. Larry Niven's *The Integral Trees* (Futura 240pp £1.95) has a brilliantly dotty astrophysical setting in the 'Smoke Ring', a vast free-fall environment: but the book contains nothing else. Lifeless characters get pushed around in a travelogue plot, with the good things far too thinly spread - a grain of caviar, a pound of suet pudding. Harry Harrison's *West of Eden* (Granada 578pp £2.50) has another too-simple plot outweighed by research: real linguists and biologists helped assemble this impressive alternate world of evolved dinosaurs, with research spilling over into a 40-page appendix. You can only groan when after all this painstaking groundwork, the victory of Red-Blooded though Primitive Americans over Vile Colonialist Dinosaurs depends on hoary sf banality, the bioengineering reptiles having invented everything you can imagine except fireproof cities and fire extinguishers.

More reissues! Gollancz offer three of Robert Sheckley's episodic novels, all £8.95: *Journey Beyond Tomorrow* (189pp 1964), *Mindswap* (216pp 1966) and *Dimension of Miracles* (190pp 1968). The first is good-humoured satire, a glorious send-up of Cold War hopes and fears; the others are even funnier but less classifiable. Sheckley, a master of insane logic, was writing Douglas Adams material long before it occurred to Adams. Further ingenious insanity appears in *The Cosmic Puppets* by Philip K. Dick (Granada 143pp £1.95 1957), long unavailable: though a bit too terse and schematic, it bubbles with Dick's engaging paranoia and dodgy reality. The gloom of Greg Benford's *Across the Seas of Suns* (Orbit 399pp £2.95) is grimmer and more technological, a slightly plodding hard-sf saga. Earth writhes under an alien invasion which is nightmarish because it's casual; meanwhile the starship *Lancer* explores the puzzle of Something Out There which hates life. (What evil lurks...? Fred Saberhagen knows.) Loaded with careful craftsmanship and clever effects, it never quite reaches escape velocity.

If it isn't reissues, it's sequels. *The Merchant's War* (Gollancz 209pp £8.95) is Frederik Pohl's follow-up to his and Cyril Kornbluth's classic advertising satire *The Space Merchants.* Alan Craddock's jacket painting is a tongue-in-cheek vision of a 50s future ... helping emphasize that *The Space Merchants* (1953) requires no sequel. Trying to outdo the original book's batty sales ploys like addictive coffee substitute and ads projected directly on to the retina, Pohl goes over the top with nonsense about careless lookers at billboards being instantly, irreversibly conditioned to drink 'Mokie-Coke'. The original 'comic inferno' ended with the hero's escape to Venus: the hero of *The Merchants' War* stays on Earth and reforms it, with a priggishness which wrecks the satire. It's easy reading, but a completely unnecessary book. Pohl also offers *Demon in the Skull* (Penguin 172pp £1.95), a negligibly improved and modernized version of his 1965 fantasy of power, *A Plague of Pythons.* The punchline's still good, but Pohl used it more effectively in a short-short story.

One sequel I'd almost looked forward to was Piers Anthony's *Bearing an Hourglass* (Granada 383pp £2.50). The first **Incarnations of Immortality** book was his best in ages; this, alas, instantly converts the innovations into formula, as again a newly-appointed demigod (here Chronos or Time) assumes his role, meets his comrades, discovers Satan to be not nice, and triumphs by realizing his own powers ... but far more feebly. Death in book one at least struggled with potent moral problems: Chronos suffers great chunks of semi-humorous fantasy which reads like rejected **Xanth** material. Death won through by logic and courage: Chronos wins by playing endless games of Twenty Questions with a dumb – in every sense – oracle which dishes out information according to the needs not of the enquirer but of the plot. The interesting ideas get buried in the dross.

Damiano's Lute by R.A. MacAvoy (Corgi/Bantam 254pp £1.95) follows on from *Damiano,* which I liked for style and unexpectedness. These qualities continue as ex-mage Damiano wanders through plague-ridden Renaissance Italy: it's not often that a major character, who you 'know' must survive to the end of the trilogy, gets offed by plague in book two. But though it reads well, the characters seem thinner, flatter, less convincing this time around. That's the trouble with writing well, Ms MacAvoy – the blasted critics expect you to write even better.

Somewhere on the twilit edge where fantasy shades into industrial archaeology, M. John Harrison goes his own entropic way. *Viriconium Nights* (Gollancz 158pp £8.95) offers seven polished stories set in and around the shifting metropolis of *The Pastel City, A Storm of Wings* and *In Viriconium.* They have a precise, exotic sleaziness, leaving you with uncomfortable images: insect-masks recur, and the Mari Llwyd (the ribboned horse-skull of folklore), and technological decay (as with the unforgettable, filthy power-weapon of the first story). I like them. I think.

More fantasy of a sort comes from that increasingly productive author J.R.R. Tolkien, with *The Lays of Beleriand* (Unwin 393pp £14.95). The book comprises poetic experiments, covering some of the *Silmarillion* ground: Turin and Nargothrond in an imitation of Anglo-Saxon alliterative verse, Beren and

Luthien (yet again!) in rhymed couplets. Thanks to ponderous notes, alternative readings and revised versions, it's quite hard to find Tolkien's own bits. A few gleams of humour come from C.S. Lewis's 15-page critique of an early draft: for the rest, poor old Tolkien lies entombed and fossilized in earnest commentary, like a set text for Eng. Lit.

Isaac Asimov is also looking fossilized, in his detective collections *Banquets of the Black Widowers* (Granada 212pp £8.95) and *The Union Club Mysteries* (Granada 240pp £1.95). Each set of stories has a rigid, formulaic setting. The starting situation is always exactly the same, a problem is propounded, and a solution issued either by Henry, modest know-all and waiter at the Black Widowers' dinner club, or by Griswold, the Union Club's immodest know-all. Both chaps strongly resemble Isaac Asimov ... especially Griswold. I generally like detective stories, but Asimov tries the patience with trivial, moronic 'puzzles'. Example: someone reveals in a dying message that he's hidden the Secret Formula *inside* a library book. The book is examined. Nothing there. Until the Great Detective thinks of looking where no-one else had suspected, *inside* the little pocket for the library card!! The prosecution rests, m'lud.

Circumpolar! by Richard Lupoff (Granada 352pp £2.50) combines alternative history (it's the 1920s; the War ended in 1913), alternative geography (Earth is the shape of a squashed doughnut), nut-cult science (the hole at the pole, lost Mu, magnetic levitation, etc) and pleasant silliness: a Great Air Race to the world's uncharted flipside, von Richtofens vs. Charles Lindbergh and Howard Hughes. It goes on a bit long and it grossly libels the Red Baron, but it's amusing and if I write any more I'll be cut off in mid-

October 1985

33 Blockbusted!

The panting reviewer gritted his teeth, dodging the huge blockbusters arcing down from interliterary space. *Kaboom!* Object 'Wolfe-399' had detonated close to his forebrain – and heavier stuff was coming. Object 'Niven/Pournelle-495' struck with stunning force! Too late to crawl to safety on three still functioning brain cells: our reviewer could only gaze helplessly as Object 'Dickson' plunged towards a terminal 692-page impact, targeted right between his eyes....

In this spate of big fat books, the one which *feels* blockbusting is Larry Niven's and Jerry Pournelle's *Footfall* (Gollancz 495pp £9.95). Their most impressive joint effort, it has the lot: politics, credible physics, well-drawn aliens, ground and space war, suspense, slam-bang action and a climax that grips like superglue. Arriving in 1995, the alien 'fithp' prove less than friendly, casually zapping the orbital welcoming party and all our satellites – whereupon it's hard to fight back. Anything launched, or moving on the ground, is a target for fithp lasers and guided meteorites. You detect a strong plug for 'Star Wars' space weaponry? Clever you. Despite minor triumphs, it steadily becomes clear that Earth's only hope is the craziest, most irresponsible spacecraft ever, kicked skywards by successive nuclear explosions (the authors *love* it). The result's terrifically exciting. The secret fithp weapon is less innovative, or even secret: N&P did all that stuff in *Lucifer's Hammer*.

Their flaws are blockbuster flaws: momentum takes 100 pages to build, several of the teeming characters are dispensable, and megadeaths are glossed over as of no interest. (Niven: 'Obliterated places contributed nothing to the theme of war.' Oh.) The tension's effective when deadpan, but sometimes N&P try too hard with lines like '*Eat hot gamma rays, foolish Centaurans!*' (which does, I admit, have a certain *je ne sais quoi*), or, at the apocalyptic launch of That Ship: 'God was knocking, and he wanted in *bad*.' Not to mention the Pournelle character's classic expression of pacifism: 'Nuke 'em till they glow, then shoot 'em in the dark.' All the same, I have to admit that I read much of it twice and ran out of adrenalin.

The Final Encyclopaedia (Sphere 692pp £3.95) brings Gordon R. Dickson's **Childe Cycle**, i.e. the Dorsai series, to a weighty conclusion – though historical prequels are still threatened. Hero Hal Mayne is the last of the 'universe-shakers' who dominate the sequence: much of the book is a prolonged rite of passage as he survives various worlds and threats while learning how to be Superman. Finally he acts, saving the universe in a somewhat undramatic fashion by, essentially, locking himself in a research library to work out the assumed Answer (while, outside, the baddies ravage unchecked). En route there's much action and debate, some overblown philosophy, and rather too many words. Over five novels and several shorts, this series has risen from vigorous pulp adventure to self-conscious worthiness ... and has, alas, got less *interesting*.

In an enthusiastically pretentious afterword, Dickson's leading apologist Sandra Miesel praises him by invoking Milton, the Bible, Heraclitus, Lévi-Strauss, and the *Tao Te Ching*, not to mention Buddhist, Celtic, Chinese, chivalric, Freudian, Hindu, Islamic, Norse and Persian myth. The Nobel Prize is apparently only a step away.

Speaking of myth-systems, *Salvador Dali's Tarot* (Michael Joseph/Rainbird 175pp £8.95) is an eccentric offering. Tarot expert Rachel Pollack introduces and comments on the 78 strange paintings of Dali's personal Tarot pack - each reproduced in perfect colour on its own page. I have no faith in fortune-telling, but the cabalistic symbolism is fascinating ... especially when refracted through the eye of a supremely dotty surrealist. Other Tarots, after all, are distinctly lacking in crutches, butterflies, ghosts and melting watches. (Imagine the resulting *Cthulhu* scenario if Marcus Rowland buys this book.) On the other hand, as art people have told me forcibly, most of the artwork here is slapdash, full of plagiarism and self-plagiarism.

Gene Wolfe practises his own brand of dottiness in the fat *Free Live Free* (Gollancz 399pp £9.95), which is frankly unclassifiable. Four seedy but enchanting characters (witch, private eye, salesman, whore) help aged Ben Free (possessor of a Secret Talisman) to defend his slum home from demolition: after a hilarious rearguard action (e.g. eight Chicago cops trying to evict a naked 300-lb lady who's prudently oiled herself all over) they seek the now vanished Free, only to be dogged by behind-the-scenes forces (or are they Forces?), leading to ... In short, as well as telling an offbeat story, Wolfe's playing games with the reader: is this stuff 'mainstream', fantasy, comedy, a detective or spy story, or what? The search ends in the enigmatic 'High Country', and in the genre you least expected; the final surprises aren't even the *kind* of surprises anticipated. I refuse to say more. It's a breath of fresh air. Read it.

Spider Robinson's *Mindkiller* (Sphere 246pp £2.25) provokes mixed feelings. It's a good read, an ambitious effort to extrapolate the sf gimmick of 'wireheading' (addiction to pleasure-centre stimulation) to a mind-expandingly logical conclusion - and to tell the story through the eyes of real people who suffer and bleed and throw up and have sex (especially that). Largely it succeeds: Robinson's a sympathetic writer when not making godawful puns. 'All human life is here' ... much more than all, in fact, since the major characters seem trapped on an emotional roller-coaster, alternating between manic hilarity and showers of tears. One can't help suspecting that this over-intensity is meant to distract you from the dodgy coincidences and out-of-character behaviour required to drive the plot ... not so much Spider as Heath Robinson.

Robinson's been called the new Heinlein (and has certainly learnt tricks from him) - bringing us to the old Heinlein, whose later grot has been severely treated here. Redressing the balance, Gollancz have reissued two of his best: *The Door into Summer* (190pp £8.95) and *Time for the Stars* (244pp £8.95), solidly entertaining 50s novels of, respectively, time and space travel. They don't creak but still purr along.

Another oldie, Clifford Simak, is still at it with *Enchanted Pilgrimage* (Methuen 218pp £1.95) and *Where the Evil Dwells* (Methuen 249pp £2.50). Such minor Simak fantasies slip down easily thanks to the old boy's charm, with everyone speaking in the same 1930s American Farmer tones as his sf heroes, robots, aliens, etc. This charm, alas, fades visibly between the 1975 *Pilgrimage* and its 1984 companion. More fantasy: Barbara Hambly's trilogy concludes with *The Armies of Daylight* (Unicorn 311pp £2.50), which polishes off the unspeakable and undefeatable Dark with reasonable flair, neat character work, and lashings of edge-of-the-seat suspense. In short, it delivers the expected goods: from hints in the previous book I'd rather hoped for the unexpected, but there you go.

In brief: *Heroes of the Equinox* and *World Without Stars* (NEL 46pp £2.50) are the witty and impressive comic-strip adventures of Valerian (Spatiotemporal Agent), as translated from French - good fun. *Starhunt* by David 'Tribbles' Gerrold (Hamlyn 'Venture 06' 252pp £1.95) began as a rejected *Star Trek* script, was novelized (with names changed) as *Yesterday's Children* in 1972, and now reappears with 60 added pages converting the ending from downbeat to upbeat. Ho-hum stuff. Michael Shea's *Nifft the Lean* (Granada 363pp £2.50), praised here many issues ago, is a lurid cross between Jack Vance and Heironymus Bosch which you should all buy *instantly* – happy nightmares! Ian Watson's light-hearted but cosmic sf trilogy makes its paperback debut with the nifty *Book of the River* (Granada 240pp £1.95). Mary Mackey's *The Last Warrior Queen* (Unicorn 240pp £2.95) may be triffic but has such an awful cover as to deter me from looking.... Enough.

News from the World SF Convention: Britain will host the 1987 Worldcon; my hot tip *Neuromancer* (soon in Granada paperback) won a Hugo award; and, good grief, one of the lesser Hugos went to me....

November 1985

34 Bah! Humbug!

With Christmas releases packing the stands in all their tinsel glitter, it's the reviewer's melancholy duty to play Scrooge and say rude things about the tarnish on each bauble. Gosh, how I wish I could be nice about everything; as a kind-hearted person I hate these cruel phrases.... *[Bah! Humbug! - Ed.]* Still, some moments make it all worthwhile, as when a burdened postman looked at me and at a Penguin parcel addressed to 'David Langford, The White Dwarf.' Your reviewer is a shade under six-foot-three. After cogitation the postman said, 'Is it a kind of pea?' The repartee which rose to my lips was unsuitable for family magazines.

The 1986 Tolkien Calendar (Unwin £3.95) is 'fun for all the family': 13 colour plates by Michael Hague, lifted from his luxury edition of *The Hobbit*. One might quibble that Hague's elves are over-chunky, and his Beorn unconvincingly gigantic (twice the height of Gandalf, who's no runt) but it's good value for Tolkien fans.

Rodney Matthews's *In Search of Forever* (Paper Tiger 142pp £7.95) is the best of the gift books - art from one who needs no introduction. His exotic, elfin paintings are backed up with sketches, photographs (some of the weirdest shapes were inspired by real-life formations of ice or rock) and an unpretentious commentary which cheerfully admits commercial problems. Budding artists can learn the secrets of 'plotting' a wrap-around cover to make a coherent picture while allowing for title, spine copy, blurb and price. Twee works like *Yendor* are balanced by passionate intensity (his Save The Whales poster hits you in the stomach); familiar props like insects and Moorcockian grotesques look better as part of a wider artistic range. Grab this and get his *Witch World* covers without having to buy the dismal André Norton books.

A new small press sends *Sceptre Mortal* by Derek Sawde (Oriflamme 294pp £2.95) - a venture into stratospheric High Fantasy. High Fantasy has a syntax and diction of its own, and is prone to debilitating bouts of Black Lords, High Kings, Elf Lords, Witch Queens, Fire Demons, Swords, Sceptres and Capital Letters, which oft join their mighty-thewed powers to forge Sentences as Silly-looking as This One. The peril of High Style is that its stiff formality can so often mean narrative arthritis, unless redeemed by rhythmic splendour (Eddison), a vein of homeliness (Tolkien's hobbits), fantastic humour (Dunsany), witty irony (Cabell), or lean poetic brevity (Le Guin). Alas, *Sceptre*

Mortal's familiar quest plot plugs tirelessly on without any of these things, paragraph after paragraph seizing up in a Spatter of Capitals. And (lots of sentences starting with And or But are another High Style giveaway) what can you make of an author who, after 258 solemnly humourless pages, offers a chapter called 'Pit of the Werebats'? Painful.

Guy Gavriel Kay's *The Summer Tree* (Unwin 323pp £8.95) inspires terror by being the first of yet another trilogy (**The Fionavar Tapestry**). Kay is a literate and economical writer, though: the mundane opening sketches relationships in brief dialogues, and for once the transition from Earth to 'a world of which our own is but a shadow' (tum-ti-tum) doesn't lead to a wholly simplistic set-up with good in the white corner and evil in the black. There are isolated outcrops of High Style, balanced by wit, humanity and such unlikely denizens of fantasy as hangovers. ('Some indeterminate fungus seemed to have taken up residence in his mouth.') Quite a promising start.

For a quick read, try *Cycle of the Werewolf* by Stephen King (NEL 128pp £4.95) - which I finished in twenty minutes, there being only 47 pages of large print in a morass of blank sheets, calendars, effective black-and-white pictures and unconvincing colour plates (both by Berni Wrightson). The latter often reveal twists King might reasonably have hoped would surprise you on the next page. This is of course a werewolf yarn, competently told despite wearying heaps of bodies before we get any actual plot; the triumph of the cute, crippled kid detective over Incarnate Evil comes as no surprise. OK, but expensive for a short story.

For the same price you can have Terry Carr's 13 *Best SF of the Year 14* (Gollancz 376pp £4.95) selections - cleverly including 1984 stories which later won Nebulas (John Varley's 'Press Enter ▮', Gardner Dozois's 'The Aliens Who Knew, I Mean, *Everything*' and Octavia Butler's 'Bloodchild') and Hugos (Varley and Butler again). I don't much like Varley's tale, whose flashy surface covers a thin and familiar technophobic theme, but most of the rest are ace stuff.

Eleven Ian Watson shorts make up *Slow Birds* (Gollancz 190pp £8.95), whose daft ideas now seem less hair-raisingly intellectual than of old - though there's some nice dottiness about a time-scoop project dredging up the philosopher Lucretius to be patronized and amazed by Modern Science, only for Lucretian physics to come along with him and invade our world. Other strangenesses include inverted, inexplicably expanded, and time-frozen worlds, a vitriolic tale of political physics which plunges Margaret Thatcher below Absolute Zero, and uneasy horror stories. Worth a look.

Still more shorts, 19 this time: *Gene Wolfe's Book of Days* (Arrow 246pp £2.25). Unclassifiable ... some straightforward, some worrying, some enigmatic and elusive, but all beautifully written. One, light-hearted but ultimately chilling, is specially for games fans: 'How I Lost The Second World War And Helped Turn Back The German Invasion'.

Software by Rudy Rucker (Penguin 174pp £1.95): the first UK appearance of this demented 1982 novel. On the surface it's a racy and blackly funny story of robots and humans-become-robots, laced with deadpan outrageousness. Brain-eating abounds, both literal (a gourmet treat) and metaphorical. Rucker is picking here at problems of personal identity. Lose your body and re-instal your software in a robot frame (complete with user-friendly SEX and DRUNK-

ENNESS subroutines), and are you still you? Is the backup copy of you in the other room also you? With destruction looming, the ex-human Cobb asks: 'Am I on tape somewhere else?' The reply is: 'I don't know.... What's the difference?' What, indeed.

Philip E. High's *Sold - For A Spaceship* (Hamlyn 'Venture 07' 175pp £1.75) is more traditional: what Orwell might have called good bad sf. High always tells the same story, beginning with rock-bottom despair amid tattered remnants of humanity. Swiftly and sometimes grammatically, the situation improves until mankind has achieved symbiosis with the ecosystem, perfect telepathic marriages with submissive womankind, and mastery of the universe. Despite writing which can be praised only as 'functional', High has qualities of excitement and compassion which make his work stand out in this series (if nowhere else).

In brief: Marion Zimmer Bradley's *Thendara House* (Arrow 414pp £2.75) is a late addition, worthy but ponderous, to the bulky **Darkover** series: new readers begin elsewhere.... *The Last Legionary Quartet* by Douglas Hill (Pan 460pp £2.95) offers lots of words for your money: a lightweight 'juvenile' tetralogy full of thrills, hardware and zap guns.... Graham Dunstan Martin's *The Soul Master* (Unicorn 293pp £2.95): one of Unwin's better fantasy discoveries, with potent and original ideas.... *Skyfall* (Panther 270pp £1.95) is Harry Harrison's potboiler of space disaster and a falling super-Skylab.... *A Pliocene Companion* by Julian May (Pan 220pp £2.50) is not the place to start reading Ms May (I didn't get the tetralogy to which this is a concordance), who comes over here as strangely arrogant and pretentious.... Granada, mindful of past injuries, have neglected to send Asimov's *Robots and Empire*: if editor Ian Marsh buys me the hardback I'll give it the praise it deserves. *[Bah! Humbug! - Ed.]*

December 1985

35 The Great Hardback Famine

I'm recovering from being a guest of honour at Britain's autumn sf convention, where serious science-fictional things occurred: a speech during which I remember proposing three new Laws of Robotics; a death threat from kindly co-guest James White because I'd done a parody of his Sector General stories which Ian Marsh will soon have an opportunity to reject; and several parties, one of which led to everyone hiding in a toilet to escape the attentions of the most appallingly boring person in the universe, whom I am not afraid to name: *[Cut - Ed.]*

Back in hungover Reading, I found the first review stack in aeons to include no hardbacks at all. Mind you, some of the paperbacks are Big - like *The Hitch-Hiker's Guide to the Galaxy: The Original Radio Scripts* (Pan 249pp £4.99). This is the perfect cure for fans worried by the differences between radio, radio repeat, record, book, and TV versions. Massive Arcturan Megafootnotes explain more, including reasons for changes, Arthur Dent's Origin Story, which TV programmes inspired the senseless violence satires, Adams' shoeshop phobia, and the ultimate significance of towels. 'Bits which were cut' appear, most of them familiar since used in books; other, weaker bits here were dropped; and Adams, then if not now a fanatical polisher, didn't add several famous lines until the records and books. (Cf. the hilarious Book One, now in its 32nd impression using the same old shoddy typography: Pan 159pp £1.95.) *Scripts* is worth it for the FX directions: THICK SWIRLING SMOKE. A FEW LIGHTS VISIBLE AND SOME MENACING BUT ILL DEFINED SHAPES. THIS IS SIGNALLED BY A FEW COUGHS FROM ARTHUR, WHO IS PLAYED BY A REMARKABLY TALENTED AND ABLE ACTOR....

Harry Harrison, a talented and able writer, shows his versatility by effortlessly turning off these qualities for *You Can Be The Stainless Steel Rat* (Grafton £1.95. Grafton used to be Granada; there are no page numbers but 339 paragraphs). Perhaps that's unfair: he cracks some good jokes, but literary ability seems irrelevant to these game books (look at the people who usually write them). Playability? Unless you get bored and go to sleep there's no way to lose, or to escape the linear 'plot' to which Harrison has merely added decorative, swiftly returning loops. Occasionally you toss a coin to find whether life or death awaits you: heads or tails lead to the same paragraph (guess what it says), inserted twice by the eerie magic of the word processor. My all-purpose review for such efforts is designed to appease the publishers: 'This one is a real page-turner!'

So is James P. Hogan's *Code of the Lifemaker* (Penguin 405pp £2.95), another step in this determined author's progress from being merely worthy and dull. The basic scenario: a million years back, a damaged alien von Neumann machine lands on Titan. Its programs being as corrupt as South American politics, the robot workforce goes awry and starts evolving – they even develop sexual reproduction. Blimey. (A first in science fiction: robot sexism! Not only do all female humans occupy subordinate roles – no female robot seems even to get a speaking part.) Cut to 21st-century investigative probe from Earth, carrying troops, exploiters and the lunatic fringe: a Gelleresque psychic (much sound scepticism here) and a fanatic debunker. Meanwhile, the robots are debating the shape of their world, a dangerous subject since they've also evolved the Spanish Inquisition.

This farrago improves as alignments shift among the Earth team, with expected and unexpected reversals, and oddities are justified by the deeply nasty political sub-plot. Hogan grapples with robot environmentalism: will Earth strip-mine the metallic biosphere for spare parts? *Lifemaker* never comes to terms with its own absurdity, but if you survive the stodgy opening it has its charms.

As does Barrington Bayley, an even more rough-hewn writer than Hogan, and sf's premier pulp philosopher. *The Rod of Light* (Methuen 193pp £2.50) follows his *Soul of the Robot*, and with tongue partly in cheek examines the Nature of Consciousness in terms of B-movie villainy. Thus: Jasperodus, continuing robot hero, is unique in being conscious, thanks to human 'parents' who donated him portions of their souls. Far more intelligent is Gargan (sic), a robot genius who though not conscious *is* bright enough to deduce that he isn't. A sympathetic and even tragic villain, he duly starts draining human souls out of the very best motives (also, of course, out of humans). Jasperodus opposes this practice on robotitarian grounds – but Gargan's team has the last word: 'Consciousness needs matter through which to act.... But does matter need consciousness? No.... We robots are proof of that. Which, then, is more fundamental to the world?' Concepts by Jorge Luis Borges, action by Doc Smith, sense of humour Bayley's own.

The humour of Peter Beere's **Trauma 2020** series escapes many readers: it's in the style and dialogue with which appalling events flow down big-city gutters a few years hence. Raymond Chandler on speed. 'As great love affairs go, ours was something of a wipe-out. Which is a surfing term meaning you scrape your balls off on the edge of the board.' The wisecracking idiom suits the non-hero Beekay, a crook, coward and (just barely) survivor whose paranoia is utterly justified. He even manages to poke shards of wit through the squalor of the sequence where he's forcibly addicted to heroin by an insane female cripple. This is volume three, *Silent Slaughter* (Arrow 202pp £1.95). 'The book doesn't stink,' says Beere. 'But it tries to.' It succeeds – conjuring up a smell that's a powerful antidote to books and TV series where violence is sanitized and good guys never get hurt, much.

For the sf reference shelf: David Pringle's *Science Fiction: the 100 Best Novels* (Xanadu 224pp £3.95). When Anthony Burgess published a book listing 99 best novels, Pringle was inspired. His selections, covering 36 years from *1984* to *Neuromancer*, are less quirky than Burgess's and, short stories excepted, would be the basis of an excellent home sf library. Most of my favourites are there, and only a scattering of dodgy selections – like Mack Reynolds, an 'ideas and concepts' man whose writing makes my teeth hurt. Most surprising omission (with an evasive apology in the introduction): Jack Vance.

The Science Fiction Film Source Book (Longman 312pp £7.95 – yes, it *is* a paperback) is David Wingrove's follow-up to the offbeat *SF Source Book*. Despite the spate of sf movie books, it's a handy list of plot summaries, with added information about producers, directors, etc. Minor glitches: the dreaded and inconsistent 'star ratings' (for Plot, Technical Skill, Entertainment and Artistic Merit) appear again, and coverage can be superficial (e.g. nothing on Hugo and suchlike sf film awards). To pick a random example, the entry on *Wizards* dismisses it as 'comic-oriented' without even mentioning the evident influence of Vaughn Bode, or Ian Miller's powerfully effective backgrounds. Nitpicking, though, is a game with no ending.

Down to the reissues. *Castles* by Alan Lee, David Day and David Larkin (Unicorn 192pp £7.95) is a gift book crammed with attractive pictures of ... well, with that title, it's not bungalows. *Lies, Inc* (Granada 224pp £1.95) is the weird, mind-boggling expansion of Philip Dick's *The Unteleported Man*. E.E. Smith has long been held not responsible for the dismal **Family d'Alembert** books, number 10 – *Revolt of the Galaxy* (Grafton 186pp £1.95) – being churned out as usual by Stephen Goldin. Rick Raphael's 1966 *Code Three*, exciting but now dated sf about 800-mph cars, is improbably released as a tie-in with *Mad Max*....

But where are my nice hardbacks?

January 1986

36 Newts That Never Were

Daily your reviewer is forced into contact with frightful manifestations from the bottomless pits of creation: publishers. Publishers love confusing mating rituals - in 1984 Sphere were taken over by Penguin, Hutchinson (Arrow/Hamlyn) by Century, and Granada by Collins, explaining why Granada books now appear as Grafton books. 'Same initial, same number of letters,' shrugged sf editor Nick Austin. Another strange practice of Granada - dammit, Grafton - is to deface review copies with huge, superglued stickers, impossible to peel off, saying A PAPERBACK ORIGINAL. This is why pictures of their books rarely appear on this page.

One false PAPERBACK ORIGINAL is Jack Vance's *Planet of Adventure* (Grafton 536pp £3.95), which appeared here in four volumes *circa* 1975 from Mayflower (Granada again). This is the **Tschai** or **Planet of Adventure** quartet, beloved by British fans for the title of volume two, *Servants of the Wankh*. The narrative is a near-triumph of ironic, exotic style over a routinely grotty space-operatic plot: Adam Reith, stranded star scout, fights and tricks his way across planet Tschai, populated by numerous enslaved/adapted human tribes and four species of inimical aliens with racial subdivisions of their own. Ho hum. The good stuff lies in Tschai's rich scents and colours, and in elaboration of style. No Vance villain would say, 'I'll get you for that.' Instead: 'Low-grade assassins will drown you in cattle excrement! Twenty pariahs will drub your corpse! A cur will drag your head along the street by the tongue!'

Ordinary conversation in Vance-land is similarly ornate. '"In what way could gibbeted corpses be consecrated to the estimable Matrons?" "By providing fodder for the Matrons' newt farms."' Actually this isn't Vance but Michael Shea, who (with permission) does an amazing job of pastiche in *A Quest for Simbilis* (Grafton 204pp £1.95). *The Eyes of the Overworld* now has two immediate sequels, this and Vance's *Cugel's Saga*. Vance can be relied on for unwavering polish, but tends to recycle old plot elements; Shea, though more rough-hewn, adds innovations plus a touch of true, murky hellfire from an imagination fuelled by Hieronymus Bosch. Since Vance was indirectly responsible for the whole D&D magic system - stolen wholesale from *The Dying Earth* - players who fail to buy these books will drop to the charisma and street credibility of a newt. 'It is their diet of sacred newts which enables the Matrons to achieve the massive solidity essential to their religious progress ...'

The funny coincidence department gives us: 'In this way we consumed a Newt we used to call Hans; it was an educated and clever animal with a special talent for scientific work ... it could be trusted with the most exacting chemical analyses. We used to have long chats with it in the evenings, amused by its insatiable thirst for knowledge. We were sorry to lose our Hans but he had lost his sight in the course of my trepanation experiments....' Thus Karel Capek's 1936 *War with the Newts*, now a welcome reissue (Unicorn 241pp £2.95). Capek's sophisticated wit converts what could be a plodding satire into something painfully funny. Discovered, given the benefits of Science (as above), bred and exploited, the man-sized Newts absorb the logic of humanity and shyly make their demands: 'Hello, you people! No need for alarm. We have no hostile intentions.... We only need more water, more shallows to live in.... That's why we have to dismantle your continents.' A classic.

Newts are scarce in the hefty, impressive *Encyclopaedia of Things That Never Were* by Michael Page and Robert Ingpen (Paper Tiger 240pp £15.95). Encyclopaedia is the wrong word: the huge pages offer an idiosyncratic collection of whatever myths and magic Page wanted to write about or Ingpen to paint. The artwork is fine (I hadn't realized the goddess Venus looked so *very* much like Princess Diana); the writing is sometimes tiresome in its paraphrase of well-known myths and fictions. Wisely, this book sticks to 'assimilated' fantasies, images which have long wormed their way into English culture: Bunyan, Carroll, Coleridge, Melville, Poe, Shelley, Stevenson, etc. Tolkien and his plagiarists are omitted; Kenneth Grahame just sneaks in, as does Anthony Hope: 'It is now the Democratic Republic of Ruritania, and Zenda is a missile base and the local headquarters of the KGB.' Good marks for production and eclecticism beyond the usual European and Greek myths: but at £15.95 there'd have to be a really yawning space on your coffee table.

The Glamour by Christopher Priest (Abacus 214pp £2.95) is true to its own weird self: not only do passages shift their meaning in the light of later revelation, but the book itself has changed. Its ending is no longer that of the hardback.... It remains *(a)* possibly sf's best treatment of invisibility; *(b)* not an sf novel.

Molly Zero (Penguin 251pp £2.50) is the latest paperback novel from Keith Roberts, which should really be recommendation enough. In Britain 200 years hence, he offers dystopia with a difference: a tattered, functioning society with no blatant nightmare of oppression but a worrying feel of control. Molly Zero 'escapes' a training school for the remote ruling class, and tastes life in the North, on the road, in London (where the rich are called 'chicos' – work it out). People muddle along as ever, but Roberts is expert with disquieting touches like the wire fence that always lies between you and the sea. There are no real villains. The ruling 'Elite' is sympathetic in its own way, struggling with the paradox of allowing freedom while maintaining stability. Roberts' simple and human story leaves you to decide whether the price of compromise, which includes all Molly's innocence, is too great.

No such subtlety from Piers Anthony! *Politician* (Granada – it says here – 398pp £2.50) is volume three of space tyrant Hope Hubris's career, and admittedly lacks the previous books' over-the-top silliness. Hubris enters Jovian

(American) politics on a platform of Hispanic (Hispanic) minority interests, solves the red-hot problem of communist Ganymede (Cuba) and negotiates with Saturn (the USSR) over a shot-down civilian spaceship, while remaining aware of the clout of Mars (the Middle East) and totally ignoring Uranus (Europe), preparatory to contesting the presidency of Jupiter (the USA), held by a corrupt machine politician called Tocsin (h'mm) ... Anthony, in other words, is handing out personal political solutions to contemporary matters, which is wearying since you're constantly translating the story back into twentieth-century terms. His heart's in the right place, but the ending is a cop-out, with the equivalent of the US Constitution being simply set aside owing to Hubris's immense popular support. Oh yeah?

Modern Science Fiction and the American Literary Community by Frederick Andrew Lerner (Scarecrow Press dist. Bailey Bros & Swinfen 325pp £26.00) is one of those extraordinary US academic productions with 169pp of notes, appendices and index: it assembles endless bitty quotes and paraphrases of what people have said about sf, and reads like newts (I mean notes) for an evaluative study which, unlike this, might reach some actual conclusions. Methuen have paused their programme of dreary new Clifford Simak books to reissue two older goodies, works that shaped my own love of sf: *Time and Again* and *All Flesh is Grass* (both 255pp £2.50). Bob Shaw's *Fire Pattern* (Grafton 208pp £1.95) struggles desperately to combine two taut action-adventures, one about spontaneous human combustion and one about telepathic aliens on Mercury: pity it wasn't two books. And Thomas F. Monteleone's *Microworlds* (Hamlyn 175pp £2.50), though more adventurous and interesting than Penguin's rival computer-sf anthology (crippled by a surfeit of Asimov stories), has the disadvantage of not appearing first.

Speaking of newts, I'd better stop while the pubs are still open....

February 1986

37 Publishers' Lore

I'm writing at the dead time of the publishing year, between the Xmas Splurge and the Spring Launches. Folklore says this is a rotten period to put out a book. When authors are told, 'We've put you on the schedule for January,' they find it as cheering as when publishers say: 'Great news - we're remaindering your book at last!'

Gollancz's latest would seem doubly cursed, since they're books of short stories. 'I'm publishing so-and-so's new collection' is pronounced by the average editor as though he/she were muttering through clenched teeth, 'Blind Pew called this morning and handed me the Black Spot.' This isn't mere superstition: the mindless hordes (you) are notoriously reluctant to buy single-author collections. You might also be surprised to hear that hardback buyers are overwhelmingly keen on glossy dustjackets, which add substantially to the cost of the book. Attempts to publish cheaper, unjacketed books have failed miserably.

Pohlstars (Gollancz 203pp £8.95) is Frederik Pohl's first sf collection for many years. The eleven stories are smoothly professional, ranging from minor gags to a mini-novel. One shaggy joke assumes that evil aliens two centuries hence will be unaware of gravitational quirks which sf did to death as plot gimmicks in the 1960s - this got published in 1983! Other tales conceal effective rabbit-punches. The mini-novel is strong on sf speculation ('oaty-boats' sucking power from ocean temperature differentials), dodgy on 2020s corporate politics (gangster/mafiosi clichés drag it back to the 1920s), good for storytelling, vaguely unconvincing in its final psychological twist. A mixed bag.

Likewise Philip K. Dick's collection *I Hope I Shall Arrive Soon* (Gollancz 179pp £8.95): the ten stories straggle from 1954 to a posthumous 1985. Though he's a lot less polished than Pohl, I like Dick better. Pohl writes as a wise guy who knows the rules, knows people are out to screw you, and knows you can't beat the system. Dick generally starts by changing the rules, continues to find 'goodness' in odd places (loonies, alien simulacra, computers), and often steps right outside the preconceived system. In his very funny and utopian 'The Exit Door Leads In', the System itself is encouraging people not to blindly obey the System.... Dick's combined screwiness and humanity fill the opening essay, switching between jokes and his worrying theory that unread chunks of the Bible were creeping into his sf. 'The existence of Disneyland (which I *know* is real) proves that we are not living in Judaea in AD 50.' Few people needed this particular reassurance. There may be no more books of previously-uncollected Dick stories, so bag this one.

There will doubtless be hordes more **Darkover** tales from Marion Zimmer Bradley: publishers love issuing books very similar to previous ones. *Hawkmistress* (Arrow 336pp £2.25), despite its veneer of science-fantasy, seems hauntingly familiar. Heroine Romilly wears breeches and gets on well with animals, but Daddy wants her to don girlish clothes and marry. One knows instantly that the chap whose advances Romilly finds most loathsome is Daddy's arranged bridegroom: and so it proves. With hawk and horse our heroine flees to find her own way in the world.... The sf factor here seems superfluous: Romilly is psionically instead of ordinarily good with animals, and eventually helps extract someone rather unconvincingly from a besieged town by the psychic equivalent of walking on tiptoe. The feminist content suffers from the period setting: stuff like arranged marriages (no longer, I believe, a hot feminist issue in America) tends to distract from more subtle inequalities.

Overall, it's a readable yarn which is essentially historical romance - for sf fans who wouldn't be seen dead with your average bodice-ripper novel, but secretly enjoy the camouflaged version.

'Science fantasy' is a useful publisher's phrase for Bradley's Darkover or McCaffrey's Pern: token spaceships and astronomy, plus lashings of Mystic Mental Powers. Freda Warrington's *A Blackbird in Silver* (NEL 302pp £2.95) is weirdly publicized under this label. Actually it's another sub-sub-Tolkien quest epic in which a tiny fellowship sets off to nobble Total Evil, here taking the form of a large and unfriendly Worm or Serpent. It's not at all badly written - just awfully standard, overdone fantasy fare. Perhaps the 'science fantasy' label came from the author's tendency to describe magic in terms of imperfectly recollected physics. 'There was no "sorcery" on the Earth, the potential energy for it did not exist.' 'The energy spins in a huge ever-increasing circle....' The writing spins out a huge ever-increasing trilogy. Beam me up, Scotty.

[Mild apologies here to Freda Warrington, who smiled sweetly on me as her boot sought my groin: her series was a mere diptych and not a trilogy at all, although I seem to recall that even later it became a tetralogy.]

With a title like *Sex Secrets of Ancient Atlantis (Illustrated)* you can hardly go wrong (Granada 220pp £1.95). Famous pseudonym John Grant has crafted another of his poignantly awful shaggy-dog narratives. The illustrations are sadly all quite printable; the text pokes fun at UFOlogy, the Atlantis myth, magic pendulums, *The Tao of Sex*, and worse. The sexual revelations are fully as astonishing as any that were published in *Imagine*. 'Ex-Government physicist Professor David Langford' is severely criticized for the vile orthodoxy of his views, and Grant complains 'I have had no reply at all to a letter which I wrote to Margaret Thatcher (who may well herself be an Atlantean agent sent to destroy our country's economy).' Need I go on?

[The reference to *Imagine* magazine alludes to its policy of deep prudery (imposed by TSR's American masters, not the healthily foul-mouthed UK editors). When they published a fantasy story of mine the fearful word 'breasts' was cut, even though the organs in question weren't bared, fondled or even made to go *spung!* - merely noticed in passing. It's only fair to add that a near-identical cut was made years later in an sf story I wrote for *Dwarf*. 'Er, we have to think of our fifteen-year-old readers' suggestible mothers.']

C.J. Cherryh goes on, and on, in *Forty Thousand in Gehenna* (Methuen 445pp £2.95), another fat volume from her ambitious Union/Alliance universe of future space politics. The basic idea is good: re-establishing contact with a collapsed human colony whose members have grown into symbiosis with aliens who think by quite different rules. There's also a cleverly nasty rationale (resembling a John Le Carré ploy) for the colony's initial failure. The trouble is that Cherryh takes 200 pages to set this up, with blow-by-blow accounts of the collapse and oodles of military-communication hokum ... after which the plot starts moving in peculiar jerks. You feel there's been too much background information and not half enough about what's happening now. An interesting read, but little is lost by skimming the first half.

As for dear old Ted Tubb's *Nectar of Heaven* (Arrow 160pp £1.75) ... long-term readers of the Dumarest series will be almost forced to fast-skim this 24th volume. Once again Earl Dumarest follows a false trail in search of planet Earth, which he long ago mislaid. Again he encounters formulaic battle, murder and sudden death, eventually outwitting the sinister brains of the nasty Cyclan. And again Tubb clears the ground for the next sequel with alarming efficiency: the woman with whom Dumarest's got involved is as usual given a nice death scene, whereupon our man *gives away* the vast wealth which would make his quest a damn sight easier. So, as always, there's a clean slate for book 25, in which I predict Dumarest will arrive moneyless on a new and savage world, urgently though somehow never very well pursued by the all-potent yet ludicrously inefficient Cyclan, and ... *et cetera*.

A footnote for those worried about loony fundamentalists banning their fantasy games: let me recommend a fat and fascinating book on their US efforts to ban the teaching of modern evolutionary biology. *Science and Creationism* ed. Ashley Montagu (OUP 416pp £7.95) has essays by many famous names including Isaac Asimov (whose *Counting the Eons* is yet another OK science-essay collection - Grafton 254pp £2.50), and reveals just how intellectually poverty-stricken the creationist movement is. Academic bloodshed on a vast scale: I loved it. It's a sadly true bit of publishing lore that a sane book like this will never sell as well as something titled, to choose an example at random, *Sex Secrets of Ancient Atlantis*.

March 1986

38 O America

According to American legend, Science Fiction is 60 this year. In 1991, presumably, it can start drawing a pension ... thanks to Hugo Gernsback's *Amazing Stories*, whose 1926 launch marks Year One for US fans and immortalized 'Hugo' as the name of a Freudian-shaped rocket trophy. Where this leaves prehistoric sf authors like Mary Shelley, H.G. Wells or Jules Verne is unclear: in sf, America rules by right of numbers. Of this month's books, 78% are from across the Atlantic and the rest pretend to be. Don't despair: several are excellent.

William Gibson swept the awards with his first novel *Neuromancer*, a tale of next-century cyber-piracy whose pace and excitement hook into your nervous system and fibrillate you to death like the killer programs he describes. The follow-up is *Count Zero* (Gollancz 269pp £9.95), set a few years later in Gibson's glittering, sleazy future. The events of *Neuromancer* are half legendary; organic 'biosoftware' is the rising new star. The cyberspace of the world data network, where *Neuromancer*'s action peaked, has changed: not only are defences ('black ice') nastier than ever, but the net is haunted by unknown presences.

Gibson spins a taut triple narrative: an industrial-warfare mercenary trying to spring the inventor of 'biochips' from his corporate employers, a nicely drawn art expert tracing works of anonymous brilliance, a wimpish teenager calling himself Count Zero who botches his first try at cyberspace piracy but is saved by Something from black ice ... all these being aspects of someone's master plan. The high-speed Gibson technique recalls Ian Fleming's – sex, violence and brand names, and many a 'carbine-format Steiner-Optic laser with Fabrique National sights.' There's even a Flemingesque monster-villain and a generous dose of streetwise voodoo. Has a girl with a headful of biochips become an avatar of voodoo's Erzulie? Are the 'presences' *only* free artificial intelligences like that of *Neuromancer*? Decide for yourself as the name Count Zero shifts meaning in a chilling cyberspace climax. This may not have the impact of *Neuromancer*'s first roller-coaster ride through Gibson's future, but it's a far better novel.

Robert Heinlein makes another come-back with *The Cat Who Walks Through Walls* (NEL 374pp £9.95), starting well with violence and flight. The hero, being a Heinlein hero, naturally pauses to marry his current lady friend before running – from an L5 colony, in a wonky spacecraft, to an unbelievable-but-funny forced lunar landing, thence in several stages across a Moon which proves to be that of *The Moon is a Harsh Mistress*, 112 years on – and finally, on page 230, after this mildly entertaining travelogue which would have served a younger Heinlein for half a chapter, we get some plot.

Oh dear.

I'm afraid it's Heinlein self-indulgence time again. What's on the menu is those blasted inter-universal travellers from *'The Number of the Beast'*, plus walk-ons from *Time Enough for Love, Glory Road, The Moon is a Harsh Mistress, Stranger in a Strange Land* and more. Everything lapses into introductions, logorrhoea and cuteness: a lurch into seven pages of dramatic finale (carefully unresolved) can't save the book. I was hoping to like it, too. Even after a merry exchange in which someone is treated with unreserved contempt for thinking it wrong that poor people should automatically *die* if they can't pay air charges on the Moon – after which, rather than debate the point, Heinlein merely reveals this wickedly socialistic person to be a traitor and spy. This is known as loading the argument.

The Memory of Whiteness (Macdonald 351pp £9.95) is the third novel by another young American, Kim Stanley Robinson, who definitely oozes talent. Confession time: the book is about music and I'm tone-deaf, so I may find it less riveting than you. I also break out in an itchy rash when addressed as 'dear Reader', which Robinson does constantly. That said, gentle lector, this is impressive for its scope and feel of connecting the two cultures: both the music and the multidimensional physics *sound* convincing. Johannes Wright is making a Grand Tour of the Solar System in 3229, from Pluto inward to the Sun, performing on the bizarre one-man 'Orchestra' devised way back by physicist Holywelkin, whose unified field theory has led to system-wide colonization. Wright is being mysteriously plotted against, while devising an ultimate 'music of the spheres' incorporating Holywelkin's equations (remember Charles Harness's *The Rose*)? The philosophical implications naturally prove to be stupendous. A few pretensions could do with trimming, but it's a worthy effort.

Philip K. Dick's 1972 *We Can Build You* (Grafton 252pp £2.50) appears here in Britain for the first time. Though not one of his best efforts, it has an uneasy power. The expected plot focus is the building of ultra-lifelike historical simulacra, e.g. Abraham Lincoln (who proves a sympathetic character) ... but this whole battery of implications and consequences is crowded offstage by the narrator's own destructive obsession with the schizophrenic girl who designs the machines. Dick's underdog humour – little people against the world – is here, but overall it's a dark book. Behind the quite irrelevant robot Hitler on the cover, Chris Foss has touchingly painted in a robot Philip K. Dick.

Eric Frank Russell is our odd one out. He was British, but cultivated a wisecracking transatlantic style for the US market, as more recently did John Brunner. *Sinister Barrier* (Methuen 201pp £2.50) is a historical curiosity from 1939, sf based on Charles Fort's famously offbeat speculations. 'I think we're property,' said Fort. Russell translated this into nasty energy beasts who herd us like sheep, and chronicled the results when the facts leak out. Painfully dated, but a must for the collector's library. Eighteen years later, Russell had improved his technique no end for *Wasp* (Methuen 175pp £2.50), a much-loved story of perverse warfare. 'By scrawling suitable words on a wall, the right man in the right place at the right time might immobilize an armoured division.' Our not very heroic hero James Mowry is filled to the eyeballs with sabotage techniques and, in a favourite Russell gambit, dumped on an enemy planet to subdue it single-handed. Fast and funny - but much less so than Granada's definitive editions, which like Dobson's hardback gained much from Russell's later (1958) revisions.

[Probably the first edition was heavily cut, rather than the later one being expanded. What was sadly lacking in this version was the wisecracking inventiveness that turned Russell's simplest chase plots into something rather special.]

Robert Silverberg's *Sunrise on Mercury* (Pan 176pp £1.95) comprises thirteen stories dated 1954 to 1979. All are exceedingly slick and competent, though I wonder whether Silverberg in 1986 now feels twinges of guilt about his patronizing attitude to 'primitive' aliens back in the 50s. The whole book goes down smoothly and tastes pretty good throughout. Half an hour later you'll be hungry again.

The best thing about *National Lampoon's DOON* (Grafton £2.50 176pp) is Bruce Pennington's cover, a lovely send-up of his paintings for the NEL *Dune* series. (Goodness knows what made NEL switch to the far less evocative artist who now disfigures the books.) Inside, author Ellis Weiner does a cut-rate version of the famous *Bored of the Rings* treatment: get in there and make as many jokes as possible, 25% of them incomprehensibly American. The idea of Doon, the Dessert Planet, whose plains are roamed by giant killer pretzels, the galaxy's sole source of the mind-bending liquid *beer* ... that's funny. There are good pokes at Herbert's pretensions: the elliptical quotations, the weird words and glossaries, the conversations in which neither party ever gets to the point (but *thinks* a lot, in italics). But with the best will in the world, a parody of a particular author gets tiresome after a few thousand words.

[You mean like this clever Langford parody you're doing? - Ed.]

Okay, I can take a hint.

April 1986

39 Starting Points

Are you the sort of reader who skips this opening paragraph in favour of actual reviews? (If you skip the whole page, I do not wish to know.) I've been thinking about the time it takes authors to roll up their sleeves and start telling the story. The longer they delay, the more putdownable the book usually is ... despite a tradition of clever-sod exceptions, from *Tristram Shandy* to *Report on Probability A*, whose literary fireworks lure you through a book which proves to have no plot at all.

Robert Irwin gets straight to his subject in paragraph one of *The Limits of Vision* (Viking 120pp £8.95). The subject is dirt. Also dust, filth, gunge, smears, stains, mould, dandruff and little waxy bits. Reading it will make you itch in places you didn't know you had. Heroine Marcia is a housewife waging a lonely metaphysical battle against these manifestations of Mucor, Spirit of Evil, as encountered in a mildew-spot on the carpet. 'Small white spot that we are, we have been elected to speak to you ...' It appears that Marcia, struggling to initiate her feminist friends into the sacred mystery of washing-up, may be slightly dotty. She also has unlikely conversations with people like Blake, Dickens, Darwin and da Vinci. Nevertheless, she wins through!

Concentrated, sinister and funny, this is a triumph of black humour. Well, off-black. As Marcia would point out, black shows up all the fluff and dust and flakes of dead skin and ...

Schismatrix by Bruce Sterling (Penguin 288pp £2.50) starts with immediate violence, slowly explained in retrospect. It's picaresque sf covering two seething centuries of change in our solar system, where Earth is off-limits and the action lies in endless scattered space habitats. The major ideological split is technological, Mechanists versus the bioengineering Shapers. The protagonist, Abelard Lindsay, survives variously as political exile, impresario, pirate, xenodiplomat, peacemaker, blackmailer, duellist, terraformer, reluctant hero ... Sterling follows the sound principle of never revealing too much: some offbeat terms ('ice assassins') are defined by context, others ('Nerve Coral Aquatics', one of nineteen alien species) don't need to be. Placid decades are omitted from the narrative, to be reconstructed from the bones and joints you're actually given.

Besides being highly exciting and crammed with ingenious ideas, *Schismatrix* paints a moving Big Picture of humanity slowly getting a grip on its own evolution. Lindsay, however unheroically, helps nudge it the right way. Excellent sense-of-wonder stuff. My only dislike is the title: Schismatrix suggests a lady who causes schisms, and I waited half the book for her to turn up before Sterling issued his own unlikely definition.

In *A Stainless Steel Rat is Born* (Sphere 185pp £1.95), Harry Harrison doesn't hang around: the legendary Slippery Jim DiGriz is holding up his first bank on the first page. Thus Harrison uses the frequent technique of starting on a high note, adding background in pages of flashback. The book rattles amusingly along, as the youthful Rat plots his way into jail and out again in search of the elusive criminal contacts he could easily have made, had he but known, at a Games Day. No sequel will match the saga's first book, but this comes close: Jim's wretched family isn't around to get in his light, the action doesn't get so excessively silly or grim as to fragment the story, and it climaxes on one of those ghastly low-tech planets in which Harrison delights.

Only on page 48 does *Killashandra* (Bantam Press 292pp £8.95) actually reach the planet where the story happens - since Anne McCaffrey needs to fill in endless background from *The Crystal Singer*, to which this is a sequel. She's on reasonable form: her world of crystal (here also linked with the *Ship Who Sang* tales) hasn't been worn smooth like Pern, and she's avoided her mistake in *Moreta* of trying to write tragedy. McCaffrey's forte is the fairy tale. Her heroines are always Cinderella or the Ugly Duckling.

Killashandra, crystal singer, rose to swanhood last book but still gets into trouble on her vaguely diplomatic mission. Only a McCaffrey heroine could wander out in search of bootleg beer, take refuge in a house then coincidentally visited by the chap who wants to maroon her in an archipelago (which he does), and later escape to another island coincidentally about to be visited by the erstwhile kidnapper, who coincidentally fails to recognize his victim through her suntan and falls in love with her instead. And so on: the plot is candyfloss nonsense throughout, but it has a certain charm. Turn off that brain. Relax and enjoy.

For tension, try Kate Wilhelm's *Welcome, Chaos* (Gollancz 297pp £9.95), a gripping, straightforward story from a fine author who has sometimes been over-subtle and elusive. In eight pages the scene is set, the well-drawn heroine manipulated to a far-off spot where a strange fate lurks. The grail or Macguffin is that sf standby the immortality virus, whose victims risk death (50% of cases) and sterility (100%). Its biggest hazard is a seeming bonus: because cell regeneration means immunity to radiation, certain persons begin to think in terms of first strikes and winnable nuclear war. Wilhelm maintains tight suspense and high-class characterization to the bitter end ... nor does she shirk the moral issues.

All right. I've been comparing these books' 'attack speed' thanks to an encounter with *The Ceremonies* by T.E.D. Klein (Pan 553pp £2.95). Such blockbuster horror novels seem to rely heavily on ominous padding. The rule is 'Tell 'em what awfulness is going to happen. Then tell 'em again. And again....' Following this exhausting tradition, it takes Klein *165 pages* to manipulate his hero into the position Kate Wilhelm achieves by page nine. Stephen King credits the book with 'a sense of deep and brooding mystery'; by then I had a sense of deep and yawning predictability. A high death toll among innocent bystanders? Yep.

A climax of nasty sexual ritual? Yep. A concluding 'The end ... *or is it?*' Oh dear, yes.

The style is, naturally, portentous. On page one we meet 'Something older far than humankind, and darker than some vast and sunless cavern on a world beyond the farthest depths of space.' Besides the thought that this is overdoing it a bit, one does rather wonder where exactly 'beyond the farthest depths of space' may be, and whether a sunless cavern there is necessarily darker than, say, one near Milton Keynes. Yet Klein's writing has been praised; presumably it's what the market wants....

Notable reissues: Robert Holdstock's *Mythago Wood* (Grafton 319pp £2.50), a magical book, recently bagged the World Fantasy Award. *The Day of Forever* (Gollancz 126pp £8.95) is the first hardback of J.G. Ballard's uneven, compelling 1967 collection. *Macroscope* by Piers Anthony (Grafton 480pp £2.95) is one of his quirky best, at last reissued here in full – Sphere's edition was slashed to incomprehensibility. [Although on mature reflection I sometimes wonder whether restoring its vast quantities of astrological woffle was entirely a good thing.]

Also enjoyed: *Lord of Light*, an early Roger Zelazny (Methuen 261pp £2.50), lumbering but nifty science-fantasy with technology propping up Hindu 'gods' and reincarnation. Brian Aldiss's *Seasons in Flight* (Grafton 160pp £1.95) offers cunningly simple stories and fables, not for those who demand 100% sf/fantasy. Ian Watson's *The Book of the Stars* (Grafton 236pp £2.50) is book two of the fun, freewheeling trilogy already plugged here. Gollancz have launched a worthy **Classic SF** paperback line, all at £2.95, aiming at literacy and enjoyability: Vonnegut's *The Sirens of Titan*, Sturgeon's *More Than Human*, Silverberg's *A Time of Changes* and Delany's *Nova*. Every six months, four more....

[About the *Nova* reissue: I fondly remembered the first Gollancz edition, with running heads giving the story's shifting place and time on every page – and asked why the typography had been changed to lose this. Malcolm Edwards of (then) Gollancz explained patiently that that version had been photo-reproduced from the US first edition, hated by Delany since the text itself was badly corrupt.... Well, *I* thought that was interesting.]

Farewell note: *Chapter House Dune* (NEL 476pp £2.95) may end Frank Herbert's galactic power-politicking, since this year he died of cancer aged 65. See column 27 for a mildly enthusiastic review. R.I.P.

Right, with these tiresome reviews out of the way I can get down to the story. Once upon a time ...

May 1986

40 A Dollop of Evil

One recurring difficulty for fantasy role-players and writers is the good old theological Problem of Evil – like, how and why? Quest after quest sets out to zap the vile though obscurely motivated Black Lord in his mountain-ringed stronghold, with such monotonous success that you'd think school careers officers would long ago have stopped recommending Black Lordship jobs. From a literary viewpoint it seems too easy: you set up a Black Lord with Abominable Minions, and the fantasy questers (be they never so wimpish) duly knock them over. Evil should be a bit closer to home than this externalized straw-man figure ... which is why Tolkien also gave us Gollum, Boromir, Saruman and Denethor.

Mary Brown's approach in *The Unlikely Ones* (Century 426pp £10.95) is to sweep Evil hastily under the carpet, with the death of the wicked witch whose curses fuel the plot. Thereafter her victims trek through yet another dewy mediaeval Britain: a cursed knight who wants his sword mended and armour rustproofed, a cursed and masked maiden who believes herself impossibly ugly (that she isn't comes as no surprise whatever), and several cute cursed fauna – unicorn, cat, toad, crow, even a cursed goldfish. Their quest: to return the property of a dragon, under the guidance of a cranky illusionist. The obstacles are remarkably unthreatening, the most notable being a castle with a terrible secret which proves to be a fondness for blood sports – good Animal Lib propaganda here – and a Sheloboid spider, too easily vanquished by D&D-style problem-solving. Later, all these obstacles without exception are revealed to have been harmless and illusory. Meanwhile, the knight's curse can only be lifted by his proposing marriage to an impossibly ugly woman....

The book has modest charm and a fresh style, but everything glides along with the happy predictability of a Mills and Boon romance. I'd rate it higher if only there were a few genuine surprises.

Unwin, of Unicorn fame, have launched an sf paperback line called Orion. *Time-Slip* (164pp £2.95) is by Graham Dunstan Martin, one of Unicorn's three best discoveries (the others being Gwyneth Jones and Geoff Ryman). In a shambolic post-holocaust Scotland, Martin's new messiah tackles the classic problem of evil with an argument crazily combining the anthropic principle (the universe is the way it is because only this universe could have produced us to observe it) with 20th-century black art – the many-worlds interpretation of quantum mechanics (every decision splits reality, so that everything happens, including the best of all possible outcomes). The forking paths of time are occasionally mirrored in the narrative; *Dwarf* readers will appreciate the way they're mirrored again in 'fantasy gamebook' choices. As Larry Niven theorized in his short story 'All the Myriad Ways', a many-worlds philosophy is hopeless in everyday life. Martin makes it blackly clear that his protagonist's religious cure-all leads to a severe upswing in the evil it explains away.

As for Scotland's survival after nuclear World War III despite the growing consensus that *no one* will survive, I suppose it's here explained by the daft theory of the book itself....

There are no evil people in Gwyneth Jones's *Escape Plans* (Orion 246pp £2.50) – just uncaring or uninformed ones. That's all you need for a nightmare future, totally oppressed by and totally dependent on information systems. Each man loves the thing that kills him: the lowest of the low want to submerge their humanity still further and become *components* of the 'oversystem'. The heroine Alice (ALIC in acronymic) is a dilettante from the orbital ruling class, who whimsically descends into the inferno of programmed India and gets stuck ... as revolution brews.

This is a terrifically compelling vision of a world where data processing systems have completely sunk in – no longer a part of the environment, they *are* the environment. Unfortunately they've also sunk into the language: Jones's welter of neologisms and acronyms is initially overwhelming, and I kept furtively turning to the glossary. Occasionally a definition appears in the narrative, breaking the spell: to *whom* in her world is the narrator explaining when she mentions a 'deeby' and then translates with 'Direct Brain Access (DB)'? But it's worth wading through the alphabet soup for the story.

'Michael Scot' is Michael Scott Rohan and Allan Scott, collaborating on *The Ice King* (NEL 252pp £9.95). Archaeologists dig up a brace of Ancient Evils, and ... no, don't run. For once the archaeology is realistic (the authors know their stuff), not to mention computerized. The ancient unpleasantness is also highly authentic, crafted with both knowledge and love of Norse myth's blacker byways. Fimbulwinter closes in on a Yorkshire village, nasties stalk the night, international data-nets ferret out the truths behind legend, a professor of archaeology goes on a desperate research trip to the Corpse Strand and Yggdrasil, and the appalling Ice King is not (in the last analysis) wholly unsympathetic. Good rousing stuff.

Another vision of evil comes from the Arabian Nights, where djinni do dreadful things in a kind of innocence but the blackest deeds are human. Seamus Cullen catches something of the mood in *A Noose of Light* (Orbit 216pp £2.50), at the same time magical and rumbustiously rude – this book tells you more than you wish to know about a djinn's sexual apparatus and proclivities. The humour and cruelty are faithful to the source: evil-doers are unremittingly punished, while the reward of virtue is often skimpy until after you're dead. Unevenly paced, but an OK read for non-prudes.

John Brunner offers a slightly enigmatic sf novel, *The Tides of Time* (Penguin 235pp £2.50). A mysterious black man and white woman enact little scenes on a Greek island, each episode further back in history, with no linkage of memory or continuity. They tell each other fables about former colleagues who've somehow been destroyed by their own desires and failings. As the repetitive chapters go by, one turns the pages faster, wondering what the hell it's all about. The final scenes explain all, in a splurge of exposition about FTL travel, fugue states, variable stars, cosmic vibes and the hypothetical Earth-soul 'Gaia': this dense mass of exposition sits oddly at the end of a slow-moving work. Brunner's philosophical contention probably needs a whole book. Here it gets about thirty belated pages, and I have to admit it's a tribute to his skill that he keeps you reading until then.

A Nest of Nightmares (Sphere 208pp £2.50) is Lisa Tuttle's first horror collection ... there are, of course, thirteen stories. Most have appeared in *The Magazine of Fantasy and Science Fiction*, which for cognoscenti is a hallmark of quality. Tuttle writes well, carefully understates the disturbing bits and knows just how to push the gooseflesh button: I'd say more, but it's difficult to type while trembling under the bedclothes.

I enjoyed Guy Gavriel Kay's now-reissued *The Summer Tree* (Unicorn 323pp £2.95), literate and gripping despite a dismayingly routine Black Lord in the mountainous background. But for deep insight into Evil, where better to look than *Artifact of Evil* (TSR 352pp £2.25) by fantasy gaming's own Dark Lord, Gary Gygax? At the very first glimpse within, my soul was purged by the brutalities visited upon the English language. To quote *White Dwarf*'s enlightened Submissions Guidelines: 'Themes to be avoided are "adventure" write-ups ...' *Artifact of Evil* is an Advanced Dungeons & Dragons campaign write-up. 'Nuff said.

June 1986

41 Reviewquest!

Reviewquest is the fantasy game in which *you* take the part of a hapless book reviewer! Yes, you alone can stand against the evil Pulp Empire, using only your quivering, naked forebrain to parry inhuman weapons: cruel syntax of no human shape, smeared with the poison of ancient, festering clichés! Which is one way of saying I sometimes get tired of bloody fantasy trilogies, and slink off to wear my other hat as half of Ansible Information, purveyors of high-class software (advt).

That said, *The Anvil of Ice* by Michael Scott Rohan (Macdonald 348pp £9.95), opening a trilogy called **The Winter of the World**, is a good read. The hero Alv (later Elof) survives the bloody sacking of his town by quasi-vikings, to become an apprentice smith of a special kind – a maker of enchanted weapons. Much fascinating research is evident here, and Rohan can look forward to seeing his smithy passages stolen for many a role-playing game campaign. There's also a grittily solid background of impending Ice Age; the characters are nicely done; the final confrontation between Elof and the representative of the Ice-powers has a nifty magical twist. We'll pass over the groan-makingly traditional fantasy reversal whereby, its leader once disposed of, a hitherto irresistible army fades away into the undergrowth in just one paragraph. Rohan clears the major hurdle of a trilogy opening: he actually makes me want to read book two! Stay tuned.

Blood Music by Greg Bear (Gollancz 262pp £9.95) is currently shortlisted for the Hugo Award – an obvious winner if there's justice in the world, which often there isn't. [The 1986 novel Hugo went instead to Orson Scott Card's *Ender's Game*, but I should add that the short version of *Blood Music* had won earlier Hugo *and* Nebula awards.] The scenario is the near future: genetic tampering ... 'Enzyme Valley' ... intelligent cells ... intelligent *disease*. A brilliant but wimpish researcher injects himself with thinking lymph cells to save his unauthorized experiment from the autoclave. Weird apocalypse follows as the cell clusters explore their world: being inhabited by germs is bad enough, but imagine being the environment of an Industrial Revolution. Bear doesn't, however, stop with the low-key horror of what North America becomes, but extrapolates further, and then further still. The finale is magnificent. Its only problem is that it's nigglingly close to the conclusion reached by an author extrapolating from a different start-point: Arthur C. Clarke in *Childhood's End*. But Bear, I think, does it better – and goes beyond even Clarke. Strongly recommended.

Brian Stableford, as consultant archaeologist at Greenhill Books, has been unearthing bygone sf/fantasy for republication. The list includes one unreadable 'classic' (*The Blind Spot* by Austin Hall and Homer Eon Flint), plus several worthwhile period pieces like *Three Go Back* by J. Leslie Mitchell (254pp £8.95; 1932). An airship is wafted back 25,000 years; a bright lady novelist, an arms dealer and a pacifist are confronted with the 'facts' of Cro-Magnon life, i.e. no war, crime, jealousy, religion or clothes. The book is slightly flawed by the now very unfashionable depiction of Neanderthals as murderous baddies (Mitchell's point was that the succeeding Cro-Magnons were nice because uncorrupted by civilization: so just who corrupted their cousins?). But it's a pleasant novel, and reminds you that while American magazine heroes were zapping greenskins with their blasters, some 1930s authors still considered sf a literature of ideas.

Two high-quality productions from small presses ... *And the Lurid Glare of the Comet* (Serconia 123pp $13.50 – try your local import shop) collects nine offbeat Brian Aldiss essays, including a fascinating 57pp mini-autobiography. The 1985 companion volume, *The Pale Shadow of Science*, is shortlisted for the nonfiction Hugo award. In Britain we have the newly founded Kerosina Press, with *Kaeti and Company* by Keith Roberts (224pp £12.50): ten stories, eight previously unpublished, plus some linking material. The £25 presentation edition comes with an extra story booklet and signed bookplate. Roberts writes beautifully as ever; Kaeti, the tough young 'eternal heroine' of these whimsical fantasies, has charm (as the author reminds us rather too often). As a whole one might call it self-indulgent ... but in a 1000-copy limited edition, why not? Self-indulgence from such as Aldiss or Roberts towers above the best efforts of many others.

This month's best totally-unknown-to-Langford author must be J.P. Miller, whose *The Skook* (Arrow 307pp £3.50) reminded me a lot of John D. Macdonald's tough, compassionate, satisfying books. The unfortunate Span Barrmann is trapped in a cave by biker cultists, to be aided through a long underground nightmare by something which may or may not be real, a crazy beast from fairytales told to his daughters: the Skook. His escape story is an epic quest in little, beset by 'extinct' creatures of the underworld deep. Meanwhile, the minor characters glow with life, from Span's semi-nympho wife to bikers who outdo Charles Manson in nasty inventiveness. Recommended.

Back in traditional fantasy, *Dragonsbane* by Barbara Hambly (Unicorn 292pp £2.95) strikes me as a major improvement on her Darwath trilogy. Normally I pass into profound slumber when invited on another quest to slay another dragon. Hambly rewrites the standard myths, though: her hero slays dragons only with extreme reluctance and by fighting dirty, the traditional witch is not only the hero's lover but a very strong heroine in her own right, and the dragon is a damned sight more sympathetic than some of its 'victims'.

In previous reviews I've hinted that Katherine 'Deryni' Kurtz is not at her best when evoking magic – except, oddly enough, in a context of ecclesiastic ritual. In *The King's Justice* (Arrow 337pp £2.95) she concentrates more on the political complexities of a mediaeval Wales that never was, and tells a good story.

It's not only a King but an author who's matured with the acceptance that it may be needful to execute an innocent man (a rebel rallying-point) or kill an enemy without giving him a chivalrous chance (which might mean the whole war having to be fought again). Paladins please note.

Michael Moorcock gives value for money in *The Opium General* (Grafton 304pp £2.95). Two-thirds of the collection is another and final Jerry Cornelius black comedy, *The Alchemist's Question*, with all the old characters swapping hip non-sequiturs as entropy bubbles over and nuclear winter seems the logical option. You either like it or not. Other stories include a serious 1979-80 trio about looming world war. Most fun: 'Starship Stormtroopers', a radical essay which finds Heinlein as disturbing as *Mein Kampf* but loses much credibility by going on to lump atheist Isaac Asimov with Tolkien and C.S. Lewis (and Frank Herbert!) as despised 'Christian apologists'....

Here's Big Isaac himself, with *X Stands For Unknown* (Grafton 270pp £2.95), yet another 17 science essays from *Fantasy and Science Fiction*, 1982-3. If you're scientifically literate you'll find the interesting bits buried in over-familiar stuff, though I always cheer Asimov when he stomps the crackpots. If not, you probably don't read books like this. That's showbiz. But for some really fascinating writing about and around science, grab Richard P. Feynman's hilarious *Surely You're Joking, Mr Feynman!* (Unwin/Counterpoint 350pp £3.95).

In brief: *A Heritage of Stars* (Methuen 219pp £2.50) is minor, recent Clifford Simak sf, which is at least better than minor, recent Simak fantasy. Patrick Tilley's *Xan* (Grafton 332pp £2.50) is a horror nasty with psychic vampire aliens, which I couldn't face reading. No room to list the other Hugo nominations.

[Har har, didn't you get one this year then? - Ed.]

Oh yes, but I was too modest to say so....

July 1986

42 To Be Continued

Something is stirring in sf publishing, something ancient and very terrible, dimly remembered only by alcoholic critics who swap their wheezy reminiscences of the bad old days. From its grave the undead horror rises, no longer a mere phantasm but a tangible form revealed in leprous morning light, a grisly revenant whose existence can no longer be denied. Partly rugose and partly squamous, first of a *ten*-book sequence, it leers and squatters beneath the gibbous moon: *The Invaders Plan* by L. Ron Hubbard (New Era 560pp £10.95). Is it all right if we change the subject now?

The Cthulhoid style leads naturally to Tim Powers' *The Anubis Gates* (Grafton 464pp £2.95), a breakneck romp through seedy back alleys of history ... the London of Coleridge, Byron (two Byrons, in fact) and the enigmatic poet William Ashbless, but also of Egyptian necromancers, the Dancing Ape Madness, the cannibal clown-king of the beggars, and a supporting cast of gypsies, doppelgangers, homunculi, time-travellers whistling Beatles tunes, and nameless sewer-dwelling abominations. What's exhilarating is the combination of dizzy pace with lurid, smoky colours and consistently tight plotting: everything in this gallery of grotesques has a part to play, and despite some weird complexities there are no loose ends. Except the question of who really wrote Ashbless's famous poem 'The Twelve Hours of the Night', a point which is left as an exercise for the reader. Profound it isn't, but *The Anubis Gates* offers terrific entertainment and much stealable scenario background for *Call of Cockburn*, or whatever that game is called.

A different kind of horror fills Gustav Meyrink's *The Golem* (Dedalus 304pp £3.50), a 1915 bestseller which inspired three films. Its atmosphere of surreal distortion recalls *The Cabinet of Dr Caligari*. In the Prague ghetto, every thirty-three years, in a room without doors, the Golem appears. The amnesiac narrator is linked to it in an obscure, cabalistic way: the golem legend runs through the book's web of melodrama and murder. It's the sort of nightmare you might have after an evening of too much lobster and Kafka. Very strange.

Another thing which gives me nightmares is overindulgence in multi-book epics. Thus: M.K. Wren's *Sword of the Lamb* (NEL 436pp £2.95) is 'Book One of The Phoenix Legacy'. Cherry Wilder's *A Princess of the Chameln* (Unicorn 275pp £3.50) is 'Book One of The Rulers of Hylor Trilogy'. Moyra Caldecott's *Guardians of the Tall Stones* (Arrow 626pp £4.95) is 'Now in one volume, her brilliant trilogy'. Hubbard's posthumous and even fatter outbreak has been reported on by the noted US critic Don D'Ammassa: 'Wait until all ten volumes are available, and then don't read any of them.' On medical advice I'm rationing my trilogy intake.

The Isle of Glass by Judith Tarr (Bantam 286pp £8.95) bears two danger signs, 'Volume One' and a plug from the ubiquitous Anne McCaffrey, but has compensating virtues. The background of 12th century not-quite-Britain is engaging enough, with elves and ecclesiarchs in conflict under an interestingly drawn Richard Lionheart: and Tarr can actually write. Her spare prose and dialogue give a period flavour without the dread excesses of gadzookery. Moreover, she's clearly a member of Black Lords Anonymous and the Society for the Abolition of Quest Clichés. After working hard against civil war, her elven hero is last seen heading on a pilgrimage to Jerusalem. I'll admit to being interested in what happens to him there.

Though, come to think of it, even the traditional quest to zap the all-potent powers of darkness can be tweaked into novelty. Adrian Cole's *A Place Among The Fallen* (Unwin 352pp £10.95) does so in one volume. The heart of darkness is not Someone but Somewhere; the routine of travelling from A to B is ruthlessly condensed; 'goodies' include decidedly unpleasant characters (e.g. a gang of murderous bigots with steel claws for hands); the denouement is a network of betrayals, and the survivors not altogether those expected. Despite some indigestible chunks of background explanation and occasional rotten dialogue ('Oh, I know you still think of me as a child, with a child's wild fancies, but I sense things sometimes....'), it's a nicely convoluted yarn.

Convolutions are what you expect from the late Frank Herbert, who with his son Brian wrote *Man of Two Worlds* (Gollancz 317pp £9.95). A superpowered alien Dreen and a wilful Earthling are forced to share the same body and – like all Herbert characters – think a lot, in italics. Herbert Jr's influence makes for more liveliness and less metaphysical stodge, but the plot oscillates way out of control: financial double-dealing and politics on Earth, battle and brothels with the French Foreign Legion on Venus (truly, I'm not making this up), existential agonizing (in italics) on planet Dreenor ... All is egregiously concluded by a superpowered yet strangely irrelevant mystic who wipes out virtually the entire Dreen race via psychic judo, while a fortuitous assassin solves the problem of the double-minded 'hero' to allow a cheery Girl Meets Alien finale. The combination of tension and daftness (Dreens are helpless against the mind-rotting Earthly herb, *basil*) makes for an odd read.

Speaking of super powers, here's Anthony Horowitz's *The Night of the Scorpion* (Magnet 159pp £1.75), a junior occult thriller. This moves well with a gallimaufry of precognitions, chases, ancient secrets, artificial satellites and the Nazca Lines of Peru ... but the climax goes disappointingly phut. I have a theory about this. When the Ultimate Evil of the Universe comes bursting through the portals that lead beyond space and time, one can believe in heroes who outwit it, or force it back at the cost of some supreme sacrifice, or invoke potent supernatural allies at a price. But it seems a pretty feeble Ultimate Evil of the Universe which, as here, can be sent packing by the direct frontal attack of two psychic kids. Evil should be made of sterner stuff.

Quick quiz: what won last year's Hugo, Nebula and Philip K. Dick Memorial awards? As a clue, here's the much-quoted first line: 'The sky above the port was the colour of television, tuned to a dead channel.' Yes: William Gibson's *Neuromancer* (Grafton 317pp £2.50), a brain-scrambling novel which has flaws but moves too fast for you to notice them. The blurb fails to mention 'cyberspace', the hallucinatory software battleground which is Gibson's trademark: it reminds me of the barracuda-infested undersea landscape in which Ian Fleming's most exciting scenes tended to happen. You may not believe in killer programs which invade the brain, but *Neuromancer*, if you once let it into your wetware, isn't easily erased.

Lightship (Paper Tiger 125pp £7.95) comprises 120 classy colour paintings by our very own Jim Burns, who has either a very enthusiastic imagination or a model with spherical breasts. Robert Silverberg (whose books inspired some of Burns' best efforts) contributes an introduction and Chris Evans a commentary, which unfortunately tends to veer aside into a 'Noddy Guide To SF Concepts' rather than discuss the actual artwork.

Robert Sheckley, as I've said, was writing superior Douglas Adams material long before Adams. Methuen offer an early novel, *The Status Civilization* (144pp £2.25), and a late one, *The Alchemical Marriage of Alastair Crompton* (185pp £2.25). The first is unsubtle, action-packed fun with satirical touches, set on a world where crime is the law and the hero soon gets into trouble for non-drug addiction. The second contains a short story's worth of plot (it *was* expanded from a short), eked out with bizarre Sheckleyisms; the result is not exactly a novel but is hugely enjoyable. 'It must be nice being a writer,' Crompton remarks; the reply is, 'It is like being a slug crawling down an infinite sheet of paper.'

Time I oozed to a finish....

August 1986

43 The Door Deliquesced

Eye-catching title, eh? For forty years sf writers have been attempting scene-setting lines as cleverly offhand as Heinlein's 'The door dilated'. Dropped casually into an early sentence of *Beyond This Horizon*, those three words pitchforked readers into a high-tech future where doors irised open (to f2.8?) and this was such an everyday event that no comment was called for. Now it's 1986 and I'm staring at the sentence - given a paragraph of its own so we'll appreciate the cleverness - 'The door deliquesced'. Subsequent paragraphs explain that yes, this door *really does* melt down into a puddle, which you must be careful not to step in, since the liquid rapidly foams back up into solidity and could lend a whole new meaning to getting your foot in the door. As Walt Willis once rather beautifully put it, 'Cor chase my Aunt Fanny round the psionics laboratory.'

This conversation-stopper is from Samuel R. Delany's *Stars In My Pocket Like Grains Of Sand* (Grafton 464pp £2.95). Delany's early books were full of poetry, brilliance and wild lack of discipline; twenty years on, not all that much has changed but the gain has been turned up on each quality. There's an admirably inventive far-future background: thousands of inhabited worlds, the information Web that links them, two major political/religious/philosophical factions (the Family and the Sygn), humans and aliens in multi-species extended marriages ... But also there are indigestible gobs of exposition, with characters lecturing each other because Delany wants to lecture the reader. He also misplaces some of his heightened, poetic prose: 'Tubes drained off the puce and fuchsia biles that, in a sort of antidigestive process, had, by their chemical actions, healed; had, by their tidal actions, exercised.' If this is how Delany wants to describe intensive care, fine: but the sentence is from the *verbal report* of a bureaucrat relating the patient's recovery, and (like many others) in that context it's unbelievable.

The story itself has a space-operatic background (who destroyed the burnt-out planet?) and, at stage centre, a homosexual love affair (oh, those sensual descriptions of cabled muscles and bitten fingernails). Neither mystery nor romance is resolved, all that being kept for Book Two - fearfully titled *The Splendour and Misery of Bodies, of Cities*. Book One is brilliant, uneven, insufferable, an important piece of sf. I haven't even mentioned the agonizing far-future pronouns, whereby I would have to refer to your editor (or indeed anyone else of any sex) as 'she', unless I fancied 'him'....

[Book 2 is still not with us in 1994. *Later:* or indeed in 2001.]

Bob Shaw's *The Ragged Astronauts* (Gollancz 310pp £9.95) is much more traditional fun, billed as the first of a trilogy - but you can trust this author, and Shaw enough the book has believable characters and a satisfying beginning, middle and end. It turns on one of those marvellously daft notions which only sf can offer: realistic interplanetary travel by hot-air balloon. Planet Land is suffering a deadly ecological threat (whose roots will be guessed ahead of time by experienced fans), and escape plans call for balloon evacuation to the binary twin Overland, which is close enough to share the same atmosphere. The airborne scenes are excellent, stirring my jaded sense of wonder. The celestial mechanics ... well, I was spared the effort of putting on my physicist's hat and doing sums, by a grandiose ploy which must have Isaac Newton developing high angular momentum in his grave. *pi*, in this book, equals 3. Therefore the universe isn't ours, the gravitational constant is different, and physicists babbling of tidal forces and Roche's Limit will kindly pipe down. Meanwhile Grafton have reissued an earlier Shaw favourite: *The Palace of Eternity* (221pp £2.50), one of the few sf novels to achieve a successful blend of physics and metaphysics. Both recommended.

Once again Arthur C. Clarke has switched on his word processor and pressed the well-worn keys labelled FICTION and KEENING ELEGIAC TONE OF VOICE, to produce *The Songs of Distant Earth* (Grafton 182pp £9.95) - previously seen as a 1957 short story and a 1979 film outline. In 1957, it was Girl Meets Spaceman for a one-night stand as his ship drops by for water: a tearful parting, and he blasts off into the night. The liberated 1985 version is much the same, with more dialogue, better props (quantum space drive, *another* space elevator, terraforming), a fistful of added elements which are barely developed and serve only to dilute the story (intelligent lobsters, incidental tragedies, disruptive effects of the visiting ship on the girl's colony world), and the identical lack of appropriate emotion. Let's face it, Clarke's characters can only manage three emotions: intellectual hunger, sorrow for bygone glories (here a nova-zapped Earth), and awe in the face of the infinite. None is really appropriate to a bittersweet love affair; with this vacuum at the book's core, the other bits don't fuse together but just lie there. Pity.

Frederik Pohl's *Black Star Rising* (Gollancz 282pp £9.95) is brisker interstellar stuff with a vein of satire. The USA and USSR having crippled each other because Reagan's 'Star Wars' nonsense has precipitated World War III (Pohl, you may gather, doesn't approve), China has moved in to administer the wrecked countries, instituting healthy, all-American practices like Mississippi paddy-fields and self-criticism sessions. Great embarrassment results when extraterrestrial invaders make the traditional demand to be taken to the President of the USA. The alien 'erks', so eager to help justice, take sides, and help us annihilate our planet, may be intended as a satire on some superpower's foreign policy. Good-natured stuff with a few sharp points.

I liked Jack Vance's *Lyonesse II: The Green Pearl* (Grafton 360pp £3.50) rather better than Volume One, perhaps because the fantasy action seems more coherent. Further quasi-mediaeval political manoeuvrings, magical skulduggery, and ornately polished dialogue; grimmer than most Vance tales, but always enjoyable for its sheer style - Vance probably writes elegantly ironic and barbed shopping lists. At least one more sequel follows.

The Blackcollar by Timothy Zahn (Arrow 272pp £1.95) is the latest 'Venture' novel of zap-happy sf, and one of the series' better offerings. Blackcollars are not people who don't wash their necks, but super-guerrillas made redundant by the fall of the Terran Empire. But there still remains one slim chance! After a few too many pages of lasers, paralysis darts, *nunchaku* and *shuriken*, our heroes win fairly excitingly through. The conclusion has a touch of political realism which almost makes the whole farrago credible. Lightweight entertainment.

Michael Moorcock's peculiar brand of sword-and-sorcery is also lightweight, but does boast above-normal inventiveness, a touch of surrealism, and a good line in doomed Byronic heroes. *The Swords of Corum* (Grafton 509pp £9.95) is a hardback omnibus of the first three Corum books, fondly remembered for the fantasy *Realpolitik* of their finale: not merely the Chaos mob but *all* the gods are summarily liquidated, leaving the world a happier and healthier place. Fundamentalists may cancel their subscriptions at this point. *The Crystal and the Amulet* (Savoy £4.95 - nice to see you back, Savoy) is part two of James Cawthorn's pictorial adaptation of the Hawkmoon **Runestaff** tetralogy, a bit confusingly synoptic in places, but powerfully drawn in sombre black-and-white. With glints of humour amid the horror, too, as witness the unfortunate slave suffering the consequences of playing *Call of Cthulhu* in the background of one sequence.

Reprints of books already reviewed: *Kiteworld* by Keith Roberts (Penguin 288pp £2.95, excellent), *The Man in the Tree* by Damon Knight (Penguin 246pp £2.95, good), *Gilgamesh the King* by Robert Silverberg (Pan 300pp £2.95, pretty good) and *Dragons of Autumn Twilight* by a committee of hacks (Penguin 448pp £2.95 - and I thought this one-time 'quality' publisher had hit rock bottom with Jack Chalker...).

I realized in terror that the deadline was here, and ran for the exit. The door detumesced.

September 1986

44 The Book Mountain

Huge piles of stuff today, a veritable EEC book mountain which will ultimately have to be fed to pigs or chemically converted to Watneys Red Barrel. Yet some publishers are rarely represented here: a private Langford vendetta? The answer, like everything about Langford, is more boring. Some outfits keep sending vast parcels of books not to my address but to *Dwarf* itself: these are purloined by typists to prop up wobbly desks, or spend months being forwarded by cleft stick. Some, like Corgi, seem to lose me from their mailing lists. Some, like Pan and Futura, send immense lists of everything they plan to publish, and want me to choose: not only do I usually forget, but it's a bit hard to empty deserved vials of wrath on a book you've specifically *asked* for ... h'mm, cunning psychology there.

Most mountainous of the current range is *The Mirror of Her Dreams*, (Collins 658pp £10.95), being part one of **Mordant's Need** by good old Stephen Donaldson. Several writers have been doing two-part series lately: it can be a better format than the trilogy, offering set-up and climax without the dread middle-volume blues (whereby, for want of any spare plot, all is padded out with a long trip to the One Tree or wherever). Donaldson has now abandoned hysterical verbal excesses to describe a world where mirrors are magic, with a interestingly non-leprous visiting heroine from Earth, and fiendish tangles of political intrigue. It kept me turning the too many pages, though I couldn't believe the Marvel Comics SF mega-warrior, or the Feydeauesque scenes in which an ambiguous mage keeps unbuttoning and stroking our heroine's bosoms *but never gets any further.* The final cliff-hanger in the besieged citadel is effective enough. However, there are so many spare plot-saving devices lying around (lethal mages, the sf warrior, a basement full of doomsday-weapon mirrors, the heroine's undisclosed but guessable Powers, etc.) that I won't lose *too* much sleep wondering how book two sorts it all out.

Slightly slimmer is Ursula Le Guin's *Always Coming Home* (Gollancz 525pp £10.95) which is: A utopian novel. A beautifully illustrated anthropological study of the Kesh, who don't yet exist. A collection of Kesh writings and songs. (You can buy a £6.95 cassette of music to read it by.) Or, says Le Guin, 'an Up Yours to the people who ride snowmobiles, make nuclear weapons, and run prison camps ... a critique of civilization possible only to the civilized.' Among many rich strangenesses it also includes a critique of its own improbabilities (as seen through twentieth-century eyes). Me, I'm still digesting it: care to join me? [Translation: didn't quite know what to make of it. Still don't, although it has its moments.]

Regulars will know I'm a sucker for Oriental fantasy. (Plugs: Robert Irwin's *The Arabian Nightmare* is being reissued as a highly publicized Penguin. George Meredith's 1856 *The Shaving of Shagpat* is an occasional Arabian treat in dustier second-hand shops.) *Bagdad* by Ian Dennis (Allen & Unwin 211pp £8.95) is an outrageously mannered performance, full of exotic dottiness. The hierarchs of Bagdad seem well grounded in existential Angst and, when not fleeing the improbable bloodbaths of the revolutionary Ripe Fruit Party, tell each other twisted little tales-within-tales like 'The Jinni and the Civil Servant'. Again, a second and concluding volume is expected.

[This was called *The Prince of Stars*, the whole story being **The Prince of Stars in the Cavern of Time**. I didn't see book two until 1999, and then wrote: 'Quirkily atmospheric, with inevitable tales within tales, wandering at random in and out of comedy, ultimately a mite inconsequential: despite various political rearrangements the tagline is, "Were you under the impression that something *happened*?"'.]

Moving from Araby to Greece, here's *Olympian Nights* by John Kendrick Bangs (Greenhill 225pp £8.95), a mildly funny 1902 romp wherein an American tourist visits Olympus as the guest of Mr Jupiter Jove Zeus – an immortal who believes in high-tech conveniences – and much fun is poked at the classical myths. Dated fun, mostly, but there are good lines here and there.

And blimey, it's another half-diptych: *Master of Paxwax* by Phillip Mann (Gollancz 280pp £9.95), which is high-class space opera with a welter of convincing aliens. These beasties are oppressed by jackbooted human empires, but plot vengeance with the unwitting aid of Pawl Paxwax, scion of one of the Rockefeller-powered galactic Families. This fast-moving adventure describes Pawl's rise. The concluding volume is called *The Fall of the Families*. Stay tuned. (One quibble: can independent evolution account for the unlikely profusion of alien species who come ready-equipped to poison humans, use them as larval hosts, etc.?)

Alison Prince's *The Others* (Methuen 208pp £7.95) is – unusually for 'younger readers" sf – set in a nasty post-holocaust anthill where people are physically and mentally programmed for their jobs. The gardener hero has garden-twine hair, secateur fingers and, presumably, terrible problems when he picks his nose. Not desperately convincing in its resolution (a totalitarian set-up reformed by appeal to external authority?), but otherwise it's tense and gritty stuff. Rather than being miraculously preserved to the finale, likeable characters can *die*.

This also applies to the amazingly prolific Piers Anthony's latest couple. *Executive* (Granada 336pp £2.95) is the fourth Hope Hubris book, with Hubris trying out all Anthony's pet political notions as the liberal Tyrant of Jupiter – a thinly disguised USA. The allegory can get a little wearying, which is presumably why the book is pepped up with massive doses of the weird exercise (combining arm-wrestling, origami and dialectical analysis) which is the author's version of sex. Somewhat more promising was *With a Tangled Skein* (Grafton 413pp £2.95), third of the **Incarnations of Immortality** series which started so well. It's thumbs-down, I fear: Anthony's ghastly fluency never flags, but *Skein* suffers from long dull passages rehashing the earlier books, and falls apart entirely at the end. Again the salvation of the world depends on depressingly arbitrary problem-solving which has *no* organic connection with the actual plot: Fate, the heroine, defeats Satan by remembering how to detect a counterfeit among twelve coins, using only three weighings, and the critic bangs his head on the wall.

The Penguin World Omnibus of SF (320pp £3.50), edited by Brian Aldiss and Sam J. Lundwall, offers representative tales from 26 countries. It's oddly like a historical collection: a language's sf moves further from the Wellsian tale of wonder as sophistication and schlock accumulate, and for all the skills of the English speakers here, the more 'isolated' authors can be closer to the wellsprings. Better to be over-naive or over-blasé? Both positions are on view here. You choose.

Towering over the word processor is an Everest of reprints. Gollancz offer volumes five to eight in their £2.95 Classic SF series, and are doing a good job despite copyright problems. Clarke's *The City and the Stars* and Heinlein's *The Door into Summer* are probably the authors' best-loved novels; I've long been fond of the Pohl/Kornbluth *Wolfbane*, here slightly revised by Pohl; and Sladek's hysterical *The Reproductive System* is another personal favourite. Meanwhile, Grafton offer Asimov's barely connected **Galactic Empire** novels as new £9.95 hardbacks: *Pebble in the Sky* is a not-bad first novel; *The Stars Like Dust* is that embarrassing one whose long-sought Macguffin, the ultimate weapon against galactic tyrants from a world subtly called Tyrann, proves (thanks to the editorial insistence of John W. Campbell) to be the US Constitution; and *The Currents of Space* is a solidly OK sample of middle-period Asimov. Strangely omitted: *The End of Eternity*, arguably the first and best of this non-Foundation, non-robot 'series'.

Other peaks climbed: *Les Diaboliques* by Barbey D'Aurevilly (1874; Dedalus 254pp £3.95), lushly warped, edging into psychological horror; *Daybreak on a Different Mountain* by Colin Greenland (Unicorn 246pp £3.50), entropic, anti-heroic fantasy; Michael Moorcock's *The Rituals of Infinity* (NEL 159pp £2.50) – immature, lightweight sf – and *Chronicles of Castle Brass* (Grafton 432pp £3.95), fun fantasy hokum; *The Book of Lost Tales 2* by J.R.R. Posthumous-laundrylists (Unicorn 385pp £3.50); Ian Watson's fine, offbeat *The Book of Being* (Grafton 223pp £2.50); and Roger Zelazny's linked *Isle of the Dead* and *To Die in Italbar* (both Methuen £2.50), the first enjoyable, the second overpopulated, jerky and disappointing.

At this stage, having fallen into a crevasse of unreadables, I'm helplessly awaiting the arrival of a St Bernard with a keg of real ale round its neck.

October 1986

45 Zero Summer

The most science-fictional thing I've read all month is a travel-agent's placard – *Coming Soon: Summer 1987! Register Now!* So that's why I got no perceptible summer this year. I should have registered for one in 1985.

There's still less available summer in David Brin's *The Postman* (Bantam 294pp £9.95, paperback to follow in January), set in North America after a mini-holocaust and 16 years of nuclear near-winter. I've long been nervous of those peculiarly American 'survivalist' types who seem quite eager for World War III and its glorious aftermath of no taxes, no liberals, and freedom to shoot whom they like. Clearly they worry Americans too: Brin's macho, kill-happy survivalists are the chief obstacle to a returning civilization.

His plot has a mythic simplicity which in synopsis reads more like mind-numbing corniness. Gordon Krantz (a sort of seedy *jongleur*) stumbles on that awesome relic of the Old Reckoning, a postman's uniform. As a symbol of lost order, this has a certain lingering power: trying to capitalize on it as a con-trick for safe passage through suspicious communities, Krantz finds himself spreading a self-fulfilling prophecy of re-established mail services. At first glance the notion panders too much to readers' own wishful thinking. Brin carries it off by showing that people in that ruined world would themselves be ripe for wishful thinking – glad to accept the half-believed lie.

The story is complicated by Krantz's intersection with another myth in the making, and then by a tangential muddle of battle, murder and enhanced super-guerrillas, all a bit of a needless distraction, but never mind. It's nicely written, sometimes moving, and ends as it should. Well worth reading.

Good old William Gibson is back with ten stories in *Burning Chrome* (Gollancz 200pp £8.95). After Gibson's massive success, this was a collection which had to appear – even if three collaborations and an over-arty first published story are needed to fill it out. They're strong, punchy tales with his glittering 'technosleaze' trademark: some are obvious precursors of the novels, and the fine title piece's hair-raising cyberspace jaunt is echoed all too closely in *Neuromancer*. Still, I like the story: it's that one about the young punks who get hold of a .45 and try the big heist, only Gibson's punks are computer jockeys and the .45 is a Russian military killer program.

Ian Watson offers his own alternative to cyberspace in *Queenmagic, Kingmagic* (Gollancz 205pp £9.95): a sort of 'gamespace'. The idea of modelling a story on a chess game isn't new to fantasy – John Brunner's *The Squares of the City* is the best modern treatment and Poul Anderson's 'The Immortal Game' possibly the worst. Watson's approach is exuberant and not over-concerned with detailed moves: a fantasy war of specialist magics, straight-line, crosswise or askew. This alone is inventive fun, but these chess-people also go in for original thought about space/time. As a result the hero and heroine, both lowly pawns, manage to project themselves through gamespace as checkmate breaks up their world, and discover the alternate physical laws of snakes and ladders, Monopoly, *go* ... The expected unexpected finale is very Watsonesque.

Raymond Leonard's *Omega* (Poplar Press 197pp £9.95) suffers badly from the fact that its theme is too familiar, one of the great sf chestnuts, on a par with stories which end 'And I shall call you ... *Eve*!' It's been done and overdone by Fredric Brown, Isaac Asimov, D.F. Jones and Frank Herbert; it's been sent up by Douglas Adams. Humanity unites to build an omniscient super-computer, innovatively called OMEGA, which will solve all our problems! Despite Leonard's vaunted engineering qualifications, the technical problems are glossed over, the vast artificial intelligence is lashed together with suspicious ease, and right from the start people are talking in theological terms. Need I go on? It takes endless pages of dreadful portentousness and worse dialogue to reach the time-worn punchline of Fredric Brown's one-pager, which (as every fan knows) goes 'Yes, *now* there is a God!'

Eye (Gollancz 328pp £9.95) is a 'definitive' collection of Frank Herbert's short sf, with the bonus of skilled half-tone illustrations by Jim Burns, plus Herbert's own mixed feelings about the *Dune* movie. It's a good anthology, free of the grotty potboilers which filled out earlier collections. I would have preferred another 'real' short story or two in place of the extract from *The Dragon in the Sea* (which deserves to be read in the context of the whole novel): otherwise, OK.

An unknown Arthur Conan Doyle novel? That's what Brian Stableford has dug up for the Greenhill fantasy museum: *The Doings of Raffles Haw* (256pp £8.95), which reminds me that you must all buy Sidgwick & Jackson's lovely softcover edition of my and Brian's *The Third Millennium* ... oops. Doyle has an old and familiar tale to tell: the Well-Meaning (but Mad) Scientist who can Make Gold, yet like King Midas finds that Wealth Is But A Curse. Fascinating for collectors and completists.

At last, the paperbacks! Geoff Ryman's *The Unconquered Country* (Unicorn 134pp £2.95) is a remarkably powerful 'alternate world' fantasy which painfully mirrors the recent history of Cambodia. It's difficult to describe: a vision of an organic civilization where even the houses live and move, where in a pun on 'labourer' the women workers give birth to industrial parts ... a symbiosis ripped apart by political upheavals which will never – can never – be explained to the people of the Unconquered Country. It packs a terrific punch. In its shorter *Interzone* form, it won two major awards. Sacha Ackerman's many line drawings work well with the text.

After being harrowed, it's fun to turn to *The Light Fantastic* by Terry Pratchett (Corgi 217pp £1.95), a direct sequel to his wonderfully dotty *The Colour of Magic*. Again Rincewind the magician cavorts across the apparently doomed Discworld, helped and hindered by the many-legged Luggage, Druids with stone-circle software problems, the nonagenarian Cohen the Barbarian, Death (who gets upset when summoned from cocktail parties) and millions more. Abandoning the glancing though often telling fantasy parodies of his previous book, Pratchett leans more heavily on one-line gags: the result isn't as pointedly funny, but still evokes more laughs than anything else around. *Especially* Thrud.

[*Thrud the Barbarian* used to be *White Dwarf's* regular comic strip.]

It's not often that I come in at the third reel, but this happened with Peter Morwood's *The Dragon Lord* (Arrow 318pp £2.95), sequel to *The Horse Lord* and *The Demon Lord*. Its plot involves shifting alliances and betrayals centred on an elaborate Code of Honour whereby (as far as I can make out) even God has lost considerable social standing and would no longer be admitted to the best clubs. Morwood works up a tense and exciting atmosphere - his horse-trappings, weaponry and dragon are particularly good - which left me disappointed by the several stylistic let-downs. It's bad enough when the inhabitants of a fantasy otherworld quote Kipling; when they start using words like 'adrenalin' and 'scenario' the spell definitely fades; and even the author realizes that 'paranoia' is a mistake. 'It was an odd, cumbersome, unAlban word ...' Near the end, drama is dispelled by the in-joke of a cameo appearance by Anne ('Aiyyan') McCaffrey, reciting from her own books. This kind of thing should be left to Terry Pratchett.

In brief: Anne McCaffrey herself returns with the paperback *Killashandra* (Corgi 346pp £2.95), sequel to *The Crystal Singer*, a frothy piece of romantic sf in the great literary tradition of Mills & Boon. As they say in *Star Trek*, it'll leave your crystals drained. Larry Niven's *Limits* (Orbit 240pp £2.50) includes some good recent short stories: it's a pleasure to see Niven sweating a interesting idea down to a few thousand effective words rather than bloating it beyond all endurance (*Ringworld Engineers, Integral Trees*). His 'Draco Tavern' thought-pieces are particularly entertaining. The collaborations with others (Pournelle, Girard, Barnes) work less well. So it goes. *Top Fantasy* ed. Josh Pachter (Dent 311p £3.95) is an above-average anthology of two dozen authors' favourite stories, which I know I needn't describe because my faithful readers will have committed last year's review of the hardback to memory. And *Dragons of Winter Night* (Penguin 399pp £2.95), by Margaret Weis and Tracy Hickman, is ... is ... er, nice weather for the time of year, isn't it?

November 1986

46 Fifth Foundation

They found me twitching and babbling in the bar at Games Day. Kindly *White Dwarf* staff attempted to rally me with promises (of beer) and threats (of *Warhammer* novelizations), but still your reviewer gibbered about robots and Lensmen and Kuhn's *The Structure of Scientific Revolutions*, while significant fingers were tapped against foreheads. This was all because of what I'd been reading on the train.

Foundation and Earth (Grafton 464pp £10.95) is number five in the trilogy, and my seizure was brought on by the thought that Isaac Asimov has hit the same problem on his intellectual level that E.E. Smith met on the physical one. Doc Smith's Lensmen were forever fighting more and more galactic-powered foes – no sooner does villainous Boskone invent an ultimate weapon than Kim Kinnison retorts with a *more* ultimate one! Asimov's 'intellectual Lensmen' are constantly uncovering deeper Secrets of the Universe: as with Smith's ever-huger megaweapons, the great revelations soon pall. They loom portentously, like Kuhn's paradigm shifts which are supposed topple whole sciences; they never match up to the hype. The strings of the Galaxy are pulled by the Foundation ... no, the Second Foundation ... no, 'Gaia' ... no, Earth ... no, in fact ... The ultimate-for-now answer is not a lemon but a robot left over from a novel set 20,000 years earlier, and really, who cares?

This isn't as dull as the fearful *Foundation's Edge*; there's more movement and colour in its travelogue of ancient, ruined worlds (unfortunately recalling similar and better travelogues by Clarke, who could make you *feel* that 20,000-year gulf as Asimov never does – cf. *The City and the Stars*). Its final line throbs with implied sequels, but Asimov seemingly intends to backtrack: promised next is *Prelude to Foundation....*

Foundation and Earth is very 1940s, bar a little discreet sex. *Heart of the Comet* by Gregory Benford and David Brin (Bantam 468pp £9.95) is very 1980s: big, slick, skilled, geared to the Halley's Comet market, and moving along painstakingly high-tech paths to the already traditional vision of a quantum leap in human evolution. On the comet's *next* pass (2060s), Earth plants an experimental community to ride the long orbit and test exploitation plans: e.g. could Mars be terraformed by comet-ice impacts? The mission is soon in trouble with unsuspected Halley life-forms, including – a little joke for D&D fans – purple worms. As expected from these highly qualified authors, the science is elaborate and convincing. Less so the characters: women tend to be 'deliciously unpredictable' with 'breasts hard and high', while the only memorable man is a hyper-Jewish super-biologist who almost single-handedly copes with every problem Halley can offer. 'You know what mitochondria are, right?' he says confidently, but don't worry – the chap he's talking to gives the answer ('in a hollow voice') for your benefit. Whopping concepts and evocative descriptions boost the novel half-way to excellence, but are defeated by the dead weight of stereotypes and lecturing. Hard sf fans will forgive its flaws.

In 1973 I bought Brian Aldiss's fine history of science fiction, *Billion Year Spree*: the new edition is *Trillion Year Spree* (with David Wingrove: Gollancz 511pp £9.95), longer by 200 pages of smaller type. SF criticism suffers from clotted academic prose and/or ungrammatical enthusiasm: this is a worthy updating of the best-written history yet seen. Not that it's infallible – I disagree with certain judgements, while it can seem very unjust that author X is dismissed as excellent in a line or two while the inferior Y is quoted at length to illustrate a point. The editors of poor old *Interzone*, Britain's only current sf magazine, are probably committing mass hara-kiri at finding themselves merely 'a pallid successor of *New Worlds*'. I was pleased and alarmed to learn from the useful index that I too have become History. Despite that, the new *Spree* is an essential reference and a good read.

[But what the hell happened to Cordwainer Smith, a major writer by any standards, who according to *Spree* is sufficiently well-known to be invoked in a description of Samuel Delany's style ('a blend of Jean Genet and Cordwainer Smith') but is otherwise not mentioned at all?]

A treat for the eye rather than the brain, *Sirens* (Paper Tiger 128pp £7.95) is Chris Achilleos's second art collection. This column has heretical views on fantasy art: I suspect Achilleos is superior in technique to Frazetta (who falls too easily into visual clichés) and Boris (obsessed with static overmusculature), but am unmoved by most of the airbrushed hyper-realism here. 'I don't know much about Art, but I know what I don't like.' Those who think of Achilleos as a painter of improbable female breasts will not be disappointed: our statistician reports 114½, 54% of them unclad. For fighting fantasy fans there's a chapter of favourites, including plugs for *Dwarf* and its Chaos Death Founders. People who like books like this will like this book.

The Lordly Ones by Keith Roberts (Gollancz 160pp £8.95) contains seven more stories from one of the finest (when on form; he's frequently erratic) stylists working in sf or fantasy. Breakdown: sf 4, fantasy 2, ghost 1. Only Roberts could write a moving and harrowing post-holocaust tale set in a public lavatory ... and then write another. Recommended.

Here's one you didn't see in hardback: don't miss *The Borribles: Across the Dark Metropolis* by Michael de Larrabeiti (Piccolo 332pp £1.95). The Bodley Head hardback was cancelled by its publishers, who got cold feet about the Bad Example set by clashes between savage street kids – Borribles – and grotesquely appalling police. (You probably remember the way your first reading of *Alice in Wonderland* compelled you to dive down rabbit holes and take drugs.) In fact, de Larrabeiti's third epic has worthy things to say about honour and trust ... in between spurts of adrenalin. Again London's underside is the nightmare background for a quest, and the tortuous journey from Battersea to Neasden has a far higher death toll than that relatively cosy toddle through Mordor. Triumph is bloody, especially in the luridly detailed Camden slaughterhouse, and expensive. Black comedy also abounds: anyone fool enough to confuse the luxuriously nose-picking Sergeant Hanks ('First class that one, looks like a well-fed whelk') with a real policeman must have as tenuous a grasp of reality as a *Dwarf* or Bodley Head editor.

James Stephens's 1912 *The Crock of Gold* (Picador 172pp £2.95) is more in the traditional fantasy vein, though not much. It's an Irish whimsy, shot through with gods and leprechauns (it should doubtless be suppressed for its subversive hints that Irish policemen can't handle leprechauns) and dotty philosophy. As the Philosopher memorably remarks: 'Finality is death. Perfection is finality. Nothing is perfect. There are lumps in it.' Bag this for your shelf of fantasy classics: it may go out of print for further decades.

The rest of the sf seems to have sunk to the bottom of the column. *Voyage to the City of the Dead* by Alan Dean Foster (NEL 243pp £2.25) offers page-turning hokum as two bickering, married scientists make their way by hydrofoil up an alien river, overcoming with ease such obstacles as the theft of their boat by hostile tribes, or attacks by ravening abominable snowmen. Just to make sure, the author has an emergency *deus ex machina* waiting to save them from the final peril.... *Dayworld* by Philip José Farmer (Grafton 322pp £2.50): another fast-moving example of a far-out social setup within which the author merely plays cops and robbers. To 'solve' overpopulation, everyone lives only one day a week, passing the rest in suspended animation. High crime consists of 'daybreaking', living outside your appointed weekday. Our hero is an arch-daybreaker with seven identities, one being a cop who pursues daybreakers, etc., etc. Terry Carr's *Best SF of the Year 15* (Gollancz 365pp £3.95) is as always well chosen, a dozen of 1985's finest stories which I've no room to list here.

Also received: *Helliconia Winter* by Brian Aldiss (Granada 393pp £2.95), fine gloomy stuff, already reviewed; *White Wing* by Gordon Kendall (Sphere 308pp £2.95), soporific militarist sf; *Swords in the Mist* by Fritz Leiber (Grafton 189pp £2.50), Fafhrd/Mouser reissue; *Footfall* by Larry Niven & Jerry Pournelle (Sphere 700pp £3.95), exciting sf despite longueurs and crassness; *27th Pan Book of Horror Stories* ed. Clarence Paget (Pan 187pp £1.95) with a token Stephen King reprint; *One Million Tomorrows* by Bob Shaw (Grafton 176pp £2.50), thoughtful sf novel of immortality; *A Blackbird in Darkness* by Freda Warrington (NEL 473pp £3.50), fantasy in which 'the daring quest continues' ... the bloody things always do, don't they?

December 1986

47 Good Stuff

I forget who said it's a magazine's duty to annoy a fifth of its readership, justice requiring that it isn't always the same fifth. Over the haggard years I've learned that any negative review will get me stomped upon, because there's no book so bad that someone won't love it. When – as this month – we get mostly good books, pins are inserted into wax images of Langford by a different fifth of the ever-loving readership ... because there's no book so good that someone won't hate it.

[According to W.H. Auden's splendid commonplace book *A Certain World*, it was Charles Péguy who said that about magazines. Now you know.]

About the most impressive is Greg Bear's *Eon* (Gollancz 503pp £10.95), which again challenges Arthur C. Clarke on his own ground. *Blood Music* took a poke at *Childhood's End*; *Eon* hurls everything including the kitchen sink against *Rendezvous with Rama*. Again a vast arcane object, the 'Stone', passes through the Solar System; again it's explored to reveal brainboggling wonders.... Bear has a nastily realistic eye for the Stone's political repercussions, and World War IV forms part of the incidental backdrop, despite the fact that the second most boggling artifacts aboard the Stone are histories describing World War IV. This thing wasn't built by aliens, you see.

The peak of weirdness is reached in the Stone's inmost chamber, whose contents are such as to dwarf mere Ringworlds and Orbitsvilles: a pocket infinity. 'The seventh chamber went on forever.' At this point the inevitable question is, 'what happened to the builders?' SF traditionally provides lousy answers, but not Bear: his space/time engineers are still in residence, a million kilometres inside the Stone, which is some 250 kilometres long. Although some of the efforts to describe indescribable technologies don't quite come off, this is impressive sf on the most colossal scale, where the concepts are bigger than universes but human beings still matter desperately. Hear that horrid grating noise? It's the sound of America's other hard-sf writers gnashing their teeth in sick envy.

Brightness Falls from the Air by James Tiptree Jr (Sphere 333pp £3.50) is perhaps this month's punchiest book: Bear aims his vast concepts at your sense of wonder, but Tiptree goes for the goolies. It's high melodrama which could be completely absurd, with its mixed party trapped on the lonely planet like the characters of a 1930s country-house murder story, to face a long night of nova-watching, loathsome crime, forbidden drugs, age-old guilt, implacable vengeance, temporal spasm and staggering coincidence. As the sky fills with the gaudy spectacle of the nova called the Murdered Star (er, yes, the last of the murderers and the last of the avengers are *both* present), various masks are ripped from 'tourists' to reveal the makings of bloodbath and genocide. Few survive for the meagre scatter of happy endings. In retrospect I don't believe a word of it, but Tiptree pours so much energy into her narrative that against all reason it sweeps you away. Phew, what a scorcher.

Over in the realms of fantasy, Gene Wolfe has begun a strange new sequence with *Soldier of the Mist* (Gollancz 335pp £10.95). You can't help comparing it with **The Book of the New Sun**, whose remote future has a similar flavour to *Soldier's* mythic Greek past. The narrator Latro is a 'holy fool' every bit as garrulous as the earlier story's Severian, not because of an eidetic memory but because he has no long-term memory; anything he doesn't write down will be lost, and his journal forms the book. (How *accurate* is it? An interesting question.) Gods and immortals are thick on the ground, visible to Latro though rarely anyone else, and forever tinkering with the course of events.

Keeping track of them needs concentration and a smattering of classical info, since Latro/Wolfe will just mention a 'man with a club' (Herakles) or a nickname like 'Earth-Shaker' (Poseidon). Sparta plays an important part but is only once named thus (in Greek letters!). Though sometimes annoying, this helps make the book immediate and alive, not just another tour through musty, shopworn legend. In other words, *Soldier* is vintage Wolfe: beautifully told, infuriatingly enigmatic, and certainly not to be unravelled on the basis of the first book alone. You will hear more of this.

Dwarf readers will be interested in Stephen Bowkett's second novel *Gameplayers* (Gollancz 159pp £7.95), a 'young adult' tale of role-playing and reality. Bowkett has a nice ear for conversation (last time I reviewed him I praised his 'schoolboy dialogue', only for it to be printed as 'schoolbook dialogue': not quite the same thing, chaps). He switches neatly between the grottiness of the young hero's life - parental divorce imminent, etc. - and the high-fantasy tone of the D&D-like role-playing game into which he regularly escapes. The tensions of the game spill over into the real world, thanks to that familiar character the nasty GM who doesn't want his puzzles to be unravelled and prefers to slaughter uppity players. At the climax, our hero wins (just) by treating a dangerous real-life situation with game-world resourcefulness. It's all rather well done, though there's a faintly moralizing note of Fantasy Games May Damage Your Mental Health.... [Which the author later told me was stressed at the request of the publishers.]

Kerosina Books, the small press, has produced its second volume: *Shades of Darkness* by Richard Cowper (Kerosina 143pp £10.95). Meanwhile, Clive Barker offers the paperback *The Damnation Game* (Sphere 374pp £3.50). These, both well-written, represent extremes of the horror genre (which in general and in theory I thoroughly dislike, though exceptions abound). Cowper's is an old-fashioned and gentlemanly ghost story, all elegance, subtlety, restraint and delicate chill, flowing along so smoothly as to resemble a long short story. Barker is determined to *really horrify* you, and pulls out all the stops including ones you hoped he wouldn't think of, as zombie after putrescent cannibalistic loose-bowelled bestial algolagnic punk zombie squelches into action at the sinister arch-villain's command.

The essence of horror is the turning of the screw. Cowper turns it with discreet style and wit, but never quite far enough. Barker wrenches it with flamboyance and effective video-nasty imagery – but so violently that he strips the metaphorical thread long before the book's over. By then each new horrible set-piece has less impact than the last, until the repulsive maggoty finale moved me to terrified cries of 'So what?'

I hadn't read Isaac Asimov's *Robots and Empire* (Grafton 508pp £2.95) when I reviewed *Foundation and Earth* last issue. This is a rather better book, following loosely from *The Robots of Dawn*: Asimov always perks up when chopping logic with the Three Laws of Robotics, and here his robots come up with a Fourth, or rather Zeroth, Law. This works out approximately as 'the end justifies the means.' For some reason the author doesn't seem even mildly worried by the implications. In addition, this is the book which completes the tortuous work of reconciling the robot and Foundation stories with such unrelated **Galactic Empire** novels as *Pebble in the Sky*, where Earth's surface is radioactive. Therefore a doomsday weapon is built and unleashed, which by continuous operation over 150 *years* will do the dastardly deed. But, enquires a particularly cunning villain, suppose somebody turns it off before then? The answer, translated from the pseudoscience, is roughly: 'Don't worry, I'm putting a padlock on the controls.' Only in sf do you find such glorious moments.

A final clutch of reprints. *The Venus Hunters* (Gollancz 142pp £8.95) is the first hardback edition of J.G. Ballard's 1967/1980 ten-story collection: no Ballard fan can be without it. Eric Frank Russell's moderately venerable (1975) collection *Like Nothing on Earth* (Methuen 159pp £1.95) comprises seven sf tales including the funny Hugo-winner 'Allamagoosa'. *The Chronicles of Corum* by Michael Moorcock (Grafton 454pp £9.95) reprints the second and final Corum fantasy trilogy, *The Bull and the Spear*, *The Oak and the Ram* and *The Sword and the Stallion*, about which it has so often been said, but never proved. Fritz Leiber's *Swords Against Wizardry* (Grafton 189pp £2.50) is the fourth in the justifiably well-loved Fafhrd/Mouser fantasy series. And *Dimension of Miracles* by Robert Sheckley (Grafton 188pp £2.50), though jerkily episodic, remains one of Sheckley's and sf's funniest books.

Suspicious I call it, so much good stuff all in a single month. Where's L. Ron Hubbard when we need him?

January 1987

48 Demand the Impossible

I pinched the title (above) from a book (below). This month's heap is indeed impossibly demanding, partly thanks to middle volumes of fantasy trilogies of which I've forgotten Volume One, partly through Unwin's habit of misdirecting books to Nottingham until about six months' output is forwarded here at a stroke, and partly because nobody should have to cope with *two* Piers Anthony outbreaks in a single column.

Guy Gavriel Kay's *The Wandering Fire* (Unwin 298pp £10.95) continues the stylish and upmarket **Fionavar Tapestry**, an ambitious fantasy sequence in post-Tolkien vein. Kay's basic stage-setting is pure Tolkien - fair land, Black Lord, everyone approaching the final test. He adds dollops of passionate emotion, a tortuous tangle of human relationships, and mythic chunks from all over the shop. And the writing's good enough to make it all work ... nearly. (There are minor glitches in naming: Kay may insist 'Aileron' is a High King, but I know he's just an aeroplane's wing-flap. Somewhere in the huge cast list is another chap called Tandem, who I like to think comes from some past epic cycle.)

The *Golden Bough*-ish themes of sacrifice and redemption are very effective, as when a sympathetic chap actually dies to end the arch-fiend's Fimbulwinter. I was less keen on the dreadfully familiar Wild Hunt stuff (though pleased to see the traditional warnings about the peril of 'old, wild magic' actually followed through - the cavalry duly comes over the hill to save the battle, and starts killing *everybody*.) The final quibble is really a question of taste. Mythic archetypes are fair game, and much fantasy concerns itself with echoing or retelling legends: all tales are the same Tale, said Tolkien, but was careful to invent his own mythos clear back to the Beginning. What Kay has done is to swipe characters from the finest legend of all, a Tale which is not his, and throw them into the already too-huge cast with promises of heavy Eternal Triangulation next book. I'd admire **The Fionavar Tapestry** more if it weren't rapidly turning into ... wait for it ... *Le Morte d'Arthur Part II*. Can the author possibly bring this off? H'mm.

Judith Tarr's *The Golden Horn* (Bantam 272pp £9.95), sequel to *The Isle of Glass*, is simple stuff without the big doomy effects: no wanton delving into the greasy mythological stockpot, just a tight focus of thirteenth-century erudition. Half-elven erstwhile monk Alf potters through the Fourth Crusade siege of

Constantinople, makes friends, finds blameless heterosexual love despite riskier hints last volume, loses (nearly) all in the sacking of Byzantium, sets his face towards Rome and book three ... This is more immediately successful than Kay's book because it takes fewer risks: an elegant Georgette Heyer romance moved back in time. In the long term? I can't remember anything of Tarr's first volume, while still retaining vivid images from Kay's.

Huysman's Pets (Gollancz 247pp £9.95) shows Kate Wilhelm in almost light-hearted mood ... one of those discreet contemporary thrillers which seem embarrassed by even a downplayed sf content. A web of non-coincidence ensnares some highly likeable characters, in particular the 'experimental animal' kids produced by the wicked tamperings of deceased geneticist Huysman. The forces of injustice are defeated by ham acting, telepathy, computer hacking and forged dollars, all very quickly and quietly and rather too easily. Nice reading, but a bit more suspense and genuine nastiness would have made for a stronger book.

Night Warriors by Graham Masterton (Sphere 410pp £2.95) is nasty all right, but short on stuff like suspense, coherence, credibility. 'The jaws clamped convulsively tight and bit away the whole of the policeman's upper lips and nostril.' 'The creature's massive member slid into her.' 'The eel had swallowed his penis almost up to the root.' 'Its claws caught the flesh of the officer's face, and ripped off everything below his eyeballs.' Thus the finest highlights (it's a tough job in the police). I shouldn't bother with the rest. [For some reason the second and third quotations didn't make it past the subeditor.]

Anne Rice's *The Vampire Lestat* (Futura 599pp £3.50) is slightly more my cup of tea: there are horrors in this 'sequel' to *Interview with the Vampire*, but not silly or gratuitous ones. Lestat unfolds a lushly decadent story of learning to be undead amid the excesses of France before the Revolution. Rice's glowing vampires have the authentic combination of lethality and sexiness so essential to the myth (which in the films tended to get swamped by blood). She's also audacious enough to propound an acceptable 'origin story' for vampirism, and to move from dark old Egyptian mysteries to the extremes of twentieth-century Dionysian ecstasy as Lestat gives his first live rock performance. Nice one.

More 'classical' fantasy comes from Barbara Hambly in *The Ladies of Mandrigyn* (Unicorn 311pp £2.95), who is no great writer but excels at freshening what writers' workshops call 'traditional narrative elements' and some of us might term clichés. Here's an Evil Sorcerer who isn't actually that good at sorcery, a Brutal Mercenary whose hobbies include philosophy and gardening, a Conquered Country which is not being laid waste but administered as occupied territory, a Female Resistance which doesn't mess around with Lysistrata tactics but demands combat training.... Add unpleasant magical gimmicks and well-drawn characters, and the result is a genuinely ripping fantasy yarn.

Over in the science-fantasy corner, Jane Yolen's *Cards of Grief* (Orbit 193pp £2.50) offers understated semi-tragedy on a world where grieving is virtually an artform. An Earth anthropologist makes the mistake of falling in love with a native Griever, and all sf precedent suggests that horrific cultural secrets will be appallingly revealed. Not so: the secrets and plot turns are merely sad, and Yolen's low, moaning narrative tone makes this not a punchy book but a memorable one.

The amazingly prolific Piers Anthony offers *Anthonology* (Grafton 432pp £2.95): 21 short sf and fantasy stories, two of which form chapters in his novel *Prostho Plus* - very irritating if you've already got it. Some display the compulsive daftness of Anthony at his best (e.g. 'Hurdle'); many could usefully have remained in obscurity; one is an incredibly and ludicrously filthy joke which would shock your editor if described here. Acerbic introductions bewail the bad taste of editors and the obtuseness of critics. From the afterword of *Golem in the Gears* (Orbit 326pp £2.50) I learn that Anthony's just switched to a word processor ... if his production rate rises further, the books will be appearing weekly. *Golem* is the ninth **Xanth** fantasy and possibly the weakest of the lot (the series is being 'rested' for a while after this [but not for long enough]). Like some legendary D&D campaigns, Xanth is so full of whimsy and casual magic that no situation can threaten for long; the storyline lurches drunkenly from pun to banal pun. (Compare the earlier books, where puns cropped up more or less 'naturally' without the plot being painfully wrenched to accommodate them.) The US mass-market readership loves it. Argh.

Robert Sheckley appears to have a similar plotline problem in *Options* (Grafton 156pp £2.50), but here, at least in theory, it's intentional. This can be read as one of those sf books which criticize sf, like Le Guin's *Lathe of Heaven* and Malzberg's *Galaxies*. Sheckley's hero is marooned without a spare part for his space drive, and despite such desperate expedients as writing himself into the book as the Man of a Thousand Disguises, the author finds himself forever 'unable' to construct a credible plot device to save the situation. Lots of fun but, for obvious reasons, not much plot.

Also to hand: *Sandwriter* by Monica Hughes (Magnet 159pp £1.75), a very ideologically sound little fantasy fable of desert ecology and exploitation, sort of *Dune* in miniature for younger readers; Fritz Leiber's *Swords and Ice Magic*, last [at that time] and darkest of the fizzy Fafhrd/Mouser fantasy series; and our title book *Demand the Impossible* by Tom Moylan (Methuen University Paperbacks 242pp £7.95), subtitled 'Science fiction and the utopian imagination'. For completist sf academics, it's a somewhat austere examination of four novels: Russ's *The Female Man*, Le Guin's *The Dispossessed*, Piercy's *Woman on the Edge of Time* and Delany's *Triton*. For *Dwarf* readers heavily into such role-playing games as Marxist Analysis and the very popular Post-Structuralism (a recent supplement to *Paranoia*), it's a riot of heteroclitic theoretical mastery and prefigurative political understanding, or so says the back cover. Who could ask for more?

February 1987

49 Bad Dreams

I rolled the dice and looked up the Critical Hits table, under *Spine*. 'Your review smashes brutally through the book's spine and ploughs on to carve a jagged smoking trail of destruction from pages 17 to 231. The shattered volume lies sundered at your feet, its future sales potential pumping uselessly forth from the severed arteries ...' This effort to make my prose more tasteful comes courtesy of editor Paul Cockburn and a freebie copy of the *Warhammer* game rules, but I don't think I've mastered it yet.

Publishers currently love raw-horror novels thick with severed arteries, steaming entrails, and mutilated parts of the body which your editor won't let me mention: numbingly over-the-top stuff which leaves no room for the spider touch of fear. Ramsey Campbell's *The Hungry Moon* (Century 293pp £9.95) is very different from the stereotype, and full of that dim uncertain moonlight where terrors breed. It has unnervingly realistic roots, beginning with a moorland village taken over by the sort of fundamentalists who frighten me: authoritarian, intolerant, brandishing glib Biblical answers for everything, and with absolutely no time for that soppy New Testament stuff about love and charity. These are the people who want to seize and burn your D&D kit, you satanic game-players, you.

As a few sympathetic characters struggle in the tightening web of paranoia, the stage is set for a different brand of darkness to seep in from the moors. A particularly unpleasant Ancient Evil, with a taste for evangelists and full awareness of the possibilities of the nearby missile base. Even at his most apocalyptic, Campbell understates the horror and leaves your imagination to work, as in the epigraph: '*... to fear the moon, to feed her as she must be fed, and never to look upon her feeding ...*' Definitely a book to make you draw the curtains and turn up the central heating.

Cheer up with Terry Pratchett's *Equal Rites* (Gollancz 200pp £9.95), his third screwy and dotty (but never, the author insists, wacky or zany) fantasy from the Discworld, about which so much has been said in *White Dwarf*. This time, an intermittently serious plot underlies the comic exuberance. A wizard passes on his staff and talent, as is traditional, to the (*seven plus one*)th son of a (*twice four*)th son. Unfortunately there's a tiny error in sex, and the young heroine finds herself equipped for a profession which has approximately as many vacancies for females as the Papacy or the Presidency of the U.S.A. Her quest for equal rites at Unseen University produces plenty of funny one-liners, plus comic-horrible scenes with the Things from the Dungeon Dimensions, as described in the hideous *Necrotelecomnicon* or *Liber Paginarum Fulvarum*: 'The whole thing had a self-assembled look, as if the owner had heard about anatomy but couldn't quite get to grips with the idea.' Good fun, but it has a transitional feel about it, with serious bits – some closely reminiscent of Le Guin-style 'balance' – and funny bits pulling different ways to some dilution of effect.

Robert Sheckley reissues keep turning up: a new novel comes as a surprise. *Victim Prime* (Methuen 203pp £9.95) is a straight though sometimes tongue-in-cheek sf adventure, recycling Sheckley's favourite satirical theme of officially sanctioned combat to the death. By 2092 the world has fallen apart in a depressingly low-key way; our slow slide to extinction is enlivened only by bread-and-circuses spectacles like the Hunt – 'Killer' played for keeps in a holiday resort. It moves well enough, but despite ingenious ploys and counterploys has a touch of staleness: Sheckley imitating Sheckley. ('Poor fellow,' goes the gossip in the Reviewers' Club. 'Douglas Adams Syndrome, y'know....')

The Greenhill classic reprints keep coming: *Tourmalin's Time Cheques* by F. Anstey (Greenhill 173pp £8.95) is the most interesting yet. I was boggled to note that this light-hearted fantasy of timeslips and paradoxes first appeared in 1885, ten years before Wells's *The Time Machine*. During a long sea voyage, Tourmalin gets the chance to deposit his boring shipboard hours in a Time Bank, to earn interest and be reclaimed when needed. When he cashes his time cheques he lives the hours he 'banked', but not in the right order: shipboard romances and scandals are hopelessly shuffled, and Anstey can only resolve things by a hoary literary device which appears in large print above this column. Otherwise, it's still fun. *Planetoid 127* by Edgar Wallace (Greenhill 148pp £8.95) is more for desperate specialist collectors: a rare sf venture by the doyen of hack thrillers. Prof. Colson communicates via 'sound-strainer' with Earth's sister planet, hidden on the other side of the Sun (oh dear), and makes financial killings because stock market events there are 'echoed' here three days later, except sometimes....

Short Circuit (Sphere 186pp £2.50) is the book of the film, by 'Colin Wedgelock', said to be an sf author whose real name you would know. The gimmick is an unstoppable, laser-toting, missile-killing robot which as a result of the traditional Frankensteinian lightning bolt 'comes alive' and decides that disassembling robots, or people, is a bad thing. Its new, self-programmed response to enemy attack is 'Run away, hide, telephone police!' I haven't seen the film [it was reportedly dire], but the novelization is taut and funny: ultimate weapons which fancy themselves at disco dancing are OK by me.

John Tully's *NatFact 7* (Magnet 208pp £1.75) is another with topical things to say about politics. Its next-century Britain, not *too* unbelievable or nightmarish, features sharper distinctions than ever before between winners ('Qualified Citizens') and losers ('Nats' on permanent national service). Dissent bubbles over at Natfact 7, part open prison and part assembly line, with a familiar cast of undercover revolutionaries, fanatics, infiltrators and one ideologically unsound sceptic (about everything) who's the most appealing character. Following the old arguments about the justifiability of violence and ultimate worth of revolution, all ends in a state of realistic confusion with just a tiny gain for the forces of good ... and Tully instructs you to think of your own moral. Punchy and hard-hitting for 'young adult' sf, but a little too slick for its own good.

Though not keen on T.E.D. Klein's interminable horror novel *The Ceremonies*, I liked his *Dark Gods* (Pan 259pp £2.50) – four stories at just the traditional length for flesh-creeping yarns about the accursed blind things which inhabit New York's sewers but are never clearly seen, or the something which looks like a black man in scuba gear and is closing in on an old literary acquaintance of H.P. Lovecraft's. The atmosphere of urban sleaze works well: as with Ramsey Campbell, the supernatural fear gets a leg-up from existing nervousness about, say, the parts of town where you wouldn't walk after dark. Low Pavement, for example, in fear-crazed, terror-haunted Nottingham. [The *White Dwarf* editorial address.]

Does anyone remember when Roger Zelazny was a hot new author who could do no wrong? The 1973 collection *The Doors of His Face, the Lamps of His Mouth* (Methuen 271pp £2.50) brings it all back, with the famous title story and 14 more. Some are jokes or trivia, and a few personal favourites are omitted ('The Graveyard Heart', 'For a Breath I Tarry'), but there are enough goodies here to prove this author had true magic in his typewriter, for a while.... The title story is a splendid homage and farewell to the whole romantic but unfortunately mistaken tradition of a wet Venus, eccentrically telling one of the biggest fish stories in sf.

Chris Drumm runs the smallest of small presses out in Iowa, producing neat and cheap booklets which are doomed to become sought-after collectors' editions: stories, essays, memoirs, bibliographies. The latest is a tiny literary autobiography from Nebula-winner Richard Wilson: *Adventures in the Space Trade* plus *A Richard Wilson Checklist* (Drumm 36pp $2, from Chris Drumm Books, PO Box 445, Polk City, Iowa 50226, USA). That's a post-free price (the John Sladek booklet *Love Among the Xoids* is only $1!) ... if you can locate a couple of dollar bills in the first place.

And while I'm at it, don't forget Britain's sf magazine *Interzone* (current subscription rates on application to 217 Preston Drove, Brighton, BN1 6FL); and *Conspiracy '87*, the World SF Convention making its once-a-decade visit to these unAmerican shores: a week of desperate sf fun in Brighton on and around the August bank holiday. [Membership details were originally included here, but it seems a trifle pointless now.]

I rolled another 16 and consulted the table. 'The *White Dwarf* rejection slip slices blurringly through your pitiful ego defences to smash with maximum impact on your forebrain, splattering through unprotected grey matter and coating the surroundings up to a distance of 10 feet with a thick spray of despair.' Oh, I shall never learn the subtleties of this.

[I should explain that the *Warhammer* game rules were full of phosphorescent purple passages like those echoed here. The Pratchett *twice four* stuff refers to the now universally known fact that eight is the magic number in Discworld – wizards draw octograms and not pentagrams, etc.]

March 1987

50 Jubilee Month

Your editor wrote to cheer me with the news that this month I'd be notching up my fiftieth *Critical Mass.* I knew there had to be some explanation for my snow-white hair, Grand Canyon-like wrinkles and other evidences of premature senility. 'We're giving you a special celebration treat,' Mr Brunton went on, and I braced myself to accept with due modesty the gift of a diamond-studded word processor or crate of champagne. 'For your 50th column we're going to let you write *twice as much*!'

Colin Wilson, my favourite dotty philosopher, has likewise decided to spread himself at length, after 30-odd years of writing. *Spider World: The Tower* (Grafton 398pp £10.95) opens a fat, far-future sf trilogy in which humankind has been reduced to slavery/outlawry by giant balloon-borne 'death spiders', apparently mutated by radiation from a passing comet. Any sf fan can instantly imagine a scenario in which the young hero develops arcane mental powers; finds himself the only person capable of killing the arachnid oppressors; is instructed in his true heritage by an aeons-old computer; and wins free thanks to a convenient buried arsenal of doomsday weapons. Rather surprisingly, Wilson's plot is *exactly* this one.

Tower opens with much ostentatious research work about deserts and creepy-crawlies, which in the great tradition of pulp sf ignores the sheer physical unworkability of giant insects. (As explained in J.B.S. Haldane's *Possible Worlds* - dated 1927.) The best bits are flashes of insight into how spiders might think. Here the musty but ripping yarn comes alive, only to trip over such wild generalizations as 'The spider is the only living creature that spends its life lying in wait, hoping that victims will walk into its trap.' Would it be pedantic to observe that sea anemones and ant lions do just the same - and that an ant lion was shown in full action only eight pages previously? Highly readable, but irritating.

(The jacket, by Chris Foss, looks oddly as though a hasty spiderweb plus token balloons have been added to an existing painting of a derelict city remarkably unlike Wilson's. Surely not...?)

I once irritated serious-minded critics by publishing a novel that cracked jokes about nukes. James Morrow's *This Is The Way The World Ends* (Gollancz 319pp £10.85) goes further, a great deal further, into a sort of manic *Slaughterhouse 5* treatment of nuclear apocalypse. Its gestures are so completely over the top as to defy criticism. The horrifically described aftermath of a megaton strike fills a chapter whose bland title is: 'In Which the Limitations of Civil Defence Are Explicated in a Manner Some Readers May Find Distressing'. With history and rationality blown to atoms, the book moves on into fantasy as six survivors are seized to stand trial after the fashion of the Nuremberg hearings, for crimes against the future. The author and his characters wisecrack their way through post-apocalyptic horror, in a way which you can take either as deeply bad taste or as an indication that minds incapable of grasping the enormity of nuclear war beforehand would do no better afterwards.

This is a harrowingly satirical book, whose main flaw lies in its treatment of the USSR. World War III, it turns out in this scenario, started by accident: but only Americans are prosecuted by the unborn, the evil Russkies being prejudged as insane and unworthy of trial. This strikes me as an insecure foundation for a scathing attack on the global arms race.

Michael Scott Rohan's above-average **Winter of the World** trilogy is unusual for avoiding the Black Lord/Evil Empire syndrome ... his cold war is against the encroaching Ice which threatens the remnants of civilization. Book two, *The Forge in the Forest* (Macdonald 408pp £10.95), has the traditional middle-volume plot of an immense journey through nameless perils - parts of which I found myself skipping, only to enjoy the vivid highlights of battle, smithcraft (in one consciously Wagneresque scene the hero uses lightning to reforge an indestructible sword which proves to be reinforced with carbon fibre; it's a smidgeon less convincing when he invents, of all things, electroplating and gets everything right first time), and above all the Powers and geography of the inhospitable Ice. Book one, *The Anvil of Ice*, is now a paperback.

Ian Watson is a deeply untraditional author; *Evil Water* (Gollancz 200pp £10.95) is his fourth collection, comprising 10 stories of sf, fantasy, horror and pure Watsonism. This collection is a shade less substantial than previous ones, but still offers fun and intellectual fireworks: alien parasites, failed timegates, transatlantic sponsored swimming, Greenham Common allegory, and an enjoyably nasty sense of humour throughout.

But Watson's is an austere and reasoned nastiness, without the lush sensual decadence of the month's most reprehensible reissue: J.K. Huysmans' 1891 classic *Là Bas* (Dedalus 287pp £4.50), also known in this country as *Down There* or *Lower Depths*. The hero or anti-hero Durtal is a thinly disguised Huysmans, indulging himself in exotic food and drink such as 'that alkermes which makes the person tasting it think he is in an Oriental pharmaceutic laboratory.' (My local pub declined to serve me this, so I can't comment.) Now he's trying to achieve the same titillation for his mind by immersing himself in first historical and then contemporary 19th-century devil-worship - which, as Robert Irwin rightly notes in his introduction, 'should not be confused with the later sanitized adventure fantasies of Dennis Wheatley ... Huysmans has given us real spit-and-sawdust Satanism.' A lurid and influential book, containing that famous description of the Black Mass ceremony attended by Huysmans himself.

The Lives and Times of Jerry Cornelius (Grafton 185pp £2.50) is a slightly more recent reprint, from 1976: oblique, fragmented stories of the hero/assassin who became a rallying point for the 1960s 'New Wave' themes of entropy and disintegration. A blurb: 'The conflicting time streams of the 20th century were mirrored in Jerry Cornelius.' An extract: 'Jerry hated needling a dead man, but it was necessary. He looked down at the twice-killed corpse of Borman, the first Nazi astronaut.' An epilogue lists Moorcock's favourite hates: Kingsley Amis, C.S. Lewis, J.R.R. Tolkien, Charles Williams, Gilbert and Sullivan, all guilty of having 'subtly corroded the quality of English thinking.' A motto for the Cornelius tales: 'Never apologize, never explain.' A review? The above is all you get.

The Best SF of Isaac Asimov (Grafton 320pp £10.95 ... publishers seem to have unanimously decided that £10.95 is now the basic hardback price) runs to 28 stories, excluding 'mysteries', which are saved for a companion volume. Most of these have been recycled many times before: 'it's my busy and efficient publishers who more or less insist on it,' notes Asimov. Some OK stuff here, but little that's unfamiliar.

And: *The Years of the City* by Frederick Pohl (NEL 375pp £2.95), in which New York appears in five clever snapshots of an increasingly optimistic future; *Orphans of the Sky* by Robert Heinlein (Grafton 143pp £2.50), the pioneering 'generation starship whose crew has forgotten its origin' story; *The Ice King* by Michael Scot (NEL 252pp £2.50), exciting supernatural thriller of archaeology, computers, Nordic vampires, and Fimbulwinter - but what a yucky cover; and *The Peace Machine* by Bob Shaw (Grafton 187pp £2.50), whose well-drawn hero tries like C.S. Forester's *The Peacemaker* to use his marvellous gadget to end war ... with similar success.

Finally, an unsolicited plug for a book I've been enjoying in my spare time while preparing this lot: *Metamagical Themas* by Douglas Hofstadter (Penguin 852pp £9.95), a heady mixture of computers, art, mathematics, philosophy, jokes and above all games. If you want something a little bit *different* from role-playing, try the twisted, self-referential game of Nomic described here ... in which all the rules can be changed by player vote, and indeed every move consists of an attempt to change the rules. To encourage you to start changing them, scoring is initially by random dice-throw; you will of course want to introduce a scoring rule that particularly favours you, but which the other players will be deluded enough to vote for.

By unanimous vote of your editor, we're now going to hurl the rulebook out of the window and do a special *Critical Mass* supplement. To boldly go where no review has gone before ...

50a A Critical Alphabet

A is for Anthologies, an endangered species except when A also stands for Asimov (who lends his name to endless collections assembled by others, usually Martin H. Greenberg). The 'public' dislikes shorts: new novelists have a slim chance, but collections from non-established authors send editors into screaming retreat.

B is for Bathos, the stylistic pratfall which awaits incautious writers of High Fantasy. Perhaps it's unfair at this late date to quote William Morris's 1897 *The Water of the Wondrous Isles*, whose heroine repossesses a frock swiped by a witch: 'Nay, ye have been in ill company, I will wear you not, though ye be goodly, at least not till ye have been fumigated....'

C stands for Critic, and bygone actor W.C. Macready summed it up: 'I wish I were anything rather than an actor - *except a critic*; let me be unhappy rather than vile!' The sentiment has more recently been echoed by Piers Anthony, Robert Heinlein and several others who seem to believe in double standards. For that almost godlike creature an Author to write dumb, offensive or shoddy work is a triumph for free speech and, where applicable, the US Constitution. Should a disappointed reader discuss the said dumbness, offensiveness or shoddiness in print ... well, there are just no words strong enough to describe such a wicked, vindictive person. SF writers, myself included, would do well to remember the observation of Dr Johnson: 'An author places himself uncalled before the tribunal of criticism, and solicits fame at the hazard of disgrace.'

D is for critical Doubts. Have I been too nice or nasty in reviews? Should I have been ruder to Gwyneth Jones's unmistakably talented but really a bit reader-resistant *Escape Plans*? (See under *E*.) Was I over-kind to Greg Bear's *Eon* thanks to its bold use of infinities? (See under *M*.) *D* is also Decisions, Decisions....

E for Endurance carries its own pitfall. Friends are aghast at my ability to plough through semi-infinite blockbusters, but E.M. Forster adds a warning ... 'One always tends to overpraise a long book because one has got through it.' Such as *Battlefield Earth*, no doubt; best to take my extravagant over-praise with a pinch of salt.

F is for Footnotes, which owing to typesetting economies aren't Fashionable. Jack Vance uses footnotes to nifty effect when setting up his exotic backgrounds; but sf's most bizarre text note comes in the Aldiss *Trillion Year Spree*, where to establish feminist credentials, collaborator David Wingrove spends 240-odd words boasting about the total non-sexism of his common-law marriage. Very scientifictional.

G indicates the Gerunds which since *The Shining* have become infallible signs of bad horror titles: *The Spawning, The Groping, The Yucking.* To hand is Tim Stout's *The Raging* (Grafton 256pp £2.50), whose blurb 'It makes a man's blood boil – to slaughter-point!' would also do nicely for *The Reviewing.*

H is the Hugo Award. Be wary of this as a stamp of quality: it's voted by a minority of each year's World SF Convention members, and is thus *(a)* American-dominated; *(b)* heavily swayed by authors' personalities and fan involvement. However, my own Hugo was for sheer merit, cross my heart.

[2000: And likewise the others that followed. I only wish I could believe this assertion myself. In several categories like editor, artist and 'fan writer', the award is not made for any specific work and memories of past years' glories can keep popular winners coasting on for a long time.]

I is trendy Information Technology, overrunning sf as writers imitate William Gibson's remarkable *Neuromancer* and *Count Zero.* Back in near-reality, Prestel's **Earthlight** sf database is giving room to *Dwarf*ish material (key *810941) ... while hi-tech *Dwarf* itself encourages submissions on disk! *Critical Mass* retains its typesetting errors because *White Dwarf* can't afford compatibility with any word processor costing more than £399.

[1992: I don't know what you'd find on that Prestel page nowadays. The point about the figure £399 – embarrassedly suppressed by the editors when this column first appeared – was that rich Games Workshop was using cheapo Amstrad PCW word processors costing that amount, while I produced the column on a PC....]

J for Juvenile is a marketing category also given the less patronizing name 'young adult'. SF which was once 'adult' can turn up with this label: a Good Thing if you're not too snobbish to read 'juveniles', because for unexplained reasons these editions are always cheaper.

K must be that strange genius Franz Kafka, and the over-use of 'Kafkaesque' to describe any sf featuring surrealism, bureaucracy, helplessness or hangovers. The critic James Agate once devised a badge with the letters PPKIBC: 'Perpetual President Kafka Is Balls Club.'

L is *Little, Big* by John Crowley, a quietly convoluted book which turns in on itself, a tale about a Tale: my most admired and re-read fantasy since *Critical Mass* began. Few readers survived Methuen's paperback, which foolishly reduced the small print of the Gollancz edition to a microfiche-sized optician's delight.

[The instant I'd complained about this tiny-print edition, a larger-format reissue turned up in the shops. Good for Methuen ... but as I prepare this collection in 1992, it's long out of print again. Hint, *hint.*] [2000: at last, a new British reissue in the Fantasy Masterworks series. Good for Millennium.]

M is Mathematics. I'm a sucker for mathematically-based sf: you don't see much, because it's hard to do. Try *White Light* by Rudy Rucker, an ex-hippy who gets high on infinite set theory to create the hugest 'world' in sf. Huger even than Christopher Priest's infinite *Inverted World,* since Priest uses lower orders of infinity.

[Rucker edited the fine 1987 anthology *Mathenauts: Tales of Mathematical Wonder*, bringing together both classics and recent gems of this tiny subgenre. I'm still looking for Clifton Fadiman's similar anthologies *Fantasia Mathematica* (1958) and *The Mathematical Magpie* (1962).]

N is obviously Novel, the unobvious point being that many aren't. Beware *(a)* the short story inflated by huge print, wide margins, terrible illustrations and blank pages; *(b)* story collections billed as novels to make them sell; *(c)* seeming novels which stop in mid-plot with the words 'Continued in Volumes II-XXIV of *Quest of the Runefork*, now in preparation ...'

O for Originality is a devilish hard thing to judge. Once I was sort of impressed by cybernetic speculations in Frank Herbert's 1966 *Destination: Void* (another 'Yes, *now* there is a God!' book) – until I found they'd been copied verbatim from a 1964 pop-science essay by Mr Cybernetics himself, Norbert Wiener's *God & Golem Inc.* Likewise I had a bit of a dispute with Bob Shaw over his very funny story 'The Cottage of Eternity', because it makes heavy use, without credit, of the joke particle-physics analysis of ghosts in D.A. Wright's 'A Theory of Ghosts' (from *The Worm Runner's Digest*, 1971). Why, asked Bob, was it all right to steal physics for sf, but not jokes? – and disarmingly added that he'd initially tried to put a credit into the story but it had spoiled the flow.

P is a book's Publicity, usually confined to an inaccurate blurb: 'The megashock novel of flesh-rending microchip horror!' is a personal favourite, from Theodore Roszak's *Bugs*, wherein large, literal bugs emerge from the computer programs and bite people.

Q is Quotation, to which I'm slightly addicted (see above, see below, see 49 previous columns). The 1980 *Penguin Dictionary of Modern Quotations* features several live [in 1987] sf authors, including Brian Aldiss defining sf as 'Hubris clobbered by Nemesis' (and two more quotes), Isaac Asimov with the Laws of Robotics, Ray Bradbury (who according to Penguin has written no memorable lines, only one memorable title – *The Day it Rained Forever*), Arthur C. Clarke ('Open the pod door, Hal,' and two others), Robert Heinlein (as with Bradbury, just a title – *Stranger in a Strange Land*. The non-modern Moses said it first in *Exodus*, chaps) ... and most unexpectedly, Larry Niven relating the best advice he ever had. 'On my 21st birthday my father said, "Son, here's a million dollars. Don't lose it."' [Perhaps apocryphal.]

R must be Robotics, with a respectful nod to Isaac Asimov for inventing the word ... and a loud Raspberry for adding, after forty-odd years, a lopsided sequel to that self-contained trilogy the Three Laws of Robotics.

S is Suppression: can I send you scurrying lewdly to bookshops by listing once-forbidden sf/fantasy? Cabell's fine novel *Jurgen* was banned in 1920 for its decorous naughtiness; Huxley's 'immoral' *Brave New World* got the chop from the Irish government in 1932; Spinrad's *Bug Jack Barron* serialization so shocked W.H. Smith in 1968 that they vetoed *New Worlds* magazine; and *White Dwarf 86* suppressed Graham Masterton's nauseating line 'The eel had swallowed his *[You stop right there! – Ed.]*

T for Translation produces more unlikely statistics. In UNESCO's top twenty translated authors for 1980, Isaac Asimov is the only living sf writer (82 translations, just behind Dostoevsky and Twain). Jules Verne outdoes him with

172 translations (just ahead of Enid Blyton and Karl Marx). Michael Scott Rohan likes to argue that Stanislaw Lem's *Solaris* 'gained in the translation'.

U is for Unnameable, Unspeakable and the University of Chicago - which as a treat for Cthulhu fans offers 'a translation of Greek magical papyri (300BC-690AD) wherein you may make the acquaintance of the Demiurge of the Seven Laughs and the Headless Demon Who Sees With His Feet. Besides infallible methods of nobbling the chariot races and making your shadow invisible,' writes my investigator R.I. Barycz.

V is for the disappointment I've christened the Vampire Effect. It works like this: a mainstream or at any rate non-fantasy-genre author achieves a shock ending by introducing a vampire (or something similar) into an apparently 'straight' story. Then a fantasy anthologist reprints it and wonders why it somehow lacks the same impact in a collection called *Fifty Great Tales In Which The Heroine Turns Out To Be A Vampire.*

W, the Wild Hunt, is about the most overused prop in fantasy. Can doomed Herne and his spectral hounds please be given a rest for a few decades? 'From a find to a check, from a check to a view, From a view to a cliché in the morning....'

X of course stands for Xanthopsia, being the jaundiced view this column takes of trilogies which contain enough interesting ideas for one and a half books, but continue remorselessly for nine. [Or twelve, or twenty, or whatever it is these days.]

You still make the final decision, gentle readers. Some people appear to think that my slightest hostile comment will condemn whole printings to the pulping vats. The despised reviewer can only read the book and try to indicate whether it seems to 'work', with due allowance for personal prejudice. (For example, I dislike the general run of modern horror novels for their tedious repetition of a limited vocabulary of nastiness - which doesn't stop me admiring a high-class one by, usually, Ramsey Campbell.)

Z for Roger Zelazny gives a small postscript on critical fallibility. Several sf pundits have praised Zelazny's description of an alien tree as wittily evocative: 'a frozen fountain of orange marmalade.' They were perfectly right but they missed the joke: the early stages of the original computer Adventure game, *Colossal Cave,* feature a cavern whose 'walls are frozen fountains of orange marble.' Zelazny stands revealed as a crypto-gameplayer....

April 1987

51 Show & Tell

Sometimes I receive stories from hopeful authors who don't realize that my influence on *White Dwarf* policy is equivalent to King Canute's on the tide. Send fiction to Ye Editor instead: he, unlike me, has limitless free time to read it. Assuming your masterpiece passes the space test (wide margins, double-spaced lines ... and remember that not putting spaces after commas etc. will brand you as one of the damned) and isn't unbelievably clumsy in spelling, syntax or diction, the editorial comments are likely to involve such litcrit jargon as: 'Show, not tell.'

The point is that an sf/fantasy author usually needs to convey the background of an invented cosmos. Clumsy authors simply *tell* you by bringing the story to a shuddering halt for a lecture starting 'Twenty years ago, the ships of the Federation had ...' and taking 2000 words to explain that, say, everyone's nose is now internally tattooed with a bar-code ID by order of fiendish DHSS galactic overlords. Less clumsy authors skip the lecture and, as part of the action, *show* you someone at the supermarket checkout, worrying about catching 'flu from the bar-code reader which has already been up 500 noses that morning. (Every rule of thumb has exceptions. If you can write an scene-setting essay as good as that opening Alfred Bester's *Tiger! Tiger!* ... go right ahead.)

In *Cuckoo's Egg* (Methuen 319pp £2.50), C.J. Cherryh is initially telling very little. Thorn, an evidently human boy, is reared in isolation by a humanoid called Duun, furry, clawed and scarred, wielder of some mysterious authority. The master-pupil relationship is the core of the book, and very nicely done. Duun is training Thorn as a *hatani*, something involving physical and mental ordeals, and games of bluff: 'There's a pebble in the pot' translates as 'Symbolically I've poisoned your food, har har.' The *hatani* are impressive, but as aliens they're very much off-the-peg ... Zen warriors with fur. Even their Guild HQ has interior decor suspiciously like the Sand Garden at Kyoto. Why is Thorn the only human on this world? The final revelations entail some background 'telling', but by then Cherryh's worked hard to make you *want* the answer to each riddle. A good read.

Frederik Pohl's *The Coming of the Quantum Cats* (Gollancz 243pp £9.95) also employs the show-not-tell technique of throwing you in at the deep end. It opens in a 1983 America where prices and interest rates seem curiously low;

beer is illegal; one can lose one's thumbs for shoplifting; Arab interests dominate the country's finance ... There are many skewed Americas in this novel of interacting parallel Earths, given a veneer of intellectual respectability by 'Many-Worlds' quantum theory and the uncertain status of Schrödinger's cat: hence the title, a bit twee for a classy and straightforward sf thriller. 'Real' people appear: in one America, Reagan is a forgotten actor; in another he's First Gentleman alongside President Nancy. Militaristic Americas invade peaceful ones with a view to behind-the-scenes assault on parallel Russias. I could predict the ending: with an infinity of worlds, any required *deus ex machina* just has to be out there somewhere! But Pohl, a reliably thoughtful author, does go one better than his semi-happy (and self-indulgent) finale. As with nuclear weapons, the crosstime technology can't be uninvented, while there's an infinity of potential new inventors....

I'm afraid Jack Williamson's *Lifeburst* (Sphere 271pp £2.95) begins with wodges of potted history, explaining how the 22nd century's space-dwelling elite have sunspots tattooed on their cheeks as badges of superiority. (Easy to fake, you think? Someone tries. The tattoo ... peels off.) Williamson has been publishing sf in the pulp tradition since 1928: his style has improved a bit over the decades, but his plots still involve utterly invincible threats (here a giant nuclear-powered, ship-eating, space insect) countered by incredible last-ditch weapons (here, as usual, courtesy of friendly aliens). Rabid megalomaniacs command space-dreadnaughts and kick-start the plot by instantly opening fire on said friendly aliens. A brilliant scientist works alone to develop the first fusion reactor, which is carried around in a cardboard box. Black holes lurch coincidentally towards the Solar System, sucking up loose plot threads like a cosmic Hoover. No character in this farrago comes to life except, briefly, the giant space insect herself - who should have known that with the odds a billion to one in her favour, there was just no way in pulp sf that she could win. This book will take you right back, probably to before you were born.

One time-honoured solution to the background problem is to drop an ignorant visitor into your future society: he'll naturally ask questions after being told 'You have slept exactly one hundred and thirteen years, three months, and eleven days.' (Edward Bellamy, *Looking Back*, 1888.) *Sun's End* by Richard Lupoff (Grafton 348pp £2.95) adds extra fillips. The hero has been handily rebuilt into a bionic superman by the time he wakes in 2089, 80 years after his accident. He's also the richest man in the Solar System (cf. Wells's *When the Sleeper Wakes*, 1899), and for no apparent reason develops telepathic powers. But though life is good in space colonies, it's grim and slummy on Earth, where the stormy Sun will erase life in mere centuries! One slim hope is offered by evidence of super-aliens on Mercury (traces only), Titan (traces only, but there's a jolly good race to get there before the devilish Russkies) and Zimarzla. This last is a new, extra-solar planet into which our hero plunges in a final ecstatic, cosmic light-show (cf. *2001*), and, well, that's it. Lupoff poses a problem: how to save 26 billion people from dying as the Sun overheats? He and his hero simply turn their backs on the question. Thumbs-down to both of them.

[In fairness, this was apparently planned as a two-parter, although Grafton kept quiet about the fact. I have restrained myself from buying *Galaxy's End*.]

With *The Princess of Flames* by Ru Emerson (Unicorn 327pp £2.95), normal fantasy service is resumed, right down to the routine enthusiastic plug from Anne McCaffrey. Decadent King Sedry and his vile brother Hyrcan are fighting the unspeakable Fegez hordes, little knowing that among the allies lurks sister Elfrid, the Bastard Princess, waiting to revenge the overthrow of their father King Lear – not his actual name, but the mad scenes are awfully reminiscent. The villains come to sticky ends and the princess gets her man. References to holograms, nicotine and coffee help weigh the story down to earth: indeed, it's a curiously unfantastic fantasy. The smelly Fegez do some half-hearted shape-shifting, and upper-class characters tend literally to glow with royalist auras or emit kingly fire (lending ambiguity to lines like 'a curse that blistered the air') ... but none of this seems vital to the tale. It's as though Emerson had written a novel of semi-historical warfare and was advised by her agent to 'fantasy it up a bit'.

Privateers by Ben Bova (Methuen 383pp £2.50) offers 21st-century US/USSR space-skirmishing with a heavy propaganda message and, to quote an American critic, '21 worn-out adventure-fiction clichés in the first 4 pages!'. *Ghost Train* by Stephen Lawes (Sphere 343pp £2.95) is another horror nasty: 'Loathsome. An unspeakable abomination. A horror buried so deep in his psyche he can remember not a single detail of what has been done to him. He stands in the railway station and shudders uncontrollably.' I've felt that way myself after British Rail bacon sandwiches. *The Black Ship* by Christopher Rowley (Century 310pp £10.95) looks like entertaining sf but is volume 2 of a trilogy, and I haven't seen volume 1 – sorry.... *The Dragon Lord* by Peter Morwood (Century 318pp £10.95) was reviewed here in paperback, not with approval, and is now reissued for rich readers who found that edition too cheap.

Finally, *Brute! Classified Pulp Nasties* (Sphere 141pp £1.95) 'is to Literature as the demented abstractions of New York subway graffiti is to Art' – verbatim from the publicity flyer. Scanning these very short stories (e.g. 18 words) in very large print with very many exclamation marks (the 18-worder uses 21), I decided the analogy wasn't quite right. In fact this work is to Literature as a pool of vomit outside a pub is to Haute Cuisine.

May 1987

52 Out of the Closet

A famous couplet by Robert Conquest goes: *'SF's no good!' they bellow till we're deaf / 'But this looks good ...' 'Well then, it's not SF.'* In case this seems like mere satire, here's Anthony Burgess reviewing a Brian Aldiss novel: '... rich, allusive, full of real people and unfailingly interesting. It is not, then, real SF.' When on the Booker Prize committee, Aldiss himself reported that several novels with sf and fantasy elements were considered, but that for litcrit respectability you had to call them something else: 'metaphorical-structural' or 'magic realism'....

That hot new novelist Iain Banks has been prowling on the borders of sf for three nifty books, *The Wasp Factory*, *Walking on Glass* and *The Bridge*. Now, under the impenetrable pseudonym Iain *M.* Banks, he's burst out of the closet with *Consider Phlebas* (Macmillan 471pp £9.95), which is unashamed space opera. Watch for the chorus of 'Rubbish!' from critics who gave Banks the thumbs-up so long as his sf images were a bit ambiguous.... *Phlebas* is manic, high-energy adventure of the sort they don't write any more. It opens with space-skirmishing à la *Star Wars*, cuts to torture, last-minute rescue, unlikely ambush ('So the Culture ships could hide in the photospheres of stars, could they?'), unarmed duel to the death, a pirate raid on a booby-trapped temple, disaster aboard a city-sized ocean 'megaship', revolting cannibalism, destruction of a mini-Ringworld by 'novalevel hypergridintrusion', etc.

Banks pumps in enough high spirits to keep this rattling along to his slam-bang finale in the bowels of an ancient deep-shelter system whose nuclear-powered high-speed trains are used for ... well, not commuting. Such seriousness as there is concerns the pointlessness of the galaxy-wide clash between fundamentalist alien Idirans and the socialist human Culture. Little subtlety, lots of fun: recommended, but read his other books too.

Keith Roberts's *Gráinne* (Kerosina 175pp £12.50) takes more of a 'discreet cough' approach to its slender sf content. Roberts always writes beautifully, but two-thirds of this book is devoted to the fairly mundane biography of one Alastair Bevan, who's editorializing in a rather affected way from his deathbed. Very late in the day, his one-time lover Gráinne achieves TV fame in an exposé series; uses the leverage to found a cult about which we're told not quite enough (fuelled apparently by her radical theory about Celtic origins, which likewise never comes into clear focus); and takes the time-honoured route to mythic immortality by dying. The final, haunting images effectively combine fairy mounds and World War III, but didn't overcome my frustration: Gráinne's barely-glimpsed story fails to conquer the dead weight of Bevan's autobiographical longueurs.

Another discreet way to disguise sf is as futurology, like Arthur C. Clarke's *July 20, 2019: A Day in the Life of the 21st Century* (Grafton 281pp £14.95). This reminded me of 1950s kiddy-science works: 'In the exciting future of 1987, nuclear piles will have made power so cheap and plentiful that electricity meters will have been forgotten!' It's optimistic, American, and hard to believe: futurologists who portray a 21st-century Utopia need to consider how today's intractable problems (overpopulation, hunger, recession, dwindling fuel reserves) are to be solved. Clarke's book simply ignores them. World War III happens, but in line with the dafter school of US military thought is confined solely to Germany, thanks to precision weapons which pinpoint and destroy only military targets. (Such as Libya?) Compare this with one interesting cause suggested in this book for the war: NATO tank squadrons accidentally straying across the East German border owing to foggy weather....

As Clarke's a very good non-fiction writer, I was surprised by the mediocrity of these essays on 2019's hospitals, roads, schools, transport, etc. It turns out that 'Ego', as fans once called him, provided only the introduction and epilogue: the 14 people who wrote the actual book are named on the back flap of the jacket, in Clarke's small-print acknowledgements, *and nowhere else*. Good grief.

Recently I reviewed an Asimov collection from Grafton; here's another from Gollancz, *Robot Dreams* (349pp £10.95), one-third of which has just appeared in Grafton's collection.... The title story is new and quite good; the rest is familiar Asimovian reprint material.

Anne McCaffrey's *Nerilka's Story & The Coelura* (Bantam 192pp £8.95) comprises two mini-novels. *Nerilka*, a spinoff from *Moreta: Dragonlady of Pern*, exists to tie up a loose thread – the need for the late Moreta's lover Alessan to be tidily married off, which would have been a bit insensitive in the book where Moreta actually snuffs it. Lady Nerilka's rise from poor little titled girl to Mrs Alessan makes a skimpy story overwhelmed by the vastness of *Moreta*'s plot, all of which has to be remorselessly summarized for *Nerilka* to make sense. *The Coelura* has the opposite problem, an alien Macguffin (flying blobs who spin sentient fabric which makes terrific clothes) which is only just barely visible: we need a good deal more lyricism about the wonderfulness of these 'coelura' before accepting the way the heroine becomes – literally overnight – obsessed with coelura-preservation. There's the seed of something interesting here, but the short format allows only a standard candyfloss ending (the coelura were never in danger at all) and a nice double wedding to finish. Hear those violins?

John Brunner's *The Compleat Traveller in Black* (Methuen 233pp £2.50) is more my kind of fantasy. These five stories began with outright pastiche of James Branch Cabell's oblique manner: 'The alteration it underwent was not altogether pleasant to witness.' But the Traveller, a demiurge entrusted with the task of confining chaos and bringing stability to the world, has a wit and personality of his own, and perseveres through further tales to the completion of his task, dealing out justice by the wish-granting which seems to be his only overt power. Very readable and re-readable.

The Hour of the Thin Ox (Unwin Hyman 186pp £9.95) is a second novel from Colin Greenland, who writes well, paints some colourful settings and works at a more interesting technological level than most fantasy authors: no magic but balloons, primitive guns, low-tech biological warfare ... After lengthy setting-up exercises, the complex tides of war bring together representatives of all three sides for a climactic battle of a very unusual nature. Greenland's real story begins in the southern jungle at about chapter 12, and continues into mystery beyond the end of the book: yet I don't think there's to be a sequel. Odd.

Wizard of the Pigeons (Corgi 254pp £2.50) by Megan Lindholm is another unusual fantasy, based on a cunning insight. Where today would one find wizards who've renounced worldly advancement to pursue magic? On the streets: next time you see that grimy lady who scavenges litter-bins and keeps her possessions in battered carrier bags, watch out - she's probably one of Lindholm's wizards. The story takes place in Seattle and on the poverty line, as something nasty from the hero's past threatens him and the city. His impulse is to run: but even if his arcane powers consist only of truth-seeing and an inexhaustible ability to feed pigeons, he *is* still a wizard.... Fresh, original, exciting.

The bulkiest of the reissues is Herbert's *The Second Great Dune Trilogy* (Gollancz 1111pp £10.95, less than 1p a page), comprising *God-Emperor* (mildly boring), *Heretics* (in which the series livens up) and *Chapter House* (now forever poised on the brink of a never-to-be-written sequel). C.J. Cherryh's *Faded Sun* trilogy (Methuen 756pp £3.95) is fine, poetic sf adventure with interesting aliens. M. John Harrison's *The Pastel City* (Unwin 142pp £2.50) is sword and sorcery with a difference: brooding, atmospheric, post-technological, intensely literate. And Gollancz 'Classic SF' reprints four more goodies: in my personal order of preference, Clarke's *A Fall of Moondust* (224pp £3.50), exciting but dated Poseidon Adventure stuff in a lunar dust-boat; Pohl's *Man Plus* (215pp £3.50), an adult, warts-and-all look at sf's fantasy of becoming a cyborg superman; Shaw's *A Wreath of Stars* (189pp £2.95) with its stunning, eerie vision of a neutrino-matter planet within our own, seen but never touched; and Budrys's *Rogue Moon* (173pp £2.95), possibly the sf novel I've most often reread: it still makes my hair stand on end with its story of men dying again and again as they challenge something inconceivably alien, uncaring and lethal.

Next month I shall once again challenge the inconceivably alien lethality of countless fantasy trilogies....

June 1987

53 Holiday Reading

I don't know what you lot read on your holidays, but I can make exclusive revelations about mine: another stack of blasted review copies. These were scanned in the alien atmosphere of Snowdonia, where one travels by exotic conveyances like *bws* or *tacsi*, and there are few gaming opportunities outside the impenetrably named *cwrs golff* and *clwb snwcer....*

According to those who take awards seriously, Orson Scott Card will win several with *Speaker for the Dead* (Century 415pp £10.95). [He did.] This ambitious sequel to his popular *Ender's Game* has lots going for it. A pleasant read; a deadly biological and anthropological puzzle (what's the life cycle of the primitive alien 'piggies' who apparently torture to death anyone who nears the truth?); religious/humanist frictions which for once in sf aren't *embarrassingly* one-sided; some genuine hate, fear and compassion.

What keeps this from being a fine book is the sense of slipshod construction. There are too many plot devices: a sentient computer network called Jane is unnecessary to the main action, and irritates by *(a)* immediately penetrating the alien mysteries; *(b)* keeping them dark from both hero and reader for no better reason than maintenance of plot tension. The biological riddle has one of the all too standard sf solutions (you know, it turns out that A metamorphoses into B, or C is symbiotic with D, or E is despite appearances just a pet of the secretly hyperintelligent F ...) and goes over the top with the gross improbability of a completely alien gene-unravelling virus which can infect humans. [There is some piffle in the next book, *Xenocide*, about the virus having been designed to infect and remodel any life whatever. See below.] Most annoyingly, hero Ender Wiggin has it all too easy. He's so damned wonderful that other characters' lifelong personality problems dissolve after mere minutes of his presence. Despite token guilt at his genocide of the sensitively named alien 'buggers' (previous book), Ender never suffers for his triumphs – even though Card is strong on suffering for everyone else, and happily cripples a young boy to add needless excitement to the finale. I was impressed by this thoughtful sf adventure, but with reservations.

Alien biological puzzles include the strange symbiosis of Larry Niven, Jerry Pournelle and Steven Barnes in *The Legacy of Heorot* (Gollancz 352pp £10.95), where life seems easy on Earth's first alien colony. 'Too easy. I don't like it,' says (approximately) one macho character: sure enough, giant superpowered flesh-hungry newts are soon on the rampage. Despite initial losses, resourceful humanity hits back with giant superpowered flesh-hungry newt guns, only to run into a predictably unexpected (see above) ecological booby-trap. Despite the resulting thrill of tens of thousands of superpowered flesh-hungry newts interminably assaulting Mr Macho's survivalist stronghold, I was tormented by the nagging thought that this would have read better at one-third the length. So it goes.

[Most egregious plot device in *Heorot*: the colonists' simple-mindedness and failure to work out the Newt Problem in advance is accounted for by their having been slightly brain-damaged when frozen for interstellar transit....]

Your reviewer has enthused too often about Robert Irwin's *The Arabian Nightmare* (Viking 282pp £10.95), that fantasy of a dark dream-Cairo which achieves the erudite fascination of *The Name of the Rose* with less neat explicability and more wit. This first mass-market appearance, fittingly illustrated with 19th-century lithographs, is very welcome. Likewise *The Limits of Vision* (King Penguin 120pp £2.95), Irwin's equally deranged exploration into the metaphysics of dirt.

From the original publishers of *The Arabian Nightmare* comes *The Illumination of Alice J. Cunningham* by Lyn Webster (Dedalus 306pp £9.95), an imaginative first novel which translates uncertain states of mind into an actual fantasy 'place' where the heroine seems trapped. Alice – significant name – manages to come to terms with life in fantasy and reality. A well-written and witty book which I enjoyed without deciphering *all* the allegorical bits. *Mea culpa.*

Academics and reference-book freaks might love the *Science Fiction Master Index of Names* by Keith L. Justice (McFarland dist. Bailey Bros. & Swinfen 394pp £29.95), a guide to sf critical mentions which would be very useful to anyone writing a Definitive Thesis. I looked up Orson Scott Card and was directed to what's allegedly the only sf reference book to cover him – a German one! I'm sure he's in *Twentieth Century SF Writers*, a monumental work which Justice never mentions. Despite other biggish omissions, the book could still be handy in its extremely specialist field.

Philip K. Dick thought *Dr Adder* by K.W. Jeter (Grafton 252pp £2.95) a masterpiece. Its energy is certainly impressively horrific, confronting the most unpleasant plausibilities of future surgical tampering used to gratify yucky longings. (Do you have the hots for amputees, or ladies with teeth in hideously unexpected places? Dr Adder can arrange it.) Whether these things *need* to be confronted is another question: I was glad I didn't confront them until several pints after dinnertime. Jeter forces sympathy for Adder by pitting him against someone supposedly viler still, an immortal Moral Majority type whom Adder, now converted to a cyborg execution machine, meets in a final electronic duel which introduces a science-fictional first – computerized pus. This one will ooze and ooze.

After scrubbing my page-turning fingers with Dettol, I attacked a heap of Gollancz's new VGSF paperbacks. *Angel with the Sword* by C.J. Cherryh (VGSF 300pp £2.95) is a nice atmospheric melodrama set on sleazy alien canals, with a likeably rude and scruffy heroine. It zips smartly along to an inconclusive ending on p250: the last fifty pages are superfluous appendices, maps, etc, indicating not merely a sequel but considerable cheek. Cherryh is inviting other writers to set stories on this world, so they need these background notes, which the rest of us could do without paying for.

Other VGSF launch books include ... *The Faceless Man* by Jack Vance (206pp £2.50), formerly *The Anome*: one of his best sf novels, featuring fine local colour and an amazingly daft religion, it opens the **Durdane** trilogy, whose later books are inferior. *Mission of Gravity* by Hal Clement (203pp £2.50) is a 'hard sf classic' - that is, despite being unbrilliantly written with all-too-human aliens, its background of life under a crushing 700 gravities is most ingeniously imagined. *Hegira* by Greg Bear (222pp £2.95) is this now celebrated author's first novel, an odyssey across a weird world which is too numbingly complex to be explained other than in a chapter-long lecture: mindboggling, unbelievable fun. *Night Walk* by Bob Shaw (188pp £2.50) explores this author's fruitful fascination with eyesight as the helpless, blinded hero invents a strange way to see, escape his captors, and save the universe.

Greenhill's worthy series of sf/fantasy classics will reportedly end soon, poisoned by the fangs of inadequate library funding. *The Blind Spot* by Austin Hall and Homer Eon Flint (Greenhill 255pp £8.95) is that strange phenomenon, a novel popular in its day for reasons incomprehensible after 66 years. You can enjoy spotting the howlers in this dotty pulp melodrama and trying to work out what'll happen next, information quite evidently hidden from the authors.

Other reissues come from Judith Tarr, whose *The Isle of Glass* (Corgi 288pp £2.50) opens the very literate 'Hound and the Falcon' trilogy of mediaeval fantasy whose final volume I'll be muttering about next issue; and Mary Brown, whose *The Unlikely Ones* (Arrow 426pp £3.50) has some charm but urgently needs a leavening of fantasy's grimmer side: the unlikely fellowship never passes through shadows dark enough to bring a contrasting glow to the happy ending's pastel colours.

As holiday relief from the above, I spent a lot of time staring at the intricate high-tech artifact which Welsh natives call a *telefision*....

July 1987

54 Nasty Futures

So you're an sf author writing about a 2087 where genetically-engineered flying pigs are replacing older forms of public transport. How do you force this bitter pill of implausibility down the readers' throats? One trick is to coat it in soporific layers of pseudoscientific justification; another is simply to describe the flight of the pig with such passion and flair that the unlikelihood is washed down by sheer force of storytelling. The first method is more traditional in sf. The second can work rather better....

Is piquant narrative flavour gives certain charm to David R. Palmer's *Emergence* (NEL 291pp £2.95). Teenage supergirl survives Armageddon, wanders emptied USA, diarizes in clipped prose. Style owes little to real telegraphese, much to Heinlein's *Moon is Harsh Mistress*: English speaker might say 'No justice' or 'There's no justice' but Heinlein and Palmer favour cutesy 'Is no justice' ... Master's Voice also detectable in references to extended marriages, *tanstaafl*, housetraining people, need for sudden-death killer reflexes, valuing of pet's life above human, etc.

Influence no bad thing. Heroine Candy likeable, convincingly competent (hair-raising emergency surgery sequences), young enough to sidestep embarrassing Heinlein version of female sexuality, wrong often enough to win sympathy. Plausibility wanes as moving tale of plain survival corkscrews into struggle to defuse evil Russki orbital bomb designed to splatter capitalist remnants. Guess who's only person able to save world? Finale close-run victory of narrative thrust over blatant plot devices (doomsday weapon access hatch big enough for space-suited 11-year-old only, Russki carrier vehicle handily reprogrammable to make safe landing ...). Is good fun.

K.W. Jeter's gimmicks are much more bizarre in *Death Arms* (Morrigan 168pp £10.95). The Jeter method of sneaking unlikelihoods past your guard is to drown them in a wash of naturalistic blood and violence: a bizarre scheme to assassinate humanity's collective unconscious emerges only gradually from the mess of gory killings, vile reanimations and terror weapons. *Paranoia* fans will love the inescapable CIA 'slow bullet' which covers a few feet per minute, can drill through any barrier, and as it nears you starts reciting: 'This is not a violation of your rights. This device legally operates under the provisions of the Expanded National Security Act of 1995 ...' Stripped of savage imagery, this would be a thin story: Jeter drives it at stomach-jolting pace to the hero's final realization that he can still save the world despite being horribly dead.

Graham Dunstan Martin's *The Dream Wall* (Unwin 231pp £2.95) has a dystopian future which goes over the top in quite a different direction, though coincidentally also featuring a dodgily plausible psychoelectronic plot to turn off human consciousness. 22nd-century Soviet Britain parodies all the worst Evil Empire fears: renamed towns (Leninpool, Engelsburgh, Marxeter), labour and death camps, secret police called 'People's Friends' forever bursting through doors at 3am to meet their growing arrest quota, etc. Over-paranoid in the hopeful era of *glasnost*? Ah, but the menacing red future is punctuated with dreams of 2007, where extremists look ready to touch off the initial British Revolution, and the 2007 hero and heroine are troubled with dreams of their 22nd-century counterparts. Who's dreaming whom? This witty nightmare has interesting ideas to offer, including a philosophical assault on doctrinaire materialism: I only wish I hadn't read it during a depressing General Election whose result was all too consistent with Martin's nastier alternative future.

More future gloom, with again a spark of hope, comes from the late Philip K. Dick in *Radio Free Albemuth* (Grafton 286pp £2.95): not communist Britain but fascist America. Dick weaves uneasy threads of autobiography into the novel, and makes it doubly disturbing – considering his own off-sane experiences – by introducing alien mentors who speak electromagnetically into good folks' brains, as in classic paranoid-schizophrenic delusions. The female government agent who entraps 'Phil' and others (seduction, blackmail, concealing drugs in victims' houses, etc) is six times as horrifying as any gang of thuggish secret police: Dick understood corruption and fear too well. I was less convinced by the visionary passages, though there's a great line when nervy politicians destroy the alien satellite: 'They shot down God.'

Dinner at Deviant's Palace by Tim Powers (Grafton 300pp £2.95) offers yet another horrid post-holocaust America, slightly resembling Jeter's wrecked, perverted world. The hero, Rivas, is a 'redeemer' rescuing brain-burned converts from a particularly unpleasant cult, looking like revivalist fundamentalist Scientology but concealing something worse. Powers's technique for putting across his unlikelihoods (alien psychic vampires, bloodsucking 'hemogoblins', robots built from prams and cocktail shakers) involves a lot of closely described pain. Rivas is no Indiana Jones who breezes in and out of peril: he keeps suffering more and more, even losing bits of himself, while improving in character from the purely mercenary bastard met in chapter one. Sizzling entertainment: but the sudden triumph over alien omnipotence doesn't quite convince.

Back in Britain, Geoffrey Household's *Arrows of Desire* (Penguin 136pp £1.95) presents a primitive and pastoral future Britain, administered by the benevolent Euro-African Federation: it falls rather awkwardly between two stools. There are traces of satire about black High Commissioners administering the Brits, fondly believing that these simple, happy-go-lucky natives regard them as all-benevolent fathers ... the Black Man's Burden, y'know. There's a hymn to Britain itself as a unique land, the love of which transcends one's birthplace or ignorance of the mostly lost English culture, even though *other* countries somehow don't attract such love from anyone. Neither theme is developed enough to save this slim book from looking unfinished. Even a throwaway joke about the lost lore of silicon chips is contradicted by the presence of sophisticated electronics, lasers, tracker-robots resembling Jeter's slow bullet, etc. Editors are supposed to spot these things.

Here are three concluding volumes. *The Hounds of God* (Bantam 334pp £9.95) ends Judith Tarr's 'Hound and Falcon' trilogy with rousing religious persecution of her elven elite in a well-researched alternate 13th century - all a bit reminiscent of Kurtz's 'Deryni' books, but Tarr is the better writer. *The Fall of the Families* by Phillip Mann (Gollancz 298pp £11.95) is the second half of a thoughtful, colourful space-opera in which devious but oppressed aliens throw off the imperialist human yoke, yay yay. The conclusion is oddly satisfying, but I was dubious about some of the psychological manipulations en route. *Master of His Fate* by J. Maclaren Cobben (Greenhill 247pp £8.95) apparently ends Greenhill's 'classic' reprint series: 1890 psychic vampirism with a scientific ('Nervous Ether') rather than supernatural rationale. Its historical interest isn't sustained by the feeble and florid writing.

The Alternate Asimovs (Grafton 349pp £3.50) should delight any new sf writer. It comprises the original drafts of three Asimov stories, *Pebble in the Sky*, *End of Eternity* and 'Belief', as rejected even by pulps like *Startling Stories*. The prologue to the original *Pebble* is so excruciatingly awful (as Asimov himself now agrees) that one can readily imagine its being rejected before the editor reached page two. Keep your dreadful unsaleable manuscripts for 40 years, goes the encouraging message, and Grafton will give you big money for them.

Don't miss Christopher Priest's hyperbolically strange *Inverted World* or Daniel Keyes's sadly moving *Flowers for Algernon* (Gollancz Classics at £3.50) - or Lucius Shepherd's terrific *Green Eyes* (Grafton 332pp £3.50), to be reviewed at length next month. You have my permission to miss André Norton's *Witch World* and *Web of the Witch World* (both VGSF £2.50), turgidly-written 'science fantasies' which must have looked fresher in the mid-sixties, before the glut of such material. Already reviewed here: *The Summer Tree* and *The Wandering Fire* by Guy Gavriel Kay (both Unwin £2.95) and *The Swords of Corum* by Michael Moorcock (Grafton 509pp £3.95).

As for the grim future ... the election was bad enough, but even I find it hard to credit a nightmare world where the Hugo nominations include *Black Genesis* by L. Ron Hubbard. Other shortlisted novels: Card's *Squeaker for the Dead*, Gibson's *Count Zero*, Shaw's *The Ragged Astronauts* and Vinge's *Marooned in Realtime*. Mind how you go. [Card won.]

August 1987

55 Sucking Them In

Recently I made the mistake of peeping into a forthcoming John Crowley novel. Just glancing at the three-page prologue couldn't do any harm, I thought.... Hours later, your reviewer returned to reality with two grudges: *(a)* against Crowley's *Aegypt* for being instantly, horrifically addictive, and *(b)* against virtually everything else for *not* being immediately compulsive reading.

One writer who can suck you in is Lucius Shepherd, whose *Green Eyes* (Grafton 332pp £3.50) opens with a serious sf interpretation of the zombie myth. Modified graveyard bacteria revive the newly dead via 'transcriptional processing of the corpse's genetic complement' ... a resurrection doomed to be short-lived as the bacteria consume the brain, burn down the optic nerve in a flare of bioluminescence: green eyes. Our 'zombie' hero predictably escapes from the research necropolis, but thereafter Shepard's plot keeps twisting away from the expected, into weird realms. In a lushly corrupt Southern US landscape, the psychic aspects of the technical miracle emerge, with developing talents of healing and perception better understood through voodoo cultists' rancid traditions. It's a richly strange, decaying world that you see through those green eyes.

Pat O'Shea's 'junior' fantasy *The Hounds of the Mórrígan* (Puffin 469pp £2.95) is high-spirited fun from the start despite being a mite heavy on the italics. The story is a long, straightforward chase with two kids pursued across real and mythic Ireland by agents of that local bitch-goddess the Mórrígan, helped in their travels by an engaging series of talking beasts and deities in mufti. I liked the Napoleonic earwig: 'If I have to be loony to be great – adieu, sanity; ze cost is but a trifle.' The comic-whimsical flavour recalls Masefield's *The Midnight Folk*; inept minions try to lure our hero to a fall by the somewhat elementary stratagem of erecting signs saying 'THIS IS A VERY SAFE ROAD. A BOY CAN CYCLE ON IT WITH HIS EYES SHUT ... TRY IT TODAY.' Things become steadily grimmer as the Mórrígan herself takes a hand, and there's plenty of inventive excitement before the end. A little kitchen-sinkish in its determined ransacking of Irish myth, but fun (as they say) for young and old alike.

Richard Grant's *Saraband of Lost Time* (Bantam 327pp £2.50) seems to go with M. John Harrison's reissued *A Storm of Wings* (Unwin 189pp £2.95). Both have a similar feel, with eccentric and rarely lovable characters pursuing chaotic courses in the decadence of a once high-tech society. Harrison was first in this field: *Storm* marks his transition from near-traditional science fantasy to oblique metaphysics. An apparent invasion of alien locusts proves to be something subtler, the arrival of a world-view incompatible with humanity's, and the philosophical infection of people who start seeing through multifaceted eyes. Fortunately, as in *The War of the Worlds*, this cuts both ways.

Harrison opens with terribly clotted prose (favourite words of the book: gamboge, nautiloid, mucoid, litharge), and *Saraband* is much more inviting. Grant's exoticism is diluted, his characters closer to the believable. What is the Overmind, that ultimate jewelled plot device created by a vanished civilization? We are never actually told outright, but obliquely all is revealed. The multi-sided power struggle has a nice flavour, as of civil servants in Gormenghast, and the hopelessly inadequate King is hilarious. Critics prefer *Storm*'s literary echoes and clever bits; but for all its excessive length, more readers are likely to finish *Saraband*.

Piers Anthony starts interestingly in *Wielding a Red Sword* (Grafton 368pp £2.95), fourth of his uneven **Incarnations of Immortality** sequence. Mym, proud Hindu prince and super-warrior, is manoeuvred into the spiritual civil service as Incarnation of War (previous books starred Death, Time and Fate), and as usual in this series, Satan hopes to take evil advantage of the new incumbent. The action is jerkily episodic and the ending a trifle hasty and contradictory, as though Anthony were typing faster than the speed of logic, but *Sword* lacks the major embarrassments of its two predecessors. [Such as mortaring large chunks of lightweight piffle – resembling PA's **Xanth** kiddy-fantasies – into supposedly serious plotlines.] What dissatisfies is the introduction of tantalizing conflicts which aren't developed. How can a devout Hindu begin to accept Anthony's massively Christian heaven and hell? No credible answer emerges.

Don't miss *Other Edens* edited by Christopher Evans and Robert Holdstock (Unwin 237pp £2.95), a collection of 14 new British sf/fantasy stories, containing excellent stuff by nifty authors from Aldiss to Watson. Me too, but you needn't read that one. Which reminds me: though I didn't write the opening of the famous collaboration *Earthdoom!* by me and John Grant (Grafton 303pp £2.95), it soon improves no end and becomes a richly lyrical study of how parodying the disaster-novel genre can swell authors' bank accounts. Could this be the finest book ever written? I confidently leave the answer to you.

For those who take horror seriously, there's no better craftsman than Ramsey Campbell. *Cold Print* (Grafton 365pp £2.95) collects his Lovecraft-influenced stories over a period of twenty years. A disarming introduction quotes hysterically overwritten early drafts ('It cannot be that abomination which I met in the nitrous vaults below Asquith Place!').... The stories show Campbell's development, from the very routine eldritch dread of 'The Church in High Street', via the midpoint of the title story's incidental use of a Forbidden Book to give a nasty porn-fancier his come-uppance, to the fine 'The Voice of the Beach'. In this last tale, a complete abandonment of the standard, all too spoofable Mythos props brings Campbell full circle to the interesting part of Lovecraft's incoherent vision: a universe of vast uncaring entities who may happen to wither our minds, but like editors are fundamentally not interested in us.

Other reissues: *The Mirror of Her Dreams* by Stephen Donaldson (Fontana 658pp £2.95) is the author's most straightforward fantasy but ends with a whopping cliff-hanger. Robert Silverberg's *To Live Again* (VGSF 231pp £2.95) reads well, a witty thriller where the Macguffin is a rapacious tycoon's mind and all the characters want its personality for their own. *Victim Prime* by Robert Sheckley (Methuen 203pp £2.50) is mostly a jaded rehash of old Sheckley themes. Jack Vance's *Trullion: Alastor 2262* (Grafton 229pp £2.95) combines space-piracy with the very implausible sport 'hussade' – like a team version of 'kosho', if you remember *The Prisoner*.

After Joy Chant's pleasant retelling of British myths from the *Mabinogion* and elsewhere, in *The High Kings* (Unwin 200pp £3.50), I lost patience with the backlog of routine fantasies. They failed the first-chapter test. I was not sucked in. You might be: 'Jonathan Wylie's' *The First Named* (Corgi 349pp £2.50) and *The Centre of the Circle* (Corgi 351pp £2.95) are Irishly followed by Kenneth C. Flint's *Champions of* and *Masters of the Sidhe* (both Bantam £2.50). Lawrence Watt-Evans offers *The Seven Altars of Dûsarra* and *The Sword of Bheleu* (both Grafton £2.95): 'Once more, Garth the overman rode his warbeast into the decaying frontier town....' Kathleen Herbert's *Ghost in the Sunlight* (Corgi 335pp £2.95) looks quite a high-class novel of dark-age Britain, while Elizabeth Scarborough's *The Unicorn Creed* (Bantam 340pp £2.95) explores the searing dilemma of a unicorn whose virgin captor is having second thoughts about this virginity lark. Other blazingly original titles are *The Wizards and the Warriors* and *The Wordsmiths and the Warguild* (both Corgi £2.95) by Hugh Cook, whose next book is not *The Wizard and the Warlord* (Corgi 332pp £2.50) by Elizabeth H. Boyer.

There are more, but even the titles are becoming curiously soporific....

September 1987

56 Dreamlands

Last night I had a terrible endless dream of having to read and review thousands of books, and woke to find it true ... but because this was a dream there were lots of peculiar and doubtless very Freudian elements thrown in, including chasms, railway carriages, bindweed, prune stones and bacon-and-tomato sandwiches. (Psychiatrists out there will please keep their conclusions to themselves.) Dreams are a tempting subject for fantasy, but a good story often isn't convincing as a dream: the *Alice* books are too logical, Cabell's *Jurgen* too consciously symbolic, *Finnegans Wake* too bloody erudite. One successful dream story, with the right non-sequiturs, surreal juxtapositions, and deliriously vivid trivia, is Kipling's 'The Brushwood Boy'. Here's another.

Bones of the Moon by Jonathan Carroll (Century 216pp £9.95) stars Cullen James, a happily married woman who in her second pregnancy starts having connected dreams. These involve hallucinatory journeys across a land called Rondua, in company with giant animals and the first child whom she chose not to have, searching for five Bones of the Moon. Glimpses of Rondua's wonders are carefully rationed, as are its oblique links with reality: a word, a name, a reminiscent event. Dream transitions replace the fantasy's traditional slow travel; dream logic spells out the personal name of each Bone but relegates major doings like 'our battle against the dancing Warm' to a sentence of offstage reporting. You're deliberately left wanting more.

Meanwhile, unpredictable flares of Rondua magic begin to erupt in Cullen's mundane life, and the dream quest moves down a dark road ('Follow the Dead Handwriting until you come to the Hot Shoes') towards the real world of urban violence. As in Carroll's fine novel *The Land of Laughs*, the apparent whimsies are heavily booby-trapped and the sudden conclusion leaves you shaken. Highly recommended.

Guy Gavriel Kay's *The Darkest Road* (Unwin Hyman 420pp £10.95) completes the ambitious 'Fionavar Tapestry', which has some claim to being the best trilogy written in conscious imitation of Tolkien. This isn't necessarily high praise: I prefer attempts to create something new, and Kay's assembly of bits from here and there suggests that a better title would be 'The Fionavar Patchwork'. King Arthur and Lancelot, hastily drafted in book two, add little to the tale. (Lancelot gets one good fight scene with an earth-demon; I groaned at his next escapade, a replay of 'The Lady of Shallott'.) Invoking the Wild Hunt twice in one trilogy smacks of desperation. And the final, expensive defeat of the arch-fiend, though sort of moving, has flaws: it seems feeble and Terry Brooksish for the all-potent unraveller of universes to fall to a common or garden cursed blade, and it's an error of judgement to make the crucial sentence shriek 'Look at me!' in italics.

The characters are generally good. The writing is OK, if a little florid in the prolonged, portentous tying up of loose ends which fills the final chapters. There are nice set-pieces: the demon fight, the proving of the dwarf-king, a voyage on a ghost ship. Kay has done well with shopworn materials; I have a sneaking hope that now he's got Tolkien out of his system, he'll write something better.

The Dragon in the Sword (Grafton 283pp £10.95) is the latest Michael Moorcock 'multiverse' fantasy, wherein the Eternal Champion wanders again through galleries of grotesques to zap unsporting Chaos and preserve the dear old Cosmic Balance. There's plenty of Moorcock's usual Bosch-like incidental invention, but his multiverse has by now been saved so many times in so many similar ways that one can't begin to take the current threat seriously. An interesting subplot features Ulrich von Bek, a fugitive from Nazi Germany who wants to cause Hitler's downfall and – by accident, and ironically without realizing it – does so. The pages turn painlessly. For Moorcock, presumably, this represents either a rest between more ambitious books or a quick fund-raiser to pay the rates. *Elric at the End of Time* (Paper Tiger £7.95) is a light-hearted pendant to two famous Moorcock series, its chief attraction being Rodney Matthews's highly appropriate paintings.

Bradley Denton's *Wrack and Roll* (Headline 406pp £3.50) is a high-energy novel of rock sf set in an implausible alternate 1979 with the Anglo-Chinese Alliance opposing the US/USSR. The manic, pseudo-streetwise narrative revolves round the hoped political clout of the band Blunt Instrument, whose clothes make punk look respectable and whose LP titles are tasteful indeed: 'After four years *Critical Mass* was still selling.' Can the force of music halt nuclear apocalypse? Only via unconvincing plot devices, but it's a good rousing read.

Famous US publishers Simon & Schuster have entered the UK market, and sf consultant David Pringle has achieved a list consisting 100% of books edited by David Pringle. *A Touch of Sturgeon* (S&S 235pp £10.95) collects eight fine stories by Theodore Sturgeon, perhaps the only long-established sf writer to have consistently worked not only with gadgets but also with strong human emotions. *Interzone: the 2nd Anthology* ed. Clute, Pringle and Ounsley (S&S 208pp £10.95) offers 15 selections from Britain's best and only current sf magazine – a good sampler if you're one of the pitiful outcasts who don't subscribe.

Several more collections are to hand, all uneven but with moments of excellence. Kim Stanley Robinson's *The Planet on the Table* (Orbit 241pp £2.95) displays a wide stylistic range, high points being 'The Lucky Strike', telling of a subtly different 1945 where one man flying in that B-29 over Hiroshima thought twice, and the unclassifiable 'Black Air' with its religious visions on a beaten ship of the Spanish Armada. David Brin's *The River of Time* (Bantam 295pp £2.50) is more conventional but contains some nice genre-mixing: in

'The Loom of Thessaly' the weaving Fates encounter spaceborne weaponry, and 'Thor Meets Captain America' offers a nasty world where Hitler *did* achieve his dreams of recruiting supernatural aid. Pity about the ambitious openingstory's offputting badprose with stucktogether wordpairs.... *Dangerous Visions* ed. Harlan Ellison (Gollancz Classics 544pp £6.95), the 1967 32-author collection which poked at all sf's taboos, remains a quirky mix of achievement and top-of-the-voice hype, of stories still brilliantly fresh and stories already moribund two decades ago.

Space is short. These previously recommended books are well worth buying in their new editions: *The Deep* by John Crowley (Unwin 176pp £2.95), *Journey Beyond Tomorrow* by Robert Sheckley (Gollancz Classics 189pp £3.50), *The Ragged Astronauts* by Bob Shaw (Orbit 310pp £2.95), *Slow Birds* by Ian Watson (Grafton 224pp £2.50), *Soldier of the Mist* by Gene Wolfe (Orbit 335pp £2.95).

The following caused me no actual pain: *A Place Among the Fallen* by Adrian Cole (Unwin 352pp £2.95), *The Stalking* and *The Ghost Dance* by Robert Holdstock (both Century £11.95, comprising 4 of the 6 'Nighthunter' books), *The Forgotten Beasts of Eld* by Patricia McKillip (Orbit 217pp £2.50), *Star Gate* by André Norton (VGSF 192pp £2.50), *The Brave Free Men* by Jack Vance (VGSF 224pp £2.50).

Consigned to oblivion: *Foundation and Earth* by Isaac Asimov (Grafton 510pp £3.50), in which disappointingly little actually happens; *The Best Mysteries of Isaac Asimov* (Grafton 345pp £10.95), hugely inferior - despite interesting new items - to *Asimov's Mysteries*; *Starclipper and the Galactic Final* by Brian Earnshaw (Pied Piper 127pp £5.95), inoffensive juvenile sf with terrible science (maximum spaceship power is '20 ergs', which amount of energy would suffice to lift this page by about 0.004 centimetres); *The Lost Road and other writings* by J.R.R. Tolkien (Unwin Hyman 455pp £16.95), more gleanings from the great man's copious waste-baskets.

Back in the discontinuous land of dreams, the most unexpected surprise of the month was Paul Kirchner's cartoon book *The Bus* (Orbit £2.95). Some of this is reminiscent of early Glen Baxter, back when Glen Baxter was funny, but these explorations of the Bus in American society are mostly original and weird [but would begin to pall, I think, as fast as Baxter did]. They are nicely sophisticated humour: consult the book for the page on which this is contrasted with unsophisticated humour. And don't tell me which sort I do in this column.

October 1987

57 Overload

Every sf publisher in Britain made a special effort for the World SF Convention over the August bank holiday. High-rise towers of the resulting review copies totter over me as I write. My postman hasn't recovered from lifting the huge crate of books sent by Gollancz....

The fattest is Greg Bear's *The Forge of God* (Gollancz 474pp £11.95), a lengthy near-future story which at first looks like a reworking of the classic problem of establishing contact with inscrutable alien visitors. Seen through a mosaic of individual viewpoints, the situation shifts perspective until the book becomes a moving and quite impressive account of how ordinary people might accept the destruction of the world. Although it's a gripping read from start to finish, much of the early material disappoints in retrospect: each tantalizing contact with apparent aliens proves to be part of a massive disinformation programme, a sideshow intended to distract a high-tech civilization from what's really going on. Since the attackers' main weapon is so completely lethal and unstoppable by pathetic Earth technology, the camouflage and the (literally) millions of lesser weapons seem pointless – photogenic rather than strategically sensible. A good nasty read, though, with a flicker of optimism: in the jungle Out There, someone is on our side.

The Urth of the New Sun (Gollancz 372pp £11.95) is Gene Wolfe's long-awaited pendant to the **Book of the New Sun** series. It opens years after the tetralogy's end, with Severian a lowly passenger in a continent-sized sailing ship travelling through space and time to another universe where he's to be judged as worthy or unworthy to bring the New Sun which could cataclysmically rejuvenate tired old 'Urth'. Tricks, traps and disguises abound, and as usual Wolfe is careful to avoid explicit answers: even more than the tetralogy, this book ends in a metaphysical quagmire where the important meanings lurk between the perfectly clear things which are actually said. Light is cast on minor points like the origin of the Claw of the Conciliator, or Severian's link with the bygone demigod Apu-Punchau, but the old enigmas remain. Fascinating and infuriating. The Ship scenes are wonderful.

John Crowley's *Aegypt* (Gollancz 390pp £11.95) is almost literally too good to be true. It's a present-day novel flirting with the whole musty fascinating complexity of Renaissance magical science; with the secret land of Aegypt and the secret histories of the world which are not found in textbooks. It opens with a 'Prologue in Heaven', as a scryer of 1582 sees a soul set out from 'ringing infinite void at once larger than the universe and at its heart', carrying an unknown message: there are to be four books, and by the end we may see the message delivered. Meanwhile the failed historian Pierce Moffett is researching the hermetic tradition and its reflection in a dead novelist's remarkable works, which include a different version of *Aegypt*'s prologue.... Meanwhile in the 1580s, Giordano Bruno carves a swathe of heresies across Europe and carries his fiery teachings towards London. *Aegypt* is the beginning of a long, strange journey, and is very beautifully written.

How does an established author come to terms with early, minor work? Some let it vanish; Asimov and Silverberg tend to reprint old stuff with slightly embarrassed introductions; Benford and Bishop have done conscientious rewrites. Brian Aldiss offers a highly ingenious approach in *Cracken at Critical* (Kerosina 192pp £12.50): make the hammy old stories even hammier, and present them between inverted commas as the efforts of a fictional sf hack. A brief framing narrative, 'The Mannerheim Symphony', encloses two mini-novels by 'Jael Cracken' - an old Aldiss pseudonym. 'The Impossible Smile' (1965) is incredibly awful, with a *deus ex machina* for every plot turn; 'Equator' (1958), an entertaining tale of alien political bluff, unreels at breathless pace as everyone runs around chasing and shooting everyone else to fill out the thin storyline. Note the careful contrast between 'Cracken's' sloppy wish-fulfilment endings and the bleak loophole which Aldiss-1987 considers the happiest way out.

There are no inverted commas around the plot devices of Gordon Dickson's *The Forever Man* (Sphere 375pp £3.50), wherein people can by sheer will-power transfer their minds into spaceships, and as a side-effect gain the ability to *(a)* see without eyes, through anything; *(b)* lift the ship's dead weight by mental force alone; *(c)* wander disembodied through space, able to see and steer along lines of gravitational stress, whatever those might be. In fact all this is necessary to Dickson's plot, in which a disembodied man and woman (inhabiting the same ship) try to understand two lots of standard sf aliens, one race being Very Boring And Literal-Minded and the other Extremely Whimsical And Near-Omnipotent. Mostly it's good, solid entertainment with some thoughtful asides - though I'm never very convinced when a grim emotional impasse is transformed into a happy boy-meets-girl ending in just a few lines of dialogue on the last page.

The Stainless Steel Rat Gets Drafted (Bantam 256pp £9.95) is the seventh of Harry Harrison's Rat books (chronologically, the second). Another lightweight romp, with the youthful master-criminal's revenge plans requiring him to suffer the horrors of induction into an army (based on Harrison's own experiences - 'I had to tone it down, the real thing was too horrible to be funny.') ... very much the mixture as before.

In *Wizardry and Wild Romance* (Gollancz 160pp £10.95), Michael Moorcock offers a characteristically quirky and iconoclastic view of fantasy. He's refreshingly rude about idols, pushes his own enthusiasms without mercy (counting the index references, one gathers that Moorcock's buddy M. John Harrison is the most important fantasy author around), doesn't pretend to give comprehensive coverage (John Crowley is barely mentioned; the popular authors Guy

Gavriel Kay, Barbara Hambly and Judith Tarr don't appear), and, unusually for a critic in this field, has a sense of humour (Terry Pratchett is deservedly praised). Moorcock's chief touchstone is style, for which he has a fine ear: good verbal effects can win his seal of approval for books which overall I reckon aren't so wonderful, while Moorcock has no time for authors who write flatly, even if like Tolkien they can achieve a notable cumulative impact. [His most irritating habit is to keep presenting short extracts as evidence of favoured authors' wonderfulness, without any indication of *why* this passage should be regarded as so wonderful.]

Moorcock likes Terry Bisson's *Talking Man* (Headline 192pp £2.50), whose quest to save the world from having never been involves a demented car-chase from Kentucky to the North Pole: enjoyably offbeat. *Tuf Voyaging* by George R.R. Martin (Gollancz 374pp £10.85) comprises seven linked stories of Haviland Tuf, eccentric cat-lover and freelance ecological engineer, who drifts around the galaxy making people's eco-problems even more complicated. Solid entertainment, with Martin's meaty storytelling overcoming some shopworn ideas. *Sector General* (Orbit 196pp £2.50) contains four more tales of James White's intergalactic hospital: its founding, and ever-intuitive Dr Conway's struggles with three implausible new varieties of alien patient. *In Yana, the Touch of Undying* (Grafton 332pp £3.50) shows the talented Michael Shea still being influenced by Jack Vance, as his semi-competent hero lurches through bizarre and lurid episodes en route to the place where immortality is supposedly available: witty and erudite, though sometimes confusingly written. *Best New Science Fiction* ed. Gardner Dozois (Robinson 615pp £4.95) is a huge compendium of the best short sf published in 1986, chosen by a fine and reliable editor.

Notable reissues include Shirley Jackson's disturbing *We Have Always Lived In The Castle* and *The Haunting of Hill House* (both Robinson £2.95); Richard Matheson's semi-classic *I Am Legend* (Robinson 151pp £2.95); Fredric Brown's dotty *What Mad Universe* (Grafton 238pp £2.95); R.A. MacAvoy's engaging *Tea with the Black Dragon* (Bantam 166pp £1.95); Robert Holdstock's powerful *Earthwind* (VGSF 245pp £2.95); Bob Shaw's eccentric *Medusa's Children* (VGSF 184pp £2.50); and Judith Tarr's very readable *The Golden Horn* (Corgi 272pp £2.75).

I also seem to have copies of Asimov's *Pebble in the Sky* (Grafton 226pp £2.95), Clarke's *The Songs of Distant Earth* (Grafton 238pp £2.50) and Tolkien's *The Lays of Beleriand* (Unwin 393pp £3.95). But nobody's perfect.

November 1987

58 Something Different

When the mighty kitchen ranges of fantasy publishing are churning out endless suet pudding, a nibble of something exotic can seem twice as good ... though too much caviar can make you nostalgic for suet pud. For me, the month's most *different* item was Alan Moore's and Dave Gibbons' comic *Watchmen*, now in a one-volume edition (DC import or Titan, £9.95). The modern myth of the Superhero is curiously powerful despite its usual silliness; *Watchmen* lovingly disassembles the mythology into bloodstained cogs and ratchets, concluding with the famous quotation *Quis custodiet ipsos custodes?* Ask Mummy to translate it for you.

It's difficult to approach Clive Barker's *Weaveworld* (Collins 722pp £10.95) with an open mind, knowing that this was a hotly sought property acquired in a £500,000 deal. Too often, colossal sf/fantasy advances lead to pretentious, substandard work ... thus *Weaveworld* is a pleasant surprise. Much of it is an exciting thriller of chases, evasions, hair's-breadth victories and defeats, chequered with passages of bright and dark fantasy. 'Dark fantasy' is today's posh word for 'horror'; Barker's considerable talents in this area lead to a few gobs of gratuitous nastiness, and also some terrific creations.

Initially the bewildered good guys and deeply knowing baddies are mixed up in a search through modern Liverpool for the Fugue, a fantasy land which is a crammed anthology of Earth's magic places, saved from an eighty-years-past threat by being woven into a carpet. At a critical moment when all seems lost, Barker achieves a fine effect by the cutting of a vital stitch – whereupon this entire country explodes into three-dimensional existence within the chief villain's house. Many complications follow, with magical effects which ring true (bar one bit of fudging: the central sorcerous plot device, a kind of reversible sausage-machine, conveniently proves to function as a photocopier too ... metaphorically, that is). One particularly memorable invention is the destroying angel which forms the final threat, a blazing, abstract and pitiable horror recalling those cosmic visions of wheels and eyes in the Book of Ezekiel. I enjoyed this exuberant, moving holiday from routine trilogies, and you will too.

You don't expect conventional fantasy from Terry Pratchett, either. *Mort* (Gollancz 221pp £10.95) is the fourth of his popular Discworld books, this time giving a central role to that eternally grim and skeletal straight-man,

Death. The Reaper makes the mistake of hiring a not very competent apprentice (Mort), to ease the workload while he investigates mortal pleasures with such bewildered enquiries as TO HEAR LOUD MUSIC IN HOT ROOMS IS FUN? Meanwhile, by interfering with the predestined assassination of a gorgeous princess whose soul he's supposed to collect, Mort throws the Discworld's operations of Time, Fate, Reality and Demented Footnotes into even more total chaos than usual. After a slightly less successful experiment in *Equal Rites*, Pratchett has sussed the combination of hilarity with a tight and tortuous plot, and the rest of us would-be humorists hate him for it.

Nearly twenty years after his previous novel *The Last Unicorn*, Peter Beagle returns with *The Folk of the Air* (Headline 330pp £4.95), which as you might expect is extremely well written - especially in the carefully rationed scenes of magic. The vaguely familiar plot comes up fresh in Beagle's hands: 1980s Californian mediaevalists, a bit like the Society for Creative Anachronism or Britain's 'Barony of the Fair Isles', throw themselves into the past only to discover that when one recreates such olden hobbies as witchcraft, the past has teeth. Soon a mock battle becomes real with the arrival of appalling supernatural aid. Meanwhile, a retired goddess (the megalithic rather than the good-looking variety) is working nearby as a lay therapist, and ends up battling the forces of evil while the hero Farrell stands around getting caught in the gears. Parts are excellent; parts are high-class padding, esoteric combat lore etc.; small portions are what certain critics call 'California crap', with that 'you should *feel*, never *think*' message which I find deeply suspect. Perhaps I'm disappointed that a writer as gifted as Beagle should only touch the surface of his mediaevalists, indulging in a few neat ironies ('God's teeth, sirrah, beshrew me, but I'll put it to thee plain, thy man's but a mewling, doddering old puppet of the military-industrial complex') but avoiding the depths of motivation which he's well fitted to plumb. H'mm.

Despite my pleas for innovation, there's nothing wrong with a good bread-and-butter fantasy novel which steers clear of the genre's frightful verbal and situational clichés. Barbara Hambly is a reliable provider of the straight goods: *The Witches of Wenshar* (Unwin 339pp £2.95) follows loosely from *The Ladies of Mandrigyn* as likeable mercenary-turned-mage Sun Wolf looks for magical training, and along with his lady lieutenant Starhawk lands in a fantasy detective story. Who or what is responsible for the supernatural killings which afflict the labyrinthine Court of Wenshar ... and why? It's easy to make a mystery when only the author knows precisely how this world's magic works; but Hambly issues enough clues for a Christie-like semblance of fairness, and the pages turn increasingly quickly.

Diana Wynne Jones favours a less straightforward approach, diverting you with hilarious invention and deadly observation of disintegrating family life as she lays fuses for her concluding fireworks. *Fire and Hemlock* (Methuen Teens 341pp £1.95) updates the old ballads of Tam Lin and Thomas the Rhymer, with a girl getting (rather remotely) involved with a musician who's somehow in thrall to a modern-day fairy queen. She has to evade subtle magical opposition without more than dim instinctive notions of what's happening; most of the time, indeed, she's struggling to recover memories erased by a sorcerous coup. There's almost too much complication in this ambitious book. When the fireworks finally begin to erupt in earnest, the change of pace from earlier, leisurely enigmas is liable to leave you battered and baffled. Read it warily.

Ian Watson's *The Power* (Headline 232pp £2.50) is one to read nervously. Grown men have pulled their own heads off at the thought of the hideously inventive Watson being loosed on a cringing horror genre. Indeed there are the usual revolting set-pieces, but the main thrust is political. After routine arguments about nuclear bases and peace camps, Watson sets off the apocalypse and moves into a bleak new territory where the suppurating Power - parasitic on humankind and with all the usual unpleasant tastes of diabolic powers - becomes the survivors' sole *ally* against something worse, the sterile wastes of nuclear aftermath. But for all his acuteness, Watson isn't immune to this genre's habitual gloating tone of 'Look, Mummy, see how disgusting I can be....' Zombie rape, crucifixion on a bicycle, all that kind of thing.

Two novels highly characteristic of their authors' current work are R.A. Lafferty's *Serpent's Egg* (Morrigan 166pp £10.95) and Piers Anthony's *Statesman* (Grafton 367pp £2.95). As so often before, Lafferty moves from determined whimsy to a bloody, religiously informed and inconclusive finale: almost any paragraph is a delight to read, but in contrast to his earlier works they don't add up convincingly.

Anthony's overall scheme in this latest chunk of **Bio of a Space Tyrant** is clear - to offer enlightened liberal solutions to world political problems, mapped by ponderous allegory on to a Solar System where Jupiter is America and Saturn is Russia plus China. It's the execution which is dire, with its humourless efforts to characterize all women by their performance in bed with hero Hope Hubris, and the extremely ad-hoc nature of the solutions. The key to peace proves to be world unification behind the Dream of Space, which from the 1980s end of the allegory is not helpful.

Also: *Less Than Human* by Charles Platt (Grafton 238pp £2.95) is moderately funny sf pastiche, especially if you think hippies are hilarious. Pohl's & Kornbluth's *Gladiator-at-Law* and Samuel Delany's *Babel-17* (both Gollancz Classics £3.95) are good reads: Earth threatened by commercial monopolies and deadly grammar from space, respectively. Philip Dick's *The Preserving Machine* (Grafton 413pp £3.50) may be the first uncut British edition of this nifty collection - does *your* copy have the 72pp story 'What the Dead Men Say'? Gosh, I'm erudite today.

December 1987

59 Forbidden Fruit

When you're sternly told not to read something, the temptation to disobey is irresistible. Earlier this century risqué authors would pray to be denounced from the pulpit, thus ensuring eight weeks on the best-seller list. Maggie Thatcher has given similar vast publicity to Peter Wright's ghost-written *Spycatcher*... I couldn't resist scanning the American edition, which reveals that *(a)* British counter-intelligence sounds just like John Le Carré on an off day, full of dodderers questioning each other about whether in the 1930s they dallied with forbidden red fruits or had it off with chaps; *(b)* Wright's alleged scientific qualifications have got distinctly unconvincing since the 40s; *(c)* despite boggling stories of incompetence, the book would have vanished without trace if it hadn't been for our kindly Government's outrage.

Another one that certain interests don't want me to read is Russell Miller's *Bare-Faced Messiah: The True Story of L. Ron Hubbard* (Michael Joseph 390pp £12.95). The Church of Scientology opposed its publication with threats and court injunctions which as with *Spycatcher* didn't claim the text was *untrue*, merely that it shouldn't be revealed. (Action dismissed in Chancery Division as 'mischievous and misconceived'). Regular readers will know I'm one of the late L. Ron's greatest fans; even so, this book amazed me. Miller, a British journalist, has done the kind of exhaustive research possible only in America, where public files are accessible via the Freedom of Information Act. (We lucky Brits just have an Official Secrets Act.) Without rancour or moralizing, Miller traces Hubbard's incredible career from pulp sf writer to guru of Dianetics/Scientology to unmistakably paranoid loony. Even before Hubbard took to issuing grandiose and provably untrue versions of his careers as 'war hero', 'nuclear scientist' etc., he was a compulsive teller of tall tales. Even before he'd built a repressive organization of his own, he routinely tried to get even with people – including his own wife – by denouncing them to the FBI as communists. As early as 1951, FBI investigators filed him as 'a mental case'.

This mightn't seem to bear on Hubbard's sf (despite snippets about *Battlefield Earth*, which L. Ron boasted he'd written in one month), but there are messages for sf fans. The 1987 World SF Convention, held in Brighton, was plastered with expensive Hubbard publicity aimed at buying him respectability as a great sf author (on the strength of his dire posthumous 'dekalogy') and patron of the arts. Many sf pundits suspect we're seeing a whitewash job, funded indirectly by a thoroughly dubious cult in the hope that cleaning up the image of its founding father will reflect favourably on, and gain recruits for, Scientology itself. Read *Bare-Faced Messiah* for a solidly researched portrait of the man whose official Holy Writ once declared that opponents 'may be deprived of property or injured by any means ... May be tricked, sued or lied to or destroyed.' In case your editor's getting nervous, I should add that this column expresses only my personal opinions.

I have a high opinion of Isaac Asimov's honesty and integrity: in sharp contrast to Hubbard, he's always been committed to truth. For decades, it seems, he's fretted about his novelization of the film *Fantastic Voyage*, whose terrific idea (medical team in miniaturized sub enters bloodstream to perform surgery from within) and nice effects suffered from a trite storyline with gaping logical holes – the worst of which, like the abandonment of a full-sized submarine inside the patient, Asimov struggled to patch. *Fantastic Voyage II: Destination Brain* (Grafton 392pp £10.95) is an attempt to rework it 'properly', as a typically cerebral Asimov novel. The pseudoscience of miniaturization spreads unchecked, and the number of references to Planck's constant must establish an sf record. The mission is slightly different, to extract crucial thoughts from a nearly dead man rather than achieve any cure. Too much of the rest is similar, but lacking that former indefensible melodrama. Taking in air at the lungs! Speeding though the chambers of the heart before the next beat brings disaster! Attacking a brain clot with laser fire! By rationalizing all this away, Asimov has thrown out the excitement with the bathwater. The replacement notions are either OK but minor (having the sub imitate the electrical signature of glucose so that cells actively welcome it in) or major but dodgy (woolly stuff about brain-wave analysis and pseudo-telepathy, topped with the supremely silly idea of detecting the nearest neuron by waving two unconnected EEG leads as a directional antenna). An impeccably idealistic finale is, alas, no compensation for the loss of the old cheap thrills.

Retailers like books packaged in neat categories: sf, fantasy, romance, gore. Michael Bishop's *Who Made Stevie Crye?* (Headline 309pp £4.95) has a cover which screams 'horror' but conceals one of those unclassifiable gems. Stevie Crye is a hopeful writer, a pleasant widow with two kids, struggling to make a living from the typewriter ... difficult when after repairs, the machine starts typing by itself at night, transcribing and distorting her dreams and fears. This modest touch of the supernatural is merely a jumping-off point. As the typewritten lies blend in with the 'real' fiction of the book, the narrative steers a sometimes horrifying and sometimes blackly funny course into the metafictional territory of works like Christopher Priest's *The Affirmation*. The writing is nifty in the extreme; the characters are successfully realistic, sympathetic, hilarious or unnervingly creepy: sometimes all of these together. Every possible double meaning in the title gets its due airing, and I defy you to predict the outrageous final chapter. Buy this one.

Blood of Amber (Sphere 215pp £2.75) continues Roger Zelazny's 'new Amber trilogy', which began with *Trumps of Doom*. The initial pentalogy had occasional classy moments amid the longueurs; but nowadays Amber feels like a D&D campaign which has been running too long, with too many unbalancing 97th-level characters. Take our hero Merle Corey, son of the pentalogy's

Corwin, who is not merely super-strong and magically gifted and able to walk between worlds, but is the only person ever to have mastered the contradictory Patterns of Amber and Chaos, giving him all sorts of handy ad-hoc abilities such as being able to call up swords, beer or pizza from nothingness, kick sand in people's faces, etc., in addition to which he carries a cuddly, sorcerously animated and prophetic strangling cord called Frakir, plus the routine set of Trumps allowing multiverse-wide travel and communication, plus some mysterious extra Trumps as emergency plot devices, and then there's this magical blue crystal stuff, and as well as that our hero's spent odd weekends constructing Ghostwheel, a supernatural computer complex of world-shaking powers, and when in spite of all this he finds himself in a particularly tight spot, Zelazny hastily makes him a shapeshifting Lord of Chaos as well.... Enough. Too much. Despite a few good wisecracks and neat ideas, Corey's plethora of powers can't revitalize the over-familiar Amber gimmickry and revenge plot.

Which isn't to say that an aged plot can't still enthral. Hwaet! 'From off the moorland's misting fells / Came Grendel stalking ...' From the 8th century, *Beowulf* still carries power; in 1981, actor Julian Glover tried to recreate the experience of listening to a scop, and devised a 'one-man performance' version in modern English, with lengthier digressions omitted. In print (Alan Sutton Publishing 135pp) it reads very well, especially aloud, and is finely illustrated by Sheila Mackie. Something to spend those Xmas book tokens on.

So now I'm discussing epic fantasy reprints first written down *circa* AD 1000. This column has drifted into the habit of ending with a condensed reprint list, usually books already reviewed here: functional but possibly tedious ... though you wouldn't want to miss Ramsey Campbell's eldritch *The Hungry Moon* (Arrow 428pp £2.95), in its third paperback printing by the time they sent me a copy. Anyone who prefers (or hates) this issue's longer reviews of fewer books, and general omission of mere namechecks, should let me know. Act without thinking! This means you!

January 1988

60 Ghost Stories

After a hard day down the mine, hacking away at the living pulp of the bookface and carving out exquisite, gem-like reviews, the last thing I want in my spare time is more of the same. (Note the tough, macho sound of that sentence. Writers are flabby types who sit on their bottoms all day, and love to cheer themselves with muscular talk of hacking and deadline-racing and writers' workshops.) Some of you think I just can't get enough terrible sf/fantasy/horror to read, and also that I'm in charge of buying fiction for *White Dwarf*. Wrong on both counts, I'm afraid ... and apologies to all whose 600-word trilogies in the great tradition of Tolkien have been returned with a terse form letter.

I've been known to say austere things when existing trilogies sprout add-on volumes: but Frederik Pohl is special, one of the few 1950s sf stars who still produces tight, high-quality work. *The Annals of the Heechee* extends the *Gateway* trilogy, which began with humanity ransacking the high-tech relics of alien 'Heechee' civilization. Book 2 told us where the vanished Heechee went, and book 3 told us why: this super-race is in hiding from the inimical 'Assassins' who are busy collapsing the entire universe in order to rebuild it their way.

In *Annals* the hero Robinette Broadhead, who suffered through the first two books and 'died' in the third, gives an ingeniously convincing description of his new life as a machine-stored intelligence amid chatty programs and other electronic ghosts. Meanwhile, the Assassins are stirring from their hideout within the weirdest object in the universe: the revelations about what they are and why they do their dastardly deeds are so cleverly inevitable as to hint that Pohl's been planning this finale for years. Though the quality of writing stays at an unflashy 'good average' throughout, this is a neat example of hard sf as it sometimes used to be. [But is still much inferior to *Gateway*.]

Pohl strikes again in the non-fact chiller *Chernobyl* (Bantam 355pp £4.95), an impressively researched fiction or 'faction' using imaginary characters to tell the real story of that 1986 reactor explosion and its aftermath. Soviets and their problems are sympathetically handled: imagine a role-playing game wherein you run Chernobyl and must choose between accepting substandard materials produced in haste to meet end-of-month targets, or delaying an already overdue reactor schedule.... Avoiding Evil Empire stereotypes, Pohl does his own country a service by reminding us that lots of Americans detest the knee-jerk, anti-commie paranoia which sometimes seems to be the US national stereotype. The technical background is all there too, in palatable form.

[Post-communist light was shed on this book in the Ukrainian fanzine *Chernobylization*, which commented that – as seems inevitable, with hindsight – Pohl badly misrepresented the flavour of day-to-day Soviet life.]

The sf world has a guilty habit of lavishing new praise and attention on its best writers, too late, when they're dead. Now the royalties can do Alfred Bester's ghost no good, I suppose his classic *Tiger! Tiger!* will soon appear in luxury memorial editions.... Philip K. Dick's reputation has grown since his death, and his oddest work is at last available as a hardcover: *Valis* (Kerosina 256pp £13.95). Initially, sf readers were baffled by its dippy metaphysics and glowingly opaque catch-phrases like 'The Empire never ended.' On second inspection, *Valis* flips like an Escher puzzle-picture: the insane revelations which in an sf novel would have to be 'true' are mere background to the blackly funny story of Horselover Fat, the brain-fried sf hack who's one aspect of Dick himself.... Dick suffered weird hallucinations/revelations late in life, conceivably because of an undiagnosed stroke, and asserted control over this internal chaos by fictionalizing it: as straight sf in *Valisystem A* (later published as *Radio Free Albemuth*, where Dick's ghost-voices became radio instructions from an alien satellite), and in *Valis* as a sort of fictional autobiography. Here a hard-headed Dick gently mocks the weird metaphysics of Fat through a series of wonderfully insane conversations and misadventures: a slapstick tightrope-dance over a pit of potential insanity, a wrestle with demons in which – both inside and outside *Valis* – Dick is the unexpected winner. Kim Stanley Robinson contributes a wise afterword.

Sometimes it's irresistible to tackle two books together. *Bronwyn's Bane* by Elizabeth Scarborough (Bantam 286pp £2.95) is a venture into the light-comedy fantasy territory whose bestselling exponent is Piers Anthony. Meanwhile Anthony himself has a crack at rustic horror with *Shade of the Tree* (Grafton 352pp £2.95) ... shade, ghost, geddit? Scarborough manages a few nicely funny scenes with her tale of a cursed princess who's unable to tell the truth, and stumbles off on a disaster-ridden quest, etc. Where *Bronwyn* scores over Anthony is in restrained description (Anthony always overdescribes and repeats himself), in snatches of believably humorous conversation (the dialogue in *Shade* is particularly awful, especially from the mouths of supposed children – and how come Anthony's modern US characters keep calling the sky a 'welkin' and talking about 'raining canines and felines'?) and in the ability to crack a mildly sexy joke without getting downright gross, ponderous and embarrassing.

Where Anthony would normally score over Scarborough would be in inventiveness (*Bronwyn* is short on interesting ideas; so, for Anthony, is *Shade*) and logic. He'd have worked much harder on the technical challenge of that curse, not letting Bronwyn get away with occasional true statements, or defy the spirit of the curse by uttering falsehood in tones of heavy irony. From Anthony we'd also expect a tidy ending, resolving problems with that inhuman fairness so often found in fairy tales. *Bronwyn* just peters out, with the curse going away for no definite reason and the heroine contracting her putative first child into twenty years of slavery – a sequel hook, no doubt, but a highly unsatisfactory note on which to end a novel. Less glibly crummy than the finale of *Shade*, though, where the Tree responsible for interminable forebodings and sinister hallucinations is converted to niceness by a spot of telepathic computer systems analysis.

Lurking behind an awful and misleading cover, Lisa Tuttle's *Gabriel* (Sphere 216pp £2.99) is a chiller which actually does chill. Dinah is a young widow, Gabriel her late husband (shown in blazing flashback as the kind of charismatic Peter Pan you love or hate but never simply *like*), and there are feathery hints of a kind of reincarnation. Tuttle concentrates on small fears, things which (as opposed to the likelihood of putrescent zombies crawling from the toilet) do actually worry people: fear of embarrassment, of losing control, of doing something shamefully out of character. The ghostly threat to Dinah contains no violence, even metaphorically, but kept me on the edge of my seat as *Shade of the Tree* never could.

Of the three great sf devices which Einstein declared impossible - antigravity, faster-than-light ships and time travel - the last is most productive of new twists. Diana Wynne Jones offers a rationale for ghosts in *A Tale of Time City* (Methuen 285pp £8.95), with a young World War II evacuee snatched into a Time Patrol headquarters vaguely like Asimov's Eternity. In doomed Time City, vivid impressions are left on the tatty and worn-out fabric of reality by important events past or future (you don't necessarily know which), a puzzle of predestination which three well-pictured and totally misguided kids unravel to save the city and the universe. Though the cavalry comes over the hill so effectively in the final chapter that one isn't sure the kids' efforts were entirely necessary, it's a pleasant read and often very funny.

If I lived in Time City, I'd be haunted by agonized ghosts of the cruelly rejected manuscripts mentioned above. Constructive advice follows. *(a)* Send a stamped addressed envelope to cuddly Sean Whatsisname at the *Dwarf* editorial doss-house, asking for *Dwarf*'s submissions guidelines. *(b)* Buy the 1988 *Writers' and Artists' Yearbook* (Black 528pp £5.95), which lists hundreds of possible markets and tells you how to submit. Though why, in a listing which includes 32 specialist publications for the blind, and 200 mostly obscure Commonwealth titles, should *White Dwarf* and all but five of Britain's many computer magazines be omitted as 'too small'/'too specialized'? I make this complaint every year. It never does any good.

February 1988

61 Back to Work

Somewhere out there are people who think monthly magazines are written the day before they hit the stands. In fact the Langford you read here is a ghostly voice from the past, still contemplating a further twelve months' reviewing after the wild debaucheries of Xmas and New Year. These debaucheries involved reading stacks of books I'd paid for and didn't have to review: some deserve a belated mention.

Russell Hoban's *The Medusa Frequency* (Cape 143pp £10.95) is a weird mixture indeed, as unsuccessful author Herman Orff suffers imaginary dialogues with his word processor and imaginary voyages into deep myth inside his own mind, where the decaying but gabby head of Orpheus keeps manifesting itself in strange disguises ('The Thinking Man's Cabbage') while the outside world throngs with stranger encounters. After flashbacks to all the women in his life, Orff emerges with the inspiration for *The Seeker from Nexo Vollma*, a pulp-sf epic described with mingled affection and contempt, ready for lucrative cerealization on the backs of cornflake packets. The book is soufflé rather than cornflakes: a light and tasty treatment of material which could be depressingly Heavy.

I also indulged myself with Rudy Rucker's *Mathenauts* anthology (Arbor House 300pp, import shops only), 23 nifty sf and fantasy stories in mathematical vein, some familiar, some quite genuinely mindboggling – Norman Kagan's classic (but until now very hard to find) 1965 story 'The Mathenauts' actually presents a delirious version of cyberspace from times before personal computers or William Gibson had been heard of. Additionally: Peter Ackroyd's *Hawksmoor* (various editions) with its unforgettably black vision of crossed timelines and sinister compulsions built into London's religious architecture, and a murder mystery called *Bimbos of the Death Sun* by Sharyn McCrumb (Windwalker 219pp £1.95), latest addition to the sub-sub-genre of novels set at sf conventions. McCrumb deploys her research with kitchen-sink enthusiasm, neatly caricaturing several sf fan and author stereotypes but striking an unconvincing note when all these wildly different and often mutually intolerant types sit down to play D&D together. In fact the dull D&D finale tends to spoil a potentially amusing squib: possibly some reference to the game is compulsory in this series, published by famous patrons of literature TSR.

Back in reality, Harry Harrison continues his *West of Eden* with *Winter in Eden* (Grafton 486pp £3.50); a third volume is scheduled. (Book 2 ends with 56pp of background, expanded from 42pp in book 1. Can we extrapolate to 70pp in book 3, 42pp of which devoted readers will thus pay for three times?) The dead weight of research which gave book 1 its worthy-but-stodgy quality is now lighter: Harrison has built up his world of savage humans and high-tech reptiles, and has more elbow room to tell a story. Somehow, though, a strong story never emerges. Several plot threads intertwine, involving groups of characters travelling from A to B or meeting up with C: much of this feels like positional play in chess, moving pieces into place for the next book's jolly exciting endgame. There's one good sf frisson as our heroes realize the nature of the excessively unconvincing biological weapon deployed against them by *dinosaur sapiens*, and one routine sf reversal as a entire cityful of inimical reptiles is overcome – almost exactly as in book one – by one man exploiting the cold-blooded foes' carefully planted weakness. These are tricks and turns of mere short-story weight, while the epic potential lies elsewhere: with the long-term inevitability of either human/dinosaur coexistence or one species' extinction, with the advancing glaciers that can't be conveniently bluffed or set fire to. Maybe in book three ...?

John Crowley's *Beasts* (Gollancz Classic 184pp £3.95) reappears as a 'classic' for the second time in the history of this column. I've always thought it the slightest of Crowley's books, but it's undeniably a fine blend of modern beast-fable and near-future sf in a fragmented USA. DNA tinkering has produced the leos, hybrids of human and lion genetic material: strange 'people' with a simplicity and grandeur which shine from the page. The tortuous political complications are orchestrated by the result of another, one-off experiment: Reynard, human/fox, a master plotter without a plan, a lost soul forever hoping to find his own identity in fables about foxes. The slightest of Crowley's works? I recant: anything by him demands to be read and reread.

Two unrelated Jack Vance books: *The Asutra* (VGSF 187pp £2.50) and *Star King* (Grafton 204pp £2.50). The first concludes the trilogy beginning with *The Faceless Man*, one of Vance's best novels for its combination of baroque sociology, colour and wit with a sympathetic hero who (as in most of the best Vance sf) is compelled to overthrow his world's rulers to preserve his own integrity. Most of the freshness leaked out of this series by book three: *The Asutra* isn't actively bad but seems perfunctory, the result of over-hasty production. By contrast, *Star King* opens a five-book series (**Demon Princes**) of which the *last* two are particularly enjoyable: Vance didn't rush to finish but waited for inspiration. This is a different brand of sf, pure space opera whose hero is a glum, dispassionate instrument of vengeance. Around this chilly and in the end rather futile core, Vance constructed a gaudy stage-set of brilliantly daft ideas, quotations, scenery and grotesques. The revenge plot is banal in the extreme [though neatly undermined by anti-triumphalist boobytraps], but the pace is headlong and it's impossible not to admire the backdrop.

Has Cordwainer Smith's *Quest of the Three Worlds* (VGSF 184pp £2.50) really not appeared in Britain before? Smith was unique, sometimes irritating with his bouts of cuteness, repetition and doggerel, but far more often achieving effects never thought of in sf before. The four *Quest* stories concern three exploits of the unlikely hero Casher O'Neill – 'On the Gem Planet', 'On the Storm Planet', 'On the Sand Planet' – plus a separate story using him in a minor role. The backgrounds are fully as garish as Vance's, though more poetic: but O'Neill is a man of ideals and compassion, and in each episode the awesome hardware is less important than O'Neill's making of the correct, unobvious ethical decision. ('Ethical' may be an unfamiliar world to the more enthusiastic hack-and-slash role-player: try looking in the dictionary.) In their far-out, mystical way, these aren't the most accessible of Smith's many linked stories: a tasty sample, though.

Further back still, from 1953 when even your aged reviewer hadn't become cynical (that came in 1954), Eric Frank Russell's *Sentinels from Space* (Methuen 227pp £2.95) is a simultaneously heart-warming and awful reminder that genre sf could be compassionate and metaphysical all those years ago. Heart-warming, because Russell's optimistic vision of the importance of life, mind and soul indicated a new direction in sf, away from mere nuts, bolts and galaxy-wrecking hyperdimensional vortices. Awful, because metaphors about 'great bright-eyed moths beating gloriously through the endless night' fit terribly into a threadbare plotline consisting largely of psychic mutants swapping clichéd wisecracks and mayhem. More modest and – on its own level – successful is his 1956 *Three to Conquer* (Methuen 211pp £2.95), a fast-paced thriller with a lone, wisecracking telepath battling alien virus invaders who infect and, as in *The Puppet Masters*, generally Take Over people. On both books, Methuen have struck a blow for sf tradition by commissioning covers you're embarrassed to be seen holding on a bus.

Still shattered and hungover from the aforementioned debaucheries, your reviewer forced himself to glance into further works which therefore may not have had a fair trial. Patrick Woodroffe's *The Second Earth: The Pentateuch Retold* (Paper Tiger 143pp £7.95) is beautifully produced and author-illustrated, but its prose content asphyxiates in the rarefied air of quasi-biblical High Style which even Tolkien couldn't quite bring off. Katherine Kerr's *Darkspell* (Grafton 369pp £6.95) opens with three pages of notes on pronouncing an invented Celtic language (if you're not going to use a real one, what's wrong with phonetic spelling?), followed by a double-page map, followed by opening text containing three rapid outbreaks of the word 'dweomer': if the language is fake-Celtic, why the Old English? To give a warm glow to D&D fans, I suppose. I lost heart at this point. Tony Richards's *The Harvest Bride* (Headline 279pp £2.95) is plugged by Ramsey Campbell as 'A supernatural thriller with a real sense of menace'; it opens with the words 'Mallory was dead. Yes, I know that's close to the beginning of another book ...', and was at once hurled aside on grounds of excessive cuteness. I must try to be nicer.

March 1988

62 100,000 Millidwarves

These anniversaries return with alarming speed: it's only a year of brain damage since I celebrated surviving my 50th column, and *Dwarf* gave me a nice picture of a birthday cake for the sixtieth (also a cardboard champagne bottle and a photograph of a large cheque). This is where, as usual, I hope no one remembers my first contribution in issue 2, or the embarrassingly pseudonymous and blackmail-worthy bits between then and my emergence with this column in issue 39. Onward, onward.

[The occasion was the 100th issue of *White Dwarf*.]

And as the latest fantasy contenders come over the last fence and into the straight, it's a rank outsider leading the pack, and yes, yes, I can't believe it, the bookies (Honest Langford, The Old Firm, Est. 1853) offered 100-1 against, but streaking first across the line despite its enormous weight penalty is nothing less than Stephen Donaldson's owner-ridden filly *Mordant's Need: A Man Rides Through* (Collins 661pp £11.95)!

This concludes the fantasy of *The Mirror of Her Dreams*, which ended on a cliff-hanger with the enemy at the gates and our heroine wrongfully accused, but with such a plethora of spare plot-devices lying around that the suspense largely concerned in which of numerous ways things could be sorted out. In volume two, Donaldson convolutes his plot further before tidying up: meanwhile the most egregious and dispensable invention, that sf mega-warrior straight out of Marvel Comics, is kept in a minor role, and the spectacular Ultimate Weapons (mirrors from which appalling nasties can be conjured) are generally left unused on grounds of ethics - at least by the good guys. Allegiances shift in an interestingly complicated way: the besieging forces of book 1 become allies, while a major 'villainess' is now praised for doing the right thing in being driven to villainy by the master plan of a Good King who only pretends to be senile in order to lure his enemies. This master plan is so tortuous and masochistic, so reminiscent of John Le Carré or Anthony Price's *Our Man in Camelot* or Thomas Covenant himself, that it has to be explained several times in order to make sure readers get the hang of it - unfortunately sounding less sensible with each new telling.

For the finale, numerous armies, mirrors and special effects are deployed; the heroine and boyfriend - both predictably revealed as magical adepts of new and different kinds - triumph over the plausible arch-fiend and his henchmen.

Donaldson's much-dreaded excursions into unexplored dictionaries are happily forgotten (though some old favourites like 'anile' appear, to remind us of what he can do). This two-volume story truly is a ripping yarn, with a nice line in magic-mirror technology and real if flawed attempts to get to grips with motivation. Why is the villain so villainous? The ultimate answer might sound a bit trite – 'Because it was there' – but with Sauron, Lord Foul and many others we never even heard the question.

Donaldson could usefully have boiled out lots of repetition, especially when in Significant Italics, and his efforts to end passages with striking sentences can be clumsy or laughable ('He felt like crowing.'), but after all my brickbats he deserves a pat on the head. This author is genuinely improving.

Colin Wilson's *Spider World: The Delta* (Grafton 304pp £10.95) also improves on its predecessor. *The Tower* was filled with irritating nonsense about biologically implausible giant spiders, thuddingly clichéd computer mentors, and routine pulp-sf doomsday weapons. Having set up these garish fantasies and laid the groundwork for a slave revolt of re-armed humanity against the death spiders, Wilson now changes gear to a more metaphorical level. This features a vital spiritual force which in keeping with the pulp approach emanates from alien vegetable demigods, but is really George Bernard Shaw's 'Life Force' from *Man and Superman* and *Back To Methuselah*, in a clever plastic disguise. Since this energy enhances everything except people – insects grow huge, sinful humanity is unchanged because Not In Tune With The Force – our hero Niall shoulders his doomsday weapon and heads for the burgeoning Delta where it originates....

Meanwhile, Wilson replays his own perennial philosophy, rousing Nietzschean stuff about concentration, forcing oneself beyond inner limits and generally achieving a Triumph of the Will. Only thus can we become worthy to grab the world back from the spiders. Niall twigs this point, throws away his ultimate weapons, and gets on the right side of the Force. The metaphor now goes ape, with the Force manifesting itself to the unfortunate spider lord and informing it peremptorily that Niall is now boss – rather short-circuiting the message about self-improvement and self-reliance. We conclude with Man (sorry, but Woman is kept firmly in her place) and Spider and Beetle going hand-in-palp into a finer future. *The Delta* is better than promised by *The Tower*, but the crudeness of its sf tropes detracts from the more interesting Wilson philosophy.

Something completely different: *The Dorbott of Vacuo, or How to Live with the Fluxus Quo* (Paper Tiger 79p £12.95) is a finely produced 'Tale of Utterly Cosmic Insignificance' written and illustrated by Patrick Woodroffe. Something that bothered me about Woodroffe's over-ambitious *The Second Earth* was that the surreal dottiness which kept creeping into his paintings didn't match the book's doomy, apocalyptic text. Now he reveals himself as a surreal and dotty writer. His shifting, grotesquely peopled world is 'an intricate web of narrative excess and gross literary tomfoolery', full of such hazards to navigation as 'busking pipe-organs, itinerant semi-detached bungalows and volcanoes of no fixed address'. The illustrations are spiffy; the text puts it in the same class of eruditely funny 'children's' books as *Fungus the Bogeyman*, which should be praise enough.

Tanith Lee is one of the few British authors who can do an original, colourful fantasy *or* sf novel. *Sabella* (Unwin 157pp £2.50) stylishly mixes the genres into the high-intensity story of a lady vampire on colonized Mars, where wolves have two moons to howl at. Though likeable, Sabella makes the mistake of killing the wrong (or possibly the right) man, goes on the run, suffers unspeakable privations, and winds up with a new lover and a new awareness. The lurid fantasy and sf images mix well, like shaken oil and vinegar, but Lee eventually takes it too far by introducing a dubious sf rationale for the vampire theme (as though you tried to mix salad dressing *really thoroughly* by adding detergent: it works, but the flavour ...). High marks nevertheless. The cover is by novelist Gwyneth Jones, which after discovering Patrick Woodroffe's writing skills is enough to make me wonder if the Renaissance has returned.

Sometimes real oddities arrive – like *The Game of the Pink Pagoda* by Roger Moss (Flamingo 269pp £3.95), which presumably came this way on the strength of the word 'game'. (Penguin once sent a whodunnit, considered interesting to *White Dwarf* readers because there was a garden gnome on the cover.) It opens with a witty non-explanation of the only game there is, condensed into selected archetypes and philosophical rules, and steadily obscures the issue with a selection of 'model games' which are mini-stories pastiching a wide range of genres and styles. Reminiscent of Calvino's *If on a Winter's Night a Traveller*, but Calvino's digressions followed a strict architecture while Moss's just seem to go on until the author gets tired. Enjoyable, though, and quite fun.

A clutch of reprints to conclude. Arthur C. Clarke's *Rendezvous with Rama* (VGSF 256pp £2.95) is a plotless sf travelogue, but a very good one. Olaf Stapledon's *Star Maker* (Penguin 264pp £3.95) is one of sf's great metaphysical works: austere, chilly, a vision in which universes change and pass like bacteria in a culture. *Bug Jack Barron* by Norman Spinrad (Grafton 384pp £3.50) is the archetypal Sixties sf novel: brash, rude, lurching, highly media-conscious, and I still like it despite vast embarrassments. Ian Watson's *Queenmagic, Kingmagic* (Grafton 239pp £2.95) offers a light-hearted fantasy-game romp with an expertly worrying conclusion.

Your editor's given me an extra page again, but fear not – it's only for this month.

• • •

The Grimoak and the Speardemon ... Darkplague of Dreadrune ... Circles of the Daggermasters ... The Treestone of Firefate ... Fellshadow ... Baleshield of Direpain ... The Skullmoon of Chaos-Spear ... The Platypus of Doom ...

That last one is actually a genuine sf title, a very strange book by Arthur Byron Cover. The others are merely typical of what arrives in fat brown parcels, every week and every month, until sometimes I start to feel rebellious.

Brassprince and the Snakesword ... Greensong Fimbulwinter ... Ghoulmirror of the Wandspell ... Fogdeath ... The Chaosweird Uprising ... The Knightscroll of Farpain ... The Doomhollow of Greenfever ...

There is something hideously predictable about the titles and even the contents of the present fantasy glut. In fact I rather like a nice rousing read which doesn't make you feel you have to be constantly on your literary best behaviour: but the words and the archetypes are distinctly wearing thin. Dragons and unicorns and elves and dwarves and the Wild Hunt; swords and rings and skulls and amulets and runes; whatever burning archetypal force used to lie in these images, its batteries are being seriously drained by over-use. To make them glow again, authors and game-writers need to put in (as it were) some serious and creative recharging work. Too few seem to have the talent or inclination. And thus:

The Quicklaw and the Heartrose ... Madsword ... Strangewand Enchanter ... The Balebride of the Runewell ... Doomlions ... Starkmoon of Blackworm ... Dwarfmagic ... The Grim Dawn of Doomfear ... Woesword of Bonewither ...

By now, if you're computerate you'll have rumbled me. In a recent fit of disaffection – 5,271,009 new fantasy titles arrived and I had a cold – I whipped up a random text generator program. When this was fed with a few hundred words culled from the fantasy backlog, it spewed out endless pages of titles which for the most part couldn't be told from the real thing. Some were quite interesting near-misses:

A Wizard of Earthgrave ... The Colour of Mage ... Sword of the Rings ... The Staffrune ... The Wounded Bane ... The One Leper ...

Eventually I got bored, and threw in some less orthodox words which led to suspect titles like *Gleetleper of Vomitspawn* or *Mindbane of Dwarfeditor*. After which I moodily turned the attention of the program to horoscopes ('ARIES: expect an embarrassing encounter with a tall, jaded, drunken book reviewer.') and computer-style prose ('The on-line RS-232 debugger mode occasionally implements an equal-opportunity iso-ASCII paper-white pop-up motherboard philosophy.') A program to generate *Sun* editorials can't be far off.

The Dragon Lord ... Soulstorm ... The Princess of Flames ... Trollnight ... Darkspell ... Drowntide ... The Dreamstone ... Swordspoint ...

No, you guessed, those are all real and arrived here in the last year or so. I have a dark suspicion that were it set to generate plot outlines, my program could gain commissions to write large numbers of trilogies. If the idea of this vast tide of unoriginality is depressing, remember that it's one of those chicken-and-egg situations in which – all together now – We Are All Guilty. The starving authors write identikit fantasy epics because the publishers demand them. The publishers package them to look exactly the same as each other, because the public (you) apparently prefers to buy more or less the same thing again and again. Members of the reading public sometimes complain that they'd read something new and different and wonderful if it were available, but it isn't, so everything must be the fault of the authors. And so on, forever.

When I look back over my own years of criticism in these pages, I reckon I've got off pretty lightly. For one thing, it's provided me with a limitless supply of bitchy opinions, the nastiest of which were collected into articles and sf convention speeches with titles like 'The Dragonhiker's Guide to Battlefield Covenant at Dune's Edge: Odyssey Two' and 'Trillion Year Sneer'. Such efforts probably helped me pick up a couple of Hugo awards last year: so I owe it all to you lot.

(Even the little parodies of sf and fantasy which I've contributed to *White Dwarf* and other places now look like being collected together and published by a new outfit called Drunken Dragon Press – and if the name sounds odd, wait till you read the Anne McCaffrey spoof. I haven't decided whether this literary event should get a glowing review or a very bad one in 'Critical Mass'. Which is more likely to make you perverse lot buy it? I wonder.)

The most soothing thing to do when criticism seems all too much is to look back at other, better critics and discover that not only did they have to work harder than me, they too felt pretty pessimistic about the state of the art. Bernard Shaw got deeply gloomy in his three years of dramatic criticism from 1895 to 1898 in *The Saturday Review*, a magazine which was presumably the cultural equivalent of today's *Times Literary Supplement* or *White Dwarf*. During those years he bunged in *weekly* essays longer than my columns, totting up to nearly 1000 pages of small print in the Collected Edition of his works. His successor Max Beerbohm stayed in the same hot seat for twelve years, and *his* collected criticisms came to more than 1700 pages. What's worse, both Shaw and Beerbohm wrote well enough to stand re-reading today, when the plays are mostly dead and forgotten. My only chance of immortality is via some anthology of Silly Misguided Quotations published by New Era early next century, in which I will be gleefully mocked for my incredible obtuseness in failing to realize that L. Ron Hubbard is the greatest writer of this or any other age.

Another bygone critic, James Agate, makes me feel even more slothful by publishing (in his multi-volume autobiography *Ego*) annual estimates of the saleable output he produced each year. 1935: 555,000 words. 1936: 505,000 words. 1937: 508,000. On average, this corresponds to writing one and one-tenth columns the length of 'Critical Mass' every day of the year, without holidays or weekends. Blimey. I did at one stage collect my first 50 columns, the product of four years' work, into an indexed booklet called *Critical Assembly* (ever such limited distribution). It looks very famished by comparison with the giant critics of yore.

Still, my collected critiques to date should be useful in my plan to make this column last even longer than Max Beerbohm's in *The Saturday Review*. Careful analysis of the past Langfordian output should provide a vast databank of key phrases to be fed into the aforementioned text generator program, which is tastefully called DRIVEL. Armed with this deep and intricate knowledge about how I write, DRIVEL should have no difficulty in generating an endless stream of insightful reviews which will make it unnecessary for me ever to open a review copy again.

Let's give the program its inaugural run right here. Stand by! History is about to be made!

'*The Weirdbane of Hyperspace* by Arthur C. Asimov (Gollafton 12pp £999.38) is without doubt indeed probably a book which arguably will be better than L. Ron Donaldson. Furthermore, it ineffably exemplifies a deep metastructure which implies a intentional load of dingo's kidneys. Recommended to masochistic real-time completists or anyone who likes pop-up motherboard menu interface debugging protocol. *Lepermage of Elfspasm* by Anne McGuin (Unpengwin 943pp £0.12p) exemplifies an intentional failure in narrative plot device protagonist character frogspawn interfacing to the battery-powered VT52 assembler network cardboard box. VIRGO: a tall, alcoholic critic will ineptly approach you one day this evening and say *Spawnflower of Rotpelvis* (Heinlein C. Collins £120pp) is the best Hubbard-compatible since *Direthrone of the Punkmage*, except perhaps ERROR TYPE B37F STRING OVERFLOW

FATAL BRAIN SPASM comparable to Tolkien at his best. EDITOR: today you will enjoy an overwhelming Scorpio-compatible syntactic on-line impulse to say, That's Enough Of This Rubbish ...'

All right, all right, but just wait until I get the program's data files straightened out. There are possibilities here.

[Ansible Information later marketed this program as 'A.I.Q.', with exciting data files to generate Shakespearean verse, hi-tech computer babble, appalling recipes, dictionary-of-quotations rejects, etc, etc. And, of course, fantasy titles.]

April 1988

63 Twice-Told Tales

It's that magic time of the year when a reviewer's fancy turns to thoughts of skiving off. Usually, long-term readers will know, I manage to catch coughs, colds and 'flu, and fill the column with a hypochondriac springtime whinge. This year, in addition to all the above, I had a close encounter of the third kind – the first kind being when you merely see a murderously approaching taxi, and the second being when you leap successfully out of its way. Horror publishers should bid high for close-up colour snaps depicting my several square feet of lurid injuries....

I did groan through a few books, most of which seem to be by Greg Bear. *Strength of Stones* (VGSF 221pp £2.95) was his second, a fix-up of shorter pieces: like his first novel *Hegira* it features a fine idea, a few well-drawn characters, and a finale which self-destructs in its determination to burst your frontal lobes with mindboggling sense-of-wonder. On a strangely isolated colony world, strangely named God-Does-Battle, people once lived in automated mobile cities. But one day long ago, the city-minds got together and – after the equivalent of the Laws of Robotics logic-chopping so familiar from Asimov – decided to throw out the unworthy inhabitants and let them revert to barbarism in the worldwide deserts. By the time of the book, the legendary cities are also running down, and we get one routine story ending with an awfully familiar sf cliché, one good one with a nice clash between a disassembled city on the march and the local Attila the Hun, and one over-the-top one. The mix is about average for Bear.

The Infinity Concerto and *The Serpent Mage* (Century 342/343pp £5.95) add up to a single, hefty novel, the same author's contribution to fantasy. Not heroic fantasy exactly: Bear makes a worthy effort to mingle the mundane and magical elements, eschewing most of the standard props like unicorns, swords, cross-country questing and magic talismans, while seeing with an sf writer's eye how a ghetto of humans and half-breeds might feel in the shifting land of the Sidhe, and not being afraid to tackle the sf problem of having the entire fantasy population arrive on Earth as their magic realm breaks up. A particular Mahler symphony and 'Kubla Khan' are potent 'songs of power' (the latter, of course, unfinished), the Loch Ness Monster is a shape-cursed and exiled mage, and the much-abused hero's magical training has the gritty discipline of Zen warriorhood. It's all very nearly a very fine effort.

The snag in Bear's thinking man's approach to fantasy is that largely it fails to sing – to conjure up 'things higher or deeper or darker than its surface', in Tolkien's words, or as you-know-who said, 'charm'd magic casements opening on the foam of perilous seas in faery lands forlorn'. Interesting and intelligent stuff, nevertheless.

Gordon Dickson's *Way of the Pilgrim* (Sphere 529pp £3.50) is another fat one, solid sf this time. Stop me if you've heard it before, but these invincible aliens the Aalaag have taken over Earth and reduced us to domestic animals, and no physical retaliation is possible since just one nine-foot Aalaag in his combat gear is more than a match for all puny Earth arsenals, and Standard Plot Device A (pinch aliens' technology, turn it against them) is ruled out too, but you knew it, the rebellious human spirit cannot be tamed, and one man almost inadvertently creates and then becomes the fiery symbol of resistance, which however inappropriately is a Pilgrim, and after much agonizing delay he saves the world by a vast and sacrificial (for other people) gesture which rather implausibly persuades the Aalaag to pack up and depart because (thinks our hero) they have been shown that humanity is forever proudly untamable, only for the final scene to reveal in one of the book's few ironies that the Aalaag take a less flattering view of us. Yes, we've read it before. The aliens are moderately good, with problems of their own; the hero is a bit of a pain, spending most of the book trying to be a self-serving bad guy with such woeful ineptitude that one is relieved for all the wrong reasons when (as foreseeable long in advance) he reverts to his true nature as a sententious saver of worlds. It passes the time pleasantly, but its bouts of worthy realism are at odds with the golden-oldie plot.

In Angus McAllister's *The Krugg Syndrome* (Grafton 218pp £2.50), the Krugg are invincible telepathic invaders who do the traditional alien thing of Taking Over Minds, only to find a bit at a time that the human condition (especially in Glasgow) is a distraction from invasion plans, while the human body is capable of much curious pleasure not available to the Krugg form (i.e. sentient trees). In essence it's another oldie, famous from a Sheckley story, but McAllister plays adroitly for giggles and produces an engaging effect of seediness. The invaded hero recalls Nigel Molesworth of *How To Be Topp* fame (even to the extent of datedness: 12-sided threepenny bits, beatniks and teddy boys are all mentioned), struggling with the dusty paraphernalia of life in a ghastly solicitor's office and a ghastlier lodging-house, intermittently recalling his Krugg destiny for long enough to move some new offender to the top of the extermination list. 'After calm and rational consideration I have concluded that the Earth would be a better and more efficient planet without the following. (1) Mrs McSnidey ...' A cop-out ending seemed possible, but the author has more sense. Any alien scourge whose most cogent effort consists of writing THE KRUGG ARE COMING on toilet walls is OK by me.

Ideal Commonwealths (Dedalus 416pp £7.95) is a quirky compendium from this offbeat publisher: four little-read classics of utopia construction, being More's *Utopia* itself (1516), Bacon's *New Atlantis* (1629), Campanella's *City of the Sun* (c.1602) and Harringay's *Oceana* (1656). The introduction by Henry Morley seemed strangely old-fashioned yet familiar: I tracked it down in his 1885 anthology of the same name and closely similar contents, and could only admire Dedalus's thrift. These weighty works of early political sf are worth examination, but unlike the next offering aren't lightweight reading for train journeys.

Don't Panic: the Official Hitch-Hiker's Guide to the Galaxy Companion by Neil Gaiman (Titan 182pp £3.95) is at first sight a surprisingly slim vol. On second thoughts, when you think how remorselessly self-consuming the Hitcher phenomenon became - how every related joke was recycled and repolished, every scrap and snippet of anecdote captured in print to annotate spin-offs like *The Original Radio Scripts* - it appears that Gaiman must have worked horribly hard to scrape up so much newish stuff. Perhaps the oddest item: a nine-page abandoned treatment of *Dr Who and the Krikkitmen*, wherein the good Doctor is confronted by the invincible terror of the entire plot of *Life, the Universe and Everything*. If you're a fan you'll already have rushed to buy this; if not, you'll have fallen into a profound stupor by about the second word of this paragraph.

Books I Did Not Receive For Review ... *2061: Odyssey Three* by Arthur C. Whatsisname (Grafton 254pp £10.95), about which I've heard fairly dismal reports, alas; *Violent Cases* by Neil Gaiman & Dave McKean (Escape £4.95), another reminder that anyone dismissing all 'comics' as juvenile trivia is talking through an orifice your editor would rather I didn't mention - very strange and original, this; *The Tale that Wags the God* by the late James Blish (Advent 290pp £12.50 import), a long overdue third collection of his sf criticism, with a good bibliography. While I have 'flu, my collaborator Brian Stableford hasn't dared call round with copies of the new, cheap Paladin edition of our *The Third Millennium* - I'm sure it's wonderful anyway, but restrain yourselves and don't buy more than six copies each.

May 1988

64 Another Mixed Bag

Christopher Priest once pinpointed the temptation lying in wait for any reviewer who tackles a mixed bag of unrelated books. This is the litcrit urge to fudge up a Common Theme, a cosmic generalization which *(a)* provides a Procrustean bed which for continuity the books are then chopped or stretched to fit; *(b)* will be totally forgotten by the time the next column's material suggests a different and contradictory theory of literature. I hope this isn't too good a description of past opening paragraphs here.

The barren land of Trilogia, famous for its sterile wastes, has developed a few oases. Most eagerly awaited is Bob Shaw's *The Wooden Spaceships* (Gollancz 294pp £10.95), successor to *The Ragged Astronauts*. Book 1 established Land and Overland, planets which impossibly (in our universe) orbit each other within a common atmosphere, and described the epic balloon migration of Land-dwellers to Overland, fleeing ecological disaster. In *Spaceships*, the plague-carrying remnants of Land society mount a crazy invasion: there's war in the 'cold arena' of interplanetary air, with balloons, bows, musketry and - literally - wooden spaceships. Rousing stuff! Meanwhile on Overland, an odd subtheme emerges, involving cursed farmlands infested with alarming insects; when in his flesh-creeping mood, Shaw can make a woodlouse horrifying.

You'd expect this to link with the ecological background, the real shadow on Overland being that unless inhabitants stop exploiting the brakka trees which are the major source of fuel and durables, the same eco-disaster will recur with (this time) no escape hatch. Instead the plot veers off through real interplanetary vacuum to a distant third world, Farland. The journey there is terrific, but to justify it Shaw introduces a plethora of plot devices: aliens on Farland, alien spores from somewhere else, an Ezekiel-style flying saucer, a superperson who recites background information in telepathed italics. The story purrs along, but if it were a car I'd say its classic lines were obscured by too many bolt-on goodies.

The Enchantments of Flesh and Spirit by Storm Constantine (Orbit 318pp £3.95) is 'The First Book of Wraeththu' - how *do* you pronounce that double 'th'? - and proves to be intelligent and well-written. God knows what it's about.... The background is a run-down future wherein our sort of degenerate humanity (which stays remarkably consistently in the background despite retaining such odd skills as genetic engineering) looks likely to be replaced by

Wraeththu, mutants who are hermaphroditic, dangerous and sexy; they'd all be rock stars if rock still existed. This is fantasy in that the mutation is contagious, like vampirism: our hero Pellaz duly undergoes 'inception' and begins life anew. Like so many genre heroes, he (now he/she) is marked for a mighty destiny thanks to inner qualities which others tell him about but which we have to take on trust: they seem to consist largely of looking *absolutely terrific* in black leather with lots of heavy silver ornaments. There are effective passages of violent mysticism and raw magic, reminiscent of the fantasies of Carlos Castaneda. (The symbolism can be equally impenetrable: chapter 8's title makes no sense at all.) Some oddities may be resolved later; the unlikeliest features of this new, punkish and anarchic race are a rigid caste system and plans for a monarchy. Maybe King/Queen Pellaz will start doing rather than being done to. Constantine, a coiner of vivid images, is evidently a writer to watch, carefully.

Today's best-selling sf book is Whitley Strieber's ludicrous tosh *Communion*, which reports a lifetime of arcane UFO experiences. (For excellent reasons, just about all experienced UFO investigators - both pro and con - distrust such 'repeaters' who claim mindboggling encounters every month.) The book you won't see on the bestseller lists is Philip J. Klass's sensible response, *UFO Abductions: A Dangerous Game* (Prometheus 200pp £13.95). Klass has accepted the thankless, unglamorous task of pointing out the consistent lack of hard evidence for fashionable 'abduction' cases, the ignored experiments in which persons carefully chosen for lack of interest in UFOs have under hypnosis produced fantasies indistinguishable from 'real' accounts elicited by hypnosis (after all, everyone's seen *Close Encounters*), the curious way in which UFO-believer hypnotists can persuade virtually anyone to recall experiences agreeing with that particular hypnotist's belief.... [This is not the Philip Klass whose sf appears under the name William Tenn.] A good overview of oddball science appears in *Pseudoscience and the Paranormal* by Terence Hines (Prometheus 372pp £12.95), written as a textbook but effortless to read, with something to annoy everyone - few will object to Hines's scepticism about telepathic yoghurt (p303), but the withering attack on Freudian symbolic analysis may come as a surprise.

Robert Irwin's *The Mysteries of Algiers* (Viking 203pp £11.95) is still further from my usual sf/fantasy stamping ground: a political thriller set in the French colony as the Foreign Legion prepares for its last stand (1959-60) against FLN insurgents. But Irwin is still dealing in metaphysics, and the tortuous reality/fantasy conflicts of his *Arabian Nightmare* and *Limits of Vision* are echoed by impossible disparities between a double-agent Legionnaire's poorly understood Marxist metaphysic and the atrocities to which it leads when pitted against dreadful opposition. 'Who wills the end, wills the means.' Our anti-hero Roussel descends step by step through a maze of means and ends, through fort, desert and Kasbah, to a conclusion full of appalling ironies that no theory could predict. Very readable, very nasty.

With nods to Verne, Lovecraft, and Tom Swift, James Blaylock's *The Digging Leviathan* (Morrigan 275pp £11.95) is a delightfully surreal mix of suburban whimsy and chthonic weirdness. Only the strange genius of juvenile prodigy Giles Peach can attain the fabled centre of the earth, either by land (hence the title) or by sea, and the convoluted but unhurried plot deals with the efforts of variously seedy, eccentric and downright bad characters to ponder the surrounding mysteries, flee through beckoning sewers, unmask the strange fish, and hitch a lift.

Another small – indeed, minuscule – press offers *The Drabble Project* (Beccon Publications 110pp £5.00; 75 Rosslyn Avenue, Harold Wood, Essex, RM3 0RG) ed. Rob Meades and David Wake, a collection of 100 'Drabbles', being stories *exactly* 100 words long. Many famous sf authors are represented, too many to enumerate; many mere jokes and frightful clichés appear; there are several genuinely nifty stories. Chesterton, an amateur of toy theatres, once remarked that on a stage so small it was simplest to do vast things – the Day of Judgement was easily staged, while character development was *verboten*. These amusing squibs tend to be like that. There is only one possible length for this review.

Paperbacks ... *Howl's Moving Castle* (Methuen Teens 212pp £1.95) is Diana Wynne Jones at her most exuberant: densely plotted, full of ensorcelled characters in strange guises, and often extremely funny, it bends the structure of the traditional fairy-tale just about as far as it will go. Highly recommended. *Dad's Nuke* by Mark Laidlaw (Grafton 284pp £2.95) sounds like routine satire, with middle-class American families investing in lasers and missile launchers to 'defend the neighbourhood', but expands the picture to show a remarkably ugly future of foreshortened lives, fundamentalist computer-brainwashing and babies adapted to consume plutonium waste – some of it almost incomprehensibly nightmarish, but leavened with an evil sense of humour. Much gentler is Bob Shaw's *Who Goes Here?* (VGSF 253pp £2.95), one of the funniest time travel stories ever, with Shaw's amazingly daft 'origin of the Mona Lisa' tale thrown in for this edition.

L. Sprague de Camp offers a loose trilogy in *The Goblin Tower*, *The Clocks of Iraz* and *The Unbeheaded King* (Grafton £2.95, £2.50, £2.75), picaresque 'light' fantasy whose hero is generally better at outwitting foes and bedding serpent-priestesses than gorily hewing limb from limb. Mildly pleasant reading, but again and again de Camp frustrates you by assembling surefire amusing situations which in the event aren't funny – they actually seem to improve in retrospect, as your own imagination touches them up. Odd.

Reprints, all good stuff: *The Space Machine* by Christopher Priest (VGSF Classics 363pp £3.50), a deadpan scientific romance combining *The War of the Worlds*, *The Time Machine* and much tongue-in-cheek wonderment. *Consider Phlebas* by Iain M. Banks (Orbit 471pp £4.95), impeccably rip-roaring space opera in which worlds are destroyed by ships bigger than worlds, pursuits cover half the galaxy at semi-infinite velocity, and nasty things happen on the Underground. Much adrenalin, little conviction.

As for the unreadables, Penguin have sent no fewer than seven bloated volumes of the turgid **Dragonlance Chronicles**. I understand these are popular. Gorblimey.

June 1988

65 On the Beach

In other periodicals you often see, instead of a regular columnist, the words 'Fred Bloggs is on holiday.' This may mean 'we've sacked him', or 'he was too drunk to write this week's piece', or 'he sent it on a computer disk which we accidentally wiped', or 'if we'd printed it, Maxwell would have sued', or even, sometimes, 'Fred Bloggs is on holiday'. I'm on holiday myself, but after a day of building sandcastles I haul out a portable computer and write furtive reviews.... Are you going to admire my dedication? I thought not.

Half a Glass of Moonshine by Graham Dunstan Martin (Unwin 179pp £11.95) is the fourth adult novel by a writer who's been getting consistently better since I allotted faint praise to his first, *The Soul Master.* This latest is one of the few intelligent books whose mainspring is the 'paranormal', having not only a good story with nifty characters but a background of intelligent theory. Its closest theoretical rival is Ian Watson's bizarre *Miracle Visitors,* which tackles the problem of inexplicability and irreproducibility with arguments from mathematical logic – our universe, as Gödel's theory shows for complex formal systems, contains unprovable truths. Martin's best-articulated approach is neurological, a matter of perception: our universe may contain truths which for excellent Darwinian reasons aren't usefully detectable. Examples are given: *Moonshine*'s cheekily Carrollian and Tolkienian chapter-headings conceal several rabbit-punches, most effectively when the amiable craziness of the Mad Gardener's Song from *Sylvie & Bruno* evokes a nightmare case-history from the pages of Dr Oliver Sacks. Initially slow-moving and thrifty with its fantastic *frissons*, the book takes the well-drawn heroine Kirsty on journeys outside rationality to a conclusion as satisfying as the rules allow – depending on the angle of your question, the final answer is *(a)* a life-saving justification of everything that's gone before, or *(b)* a lemon. I enjoyed this one hugely.

Moonshine has been given Unwin Hyman's new 'posh' look, apparently reserved for work not easily forced into genre pigeonholes. It's a striking design: broad white bands above and below a central picture whose dominant colour is picked up in the initial letters of the title. In the same format are two good short story collections, Garry Kilworth's *The Songbirds of Pain* (187pp £2.95) and M. John Harrison's *The Ice Monkey* (144pp £2.95). Kilworth is a highly effective short-story writer with a particular gift for exotic locales and nerve-tingling insights. Harrison's main theme here is top-class kitchen-sink fantasy, inner-city sleaze with ambiguously nasty implications; in *The Ice Monkey*, the individually fine stories add up a little oppressively, and outdoor pauses are needed to clear one's head of the cumulative metaphysical stench.

Gollancz indicate their front-runner books with colour covers (to the discomfiture of authors who only ever get the grotty standard design): one such is Greg Benford's *Great Sky River* (326pp £11.95). This features electronically enhanced humans pursued by an inimical machine intelligence across a dying world near the central black hole into which our galaxy is gurgling like bathwater: ambitious stuff, conscientiously worked out, and I wish I could enjoy it more. Benford's future people are such dim and unsympathetic hicks, so lumpish in their slang and so wilfully determined not to use the wisdom of the ages built into their augmented memory banks, that the pursuing 'Mantis' machine fully deserves to win. This is theoretically a good book, but something's gone wrong in the execution: the skilled imaginings (think of a vast electromagnetic intelligence anchored in and powered by the black hole's stormy accretion disc) can barely fight their way through meticulous but uninspiring prose.

By contrast, though Garry Kilworth has little new to say in *Cloudrock* (Unwin 160pp £11.95), and his low-tech tribes are shackled by still less defensible practices like ritual cannibalism and incest, the colourful story exceeds its modest ambitions and - in a word - works. This closed-environment tale of a jungle in the sky gains power not from scientific thinking (the setup is just barely plausible) but from psychological and anthropological conviction. Oddly enough, Kilworth's primitives sound both more convincing and more literate than Benford's enhanced folk: their difference is conveyed through omissions and tone of voice, rather than a mass of jargon.

Michael Scott Rohan and Terry Pratchett continue their fantasy sagas with the **Winter of the World** conclusion, *The Hammer of the Sun* (Macdonald 502pp £11.95), and the fifth Discworld farce, *Sourcery* (Gollancz 243pp £10.95). Rohan's trilogy is well above average, marred only by sluggish transitions involving rather too many words: as soon as our Mastersmith hero settles down to his forge again, the inventiveness is compelling. Having previously sussed carbon fibres and electroplating, he now goes on to invent weather control, Greek fire, distillation, napalm, powered flight and the solar furnace, while casting impressive mythic shadows as crippled Vulcan and, later, Thor. As for the Hammer of the Sun itself, the final masterstroke against the Powers which plan an eternal ice age ... it's so outrageous that Rohan hints at its full nature only indirectly. Clue: think *tactical weaponry*.

Sourcery [sic] is also outrageous, if a fraction less triffic than its predecessor *Mort*. I'd describe it, but I don't think your feeble minds could withstand being told of a magical disaster so appalling that even the bedbugs flee Unseen University, taking their mattress homes with them; of the horse theft resulting in One Horseman and Three Pedestrians of the Apocalypse (we also discover Pestilence's favourite tipple, a small egg nog with a cherry in it); of verse rewrites to make Omar Khayyam rotate at 15,000 rpm in his grave; of eldritch footnotes and abominable puns beyond the grasp of sanity.... All right, read it; don't say you weren't warned.

The Misenchanted Sword by Lawrence Watt-Evans (Grafton 332pp £2.95) is an absolutely bog-standard fantasy novel. In a haze of magical absolutism and spell levels suggesting a heavy RPG influence, our hero acquires a charmed/cursed sword which preserves him from death and when drawn the first 100 times gives him an infallible kill, but (isn't there always a But? isn't it always ridiculously arbitrary?) will then smite *him* and give the next user 99 sure kills until (pow!) the one after that gets 98.... This 'countdown' plot device resembles Robert Louis Stevenson's 1893 'The Bottle Imp', which was satisfyingly concluded in about 30 pages. Watt-Evans takes 332 pages to avoid any exploration of the long-term events he's set up. For a while it does seem that he's going to tackle seriously the hero's Tithonus problem – the sword keeps him alive, not young – but all is solved by a second and not even hard-won dose of magic, a conclusion which is both unsatisfying and flabby. Inoffensive; instantly forgettable.

Slow Fall To Dawn by Stephen Leigh (Headline 165pp £2.50) is a first novel: worthy but slightly overwrought sf with distant echoes of Frank Herbert, e.g. much mental debate (here kept to a reasonable level), a feudal, Guild-based future society, and unlikely excuses for swashbuckling swords and daggers when lasers and sonic weapons exist. The action centres on an Assassins' Guild which sportingly rigs the odds so 15% of the contracted victims escape; it seems less sporting for them to require payment for failures. When a politically important kill joins the 15%, the Guild's essential neutrality is called into question, and the story takes off from there. I boggled on finding that not one of these frightfully honourable people questions the morality of assassination, and became altogether incredulous when this obscure planet's offworld embassy starts talking turkey with the assassins, like a British Raj civil servant giving serious consideration to the officially sanctioned export of Thuggee to Victorian England. Leigh writes adequately but not quite convincingly.

Lastly, a worthy reissue: *The Intrepid Enchanter* by L. Sprague de Camp and Fletcher Pratt collects all their humorous fantasies about Harold Shea, the incautious academic who travels to fictional worlds via 'syllogismobile' to mess up the action of Norse, chivalric, Finnish and Irish myth. Neither author achieved quite this light touch when working alone. If I had a collaborator, maybe we'd think of a witty conclusion for this column, but instead I'll just note that the cover – in Ian Miller's quirky steel-engraving style – is a welcome change from facile airbrushed grot.

July 1988

66 Enthusiams

Oh, I hate months like this: you lot all complain when there aren't enough books which merit the real fire-and-sword genocide reviews. What's more, I've just returned from a night of bribery and corruption in London, during which I bummed drinks off Robert Irwin (working on a fantasy of mediaeval England), Terry Pratchett (busy sending up ancient Egypt in a Discworld book called *Pyramids*), Rob Holdstock (sequel to *Mythago Wood* due out real soon now) and William Gibson (see below) ... as well as a number of low life-forms such as editors. This is major graft. How can I be scathing about any of them now?

Everybody's talking about *Mona Lisa Overdrive* (Gollancz 251pp £10.95), which completes William Gibson's 'cyberspace' trio without, claims the blurb, being a direct sequel. You'll still be fairly baffled by it unless you've read *Neuromancer* and *Count Zero*. Gibson's technical skills continue to grow, with multiple plot threads weaving through next-century urban sleaze to a final resolution which makes sense of the fruitful but baffling voodoo/AI 'presences' in the world data network. This time we meet London and Japanese crime barons, a demented scrapheap artist who builds custom killer robots, an intricate kidnapping plot, several dead but still functioning characters including Lady 3Jane Tessier-Ashpool from the first book, a pocket universe which is the computer version of Borges's 'aleph' ... and one deliberately loose end which goes on and up and out in a familiar but satisfying sf conclusion. On the negative side, the *Neuromancer* shock of novelty and gritty *film-noir* style has naturally worn off a bit, and Gibson's actual science is always dodgy. (Here he implies, and comes dangerously close to saying outright, that cyberspace communications aren't constrained by special relativity - to which I say Hum and Ahem and Come Off It, Bill). It is nevertheless ace stuff.

Likewise *Life During Wartime* by Lucius Shepherd (Grafton 383pp £10.95), a book whose impact is in another area - hitting through the guts and earthy senses rather than Gibson's largely visual imagery. It begins with US soldier David Mingolla in a Central American war which echoes Vietnam but is science-fictional too, with drug-enhanced psi powers used for prediction and assassination. Shepherd's evocation of Mingolla's new-found abilities and concomitant sex life is strange indeed: lush, rank, feverish, hallucinatory, skin-crawling and very dangerous. It emerges that psi-gifted families have been manipulating history from some time, ineffectually, since they're addicted to playing Montagues and Capulets. Mingolla becomes a key figure in attempts to settle the feud, end the war and put the world to rights, but the negotiations in Panama are a cauldron of raw emotion, power and horror. In the end, limp and enfeebled, I wasn't sure that I'd ever sympathized with Mingolla's semi-permanent state of violent rage: he rarely analyses, never explains, just reacts. Shepherd is a hell of a writer, though, and this is a major book by any standards.

Scudder's Game (Kerosina 175pp £12.95) is the first in some while from D.G. Compton, a fine, underrated author. But history has played a black joke on *Scudder*, which surely wasn't written recently: there's an air of post-60s reaction in its background of a population crash thanks to unlikely gadgets offering souped-up sex *plus* contraception in one hygienic package. The precision characterization and the sad fate of a lonely rebel against this grey Utopia work well. However, just as future-war stories have needed since 1945 to make allowance for nukes, a 1988 story with Compton's theme simply can't convince without taking into account the horror of AIDS. With such unreality in its foundations, the plot topples.

A Malady of Magicks by Craig Shaw Gardner (Headline 235pp £2.99) is that peculiarly American product, the Theoretically Funny Book. A wizard allergic to magic is a theoretically funny idea, and his idiot apprentice reports a series of theoretically funny escapades and pratfalls, which do raise the occasional mild smile, but no more. Gardner has the funny ideas, you see, yet lacks the verbal skill, timing and precision to make anyone but easily amused blurb writers fall off their chairs laughing. The fallacy of the T.F.B. is the assumption that humour is an easy, sloppy option, rather than something particularly hard to write well. There's a Josh Kirby cover to hint that this is aimed at the Terry Pratchett market (whether it hits it is another question): in one accurately rendered detail, the top hat on the dragon, Kirby illustrates precisely how Gardner tries just too hard and unsubtly for laughs.

[Crushing Terry Pratchett remark overheard when a fan offered him an inadequate joke for his next **Discworld** book: 'Oh, that's a bit *Craig Shaw Gardner*, isn't it ...']

It's always a relief to unearth a high-class fantasy; I worry sometimes that like the malady-afflicted wizard I'm growing allergic to the stuff. John James's *Votan* and *Not for All the Gold in Ireland* (Bantam 240pp £2.75, 348pp £2.95) are hugely enjoyable excursions through the Dark Ages, where Photinus the Roman/Greek muddies the wellsprings of mythology by, among other things, entering a crummy little village called Asgard where they contract his name to Votan, and ... It's all exuberantly energetic, with some parts funny (Photinus is no mean con-man) and some grim: when Loki names his new spear 'Mistletoe Twig', memories of Norse myth make you realize that Balder would do well to leave town. The second book, richer and darker, rambles over Britain and Ireland with more con tricks, some wonderful Gaelic-style speeches, an electrifying moment at Glastonbury and a behind-the-scenes look at the story of Cuchullain ... not to mention a particularly outrageous final page. Recommended.

David Gemmell tries a similar exploration of the raw material that might have lain behind myth, in *Ghost King* (Century 266pp £6.95), where the mythos is Arthurian. Somehow, though, it's not a mythopoeic book: Photinus's adventures could be felt to cast enormous shadows, but here the significance is artificially imposed by a lot of stuff about immortal god-magicians, which goes over the top into bathos. 'How that must pain you, Taliesan. Or should I call you Zeus? Or Aristotle? Or Loki?' Another character has in the past been Athena, Freya and Astarte; Achilles, Aeneas, Ares and Gilgamesh also crop up. Interesting historical research, clever ideas like the use of the lost Roman Ninth Legion, and even the Arthurian story itself, get lost in the undergrowth as the viewpoint hops all over the place and far too much casual magic is thrown around. The novel has good bones but a confused surface.

A couple more well-produced art books from Paper Tiger: *The SF and Fantasy Worlds of Tim White* (143pp £7.95) and *Medusa* by Chris Achilleos (144pp £7.95). It's tempting to mumble about my total lack of artistic insight and pass over these.... The White book consists almost entirely of colour plates, some a bit routine but some showing a nice ability to handle high technology and exotic natural landscapes in the same scene: usually, one or the other gets sacrificed. Achilleos takes a vaguely instructional approach, with lots of rough sketches and photographs showing (e.g.) the development of a striking Judge Dredd – actually Judge Anderson – picture for some GW product. But had I paid for this third Achilleos book I'd feel cheated by the reappearance of so many illustrations from the second, *Sirens*. Feminists should also steer well clear.

Reissues ... I'll reread George R.R. Martin's picaresque eco-fables in *Tuf Voyaging* (VGSF 374pp £3.50), because although the plotting's a mite shopworn there's a nice vein of deadpan humour. I'll skip *The Legacy of Heorot* by Niven, Pournelle and Barnes (Sphere 400pp £3.50): every character is so witless and two-dimensional that you don't care who gets eaten by giant cannibal newts.

August 1988

67 The Entropy Circuit

Imagine this mind-stretching thought experiment, guaranteed to explode your forebrain with galactic concepts and cause Sense-of-Wonder to squirt in twin streams from your ears. X is a lifelong sf addict. X has read more sf novels than he's had hot dinners. The doorbell rings, and gosh wow, it's every sf fan's dream: a big parcel of new hardbacks, none of them yet in the bookshops, sent free of charge by a leading publisher! X looks at it jadedly, and puts off opening it until some other time.... The reason for this bizarre and paradoxical behaviour is, alas, that after six years of such parcels and close on seventy monthly *Dwarf* columns, X feels bleary about the whole thing. He will not be doing it much longer. Try to have compassion. He is the product and victim of his environment. Not he but society stands condemned. We are all guilty.

Meanwhile ... *The Wave and the Flame* (Gollancz 358pp £10.95; VGSF £3.50) and *Reign of Fire* (Gollancz 382pp £11.95), by Marjorie Bradley Kellogg, form a complete SF story which begins promisingly. The flavour vaguely recalls *Dune* (lots of cave-dwelling 'primitives' who are really mind-wrenchingly sophisticated and hi-tech), with a wider and fouler range of weather. This is a 'weather as hero' novel. Enter Earth's survey ship, carrying a majority of eco-conscious but ineffective scientists plus one exploitative bastard with lawyers, guns and money, and things are bound to hit the fan. As a goodish read at dead centre of the hard sf mainstream, it kept me happy for several hundred pages.

But. Hard sf shares some fruitful constraints with the detective story; plenty of sf tales *are* detective stories in which the villain might be a recessive gene, a dimensionless constant or a gravitational quadrupole interaction. Here the frequently stated puzzle is the deadly weather of the planet Fiix, which baffles scientific analysis and seems explicable only in terms of native myths about eternal struggle between goddesses of fire and water. A creation myth offers tantalizing clues that this conflict might be a metaphor for some weird state of affairs grounded in celestial mechanics, and with a NASA atmospheric scientist – William B. Rossow – collaborating on both books, I was ready for a brilliantly ingenious revelation. I do wish I'd stopped before reading it.

What we get, alas, is a cop-out compromise which without vanishing wholly into mysticism goes halfway there for a preposterous 'rational' solution whose mechanisms aren't even sketched out. Instead it's that old standby, Forces Beyond The Comprehension Of Mere Earthly Science (if said forces can't be detected by any physical instruments, how on Fiix do they affect that very physical thing the weather?), hyper-technology which can soak up ground-zero nuclear explosions without turning a hair, etc. Boo, hiss.

[The general impression conveyed was that atmospheric physicists do not concern themselves a great deal with old-fashioned stuff like the laws of action and reaction or conservation of energy.]

Much attention and several stomachs were aroused by Ian Watson's *Interzone* story 'Jingling Geordie's Hole', whose theme your editor would prefer I didn't dwell on here. [Somehow I didn't think Exciting Tales of Buggery would pass the *Dwarf* censor.] Constructing a novel around it, the ingenious Watson came up with *The Fire Worm* (Gollancz 207pp £10.95), which presents the story as the narrative of someone hypnotically regressed to a 'past life', moving through elegant mirror-mazes of lives within lives to the origin of the story's Something Nasty – involving the Great Art of Ramon Lull (?1232-1315) as practised by an alchemical impostor, and the conjuration of a legend-attested Worm in a 'mediaeval Chernobyl' whose fallout still lingers. Very ingenious, but when we've toiled through all Watson's intellectual hoops, the finale returns us to within disappointingly close range of the short story's.

Almost simultaneously, Watson offers the richer and more cohesive *Whores of Babylon* (Paladin 302pp £3.95), with a reeking amalgam of all the cities that were Babylon recreated in the Arizona desert, full of volunteers role-playing a deadly serious game of ancient life which includes sacrifice, torture, branding and slavery. Borges's story 'The Lottery in Babylon' showed Babylon as the universe as the board of an infinite game of chance: Watson embroiders on this in what looks like conscious homage, spicing it with offbeat philosophy and electronic trappings. The textured ambiguity of Babylon works rather better than *The Fire Worm*'s slick paradoxes and strange loops, maybe because from this author it's less expected.

Here's an oddity: Philip K. Dick, whose output (like Tolkien's) has been steadily rising since his death, has at last published his 1966 children's book *Nick and the Glimmung* (Gollancz 141pp £7.95, ill. Paul Demeyer). It's quirkily funny and sinister in a mild way; it uses several of the author's patent ideas and aliens; no Dick fan can be without it. I have a suspicion that Dick wasn't quite sure of his 'younger reader' audience, though: here he seems to be talking down to them, there writing over their heads, and at the end leaving a plot-thread unresolved. Fun, but if Dick were still around his editor would surely have asked him to polish this some more.

Roger Zelazny's interminably open-ended Amber sequence continues in *Sign of Chaos* (Sphere 214pp £2.99). My old criticism still holds: if this were a D&D game, everyone would be loaded down with Bags of Holding, Pockets of Colossal Extension and Steamer Trunks of Universal Capacity just to carry all their plethora of magical powers, weapons, talismans, spells and disguises – not to mention the hefty *Who's Who in Amber and Chaos* required to keep track of the hero's numberless cousins, uncles, aunts, blood-foes, creations, demonic allies, etc. *Sign* opens with an amusing variation on Amber's gimmick of Shadow-travel, moves rapidly through expected mazes of intrigue, and ends with the socko revelation that so-and-so is really ... well, irritable thumbing through two previous books did at last confirm that the unmasked character *had* previously been introduced and so probably isn't a misprint for the one whose name differs by exactly one letter. Sloppy work, Mr Zelazny.

In *Far As Human Eye Can See* (Grafton 214pp £11.95), Isaac Asimov presents the 313th to 329th of his monthly essays for *Fantasy & SF*. Yes, yes, I do envy his stamina, and what they pay him. It's tempting to say this is exactly like every other Asimov science collection: actually, on inspection, it's a shade below average owing to many articles on chemistry. Polymath Asimov is highly qualified in this subject, and perhaps this encourages him to be - well, hardly less lucid but discernibly more tedious. He's still a good teacher, though never an inspired one. Example: essay 1 discusses synthetic elements; its final page and a half merely list such elements, and the resounding punchline at the very end goes, 'Only the elements beyond atomic number 102, of which only a few isotopes are as yet known, have none with a longer half-life than francium-223.' Not only a unusually dull and clumsy sentence for Asimov, but a hell of a flat way to end a popular-science essay: compare the last line of almost anything by J.B.S. Haldane, Stephen Jay Gould or Carl Sagan.

Don't miss John Brunner's reissued *The Shockwave Rider* (Methuen 288pp £3.50), a 150-proof distillation of computerized future shock which anticipated trendy 'cyberpunk' by nearly a decade, and trendier real-world virus programs by longer still. *The Darkest Road* by Guy Gavriel Kay (Unwin 420pp £3.50) concludes in paperback the trilogy which is about as good as you can get in its dubious genre of imitation Tolkien larded with great dollops of Arthurian and other legends. Jack Vance's strength and weakness, fine background invention plus feebleness of plot, are nowhere better shown than in *The Palace of Love* (Grafton 236pp £2.95): every snippet of irrelevant detail sparkles - look at pages 16-18 on the poison-planet Sarkovy, for example - while the storyline is limp beyond belief and the current Demon Prince's unmasking a distinct anticlimax.

Finally, my 'Return of the Killer Breakfast' award for covers which convince one not to read the book was decisively won by Sphere for Guy N. Smith's *Fiend* (disembowelled fatso hollowly grinning/bleeding at reader) and Robert R. McCammon's 956pp *Swan Song* (Cthulhu-cum-Werewolf sticking out a fly-blown tongue at you). To coin a better final line than Asimov's, Urrrghh.

September 1988

68 From A to Zombie

Faced with coruscating brilliance, one can only gush over the wonderfulness of the greatest literary triumph since *War and Peace* or the discovery of the semi-colon. Such an epochal landmark, transcending the feeble term 'book', is *The Dragonhiker's Guide to Battlefield Covenant at Dune's Edge: Odyssey Two*, from god-like publishers Drunken Dragon Press, 84 Suffolk St, Birmingham, B1 1TA. Not since the Epic of Gilgamesh or the Book of Genesis has such ... *[I suppose this is the Langford sf parody collection? Ed.]* Curses, now I've forgotten the rest of my impartial critique. After this column I shall stalk off in a huff.

In today's lemming-rush of formula fantasy, it's nice to find something different like Sheri S. Tepper's *The Awakeners* (Bantam 476pp £12.95). This is 'science fantasy', its magical exotica built on an understated sf background of clashing ideas and ecologies on a weird colony planet. Zombies (popular this month), alien conflict, immortality and cruel theocracy sound routine: Tepper scores by showing the colour and complexity of a real world with real politics. Her narrative mosaic has many characters, many factions, with no stereotyped Evil Lord and likewise a happy lack of elves, dragons, spells, rings and the Wild Hunt. No-one's wholly right or wrong, the most painful tragedies result from ignorance rather than Evil, and even the nastiest race is so because caught in an evolutionary trap. Despite sluggish development of narrative tension and a cast so large that it's bothersome remembering who's who, I liked this for its freshness – its dextrous avoidance of crudities, clichés and lecturing condescension. Piers Anthony could learn from it.

On Stranger Tides by Tim Powers (Grafton 352pp £11.95) contrasts neatly with *Awakeners*. It immediately hooks you and drags you along in sympathy with one central character's appalling misfortunes on the Spanish Main ... and escalates from there to closing mega-thrills so determinedly spiced that your palate is left almost jaded, overdosed on additives – like the junk-food tradition of Woman as Plot Token, existing only to be Threatened and Rescued. Where Tepper's plot unfolds in expanding patterns, Powers's accelerates at insane speed through delirious scenery to a shattering brick-wall impact. His 1718 pirates have learned voodoo lore from Caribbean islanders and use it to nasty effect. Our clerkish hero, pirate against his will, is sucked into the horrors (not only the cover's zombie-crewed ships but a genuinely nightmarish search through darkest Florida for Ponce de Leon's fountain of youth) until he learns some painful, scarring tricks of his own. Compulsive stuff.

UFOs remain compellingly lucrative, for some; Gary Kinder's *Light Years* (Penguin 266pp £3.50) allegedly reports 'the best documented, most credible UFO case ever.' On the sceptical side, Martin Gardner's *The New Age: Notes of a Fringe Watcher* (Prometheus, 10 Crescent View, Loughton, Essex, IG10 4PZ, 273pp £14.95) comprises 33 essays/reviews distrustful of extraordinary claims which aren't backed by extraordinary evidence. Kinder rummages for such evidence in the mass of shoddiness invariably surrounding major reports. Few UFO believers can swallow his 'contactee' Eduard Meier's stories of over 100 personal sightings and close encounters. To illustrate shoddiness: much is made of an astonishing metal fragment which reputedly couldn't have been manufactured on Earth. Solid evidence at last? Well, no, overnight it got lost! It's sad to see Kinder refusing to read beyond 'a small portion' of sceptical literature, and eventually bowing not so much to evidence as to the sheer mass of claims, including thoroughly refuted ones. Of course no writer could be influenced by knowing that his conclusions, pro or con, decide whether or not he's pushed as a best-seller....

Gardner too arouses a sad sympathy. He's been arguing for common sense since the 1950s, a depressing and thankless task: forever citing the same old boring disproofs and appeals to reason, while the loonies not only shift their ground weekly but carry on citing old rubbish like astrology as though it was never in doubt. (To digress: Heinlein's best-ever sf prophecy is in *Stranger in a Strange Land*, where the only way to influence the mediocre leader of the Western world was via his wife's astrologer!) Amazing that Gardner still retains a sense of humour in this uneven but worthwhile collection.

Arthur C. Clarke has apparently reached the undead stage at which other people write his books. Certainly, despite godlike aliens and undersea mystery, *Cradle* (Gollancz £11.95 309pp) doesn't read like Clarke – who's credited as 'director' while hitherto unknown co-author Gentry Lee is 'producer'. No sad cadences or dying falls: lyrical techno-prose has given way to dull exposition, often irrelevant (padding about passwords, security, computers, adventure games) or unfocused (aliens, described from an omniscient author-viewpoint, boast 'rows of orifices of unknown purpose' – unknown to *whom*?). The characters have terrible flashback problems and luridly overwritten sex lives, contrasting with Clarke's coy unease about naughty parts. *Cradle*'s plot is pepped up with mildly exciting but forgettable chase/caper elements, while losing poignancy, mysticism and awe ... the Clarke trademarks one remembered.

Some people don't know when to stop, and most of them are Piers Anthony. *Being a Green Mother* (Grafton 399pp £3.50) concludes the five-book 'Incarnations of Immortality', which started promisingly but became ever more sprawling, sententious, and apt to tackle ultimate questions in terms of stupefying banality. Here Anthony imitates Heinlein's later self-indulgence by rehashing at zombie pace the tangle of family relationships from four previous books. He offers what James Blish termed an idiot plot, one whose functioning requires major characters to be idiots, including the heroine and Satan. The reader is merely treated as one. This heroine is terminally capricious and wimpish; after oodles of non-plot occasioned by the fact that the main story is too slight for a thick book, she literally destroys the world in a tantrum.

(*Q*: What does Mummy say to a daughter who's just obliterated humanity? *A*, from the Piers Anthony Book of Etiquette: 'I think we should talk, dear.')

The finale is arbitrary, embarrassing, and so question-begging as to look irritatingly unfinal. For feminists, there's a treat when our enlightened lady meets a superstition about defilement and magically senses its truth: 'Anyone who drank in it would be sickened, and clothes washed in it would remain unclean. The soul of the water reeked of its special pollution.' Why? The buried water-pipe had been walked over by a ... woman. Oh God.

Some writers hack their zombie way to solvency, some laboriously practise craftsmanship, some radiate unfair genius even at their cockeyed worst. R.A. Lafferty, Scribbling Giant, is in the third category, forever answering Ultimate Questions with hilarious tall stories which sneak around and rabbit-punch you while you're laughing. *East of Laughter* (Morrigan, 84 Ivy Ave, Southdown, Bath, BA2 1AN, 176pp £10.95) isn't his best work, which is diffused through many short stories, but offers subversive metaphysics, swarming stranger-than-truth characters which no one else could have created, and – despite the doomy promise of his familiar narrative pageantry, numerology and Catholic echoes – a cheerfully daft finish. Minor genius? As he observes, 'I doubt whether really small giants will ever become the fashion.'

Who could resist *The Return of the Shadow* by J.R.R. Tolkien (Unwin 497pp £17.95), being mercilessly annotated early drafts of *Lord of the Rings*, as far as Moria? Me, for one.

This, despite your editor's tearful pleas, is the last monthly 'Critical Mass'. With the six-year mark approaching, I'm now reduced to zomboid numbness by the mere sight of review copies, and plan to spend several recuperative weeks reading detective stories and whisky labels instead. Rather than self-pitying farewells, let's end with a Good Cause. The organizing body of the 1987 World SF Convention – held in Britain – is fighting financial collapse, not unconnected with lack of sponsorship from UK publishers. Bankruptcy could mean a gap of decades before Britain is trusted to host this colossal sf/fantasy event again. Well-wishers (and I was glad to say Hello to lots of you there) can gain great good karma by sending the price of a paperback to 'Conspiracy' c/o [address omitted; this is old history; the disaster was averted]. I promise I don't get a cut.

Bye-bye, all. It's been fun.

October 1988

[That saw the end of my *White Dwarf* stint. Before long, 'zomboid numbness' dissolved with the offer of more money, and I returned to plague mankind in the new magazine *GM* (*GamesMaster*) – with the column title subtly varied to 'Critical Hits'. My monthly sequence continued 'uninterrupted' since the *GM* printing schedule was very much quicker; they also took copy on disk, and I marvelled at all the extra hard work they had to do to continue the tradition of mucking up my punctuation, omitting words and adding typos each issue.]

69 Now Read On

THE STORY SO FAR: Some games fans may remember the hated name Langford from six years of book review columns in a magazine called something like *Albino Of Restricted Growth*. That all ended amicably when, alerted by failing eyesight and hairy palms, I decided to stop abusing my health through over-indulgence in fantasy trilogies. My happy retirement had barely reached its third bottle when *GM* tempted me with promises of a looser format, voluptuously non-sexist groupies, and lots of independent systemless role-playing fantasy money. *Now read on....*

An awful lot of story-so-far is needed for Isaac Asimov's new *Prelude to Foundation* (Grafton 461pp £11.95), although it slots into his interminable History of the Future *before* the other books with 'Foundation' in the title. As known to every sf reader whose fictional researches go beyond the *Sunday Sport*, the technocratic Foundation is set up as antidote to the fall of a Galactic Empire suspiciously like the Roman one - this fall having been predicted by ace guru and 'psychohistorian' Hari Seldon. Typically for Asimov, the books have vaguely intellectual quest/detective plots, with big questions and big trite answers. *Q:* Can the historical inevitability of Seldon's Plan save the Foundation from this threat, and that, and three more? *A:* Yes, yes, and three times yes. *Q:* What can save the Plan from the mutant superman who defies psychohistorical prediction? *A:* Aha, there is this hidden *Second* Foundation.... *Q:* Hidden where? A: Here, no, there, no, there, no, *there*, no, no, I was kidding, it's really *there*!

That summarizes the original 1940s stories, inevitably dated but fast-moving and fun. In the 80s, Asimov's sequels got out of hand, increasingly bloated and vacuous, each ending with a feebler revelation than the last. Meanwhile the series expanded backwards with the incorporation of the earlier 'robot' books and some depressing stuff about every plot-string being ultimately pulled by offstage robots. This accounts for gloomy critical speculation that Hari Seldon, onlie begetter of the Foundations, would turn out to be another bloody robot....

Prelude is all about the young Seldon. It's risky to over-expose your white-haired guru in this fashion: Tolkien never showed us the early apprenticeship and sex life of Gandalf, but Asimov has no such qualms. Pursued through strangely stereotyped regions of planet Trantor, Seldon emerges as a bit of a wimp: not too bad at unarmed combat (mathematical expertise is hard to convey, so I suppose this was the next best thing), easily manipulated by everyone else in the plot, but – thank goodness – not a robot. No robot would be so daft as to risk its neck violating sacred taboos in the vague hope of maybe picking up some possibly nonexistent information which might just bear on an idea not yet properly formulated. *Prelude*'s big question isn't, 'Will Seldon invent psychohistory?' (we know he must) but, 'When will he get his great creative insight?' Here there's genuine suspense: it could be on any page from about 400 to the last (461), and only my disappointment with the inspiration's remarkable unexcitingness could persuade me to give away this, the book's major secret. *Answer:* page 440.

It's slightly more fun to play Spot the Hidden Robot among the smallish cast list. To equal my 100% score, you must remember the *Robots and Empire* rewrite of the Laws of Robotics, whereby robots can now hurt and disobey people all they like provided it's for a good enough cause. After the astonishing, mindboggling revelations, *Prelude* fades into the sunset with an ending to satisfy all you connoisseurs of Mills and Boon. I wonder how awesome the mentor-figure of *Lord of the Rings* would have seemed after a prequel with the final line, 'Kiss me again, Gandalf. – Please.'

Turning hastily from sf, here's David Pringle's *Modern Fantasy: the 100 Best Novels* (Grafton 278pp £14.95). The best fantasy games aren't necessarily based on the best fantasy, but everyone loves a booklist. When not nodding happily at the discovery that a personal favourite is featured in this sensibly chosen Hall of Fame, you're enjoying exhilarating shrieks of rage at some unspeakably boneheaded inclusion or omission. Pringle does us proud on the first count, and generously allows much scope for the second. Here, compiled from his enjoyable book, are some lists of my own.

Influential Authors Omitted Merely Because Pre-1946 include Ernest Bramah, James Branch Cabell, Lord Dunsany, E.R. Eddison, William Morris, etc. Cabell and Dunsany were in fact still publishing lesser work in the 1950s; but Robert E. Howard of Conan fame gets in on a publication-dates fiddle despite dying in 1936.

Nifty Fantasies Which You Didn't Read Because They Looked 'Mainstream' include books by Peter Ackroyd, Kingsley Amis, William Burroughs, John Fowles, Michael Frayn, Alasdair Gray, Doris Lessing, Brian Moore, Flann O'Brien, Christopher Priest, Thomas Pynchon and Iain Banks.

Most Over-Represented Author. Fritz Leiber deserves two of his four entries, for the horrific *Conjure Wife* and the exotic/humorous *Swords of Lankhmar*; but his *The Sinful Ones* loses a fine idea in a mere potboiler and – I'm going to be unpopular for this – the urban-nightmare qualities of *Our Lady of Darkness* fade into triviality by comparison with Ackroyd's *Hawksmoor* (also here).

Most Blatant Double Standards. Mervyn Peake's Titus trilogy gets a separate entry for each volume, while Tolkien's trilogy is disposed of in a single entry (and ditto multi-book efforts by Blish, Donaldson and Kay). Is this justice? Yes, to the extent that the Peake trio is discontinuous; but no, because I don't think book 3 (*Titus Alone*) rates inclusion as a separate item.

Most Stupefying Editorial Courage is shown in the 'humorous fantasy' subgenre, when after admitting pleasant efforts by Poul Anderson, Gordon Dickson and the de Camp/Pratt team, Pringle not only excludes Terry

Pratchett but relegates him to an omission-list featuring such awful failed humorists as Piers Anthony, Robert Asprin and Jack Chalker.

Best Unexpected Genre Inclusions. Avram Davidson's *The Phoenix and the Mirror*, R.A. Lafferty's *Fourth Mansions*, Rudy Rucker's *White Light*, Michael Shea's *Nifft the Lean*, Gene Wolfe's *Peace*.

Deplorable Omissions-By-Fiat. Our editor quailed at the extra slog of researching translated or 'children's' fantasy. In the first category we lose Italo Calvino and Gabriel Garcia Marquez; I'd also have been tempted to smuggle in Jorge Luis Borges for all that he never wrote a novel. The second category excludes such revered writers as Diana Wynne Jones and William Mayne, though juveniles by Alan Garner, Ursula Le Guin and C.S. Lewis somehow creep in – double standards again.

Forgivable Omissions. Introducing this work, Brian Aldiss whinges about the non-inclusion of William Golding's prehistoric fantasia *The Inheritors*. Many fans will likewise boggle at not finding Gene Wolfe's **Book of the New Sun**. Same reason each time: our hero editor judged both to be on the sf side of the border, and had already put them in his *Science Fiction: The 100 Best Novels* (Xanadu, 1985).

Most Grudging Entry. See Pringle's editorial comments on the lumbering, knurred, ravaged-nostrilled, spleen-bedecked, leprous, argute and refulgent lucubrations of Stephen R. Donaldson. Very naughty of him. Tee-hee.

That's enough lists. Indeed, that's enough Langford for now. One last recommendation: don't miss Russell Miller's scarifying but hysterical *Bare-Faced Messiah: the True Story of L. Ron Hubbard*, out in paperback at last despite Scientological litigation (Sphere 521pp £3.99).

November 1988

70 Conventional Aberrations

Fooling around in sf gives endless opportunities for relaxation at science fiction conventions. Relaxation as in 'relaxed as a newt': whether dozens or thousands of fans attend, it's an unbreakable tradition that the event's cultural centre is the hotel bar. Appalling results of this tradition are fortunately rare, though I was once badly molested by a Tolkien authority in whose masterwork I'd pointed out a mistake. While this enraged hobbitomane tried hard to twist my ear off, the convention organizers soothed hotel staff by explaining, 'It's all right, he's a professor of mediaeval literature.'

Yes, bizarre things happen at conventions, and this month's example comes from the 1987 British national event. Despite feeble protests, I was lured for the first time since 1976 into something very like (drops voice to guilty whisper, places blanket over head) a role-playing game. The idea of 'Alien Encounter' was that audience volunteers were thrown into First Contact with an 'alien' of unknown motivation, and allowed to cock up the likelihood of Earth's acceptance into the Extraterrestrial Economic Community. SF authors scripted the various aliens' behaviour; the unfortunate volunteers had to use their own wits, ho ho. Fun to watch, for sadists.

Here's my own disgraceful contribution, which was tastefully entitled 'The Betelgeuse Blow-Job'.

In this scenario you are Vrdn'tgrn, an alien undergraduate in your freshthing year, dumped on this primitive world with a Mission to perform. Betelgeuse University has lots of offbeat traditions and initiations, and you are stuck with the challenge about to be described. If you succeed, you will gain almost immeasurable *pffnokker* (untranslatable Betelgeusan concept with overtones of free beer, celebrity-guest-on-Wogan status, and being president of the Oxford Union). If you fail, you will spend the rest of your student life covered in the most ignominious *glwb*.

What you're like: very humanoid though visibly alien in a low-budget way (deely-boppers, green makeup, etc). No problems with air or gravity. Internally you have some important differences, the main one being that the things fans correctly assume to be your ears are also reproductive organs....

Your aim: aural sex! Amongst your race, genetic information is exchanged by coded sonic transmissions ... or to put it another way, loose talk.

Interfertility with *Hom. Saps.* will have to wait until they can be taught to speak fluently in your genetic code; but you're not here for that, just for fun. All you need is to get one of your human contacts to talk to you *privately and uninterrupted* for a minute or so, and the solar system will move for you. In addition, you'll have passed the student initiation.

How you behave: alas, somewhat repressedly. Those hearty types from the *fnurb*-ball team would enjoy this no end ... but despite being intelligent and fun-loving, you're a seething mass of youthful inhibitions.

• All this loose-lipped promiscuity on Earth shocks the hell out of you. When in a group you confine yourself to sign language only. (In this area you're reasonably bright and inventive. Whether the Earthlings are is another question.) The contactees will doubtless talk amongst themselves even if they wrongly deduce you're deaf: abandoning the Prime Directive, you hand out, demonstrate, and try to persuade them to use, Oral Protectives. These bear a strange resemblance to bubble-blowing kits: you're quite happy to listen to human conversation when it's 'decently clothed' in bubbles.

• You want a private bout of aural naughtiness. A crowd inhibits you. Privacy for you means that no one else is *listening*: if the other contactees are at a reasonable distance, or have their hands over (or, disgustingly, their fingers in) their ears, you're ready to go ahead. But naturally you won't want any prudish bubbles during your big moment....

• Of course you may have a problem when and if the excitement really starts to mount. Your sensual moans (in genetic code) and lascivious writhings may persuade the Earthling who's t*lking to you that something's wrong and that he/she should stop. *Coitus interruptus* is not considered a barrel of fun on your world either.

• Successful consummation will leave you limp with gratitude despite post-conversational *triste*. At your discretion you can present the group with some spare text from your university studies, *Phlmgrooper's Omnibus of Perpetual Motion Machines* or *Theory and Practice of the Deusexmachina Interstellar Drive*. They will have a fun time translating it, for the next century or so.

• If they blow in your ear you'll follow them anywhere.

Enough of that – the above should suffice to ruin plenty of Christmas and New Year parties. Between disgraceful lapses, I've promised to mention the occasional book....

Jonathan Carroll is an author who deserves your attention despite, or because of, being weirdly difficult to classify. You could call his books psychological-fantasy-mystery-horror stories, with an elusive magic in the writing and vivid characters reminiscent of those larger-than-life creations of the late Theodore Sturgeon. Carroll's first, *The Land of Laughs*, baffled publishers and suffered from desperately misleading cover designs: the American paperback resembled a twee, Oz-style children's book, the British one looked like routinely grotty horror. More sensibly, his present publishers have opted for colourfully surreal jackets on *Bones of the Moon* – one of my 1987 Best Books – and the latest, *Sleeping in Flame* (Legend 244pp £10.95, or £5.95 paperback).

This time, Carroll's favourite elements emerge quickly enough: a setting in Vienna (where he lives), a relish for life, places and food, a moving second-time-around love affair ... and something nasty in the woodshed. The blackness from the hero's past has such weird ramifications that few writers could have made it work: our man's life seems prefigured by past incarnations going back to a bit-part from the Brothers Grimm, his diminutive father may or may not be a famous character with a very silly name, and the conclusion is an outrageous psychological rabbit-punch. I'll read this one again.

One I've read before: Rudolph Eric Raspe's *Baron Munchausen* (Dedalus Classics 268pp £4.95), that legendarily daft collection of tall tales from 1785. The Baron's journeys around and through the world by eagle and volcano, and to the Moon by beanstalk and whirlwind, make this a must for fans of Piers Anthony and other unconvincing sf.

I can't do justice to story collections: a decent short needs as much comment as a novel, and space forbids. *Terry's Universe* ed. Beth Meacham (Gollancz 245pp £11.95) is a memorial to one of sf's best-loved editors, Terry Carr, who died in 1987. Twelve writers contribute stories (Fritz Leiber's is a tantalizing extract from a coming Fafhrd/Mouser novel) and Harlan Ellison, unable as so often to get his fictional act together, says emotive words instead. *The Orbit Science Fiction Yearbook* ed. David Garnett (Orbit 336pp £4.99) is cheering to see, not merely for its fine stories and trenchant critical comment, but because at last we have a supposedly regular British anthology of each year's best short sf. (It's over a decade since the Aldiss/Harrison *Year's Best* ceased publication. [And, alas, all too soon *Zenith* itself was given the chop.]) Garnett fails to include my own 1987 story, but does a good job despite this one awful lapse.

December 1988

71 The Omnipresent Pratchett

Of all the writers I actually know, Terry Pratchett has displayed the highest profile of 1988. It began with the year's first sf convention, Microcon in Exeter, where friendly student hosts struggled in vain against the university venue's malign anti-barmen, who stalked the halls searching for drinks and taking them away from people. It was Terry who saved the attending writers with his emergency convention kit, a briefcase of lemons, tonic water and gin.

Wherever two or three sf fans are gathered together, Terry Pratchett miraculously appears, often in tasteless leather trousers. Examples of spontaneous Pratchett were reported at every British convention of note and also the 1988 World SF Convention in New Orleans, whence I heard unsavoury tales of addiction to bucket-sized banana Daiquiris.

His energy remains appalling. The sixth Discworld book is out; the seventh (*Pyramids*) follows in May; the eighth (*Faust* [alias *Eric*]) is finished and the ninth (*Guards! Guards!*) nearly so, while our author wanders convention bars trying out jokes intended for the tenth, and in between has also written a children's book [*Truckers*]. Blimey.

For now, we have *Wyrd Sisters* (Gollancz 251pp £10.95), another exceedingly funny concoction which shows the Pratchett ability to pinch stock materials and reassemble them with warped Discworld logic. Tom Stoppard converted *Hamlet* to *Rosencrantz and Guildenstern are Dead* with star parts given to attendant lords; *Wyrd Sisters* re-examines *Macbeth* from the viewpoint of three witches, including redoubtable Granny Weatherwax.

Hamlet creeps in too, and a million other productions like *Waiting for Godot* and the seminal *Duck Soup*, plus Shakespearean properties: strolling players, a storm waiting for its big theatrical break, substituted identities and a scene-stealing Fool. The author's 'wide but superficial' (his words) erudition is more visible than usual in this riot.

I think I fell off my chair most painfully at the Ideologically Sound Cauldron Scene, influenced by a progressive young witch. *'Whole grain wheat and lentils too, In the cauldron seethe and stew ...'*

After the World Fantasy Convention in London (where Stephen Donaldson filled me with heart-stopping terror by saying, 'I read your review of me.'), *Wyrd Sisters* was launched at a Hallowe'en party, together with Robert Holdstock's

Lavondyss (Gollancz 367pp £11.95) – a sequel to the much-praised *Mythago Wood.*

Lavondyss is a book which demands rereading, and for that matter a rereading of *Mythago Wood* too. In both, Holdstock shows an amazing ability to plug into the raw stuff of myths – shaving away endless layers of storytelling embellishment to reach something brutal and numinous that lies at the core.

The dense, shadowed, creepy heart of Ryhope Wood opens inward into larger realms, primary places where 'mythagos' emerge from shared racial dreams. Anyone penetrating these 'geistzones' is liable to be absorbed into the beginnings of myth: not replaying old stories but becoming their origin. It's a subtle, disturbing, powerful idea, and much more complex than my too-brief summary.

Lavondyss charts the progress of Tallis, a girl shaman moving slowly from 1950s England to the inner realms in search of her lost brother. Much of it is amazingly good, like her growing awareness of elusive power and a magical apparatus of masks and totems which 'work' via fine shades and perceptions – nothing reducible to any crude table of spell effects or power points. And the final vision has a shocking, unexpected force.

But unlike *Mythago Wood, Lavondyss* seems to begin too far from the realms of common sense. It's hard to believe that this thirteen-year-old seer wouldn't be taken rather frequently to the doctor for persistently weird speech, behaviour and 'hallucinations'. There's also some confusing play with flashbacks, repetition and changing point of view, all getting in the way of that compelling journey to the heart of myth.

Minor flaws, I'd say. *Lavondyss* is a book of great power. Read it.

Had you attended the World Fantasy Convention you could have simultaneously met Messrs. Pratchett and Holdstock, fallen over the slumped bodies of myself and *GM*'s Wayne, and sat at the feet of Diana Wynne Jones – another author whose popularity keeps growing. Her latest is *The Lives of Christopher Chant* (Methuen 252pp £8.95), extending the very loosely connected series about the alternate-world civil servant in charge of Magic and Social Security: Chrestomanci.

After saying the usual things about never-failing inventiveness and sense of fun, I must add that this story of the enchanter's youth is singularly bloodthirsty. The villain goes in for butchery on a scale unprecedented in 'juvenile' fantasy, while wince-making viewpoint accounts of impalements, burnings, broken necks and smashed skulls are made doubly so by a magical need for the unlucky victim to suffer each calamity twice.

Also here: a decidedly offbeat approach to astral travel, a Living Goddess with (sometimes) four arms and (always) a passion for Angela Brazil, much smuggling and double-dealing in several different worlds, a levitating roof, and an unspeakably hellish cat called Throgmorten. Nifty entertainment.

Next came the annual Novacon in Birmingham, featuring most of the above plus guest of honour Garry Kilworth, whose latest is *Abandonati* (Unwin Hyman 162pp £12.95). Instead of the exotic, colourful locations we expect from him, this delves into the muckiest depths of street life.

Abandonati are street people, sleepers in doorways and scavengers of litter bins. With dollops of grim humour the book describes a world from which the rich – i.e. anyone who can afford *GM*, shoes, food – have inexplicably vanished. One unstated but obvious message is that viewed from gutter level, we 'rich' have in all the most important ways already disappeared.

Life goes on, just barely, for the brain-wrecked wino hero. The best-fed people are cannibals; the most happy and affluent are former gypsies; a handleless mug and a greasy pack of cards are potent tokens of exchange. It's a moving little book.

Now here's a fact of mindboggling improbability to those who know the publishing business. All four of the above books have good covers which the authors like! In a world where art departments work long and hard to devise ugly, inappropriate, and barely distinguishable jackets, this is cheering. Loud huzzas for the artists, respectively Josh Kirby, Alan Lee, Cathy Simpson and Dave McKean.

Speaking of artists, Britain's gallant small-press publishers always try hard in this area. John (The H-Bomb's Thunder) Brunner's *The Days of March* (Kerosina 309pp £14.95) is a warts-and-all novel about the early days of CND, massively worthy but distinctly short on plot, and competently illustrated by Richard Middleton. James Blaylock's *Homunculus* (Morrigan 244pp £11.95) is bizarre Victorian fantasy, alternately mystical and hilarious, with eccentric 'period' illustrations from someone called Ferret who can't tell a cocked hat from a top hat. I'm glad to have this collector's edition of a good book; cheapskates and abandonati can skulk off looking for the paperback (Grafton 301pp £3.50).

With all the conventions of 1988 safely behind me, I enjoyed a few pints of relaxation at the British SF Association's London pub meeting and was surprised to find it (almost) the year's first sf event which didn't feature Terry Pratchett. But later, on a platform of the Central Line, I heard a balding, bearded voice say 'Hello Dave!' behind me, and turned to find there was indeed no escape....

January 1989

72 Gut Loathing

Publishing is strange, full of eccentricities from bygone days. SF author Richard Cowper used to claim that his first book contract contained the clause, 'In ye euent of tardie deliuerie, ye Scribe shall be flogg'd.' A true example of the industry's endearing daftness concerns my last novel, *Guts*.

This was a spoof horror epic written in revolting collaboration with my taste-challenged pal John Grant. Real horror authors did us proud with quotations meant for a suitably bloodstained cover. 'I have seen the bowels of horror fiction, and their names are David Langford and John Grant!' retched Graham Masterton. 'Makes *Night of the Crabs* look like Beatrix Potter!' gibbered Guy N. Smith. 'The first horror novel I don't even dare to read!' quavered Ramsey Campbell.

Alas, although *Guts* was commissioned in advance, completed in 1987, enthusiastically accepted and paid for, it proved to be the horror novel they don't even dare to publish. For eighteen months there was silence. As I write, the last weeks of the contracted publication period are trickling by. All bets are then off; we'll have to market the ruddy thing all over again, to some less timorous outfit.

What went wrong? Too complex to explain: a tangle of internal politics at the publishing house, making it hard to blame our hero editor. My frenzied public must wait another year, or decade, for *Guts*. [At last: Cosmos Books, 2001!] Meanwhile the horror boom continues unabated, although in posher circles it's polite to call it 'dark fantasy' and to make no tactless reference to chainsaw massacres, zombie gang-bangs or (as in *Guts*) exploding entrails.

If like me you prefer your fear and loathing at short-story length, Robinson Publishing offer a solid selection of wintry chillers: *The Mammoth Book of Short Horror Novels* ed. Mike Ashley (518pp £4.95), *Christmas Ghosts* ed. Kathryn Cramer & David Hartwell (282pp £5.95), *The Best Horror from Fantasy Tales* ed. Stephen Jones & David Sutton (264pp £11.95), and best of all, Robert Aickman's collection *Cold Hand in Mine* (252pp £3.50). Every Aickman story is a reminder that a good writer doesn't need gory stage-props to create that lingering aura of chilly unease.

So ... is Brian Stableford's vampire novel *The Empire of Fear* (Simon & Schuster 390pp £11.95) another formulaic horror epic? No indeed. Despite a smokescreen of ritual and 'sabbats', the immortal vampire aristocracy of this alternate-world 1623 has been created by biological rather than supernatural change. Traditional Victorian vampirism was a heavily sexy metaphor for what couldn't be written about, i.e. sex; rationalist Stableford has a slightly different unthinkable in mind.

In the first section, which is incidentally the culmination of a tortured love story, one of this world's few scientific thinkers conducts a suicidal experiment in anti-vampire biowarfare. His talisman isn't the cross but the newly invented microscope.

This torch of reason is passed to his son Noell, who makes a gruelling heart-of-darkness journey to the African wellsprings of the vampire plague. Here heroism doesn't lie in moral worth but using one's intellect: from the appalling initiation ceremonies of the vampire elders, Noell deduces their essential secret.

The message isn't that there are things with which mankind wasn't meant to meddle, but - much more modern - that it's supremely important to understand seeming horrors. Vampirism itself turns out to be neutral; the empire of fear is a tyranny of ignorance. *Empire*'s baddies, including the immortalized Richard Lionheart and Vlad the Impaler, are the despots who like large sections of our Government prefer truth to be hushed up, in case it makes you free. There are grisly parallels with the transmission method and superstitious terror of the 1980s scourge which also supposedly came out of Africa.

Despite a slightly indigestible lecture towards the end, when the scene shifts to the alternate 1980s and vampires are re-explained in terms of modern genetics, this is a classy, thought-provoking book - Stableford's best fiction yet.

Meanwhile, without being the talented Michael Bishop's best yet, or Philip K. Dick's either, the Bishop novel *Philip K. Dick Is Dead, Alas* (Grafton 411pp £3.99) is a creative pastiche which Dick ought to have written and would have liked to read. Confusing? Of course: a surreal and paranoid confusion about reality is the Dick trademark.

In *this* alternate timeline, the diabolical President Nixon is in his fourth term, and after winning in Vietnam is running Amerika as a barely disguised police state. Philip K. Dick died in this 1982 just as in our own, after making it as a mainstream author whose sf never got published. Now his ghost keeps bubbling through the structure of reality with a master plan for the world's redemption - through the funny, eccentric, oppressed people-in-the-street who just as in a real Dick story are the ineffectual heroes.

Bishop's shuffling of realities is more controlled than Dick's own (in some PKD books like *The Three Stigmata of Palmer Eldritch* it's impossible to work out which sections are 'real' and which hallucinatory), and so is his grammar. He uses a few too many words, making this the fattest book Dick never wrote, but the plot has the right sort of lunacy. A nice work of homage.

Incidentally, I'm deeply grateful that the Bishop novel is a one-off fireworks display, not just the first of some multi-authored series to be called (say) 'Philip K. Dick's Whacky Realities'. Too much to believe? Recently we've seen obscure author Gentry Lee writing the bulk of a supposed Arthur C. Clarke novel, *Cradle* (lousy, incidentally). Worse is coming: America now offers series like 'Roger Zelazny's Alien Speedway' and 'Isaac Asimov's Robot City'. The famous name gets put on the cover and hypes up the sales; unfamous journeyman authors do the actual writing. Anyone want to write 'Dave Langford's Hatchet Reviews'? I'll only ask for 75% of the revenue.

Speaking of Isaac Asimov, note that his *Fantastic Voyage II: Destination Brain* (Grafton 480pp £3.99), though billed as a 'sequel to the classic *Fantastic Voyage*', isn't. *Voyage* began as an amusing but scientifically illiterate 1966 film. In his flattish novelization, Asimov managed to clean out the screenplay's grosser idiocies. But for years it nagged at him: he wanted to Do It Right, and this book *replaces* the original.

Unfortunately, rigorous Asimov can't bring himself to believe in the technology of miniaturizing crew-carrying submarines to play Twenty Thousand Leagues Along The Bloodstream. Acres of woffling non-explanation are devoted to circumventing this, but not, alas, into making the new 'scientific' plot-twists sound other than totally daft. If Asimov were commissioned to write a novel pushing 'creation science' (which he rightly loathes and rejects) it would come out no less lacklustre than this.

Asimov is one of the lucky few who can publish whatever they like. Most of Dick's 'straight' novels stayed unpublished in his lifetime, appearing only recently – e.g. *Mary and the Giant* in 1987 (Gollancz 230pp £11.95). Stableford, a British author, never found a British publisher for one of his best novels; another, *The Walking Shadow*, sold out so quickly that the publishers were annoyed by the need to reprint after only a few weeks, and petulantly decided not to.

Yes, I'm not alone in sometimes feeling – however unjustly – that publishers hate my *Guts*.

February 1989

73 Loaded Dialogues

'I don't know how you can *read* that sci-fi and fantasy stuff,' you have probably heard someone say, in tones implying that you also bite the heads off small furry animals and keep coal in the bath. The bizarre thing is the way in which people struggle to reinforce these literary ghetto divisions from both sides.

'This novel's really good,' I remember saying to an sf fan in a second-hand bookshop.

'But it's a ... *detective story!*' he gasped in stark terror.

'Ever so science-fictional, though,' I explained. (It was one of Peter Dickinson's: *The Poison Oracle*, plug, plug.)

'Er,' the sf fan quavered, retreating: '15p is a bit much to pay.'

Much more forthright was the lady fan to whom I mentioned that John Fowles's last novel *A Maggot* was of great interest to sf aficionados. 'I'm not reading *him*,' she exploded. 'He's a *novelist*!'

But to the diehard sf addict, there are things more terrible and threatening even than crime writers and 'mainstream' novelists. I made the mistake of telling one such chap that for my Xmas 1988 treat I'd reread three favourites: an 18th century novel, a 1930s detective story and a 1980s fantasy (actually John Crowley's excellent *Little, Big*).

'*Fantasy!?*' he spat. 'You traitor. Fantasy is a terrible cancer which pollutes the precious bodily fluids of true sf.'

'Well, a lot of those fantasy quest trilogies are pretty dire,' I allowed. 'Especially the ones that go over five volumes.'

'*All* fantasy is intellectually corrupt. It's cheap escapism which denies the real scientific principles of the real world.'

I thought a bit. 'Ah. What you want is fiction which takes proper account of the established laws of physics and mechanics as we know them today.'

'That's right,' he said stoutly. 'Real Science Fiction.'

'So obviously you despise all those ludicrous fantasy stories about free power, perpetual motion and immortality, which go against thermodynamics; and reactionless space drives, which violate the conservation of momentum; and matter-transmission, anti-gravity, faster-then-light spacecraft, ansibles and time machines, all flagrantly in breach of relativity.'

'That's different,' he said. 'It's a question of ... the scientific attitude, the world-view in which everything in the universe is rational and can be known.'

'Except,' I sniggered deplorably, 'that there's a famous theorem by Gödel which proves that even the abstract universe of pure mathematics is riddled with undecidables ... true facts you can't ever know are true.'

The argument went on. A lot of it seems to be prejudice about what you actually call the plot devices: floating a rabbit out of one's hat by a *spell* is mere shoddy fantasy, while doing the same thing by *psychokinesis* is sf and therefore OK.

In the end my pal won the debate by teleporting beer all over me and stamping out of the room. I was left wetly thinking that for *GM* readers, that was a good finale: the beer-flinging climax to the conversation was psychologically correct even though in fact I made it up. Narrative truth doesn't demand morbidly pedantic accuracy....

One of that hardened sf fanatic's favourite authors is Hal Clement, a writer whose hair has square roots and who was born with a silver slide-rule in his mouth. *Still River* (Sphere 280pp £3.50) shows him at his most erudite, not to say readable.

I won't insist that you need a doctorate in physical chemistry to tackle this one, but from time to time I felt handicapped by having a physics degree only. In brief: five research students from different worlds are dumped on the extremely weird planet Enigma, to fathom its arcane behaviour as their practical exam. After many mishaps they succeed.

Unfortunately the writing and characterization are flatter than the Euclidean plane. In endlessly protracted journeys through seething underground tunnels, there's barely a single vivid image to give life to the slow exposition of Enigma's gurgling internal oddities. Only one character – one of the aliens – comes alive a bit by virtue of a mild case of paranoia; even this doesn't lead anywhere.

Still River could have been gripping if told at a quarter of the length by Arthur C. Clarke or Greg Benford. But this time Clement seems just too busy with his textbooks and equations to bother with narrative suspense. I finished it with a single crumb of satisfaction – that I'd guessed before starting that the title was a pun.

'Just the sort of dumb reaction I'd expect from a low, crawling, fantasy lover,' I hear my hard-sf friend say....

Secretly he'd probably get a lot more enjoyment from Clifford Simak's collection *Brother & Other Stories* (Methuen 165pp £2.95). Simak more or less invented his own genre of Folksy American Midwestern Pastoral SF, and was more concerned with moods than how his sf stage-props actually worked.

His robots, for example, don't sod around picking loopholes in the Three Laws: they're too nostalgic, compassionate and kind to ants. The speed with which Simak characters leap intuitively to correct answers can be a mite unconvincing, but (unlike Clement's lecturing) doesn't plod. None of the four stories here feels over-long.

Be warned, though: they're definitely minor work, and the loathsome editor does his best to give away all the plots in an introduction. If you're new to Simak I'd advise starting with one of his novels instead: *Way Station*, *Time and Again* or, not quite a novel but justly celebrated, *City* (Methuen 255pp £3.50).

Famous sf author Samuel Delany offers a new edition with a new introduction – in fact by a pseudonymous Delany – of *Tales of Nevèrÿon* (Grafton 335pp £3.50)....

Hard SF Fan: Aha, caught you! Sneaking in another horrible lowbrow work of fantasy, eh?

Myself: How many fantasy epics do you know that are full of semiotics just like *The Name of the Rose*, with an approving quote from Umberto Eco Himself on the back?

Fan: I didn't read *Name of the Rose*, it was (ugh) mainstream.

Delany's weirdly analytical fantasies are beautifully written (most of the time), heavily didactic (some of the time), but completely unlike anything else around. The stories shouldn't be missed; try to ignore the pretentious apparatus of esoteric epigraphs and an appendix (by another and even more pseudonymous Delany) about 'the modular calculus'.

Brilliant and original stuff, honest. Mind you, at least one of the sequels is terrible.

Finally ... One of the last sf events of 1988 was a noisy, sweaty party-cum-auction intended to raise funds and avoid the looming bankruptcy of the 1987 World SF Convention organization. Apart from the appalling sight of Iain Banks drunkenly balanced on a shelf six feet off the ground, your reviewer strategically doesn't remember the party's most embarrassing scenes – bar one.

I was talking to an sf author who shall be nameless, but whose eyes bulged as they suddenly focused beyond me. 'What,' the author croaked, 'what is *that* apparition?'

Nervously I turned round and looked. 'Ah,' I said. 'I must introduce you to the famous and influential *GM* editor, Wayne....'

[*GM/GMI* co-editor Wayne's appearance and dress were highly distinctive, involving leather things, viciously studded things, artfully torn things, and a nova burst of bleached hair.]

March 1989

74 Megalomania!

SF writers are deeply addicted to the business motto 'Think Big'. If you're going to blow up a continent as part of your plot's love interest, why not do it properly and detonate the planet? The galaxy?

Likewise, if you fancy writing about a *big* artifact, why not make it absolutely bloody mega-colossal? It might be fun to compile a list of famous big constructions in sf.

Well, forget Ringworlds and Orbitsvilles, those merely (sniff) possible objects. I mean, for goodness' sake, they're finite! The three biggest urban development sites in sf are probably:

- Rudy Rucker's infinite place Cimön, in *White Light*, which stretches past ordinary infinities through and beyond the 'inaccessible numbers' and other domains which mathematicians take too long to explain.
- Christopher Priest's *Inverted World*, a hyperboloid which extends to (a conventional) infinity at both poles and all around its equator. Since the sun is the same weird shape, the planet therefore rather embarrassingly intersects its own sun....
- Greg Bear's 'Way' from *Eon*, a tunnel infinite in one dimension only, whose detailed space-time engineering makes it the most plausible Big Place yet.

Having thus Thought Big, Bear now strives to Think Bigger and outdo *Eon* with its sequel *Eternity* (Gollancz 399pp £12.95). He's a destructive little chap, having already polished off the Earth three times via biological transformation (*Blood Music*), nuclear holocaust (a minor subplot of *Eon*) and alien doomsday weaponry (*The Forge of God*).

How to follow these acts? Clearly Bear has to destroy the universe, which he does perfunctorily quite early in the book, and bring his own infinite Way to infinite ruin. It's a skilled, mind-blowing read, with some nicely chilly aliens, but nevertheless it left me with an itch in the cerebrum and a sour taste in the medulla.

The itch? The reason the Way must be destroyed is that, skewering its way to the end of space/time, it's mucking up the orderly closing down of the universe. (Hurry up please, it's time....) But if it 'is' once at the extreme far end of time, isn't it still 'there' no matter 'when' it's destroyed?

The sour taste comes from the way that the Clarke-like sense of boggling horizons, which ended *Eon* and gets a brief airing early in *Eternity*, is thoroughly upstaged by Bear's final act of destruction. The nicer characters are nicely pensioned off, and the gates to infinity are slammed shut. Ambition should be made of sterner stuff.

There are doors to strange places in Gene Wolfe's *There Are Doors* (Gollancz 313pp £12.95), a slightly surreal novel which achieves the difficult trick of making you doubt the hero's sanity even when the sf label on the jacket hints strongly that his weird experiences are 'real'.

In brief: nondescript salesman falls in love with quasi-goddess from elsewhere, her strangeness rubbing off on him and enabling him to pass without knowing through those Doors, in pursuit. Parts are funny, parts are hauntingly weird, and there's a thoroughly nasty sf notion lurking at the edge of the plot. As usual with a first reading of Wolfe, even this minor work, I suspect I haven't got to the bottom of it. (Translation: Wolfe excels at making me feel thick.)

A new Roger Zelazny, and not another blasted Amber book: *A Dark Travelling* (Hutchinson 109pp £6.95). In its US edition I thought this a bit lightweight - a nice idea or two but not enough tension or development, or for that matter words (those few pages are in big print). Here it's published as a children's book, which makes sense.

This is a slickly competent parallel worlds story in which fantasy and sf elements are blended: both gadgets and witchery are used to swap worlds, the worlds themselves being 'lightbands' or 'darkbands' depending not on the output of the local sun but on whether the rulers are goodies or baddies. Yes, it's really that simplistic.

So our hero, a teenage werewolf who's due for a nasty moment of puberty at his first full moon, joins forces with a witchy sister and a ninja pal to save the (or a) world from nameless technomagic, and guess what? They succeed, a little too soon.

Apparently the American series was meant to provide a showcase for hordes of standard sf themes: Zelazny did parallel worlds and Robert Silverberg, in the companion *Project Pendulum* (Hutchinson 139pp £6.95), did time travel. The latter took about fifteen minutes to read and makes Zelazny's effort look densely plotted and overburdened with tense drama. Young readers would do much better to find a copy of *The Time Machine*.

Something completely different. One of sf's weirdest talents is R.A. Lafferty, who tells profound and/or bloodthirsty stories with high hilarity - tall tales which he dares you not to believe. Now the story of his life and times is appearing in instalments, and gorblimey: it reads just like his fantasies.

Hero publisher Chris Drumm is the man responsible. Lafferty's non-fact history *In a Green Tree* has four volumes; Drumm has now published eight chapters of book 1, *My Heart Leaps Up*, in four booklets (54pp \$2.75, 44pp \$2.75, 53pp \$2.95 and 49pp \$2.75, post free from Drumm Books, PO Box 445, Polk City, Iowa 50226, USA). All contain unclassifiable gems from one of sf's few genuine Living National Treasures.

For a while I've been meaning to annoy the 'only printed words can be true Art' fans by mentioning comics. Something comics fans have probably been saying long and loud is that certain 'collected works' books now being heavily pushed in the shops look suspiciously like rip-offs.

Take volume 9 of Alan Moore's nifty *Swamp Thing* (Titan £5.95), whose introduction gets up my nose by flaunting such (deliberately subversive?) terms as 'lush' and 'floral' and 'hallucinogenic intensity', while as in previous volumes avoiding direct mention of the word 'colour'. These non-cheap reprints omit the originals' colour. Not lush at all.

Comparisons with the *Watchmen* book, or imported US *Swamp Thing* collections (lots more pages, full colour, comparable cost), suggest that these reissues are monstrously overpriced. And whether or not you enjoy comics, it's clearly artistic sabotage to drop a major feature like colour. When Titan start reprinting novels, will they edit out the adjectives?

Speaking of comics brings one to Harlan Ellison, who spies inform me has just received a terrific panning in *The Comics Journal* for pontificating not wisely but too loudly on the subject in *Playboy*. This reminds me of the legendary essay on Ellison's 17-year [2000: now more like 30-year] delay in completing his much-hyped and oft-promised anthology *The Last Dangerous Visions*....

In 1987 Christopher Priest published a preliminary version of *The Last Deadloss Visions*, a polemic about *LDV*'s saga of missed deadlines and broken promises. In 1988 the booklet was finalized with additional material - making it, incidentally, eligible for 1989's nonfiction Hugo award, a notion I gleefully pass on as bound to enrage many [alas, it wasn't nominated].

To read the whole story, including the death threat, send £5 for a copy to Priest c/o Ansible Information, 94 London Road, Reading, Berks, RG1 5AU. Like the Drumm booklets, you won't find this in W.H. Smith's.

[Update, 2000: Send no money, please. *The Last Deadloss Visions* was withdrawn with the appearance of a professionally published version of Priest's polemic as *The Book on the Edge of Forever* (Fantagraphics Press, 1994). This was indeed shortlisted for the nonfiction Hugo in 1995, but fell four votes short of winning.]

April 1989

75 Clarke Award Guilt

The awards season's here again, meaning frantic catching-up efforts from lazy sod reviewers (no names, now) who wish to retain job security by pretending to have read all the Important books long before they were shortlisted for prizes....

By the time you read this, the Arthur C. Clarke Award will have been announced and excitedly ignored by media worldwide. Seven books are shortlisted and I've read five, which isn't too bad.

Already reviewed in this column or its pallidly diminutive predecessor: Michael Bishop's *Philip K. Dick Is Dead, Alas* (good if over-long pastiche), Lucius Shepherd's *Life During Wartime* (fragmented but brilliantly potent and colourful), Brian Stableford's *The Empire of Fear* (instant classic of scientific romance) and Ian Watson's *Whores of Babylon* (very unreliable-reality, very Watson).

To conceal the fact that I haven't read Gwyneth Jones's *Kairos* and Rachel Pollack's *Unquenchable Fire* – not so much through vile sexism as because everyone ganged up on me and said 'Gosh, these are hefty and demanding and not to be read at *your* usual breakneck pace' – let's hastily discuss the remaining nominee, *Rumours of Spring* by Richard Grant (Bantam 458pp £3.50).

Er, I liked it. Grant, I'd guess, has fondly studied John Crowley, Mervyn Peake and M. John Harrison, five-sixths of whom are good influences. Also he's written the first decent science-fantasy to make use of Rupert Sheldrake's fabled morphogenetic-field theory, which like anti-gravity and time travel may be dubious science but makes interesting sf. As a gentle dig, Grant offers a character called Sheldrake who's full of hopeless herbal remedies and sympathetic magic.

In *Rumours*, the morphic fields 500 years hence have got out of hand and become a forced draught of evolution in the world's last forest, which looks set to grow without limit and generally Take Over. Against it is pitted a dotty Crusade of delightfully ineffectual characters struggling with decaying technology. Much of this is very funny.

At the heart of the story Grant manages to have his cake and eat it too, with that Sheldrakean plot-device twining three world-views – scientific, mythic-animistic, narrative – into a double reverse Gordian knot. Tachytelic evolution? Woodland spirits? Either, or both. One to read again, award or no award.

The award reminded me to take a belated look into Clarke's own *2061: Odyssey Three* (Grafton 302pp £2.99), quite rightly not shortlisted for anything. As a very lightweight read it's pleasant enough, if you skip the chunks of 'history of the world since 2010' padding and the hollow bonging portentous lines which end most chapters.

What's left? Some travelogue material about a trip to Halley's Comet, replete with worthy facts and schoolboy humour, and a chase after a mountainous Macguffin on Europa. Clarke is excruciatingly coy about this gigantic object, explaining first that it looks like ice but isn't, and then that it's frightfully interesting to persons of nudge nudge *South African* descent, and then dropping hints about the names of old Beatles songs, and then ...

So help me, 158 pages elapse between all this and the socko end-of-chapter revelation of what this 'magic mountain' is made of. Pausing only for the obligatory mystical bit in which the original enigmas of *2001* are made duller and more mundane, Clarke lays foundations for yet another sequel and signs off. The blurb says this 'tells of humanity's evolution towards the stars'. It doesn't.

A Gwyneth Jones book I *have* read is *The Hidden Ones* (Livewire 151pp £3.50), featuring the best-drawn punkish teenage heroine I've met in sf. Adele is prickly, unregenerate, severely bruised by life, terrified that her erratic mental abilities (poltergeist stuff, mostly) will get her slung into another institution. This indeed is the threat used against her by virtually every adult in the book, except one smiler who has more subtly exploitative plans.

There's a plotline about a rural fast-buck merchant whose nasty scheme for the local environment is just slightly too easily if not tritely defeated. Worthy stuff, no doubt, but it's Adele who sticks in your mind (and sneers at its contents, and starts hurling the furniture about ...).

Like Sheldrake's fields, Adele's telekinesis is a notion from the murky fringes of science. Sheldrake is cautiously mentioned in *The Cosmic Blueprint* by Paul Davies (Unwin 216pp £5.95), a good, readable survey of the quiet scientific revolution now taking place far in from the fringes.

Instead of a clockwork universe ticking in Newtonian cycles, they're talking about infinite chaos and unpredictability emerging from the simplest of starting points ... and about higher levels of order and organization growing from chaos. Davies offers a glimpse of an optimistic, evolutionary arrow of time which is a cheery change from the all too familiar entropic arrow that points to nothing but a final chucking-out time. From my regrettable viewpoint as an sf writer, this looks like a marvellous source of story ideas. Pinch a few for your own sf scenarios.

One cavil: the illustrations are awful, murky scraps of graph paper and palsied sketches apparently drawn while the train was going over points. Unwin should have invested a few bob in nice graphics.

Speaking of which, I could almost kid myself that my bitching has influenced that luxuriously priced *Swamp Thing* comic reprint series. Volume 10 (Titan £5.95) contains the first admission that, yes, the originals were in colour, and – by implication – yes, the person who did the colouring (Tatjana Wood) has until now been expunged from the records.

Other aspects of the comics scene bother me too. Self-confessed rising megastar Neil Gaiman thrust his and artist Dave McKean's *Black Orchid* at me

(DC import, around £2.55 per book). Yes, I thought again, this shows that comics *can* be highly literate and *can* have beautiful artwork ... but surely the best stories are self-contained?

DC don't work that way. If they published sf novels, writers would have to work within the fundamental 'history of the universe' laid down by Doc Smith or whoever. No one would be allowed to blow up the world in a story, because it would muck up the continuity of other 'simultaneous' tales. Established heroes and villains would be expected to get cameo parts in new books.

There's plenty of this in *Black Orchid*, mildly ho-hum when I recognize the cross-references and bloody annoying when - not having spent all my days reading these things - I don't. So I show some sceptic this trilogy as an example of genre improvement and fresh originality, and he opens it at random and hurls it across the room with a cry of 'It's got sodding *Batman* in it!'

Meanwhile I'm still trying to find time to read S*lman R*shdie's *The Satanic Verses* before someone sets fire to my copy. As I write, there are further demands that Britain's stupid, antiquated blasphemy laws should not be sensibly abolished but extended to all religions. Including voodoo? Satanism? Scientology?

May 1989

76 Secrets of Publicity

Publishers, as writers know from bitter experience, work hard to avoid publicity and discourage favourable reviews, which only make the authors uppity. Here are some of the tricks which keep enthusiasm to a minimum.

• If a reviewer obviously likes your author, quit while you're ahead and don't send the author's next book. In this way, publishers tried to avoid *GM* coverage of Terry Pratchett's and Diana Wynne Jones's last novels. I cheated and bought copies, but the reviews were grudging, grudging.

Ditto my comments on Robert Rankin's unclassifiably funny *The Sprouts of Wrath* (Abacus 248pp £3.99), not received for review. Again nameless occult and sidereal forces converge on that most ancient of sacred sites, the Brentford gasometer. Again Rankin's shifty, beer-swilling eccentrics confront fates worse than regular employment. Again Langford fell out of his chair a lot. But grudgingly.

• Go for the reviewer's weak spot. An overdose of Piers Anthony has left me notoriously apt to break out in a rash at the least exposure to puns and tweeness. Esther M. Freisner's new fantasy may be jolly triffic despite the unicorn (not to mention the pert-bottomed prince in tights) on the cover, but can one really bring oneself to open a book called *Elf Defence*? (Headline 234pp £2.99.)

• Deal mortal blows to the brain by sending 'shared world anthologies' in which many writers set stories in the same fictional 'universe'. Once interesting as an occasional gimmick, this has become an entire naff publishing category. Even if good stories are contributed, the collection will always be sunk by the leaden efforts of other writers who don't play well in these away matches.

Case in point: *Tales of the Witch World* 'created by' André Norton (Pan 343pp £3.99), with a cast of thousands. Verily, popular Norton is for her fantasies melodramatic, with syntax backward and writing turgid, mayhap too faithfully here imitated. I'm sending the blurb to the Advertising Standards Authority. 'Comparable with and often surpassing the works of J.R.R. Tolkien', indeed.

• Send lots of short story collections. No, there's nothing inherently repugnant about shorts, which some still reckon are the lifeblood of sf. Unfortunately it takes as long to comment sensibly on each short as on a novel. One cunning retaliatory ploy is to concentrate on the title story, as follows ...

Dark Night in Toyland by Bob Shaw (Gollancz 190pp £11.95, 15 stories) has a grimmer tone than previous Shaw collections despite several very lightweight pieces; the title story is a pitiless sf examination of death and religion. As in good tragedy, the ending can be seen coming a long way off but stays effective.

Salvage Rites by Ian Watson (Gollancz 223pp £11.95, 15 stories) shows Britain's premier sf 'ideas man' flinging out endless notions, about half of them worth making into stories. The title piece, which coincidentally echoes Shaw's, is a nice bit of Grand Guignol yuck whose agreeably nasty finale doesn't actually make a lot of sense.

The Toynbee Convector by Ray Bradbury (Grafton 277pp £12.95, 23 stories) is all Bradburian whimsy and poetry, not perhaps for hard sf fans. The title story is that old one about hoaxing the world into being nicer, as in several Sturgeon shorts, a *Twilight Zone* episode, and *Watchmen*. It's moving for just as long as you can avoid contemplating the stark unlikelihood of anyone *believing* the feeble deception involved. As usual, Bradbury improves as he gets further from straight sf.

• A nasty ploy if you want to sink an sf/fantasy book is to have it sent out by Pengelly Mulliken Publicity ... perfectly nice people whose name unfortunately gives reviewers agonizing bouts of Pengelly Mulliken Tension (PMT), since past experience has shown that parcels from their address often contain appalling books by L. Ron Hubbard.

This time, opening the jiffybag cautiously with tongs and asbestos gloves, I found *Robert E. Howard's World of Heroes* (Robinson 424pp £3.95, 10 stories). Assorted Howard heroes tackle a variety of 'loathly demonic things that crawled hideously up from hell'. What passes for criticism in the fantasy world usually overrates Howard's writing on the strength of historical importance - he *invented* sword and sorcery, including the famous phrase 'mighty-thewed' - but these vigorous pulp adventures are infused with loony energy borrowed from his own distinct dippiness.

[To clarify: Howard invented the S&S *genre*, but credit for the actual term should go to Fritz Leiber.]

• If the American title isn't sufficiently off-putting, change it to something worse. Thus Spider Robinson's three *Callahan's Crosstime Saloon* collections have been boiled down for British consumption as *Callahan's Crazy Crosstime Bar* (Legend 351pp £3.50, 12 stories).

Robinson's an odd case. So many sf characters are soulless ciphers that it seems churlish to complain of someone going too far in the other direction, but Robinson really lays it on with a trowel - no, a JCB.

Callahan's Bar regulars ooze empathy in glutinous streamers, like ectoplasm. They love each other, and they love telling each other how much they love each other, and they all laugh long and loud at the same tall stories and lousy puns, and they have this wonderful sort of caring group mind, and often the bones of a perfectly good story get lost in gooey accretions of schmaltz.

Robinson's learned a lot from Heinlein, much of it good, but including Heinlein's special rule that there *is* such a thing as a free lunch if you're one of the Right People, who get away with murder while reserving the right to liquidate outsiders for high crimes like bad table manners. (There is a word for the political theory based on this attitude, but it's been over-used of late.) The stories are readable and fun, but leave this aftertaste....

How can you ensure a favourable review from the likes of capricious me? Easy. First invite me to a *big launch party* with *lots of free champagne*, as Unwin Hyman did recently. Also, make sure the book being launched is as good as Garry Kilworth's *Hunter's Moon* (Unwin 330pp £12.95).

This is 'a story of foxes', much more sympathetic creatures than, say, the rabbits of *Watership Down*. It's very carefully researched, and Kilworth avoids the usual major implausibility of imposing an epic plot: real animals don't go on epic quests, and his foxes are real.

What do they do? Just try to live: through the last days of hunting in their wood, through redevelopment and the transition to urban life, through shoot-everything-in-sight rabies scares, through the terrors of dogs, cars, poison, all the machinery of civilization.

En route we learn a lot about the vividly three-dimensional and smelly foxes, their haunts, habits and food, their relative frailty - even a cat can give one a hard time. Kilworth adds some poetically appropriate myths, rituals and eschatology. There are minor lapses when the communications between foxes get faintly soap-operatic or where a bit of humour jars ('Vixens - who could fathom them?'), but in general they're emphatically animals, not people in funny suits.

This is a fine, moving book which I hope will swell the ranks of hunt saboteurs. Nice one, Garry.

June 1989

77 More and More Clarke

Let us now praise famous men. Arthur C. Clarke's *Astounding Days: a Science Fictional Autobiography* (Gollancz 224pp £12.95) is pleasant enough, and more readable than Asimov's blockbuster chronicle of every shopping list and bowel movement of his life ... but it does feel insubstantial. The trouble with literary autobiographies is that despite gaudy claims of past occupations ('lumberjack, nuclear physicist, short-order cook, pimp, President of the USA'), the typical author's life consists of sitting on one's bottom, growing ever more flabby and pallid as the years flit by.

Clarke's bright idea is to invite you for a ramble around his 1930-45 copies of *Astounding SF* magazine, with much humorous nostalgia and many a chatty anecdote. What a nice but tiresome old chap, you think as he repeats himself in many pages of reprinted material, and calls unnecessary attention to his trophies: he's genuinely world-famous and shouldn't need to shore up his ego with dragged-in references to this award and that bestseller and how - for the umpteenth time - he gets invited to address the UN.

He has some fun with terrible old stories and their scientific howlers: cold rays, planets inside atoms, the 'ultimate prime number'. But rather too many *good* stories are merely mentioned without comment. Like *1066 and All That*, this is only a sporadic collection of the history its author happens to remember.

Best bits: memories of the British Interplanetary Society's early enthusiasm. 'Mrs Edwards put her foot down on hearing of our intention to cast lead weights in her best saucepan.'

Worst omission, something essential for a book as rambling as this: an index. Slapped wrists to all at Gollancz.

Most unbelievably tasteless remark: 'And perhaps if NASA had remained faithful to the Greek pantheon, its luck would not have run out on 28 January 1986.'

Meanwhile, the Clarke Award for sf was this year won by Rachel Pollack's *Unquenchable Fire* (Legend 390pp £3.99). This is a future fable set in the afterglow of a sort of Second Coming, in which the hot colours of Latin-American magical realism have now lit up boring old North America.

It's an age of everyday miracles, where divine manifestations are liable to knock you down in the street, and small-town Americans worry about demons rather than Reds under the bed. The heroine is unfortunate enough to be selected by Something as the mother of a new prophet, and is not best pleased by this. Pollack's witty picture of the transformed USA is haunted by darkly primal imagery and shades of Yeats's 'Second Coming'. Recommended despite a surfeit of bodily fluids.

Traditional 'hard' sf is represented by Stanislaw Lem's grimly uncompromising *Fiasco* (Orbit 322pp £4.99). Once again (see *Solaris* and *The Invincible*), a human exploration team confronts a planet-sized enigma that can't or won't communicate in our terms. What to do?

In *Fiasco* the humans feel very much in control: the alien Quintans have a technology within shouting distance of Earth's today, while 'our' side boasts a later generation of world-wrecking sidereal energies. No problem.

But the Quintans seem too busy fighting each other to talk. Slowly it dawns on you that the murderous battleground to which they've reduced their entire solar system is Lem's own careful extrapolation of today's 'Star Wars' defence proposals. Meanwhile, step by logical step, the boys with the ultimate weapons decide that a show of force is the only way to gain the Quintans' attention. Once they've started down that path, they find it hard to stop.

Fiasco takes ages to get going: the opening is a good but barely connected short story whose existence is only part-justified by links to the blazing finale, when the most innocent and heroic (and over-thick) character of all makes the expedition's last mistakes. A solidly depressing read. [But see further thoughts below.]

I tend to be depressed by Tolkien spin-offs, and here's another, *The Hobbit* again! But wait: it's *The Annotated Hobbit* with notes by Douglas A. Anderson (Unwin Hyman 337pp £14.95), and a very nice piece of book production too.

This sort of thing depends on the quality of the marginal notes: for classy examples, see Martin Gardner's *The Annotated Alice* and *The Annotated Snark*. Anderson does a reasonable if lacklustre job, but ultimately doesn't seem to have worked hard enough. (Maybe only pedants would complain that he fails to tag a quotation from the Duke of Wellington in an included Tolkien letter; but too many simple, obsolete words aren't annotated.) It's interesting to see illustrations from countless editions of *The Hobbit* – almost as many artists seem to have tackled it as *Alice*. Tolkien complained of 'frightful' Swedish and 'foul' Portuguese artwork, and on the evidence here he had a point.

Completists will find much of the 'note' material suspiciously familiar (especially from the *Letters* and Shippey's *Road to Middle-Earth*, heavily pillaged here), but then completists probably bought this five seconds after publication.

Ellis Peters's twelfth-century 'mediaeval whodunnits' seem popular among sf/fantasy fans, since they do after all depict an alien world. I've been reading them on and off with growing disaffection. The series started well with *A Morbid Taste for Bones*, a good mix of monastic piety and black humour. But it's gone on too long.

The trouble is that Peters has fallen into a dreadfully predictable formula of Romance Fulfilled. It becomes increasingly clear that the prime directive of her plots is to get the book's inevitable Young Lovers happily married off (ahhhh ...). A practised killer may have all the time in the world to ensure his victim is done for, but if the victim is one of the Young Lovers he will miraculously survive.

The latest into paperback, *The Confession of Brother Haluin* (Futura 205pp £2.99), falls apart completely as a whodunnit. You simply apply the prime directive as above, and it's instantly apparent that the Young Lovers – who as supposed half-siblings can't shack up together – must therefore turn out not to be related, whereupon all the rest of the plot is laid bare. The wit that animated these books has dissolved in sentimental, melodramatic sludge. If interested, stick to the early ones.

A friend once spent years puzzling over that favourite blurb-writer's word 'Kafkaesque', until finally he read Kafka and decided, not altogether fairly, that it meant 'boring'. *Mr Narrator* by Pat Gray (Dedalus/Hippocrene 155pp £4.95) is billed as both Kafkaesque and surreal, which would make my pal run a mile. Wimpish businessman entangled in barely exaggerated toils of Arab finance, politics, sex: some good scenes and witty passages, but the narrative never really breaks loose to become a Universal Statement in Kafka fashion, and vanishes routinely up its own fundament.

Reissues not to be missed ... *Dying Inside* by Robert Silverberg (VGSF Classics 188pp £2.99) takes the 'mainstream' chestnut of a man whose powers and potency are deserting him, and makes it new with the strong sf metaphor of a telepath whose talent is fading. Lucius Shepherd's brilliant *Life During Wartime* (Paladin 383pp £4.99) keeps just missing the awards it deserves. And Philip K. Dick's *The Divine Invasion* (Grafton 270pp £2.99) is ever so Philip K. Dick.

Look back at the prices above. Publishers' wisdom, apparently justified by experience, is that readers who think £3 rather too expensive can be suckered into paying £2.95. Now, by mysterious mutual consent, the £2.95 is becoming £2.99. You are supposed to be too dim to notice.

July 1989

78 Bladder of Doom

No longer can I claim total ignorance of these terrible things which happen elsewhere in the magazine, and which I understand are called live role-playing. Now I too have descended into cavernous gloom, amid the savage clash and parry of rubber swords....

This was all an eccentric launch party (that's *launch*, printers, not lunch as it became last time I used the word) for the Joe Dever 'Legends of Lone Wolf' spin-off material. My old pal John Grant co-wrote the novels, so I accompanied him on his heroic quest for publicity.

All the best epics involve gruelling journeys through pitiless conditions, and London Transport deserves credit for forcing us to stagger from Paddington to Charing Cross during a heatwave. Shrivelled and sweat-drenched, we finally attained the Chislehurst Caves, and it all went ape.

'You,' I was told, 'are Sir Conrad, a knight who prefers the banqueting hall to the battlefield.' I begged to be something more like Langford Hackrender, barbarian scourge of the pulpsmiths, but this was not permitted. Shepherded by persons in arcane robes or knitted chainmail, a band of literati and media hacks bore their hurricane lamps nervously into the tunnels.

The subterranean journey was punctuated by loud encounters which were doubtless thrillingly choreographed if one had been able to see anything. I particularly enjoyed the sadistic spectacle of a Radio Midlands chap being stripped of his symbiotic tape recorder and thrust whimpering into the darkness to hit things with a padded stick.

Our quest's goal was a dank, lamplit cavern where the party was plied with lethal cocktails and such delights as 'swamp viper', which I found too late was smoked eel ... backbone, skin and all. As the booze flowed freely, several guests got very thoughtful about warnings that *(a)* no one should stray out of sight for fear of being lost in 22 miles of caves, while *(b)* there were no toilets down here. I cast a diplomatic veil over the ensuing scenes.

More role-playing fun lay in store as the now sodden visitors were invited to win a grand prize by solving riddles which costumed characters would pose on request. I'm afraid I blew it. Approaching a hideously made-up dwarf wielding an inflatable axe, I started with 'Excuse me, good sir,' and at once she took huge offence.

Egged on by evil John Grant, I tried again: 'Hello, costumed person, tell me your riddle.'

'I'm not in costume, you bastard,' said Wayne.

As Messrs Dever and Grant were dragged piteously off to sign 1000 copies of the Beaver 'Lone Wolf' novels (review contract for these masterworks seized by eager Alan Crump, *GM*'s other book critic), I located a native guide and headed back towards the sun, falling over from time to time.

Here is a completely serious novel of the future, *Island Paradise* by Kathy Page (Methuen 192pp £11.99). This shows a world ruled by a new and awful moral balance in which war and killing are unthinkable, but by way of compensation you're expected to shuffle off voluntarily soon after your retirement. It's thoroughly gloomy and exceedingly well written.

But I think I detect uneasiness in the author, as though she were uncertain of how to handle sf. Euphemisms about Timely and Untimely exits, the former being the Price of apparent utopia, are relentlessly Repeated in Capitals to hammer the point home: who in 1989 goes significantly on and on about capitalized Pensions and Funerals?

Then we hear about importing power from planet 'Three'. Quite apart from the economics of this (spaceborne solar collectors make far more sense), it seems fairly daft to suggest that people won't carry on calling it Venus, or Mars. Page appears more concerned to steer clear of the sf slums than to retain credibility. Surely any old hack could work up something more plausible than her picture of a totally unguarded 'please take one' nuclear stockpile.

I'd rather read Page, whose characters are niftily drawn and who can write most of the sf crew under the table. Nevertheless, that embarrassed fudging of sf tropes leaves her world unfocused; it has not been clearly thought through.

One of those old, er, traditionalist sf authors is Gordon Dickson, whose *Chantry Guild* (Sphere 428pp £3.99) adds another doorstop-weight to the seemingly endless Dorsai series.

Dickson is an interesting case. Like Poul Anderson, he started with escapist space-adventure novels and then began to get Heavy. [But, as I wrote in *Foundation*, he tries to add this increasing philosophical weight to the jerrybuilt fabric of his earlier sf action-adventure novels, rather as though a colossal bronze mask of Tragedy were to be erected atop a pinball machine.] The Dorsai or 'Childe' cycle is now supposed to be a panorama of human evolution, with a plot gimmick that justifies traditionally stereotyped characters: the race has split into specialized breeds of soldiers, fanatics, mystics, physicists, lavatory attendants, etc.

In theory you get a vast panorama; in practice you get action-adventure with interspersed dull bits about the meaning of it all. I rather lost patience with *The Final Encyclopaedia*, whose hero abruptly realized that to save the universe he needed to ... lock himself in a library and meditate. The book ended as he triumphantly slammed the door. *Chantry Guild* is the sequel.

(I forgot to mention that for those unconvinced by one chap holding the fate of the whole universe in his hands, Dickson keeps explaining that he merely represents huge historical forces. Any reasonably astute historical force would, you'd think, hire more than one representative.)

So hero Hal Mayne awaits the spiritual insight which will save the plot. In hope of finding it he visits some mystics whose habit is to plod in endless circles: this proves wondrously inspirational. Dickson injects only a modicum of excitement via external threats (too easily disposed of) and flashbacks, and in 428 pages advances the situation by one small step. The universe-busting arch-fiend still prowls outside, undefeated, unchallenged, exactly as at the end of *Encyclopaedia*. Oh God, this means another sequel.

Being Invisible by Thomas Berger (Mandarin 262pp £3.50) was something of a relief after all those world-shakers. Its protagonist is essentially a wimp, trapped in a horrible job writing naff advertising copy, surrounded by oafish colleagues and intimidating women; and one day he discovers the knack of invisibility.

The result is low comedy rather than H.G. Wells's brutal moral fable, but Berger keeps his story 'realistic' and some of the laughs ring true. It gives an extra comic edge to the narrative when awful, tragic or humiliating plot-turns are clearly always on the cards. SF author Bob Shaw once noted that if you really want to make people laugh, you should describe in unsparing detail one of the most dreadful things that ever happened to you. It never fails.

This applies too to Terry Pratchett's *Pyramids* (Gollancz 272pp £11.95). One thinks of the Discworld books as being jolly little romps, but they gain comic strength from repeatedly dealing with final things like death ... not to mention, of course, DEATH.

This time the hero is an assassin, a deceased pharaoh gets to watch (in spirit) his brains being extracted through his nostrils, an innocent bystander loses a hand, 1300 unhappy mummies reveal how thoroughly rotten they've found the afterlife, several people are fed to crocodiles, and I can't even bring myself to explain what happens to the tortoises. Basically, we are not talking P.G. Wodehouse here. Horribly funny and well up to standard.

I'd have been much more nervous if Pratchett had scripted that psychodrama in the Chislehurst Caves....

August 1989

79 Diabolus Ex Machina

One easy way to get the thrill of being an insider is to report on books for publishers, so that when something finally reaches print you can sniff, 'Ah, *I* read it in manuscript, of course.' The smart printed version always seems better than that original pile of grimy, fly-specked paper; there's a distinct danger of finding a good book unsatisfying just because the MS looks all tatty.

I wondered whether this had happened a bit when in 1987 I read Barry Hughart's *The Story of the Stone* (now Bantam 236pp £6.95). It's a sequel to his *Bridge of Birds*, a highly enjoyable romp through the old China of legend (rather than of mere boring history), which as well as incidental knockabout fun and ribaldry has a wonderful high-fantasy finale. The new book is OK but never quite soars in that way.

For *Stone*, Hughart has stirred in lots of tasty ingredients - some of them a shade too familiar from *Bridge*. Again you get underground maze-solving, ancient crimes whose solution emerges from ancient folklore, the narrator's naughty dalliance with someone too wonderful for this earth, a final scene of transcendence, etc. All the bits pass muster, but as a whole *Stone* is a shade too over-elaborated ... even over-sophisticated. Some of the best things in *Bridge* were the old and simple ones, like the fairytale 'tell me three times' repetitions.

Thus even in its nifty published form, Hughart's second book is still faintly disappointing by comparison with his first. It remains a good read, full of good things. By the way, if you like this non-factual Chinese background, hunt for copies of Ernest Bramah's incomparable 'Kai Lung' books. (One was reissued by Oxford University Press quite recently, with a blurb which successfully concealed any hint that the book is funny.)

Angel Fire by Andrew M. Greeley (Legend 304pp £12.95) sounds interesting. A maverick biologist gets the Nobel Prize for evolutionary theories which hint at the possible development of beings very like angels; mysterious assassins dog his journey to Stockholm; a luscious and literal guardian angel turns up to protect him.

The result is readable but not quite satisfying. It cries out for an infusion of some author like Thorne Smith to pep up the feebly naughty bits, or John D. MacDonald to give colour to flabby characters. Clichés and implausibilities abound: vile Irish brogues, East Germans who are all Nazi torturers, Englishmen who say 'sheem' for 'scheme' (Greeley must be thinking of the variant pronunciation of 'schedule'), and daft Thatcherite projects to harness the energy of angels which no one believes to exist.

Tension is provided by far too many cloudily motivated attempts on our unlucky hero's life and/or knowledge ... threats which after the first couple are visibly futile, since omnipotent, invulnerable, teleporting, time-travelling, bilocating 'Gabriella' can frustrate them all with the twitch of a spiritual finger. It's a pleasant enough page-turner, but unbalanced, like a D&D game with a party of six beginners and one 200th level mage. The happy ending goes on for twenty pages of treacly superfluity after making its point.

When you've been around for a bit in the writing business, you make the alarming discovery that your infamy has spread wider than you knew. I said loud and rude things on seeing one of my parodies shortlisted for a 'Girgamesh Award' in Spain ... not having been told (or got any money from) the fact of its even being *published* in translation.

The Girgamesh criterion of 'first Spanish publication in 1987' made for some strange bedfellows, with ancient Leiber books and mid-period Ian Watsons up against newish stuff from Silverberg and Bear; the 1980s Silverberg very properly losing to Silverberg-1972; and best of all, Clive Barker tying with that other rising horror megastar Walter de la Mare. Who died in 1956.

It was nice to see the dear old Nicholls/Langford/Stableford *The Science in Science Fiction* winning another of these awards, though I still haven't seen a copy of this Spanish edition, or the German one, or the Swedish one which rumour said was being heavily rewritten to replace parochial references to British and American sf with matters of more widespread global importance, i.e. Swedish sf....

Second Variety by Philip K. Dick (Gollancz 395pp £12.95, 27 stories) is volume two in the collected stories of the sf writer who :: reality transform :: butterfly dreams :: Zen override hallucinatory meta-God loop :: kipple and potsherds :: we are completely surrounded by vugs :: different, unique and impossible to summarize.

You could say the same about Samuel Delany's **Nevèrÿon** books - all Grafton paperbacks whose titles contain weird accents that our printers would rather not know about. They look like fantasies but are deeply subversive. *Tales of Nevèrÿon* and *Neveryóna* are thick with anthropology, semiotics (*you* know: a semiotic is half an otic), conscious artifice, and Delany's trademark of fanciable young men with bitten fingernails. *Flight from Nevèrÿon* climaxes in 'The Tale of Plagues and Carnivals', its fantasy plague cross-cutting with Delany's personal dismay as his New York gay community was decimated by AIDS. It hits hard.

Small press spot: *The Many Worlds of Larry Niven* is a very complete-looking bibliography from Drumm Books (63pp $4.50, address in column 74). I tried without success to catch it out in likely omissions like Niven's fanzine articles or obscurely published nonfiction. But the title of his first novel is mistyped on page 1 and twice more on p63, so there.

As usual, my word processor is overshadowed by a vast and teetering tower of stuff I can't actually face reviewing. (Warning to publishers: all fantasy/sf gamebooks fall into this category.) The most off-putting current title, by a short head, is *The Devilgod in the Empire of the Universal Master* by Collins Jallim (Book Guild 160pp £10.50).

But the star prize for resistibility must go to James V. Smith's *Beastmaker* (Grafton 336pp £3.50) The cover shows the book's *diabolus ex machina* – 'It Lives To Kill!' – possibly the silliest-looking unspeakable horror to be portrayed on a paperback. Little bulging round eyes, cute stubby horns, carrot-sized claws, rows and rows of grinning pointy teeth, lashings of saliva, grey fun-fur, *and* a faceful of scales, all leaping out at you in glorious bas-relief. Could any book live up to the hilarity of this monster? Well, I checked the back page for that guaranteed laugh-line 'THE END – OR IS IT?', and yes, in paraphrase it was there....

To provide the obligatory mention of Terry Pratchett, he confides: 'I'm giving Discworld a bit of a rest, you'll be madly interested to know. Not because the ideas aren't coming, but because this angel appeared to me and said, "Look, you don't have to write two a year, honestly"; so I'm working on some children's books and other stuff.' A stay of execution is thus granted to vast and fear-crazed Scandinavian forests.

Lastly, it would be wrong for me to review *Dark Fantasies*, edited by Chris 'Slime and Chainsaws' Morgan (Legend 319pp £5.95), an undoubtedly ace collection of sixteen subtle (as opposed to raw-liver revoltingness) horror stories by people I know, including me. In fact, to maintain my impartial attitude to this incredibly brilliant anthology, I haven't yet read it.

September 1989.

80 The Critics' Mafia

In the skimpy tradition of humorous sf, John Sladek occupies a special place for his satirical novels, usually set in a bizarrely mechanized American Midwest of the future. 'I feel I ought to do my part in helping machines take over the arts and sciences, leaving us plenty of leisure time for important things, like extracting square roots and figuring payrolls.' His books have got steadily grimmer and closer to the present, until ...

Bugs (Macmillan 213pp £12.95) demonstrates the 'discreet cough' school of sf packaging, which seeks to woo a snobbish literary establishment by concealing any clue that this might be sf. Even Sladek's other sf novels are discreetly mentioned only as 'works'. Inside, the same Midwestern black humorist is at work, informing us that most people don't think but just run consciousness and conversation programs, often to hilarious effect but baffling Sladek's far more creative robots.

The naive English hero plunges into an American nightmare of ghastly jargon, a deranged computer industry, the 'Presidential Sanity Hearings', fast-food restaurants to chill the blood, and the quest to build a military robot: 'Most important of all, it needs to be someone the men can look up to.' When the robot reads *Frankenstein* it naturally starts to get gloomy ideas about its future.

The plot is hysterical and unsummarizable, with many effective running gags. But beneath the hilarity are echoes of *Gulliver's Travels* and *The Island of Dr Moreau*, where the hero returns to see his fellow-men in a new light, as barely disguised animals; or in *Bugs*, as empty robotic shells buzzing with insect data-bits. You laugh and you shiver.

Killer Planet (Gollancz 105pp £8.95) looks at first glance like a new departure for famous and lovable Bob Shaw ... it's a 'younger readers' sf novel. The opening has an uncertain feel, with very much cruder construction than expected from Shaw: painstaking explanations of sf terms, a lone diehard idealist pitted against the entire (and of course wilfully blind) Stellar Authority, a major coincidence to kick-start the plot.

However, once we reach the stormy hell-planet of the title it's sort-of-exciting stuff with many a spurt of adrenalin, reading rather like an escaped episode from the same author's *Ship of Strangers* sequence – which is no bad thing. Two ingeniously daft sf coups ('Faraday!' he half-shouted. 'Faraday's Cage!') and one crushing dose of Gritty Reality do more or less compensate for a somewhat painfully spelt-out Moral. Lumbering, old-fashioned fun ... in fact I suspect it will appeal more to old fogeys who remember Kemlo and the awful sf of Captain W.E. Johns than to the sophisticated present-day kids who are its supposed audience.

Very much older, a 1960 novel set back in the dying Ice Age, Roy Lewis's *The Evolution Man* (Corgi 160pp £3.99) reads as though written yesterday and looks suspiciously like an influence on the writer who's coaxed it back into print - you know, whatsisname, fellow with the turtles and Luggage and HOLLOW CAPITALS.

This hilariously deadpan satire takes us through the Pleistocene invention of all sorts of appalling things, all by the same remarkably articulate ape-man: fire, spears, marriage, arrows, cookery ... It's left to his rather less brilliant offspring to devise the even more fearful spin-offs, like religion, politics and national security. Grab this gem before it goes out of print for another 29 years.

Robinson Publishing keep doing voluminous anthologies like *The Mammoth Book of Golden Age SF* (504pp £4.99; 10 stories), edited by that interminable trio Asimov, Greenberg and Waugh. As a selection of clanking 1940s sf, this one is OK provided you're an absolute newcomer. Anyone who's been around more than about five minutes will own most of the stories here: four have long been incorporated into well-known novels. It seems peculiarly discreditable to sneak in an episode of *Foundation* itself, disguised under the 1944 magazine title.

With a sigh of relief I turned to Barbara Hambly's *Immortal Blood* (Unwin 306pp £3.50), neglected on its appearance because of a naff vampire cover and mislaid until just now. Hambly continues to bring a reliable freshness to mouldy old themes: here a don and retired spy is hired not to hunt vampires, but as their agent to find out what rotten imitator of Prof. Van Helsing is murdering the vampires themselves.

The plot zips happily along with the proper number of expected/unexpected turns. I enjoyed it despite lapses in early-20th-century background. (Did anyone still call a crowbar a 'crow' in this century, and could 'spanner' ever have been a synonym for this tool? Was Liverpool Street Station ever called Liverpool Station? The author of *Alice* never rose to be 'Professor Dodgson'. Etc.) Strange that the very rational hero, who *knows* that sunlight destroys vampires, never investigates magnesium flares or electrical discharge tubes but instead buys silver charms recommended by superstition alone.

I usually try to set aside a spot to put the finger on some real clunker which made me shriek with boredom. Unfortunately I'm reviewing *Information Technology: Agent of Change* by Murray Laver for another publication altogether. Tough luck, masochism fans.

Instead, it's confession time. Grim-jawed members of the Critics' Mafia recently backed me up against the wall and posed hard questions like, 'How come you didn't slag off Lem's boring and aptly named *Fiasco* in July?'

'I am not infallible,' I whimpered. 'I'd written too much and had to edit my column in a hurry, thus losing certain comments about Borges' and indeed Lem's clever practice of *not* writing some tremendously heavy novel but instead reviewing the book as though it had been written - putting across the ideas without all that dreadful slog for the writer and reader. *Fiasco*, I failed to make clear, would have benefited vastly from this treatment. Please, take away that L. Ron Hubbard dekalogy now....'

They let me off with a reprimand, on condition that I made this public confession. It's a hard life in the Critics' Mafia.

Speaking of which, every sf critic called David has been trembling in fear of being the next book reviewer over at *White Dwarf*. I lasted nearly six years there. David Pringle stuck it out for mere seconds. Now David Barrett has thrown in the towel thanks to a problem I never met myself but thought I could see coming: pressure from the Games Workshop hierarchy concerning the column's actual content. (To paraphrase: 'More downmarket adventure juveniles, please; stop reviewing this good stuff.')

This, to anyone who thought about it, has clearly been on the cards ever since GW planned its foray into **Warhammer** game spin-off novels. I'd like to see an announcement in *Dwarf* that the next sf reviewer will be perfectly free to praise, condemn or ignore these publications on their individual merits. Otherwise... well, I rather like to think the column was respected for its independence. If all GW books must (like their games) be uniformly praised, who'll be able to trust *Dwarf*'s coverage of 'rival' publishers?

[In the end *Dwarf* simply dropped the book reviews.]

Personally I've no quarrel with *Dwarf*: they always treated me well and paid up faster than some magazines I could mention. However, since leaving I've been a bit miffed at the way *my* column title 'Critical Mass' has been pinched and imposed on later reviewers who would have preferred their own. Not quite cricket, chaps. Couldn't you afford some new artwork?

A fearful challenge confronts me for next month, in the shape of two sodding great enormous blockbusters, both just arrived, both merely the first parts of vast series: *The Dragonbone Chair* by Tad Williams and *Chung Kuo: The Middle Kingdom* by David Wingrove. Together: 1155 pages. Wish me luck.

October 1989

81 The Greasy Stockpot

I promised to report on certain mighty blockbusters, beginning with Tad Williams's *The Dragonbone Chair* (Legend 654pp £14.95), which is of course but the first volume of a presumable trilogy.

One can see that the road will be long and arduous; to add to the challenge, obstacles have been set in our path. The publishers do their bit with shrill quotations from uncritical reviews in *Locus* ('The fantasy equivalent of *War and Peace*', a judgment doubtless based on micrometer measurements of thickness) and *Xignals* (a US publisher's house magazine which exists only to puff their own books).

Then the author tells us that this is book one of 'Memory, Sorrow and Thorn' ... which looks irritatingly like a semantic selection error and begs for parody: 'Rage, Despair and Fungus'. (In chapter 34 the names finally turn out to be those of magic swords which the good guys must collect at the sedate rate of one per fat book.) Next comes an off-putting 'Author's Warning' which can readily be decoded as saying, 'This may seem full of terrible fantasy clichés, but it's much more original than it looks, honest!'

Fear not, there is no dangerous originality here. This is a long, soothing dip into the warm and greasy stockpot of post-Tolkien fantasy, larded with Prophetic Dreams, Interminable Journeys (on foot, of course, and studded with Regular Peril), a Dark Lord (distinguished from Sauron largely by having two Red Eyes and not just the one), Evil Henchmen (distinguished from Nazgûl by numbering five rather than nine), Magical History (innovatively revealed in the 32nd rather than the second chapter) and Familiar Situations.

Actually it reads very well, although the Council and Siege stuff beginning around chapter 32 contains too many wince-making echoes of Tolkien's plotting and phraseology; and I boggle at the race of Sithi (i.e. Sidhe or sodding elves) using vast furnaces and foundries to forge *wood*; and readers aware that trolls are big, vicious heavies will be disconcertingly wrong-footed by Williams's contention that trolls are child-sized, humanoid, resourceful and cute (it's a wonder they're not called h*bb*ts).

I appreciated the efforts to work up a credible political situation, and rather enjoyed some of the descriptive set-pieces, like one castle's gormenghastly cellar-labyrinth. Ultimately, though, the history and mythology lack deep roots. A high level of inventiveness is not required to make up months like Novander and Decander, or weekdays like Drorsday; as a thumping hint we're also told about Dror's Hammer.

In short, while not contemptible, this is a product rooted in the thin, depleted soil of all too much commercial fantasy. So what's new? It's big, undemanding, reasonably literate, and will occupy a long train journey without imposing the hideous mental strain of coping with actual innovations.

[I'm told that the later books had some good twists and reversals.]

Freshness also depends on the narrative slant. Fay Sampson in *Wise Woman's Telling* (Headline 229pp £2.99) has a go at the worn old Arthurian legend, but injects new life – first by having the story told by a garrulous minor character, the wise woman and midwife who delivers Arthur and his half-sisters, and second by making Morgan (le Fay) the focus of interest.

The undercurrent of paganism has a grim and messy conviction about it, and likewise the Dark Ages brutality. The extent to which magic 'works' is left hazy, allowing this to be marketed as Historical Fiction. By the end, young Morgan is already warped: an ugly duckling with a beautiful mother and sisters, neglected by a father and then a stepfather (Uther Pendragon) only concerned with male heirs.

We know tragedy must follow. After Malory's and T.H. White's pictures of Morgan as a conventional villainess, it's a change to see something of her viewpoint. If she comes convincingly through puberty and sorcerous initiation in the forthcoming *White Nun's Telling*, this will be a series to watch.

Chung Kuo: The Middle Kingdom by David Wingrove (NEL 501pp £7.95) is another one to get compared with *War and Peace* – the finished series, gasp the awestruck publicists, will be four times as long. Well, yes, and David Langford is *much taller* than William Shakespeare.

This is a genuinely ambitious future history, an sf political thriller set 200 years hence in a world run by the Han (Chinese), who have rewritten the past to eliminate Western culture. Officially, a lid has been jammed down on technological change; unofficially, the Caucasian subject peoples are boiling with new inventions in genetics, spaceflight, etc. The world's hive-cities are filling up, and something will have to go pop.

Initially the book is a shade off-putting, with its portentous epigraphs, welter of similar-seeming Chinese names, choppy narrative (Wingrove likes fragmented sentences. Likes them a lot. Especially for melodramatic bits. *Especially then*) and over-flaunted research work. Unrolling an edict, a character explains, 'These are their seals. The *Ywe Lung*, symbol of their power ...' This helpful translation is not in fact the sort of thing you say when showing someone his death warrant.

Nevertheless the story develops into quite a page-turner, clumsy but thick with plots and assassinations. The sf themes work reasonably well with the politics, my chief cavil being that when you have 36 billion mouths to feed, you surely grow mushrooms in your world city's basement rather than leave it 'wild' for tribes of degenerate trogs (see also Brian Stableford's *The Face of Heaven*).

Wingrove rather cunningly works against our prejudices by giving the Han rulers far more dignity than the beastly opposition: the 'Western' faction leaders are, almost without exception, nasty pieces of work. There is lots of skippable blood and violence to help establish this point.

At the close of this first book, nothing is resolved; loose threads proliferate; two characters who will be major shapers of the plot (according to publicity sheets) are still brain-damaged kids. One can't prejudge a seven-book sequence, but although I think Tolstoy's position in literature is entirely safe, *Chung Kuo* could yet grow into something worthwhile.

For light relief, try Tom Holt's *Who's Afraid of Beowulf?* (Orbit 206pp £3.99), which isn't a sequel to his Wagnerian farce *Expecting Someone Taller*, but a similarly daft treatment of epic strife between revenant Vikings, sorcerer-kings, BBC film crews, the London Underground and the National Grid. It made me chuckle a lot, if not quite as much as Holt's first book. For games fans there's the added challenge of working out the rules of Goblin's Teeth, as played by two chthonic elementals throughout the book. 'Four ... Double Rune Score. I think I'll have another longhouse on Uppsala.'

These days, short sf/fantasy stories are rarer than novels, but there are still enough to fill two hefty Best of 1988 collections with minimal duplication (two pieces). Gardner Dozois's American selection is the fat *Best New SF 3* (Robinson 596pp £6.99); for Britain, David S. Garnett offers *The Orbit Science Fiction Yearbook* (Orbit 347pp £4.99).

Much though I love and accept large glasses of beer from Garnett, Dozois wins on several counts. Size: 28 rather than 12 stories, and many more words for your money (larger pages, smaller type). Chauvinism: 3 rather than zero British items. Acclaim: 9 Hugo-shortlisted stories (including my favourites, Eileen Gunn's 'Stable Strategies for Middle Management' - yuppie climbers meet *The Fly* - and Lucius Shepherd's 'The Scalehunter's Beautiful Daughter', the latter probably too long for the Orbit book) rather than only one.

Still, both collections are worth your money. And Garnett's contains bizarre extras, notably Brian Aldiss's farewell to the late Salvador Dali (and his ocelot), and the editor's own caustic look at the year in sf, by comparison with which I am a starry-eyed optimist brimming with uncritical love for everything, even Piers Anthony.

November 1989

82 Page-Turners vs Slow Reads

Last month I sounded breathless; *GM* had maliciously been rearranging its copy dates, and while you lot could recover for a leisurely month between my last two columns, I only had a week from one deadline to the next. Such are the Mysteries of Publishing.

Herewith some afterthoughts on a phrase used then: 'quite a page-turner'. This sounds great, as though the book is of such stupefying brilliance that it grabs you by the scruff of the neck and forces you to page through at compulsive speed. Conversely, 'a slow read' doesn't sound very exciting, does it?

In terms of quality and durability, it can often be the other way around. A 'country ramble' novel that tempts you to read slowly and relish every page might well score over a 'motorway' book which goes fast because it offers nothing to detain you anywhere - where the only thing to do is zoom on through featureless prose to the next major plot intersection.

A good uncontroversial example of storytelling that works at either speed is the Ursula Le Guin *Earthsea* trilogy (reissued by Gollancz at £9.95 per book, an Xmas present I wish I'd had way back). There's plenty of plot to gobble down, but sentence by sentence the writing offers enjoyment no matter how slowly you wander through.

Conversely, my vague unease about that 'page-turner' *Chung Kuo: The Middle Kingdom* (last issue) came into focus when I realized it's a motorway full of potholes. The leaden and undistinguished prose persuades you to scan it at increasing speed, whereupon you keep running into bumpy details which require more attention, and momentum is once again lost. Stop, start, stop, start ... very exhausting.

Much more fun is *The Player of Games* by Iain M. Banks (Orbit 309pp £4.99), an unashamed space opera whose easy style and control of pace looks effortless until compared with the opposition; it's a Rolls-Royce journey through Disneyland.

This is set in the universe of *Consider Phlebas*, whose grand space-operatic gestures didn't quite fit the claustrophobic finale and the doomed protagonist who all along was fighting on the wrong side. *Player* is much sunnier in its depiction of the right side, the Culture, a galactic society of unlimited energy which unlike most sf utopias sounds huge fun to live in. In it lives supergameplayer Jernau Morat Gurgeh (for short: Banks has a weakness for ludicrous names, and I'll spare you the rest).

Gurgeh is lured by an obvious set-up into a journey beyond the Culture to play in the horrible Azad Empire, whose structure is mirrored in their vastly complex game of azad. Thanks to this one-to-one mapping, everything Banks writes about the Empire is information about azad, and vice versa: an intricate system of dog-eat-dog viciousness, surpassing even the legendary horrors of the City of London in the barbaric era of Thatcher.

Goaded and abetted by highly engaging and/or maddening machine intelligences, Gurgeh must claw his way to the top of the Empire game and challenge the ruler himself in a deadly playoff on the lethal Planet of Fire, etc. Killer gambits are not confined to the gameboard, and great wads of cards bulge in every visible sleeve. Yes, it's *that* plot again, and I've never seen it so enjoyably done.

Man in His Time (VGSF 328pp £3.50) is Brian Aldiss's *Best SF Stories* (1988) with a new title and introduction, perhaps to distinguish it from two previous 'Best Aldiss SF' collections (some swine suggested it should be called *The Third Best SF Of...*). The new *A Romance of the Equator* (Gollancz 345pp £13.95) assembles his best fantasies, with an introduction which mildly deplores this fantasy/sf pigeonholing and threatens a further volume, *Best Nondescript Stories.* Both collections are superlatively good; I liked the fantasies better only because more of them were new to me.

Entirely new to me is Rosaleen Love, whose collection *The Total Devotion Machine* (Women's Press 167pp £4.50) is full of fun and irony, sometimes very black, always sharply pointed. Certain readers seem to think Women's Press books are all boring rants about the evils of men; this one is more typical in being wittily acid about both sexes. Highly recommended.

Douglas Hill's *The Fraxilly Fracas* (Gollancz 220pp £11.95; simultaneous paperback) is billed as the first *adult* sf by this popular children's writer. You could have fooled me. It's a simple-minded adventure, the sort of thing which Harry Harrison sometimes – by no means always – manages to make work by sheer energy.

Interstellar courier Del Curb, a diluted and substantially more thick-witted avatar of the Stainless Steel Rat, fumbles through a plot which announces its proud escape from the children's list by including discreet s*x scenes, drooling mentions of women's br**sts, and real grown-up sneers at poofdahs. Oh, and it concludes with a tiresomely protracted battle in which lots of spear-carriers get mown down with blasters.

The best thing about this is the good it does the reader's self-esteem. Like a superbeing filled to the gills with the magic drug which is the story's Macguffin, you find yourself eerily able to predict plot turns forty pages in advance, and increasingly snappish when (as always) they come as a total surprise to Curb. If it weren't for the naughty bits and some rather anaemic violence, this would be strictly for the kids.

I popped into last week's *GM* pub meeting (August – that's how long this stuff takes to reach you) and Alan Crump felled me to the ground with cries of, 'You bastard, you reviewed *Who's Afraid of Beowulf*: I'd already done it in issue 9.' Spitting out teeth, I explained that my review was *(a)* justified by the new paperback edition, and *(b)* much better than his. When I recovered consciousness, a passing reader suggested that hardback reviews should include a note of when the affordable version would appear. If only publishers would tell us. Expect a minimum one-year lag.

Some recommended reissues: *Cloudrock* (Unwin 160pp £3.50) and *Abandonati* (Unwin 162pp £3.99) by Garry Kilworth. *On Stranger Tides* by Tim Powers (Grafton 397pp £3.99). *Durdane* by Jack Vance (VGSF 617pp £3.99) – a fizzled-out trilogy worth it for the first book *The Faceless Man* alias *The Anome*.

Deryni Rising by Katherine Kurtz (Legend 271pp £3.50) is the first in that popular yet oddly lacklustre fantasy series. Why lacklustre? Ursula Le Guin explains, in *The Language of the Night: Essays on Fantasy and SF* (Women's Press 210pp £5.95). This includes her classic essay 'From Elfland to Poughkeepsie', bashing Kurtz and others who take the wine-flask of high fantasy and fill it with stale stylistic Pepsi. Most of the book is essential reading, though Le Guin can lapse into a sort of annoying Zen impenetrability which seems more like pose than communication.

Finding my wife laughing uncontrollably over a novel, I wondered if some new rival to T. Pratchett had appeared. But, drying her tears of mirth, she warned that you do need an Egyptology degree to appreciate all the wondrous unintentional humour of Anne Rice's *The Mummy, or Ramses the Damned* (Chatto & Windus 436pp £12.95), starring a revived mummy who unlike other ancient Egyptians is a tall, blue-eyed, wavy-haired hunk. Mummies, who can figure 'em?

To end the year, there's always another Tolkien calendar (Unwin). The 1990 illustrator is Ted Nasmith, whose landscapes look spiffy but resemble Canada (where he lives), not Tolkien's English vision. The hobbits are averagely cute (but pointed *ears*?), Gollum wisely shirked, Treebeard unwisely attempted, Legolas camp beyond belief; Aragorn's 'travel-stained' threads are clearly fresh from the laundry. The Nazgûl, nobbled at the Ford, have visible skull-faces and hands (shome mishtake surely), while in the background Glorfindel is blatantly ignoring the carnage to pose with his best profile forward. Ho hum.

December 1989

83 Various Magics

Some review books are shiftily put on the When I Get Around To It pile (sometimes known as the Oxfam Stack or the Trilogies' Graveyard); others are snatched from their wrappings and eagerly gobbled even when I should be doing something else. Yes, I know, this is fearful prejudice and discrimination. Please don't tell publishers.

Anything by Jonathan Carroll comes into the second category, and here is *A Child Across the Sky* (Legend 268pp £11.95), in similar vein to his *Bones of the Moon* and *Sleeping in Flame*. The Carroll 'formula' involves colourful people with warm relationships and lovable eccentricities (sometimes vaguely reminiscent of Theodore Sturgeon), usually living in or visiting Vienna (where Carroll lives), their over-egged brightness and warmth contrasting powerfully with the supernatural darkness or insanity which seeps from outside.

Child makes unconventional use of familiar horror props: the imaginary companion, the angel of death, fears of pregnancy and cancer, and horror movies themselves. It addresses the big question of whether gut-wrenching horror can really be art, to which George Orwell replied that certain works might simultaneously be brilliant creations and worthy of being burned by the public hangman. Carroll's convoluted response is both shocking and ambiguous.

Though I could have done without the cross-references to his last two books, this is compulsive reading, and unlike anything else around.

If anyone wants an immensely complex and consistently daft magical system for some RPG game, astrology might fill the bill – not so much the superficial nonsense in newspaper horoscopes as the esoteric, in-depth nonsense which lies behind. *Astrology: True or False?* by Roger Culver and Philip Ianna (Prometheus 228pp £10.45) is a semi-technical look through scientists' eyes at the roots of the alleged 'oldest science'.

And?

The intellectual underpinnings of astrology would appear to be shabbier than even I'd believed. There's no testable theory of why it should work, let alone proof that it does; no explanation of why Uranus, Neptune and Pluto never disturbed the calculations of astrologers before their discovery, as they did those of mere astronomers; no justification of significant angles like the trine (120 degrees) other than numerological neatness; no consensus, even, about the zodiac, its constellations (e.g. the simple, observable facts that there are more than 12 and some are bigger than others) or the 'Age of Aquarius' (beginning in 1781, 2740, or somewhere between).

However, astrology is testably and verifiably a great money-spinner, and one must deplore this book's scurvy attempt to persuade the gullible not to invest in worthless predictions. Even charlatans have to live.

Cradle by Arthur C. Clarke and Gentry Lee (Orbit 373pp £6.99) is, despite the price, a paperback reissue. This oversized 'C-format' is supposed to be prestigious; nice for authors but a pest when you have to wait another year for an affordable paperback (I reviewed the hardback aeons ago, in my final *Dwarf* column).

Not to worry: *Cradle* is a shatteringly disappointing sf novel, well worth missing. The Clarke flavour is faintly detectable, but only in the sense that a reconstituted freeze-dried curry might fleetingly remind you of real tandoori cuisine. How did this literary fast-food merchant Gentry get hold of the ageing but respected Clarke fiction franchise?

In *The Treason of Isengard* (Unwin Hyman 504pp £17.95), the even more aged – indeed, dead – J.R.R. Tolkien stirs again into a ghastly semblance of life and shambles gruesomely towards the bookstands, under the cruel compulsion of his merciless necromancer son.

Yes, Christopher 'Reanimator' Tolkien has once more dabbled in forbidden first drafts with which Man was not meant to meddle. After extensive backtracking he continues and laboriously annotates the early *Lord of the Rings*, from Moria to Theoden's hall. Crushed by the numbing weight of seven such volumes (to date), deafened by the eldritch cries of academic thesis-mongers, sanity crumbles and one acknowledges that *someone* must think this vast prose mausoleum worthwhile. That is not dead which can eternal lie; they'll look nice on anyone's shelf, imposing, scholarly and unread.

Amongst the living, Keith Roberts is conceivably Britain's finest sf/fantasy author – when he's on form. So often, he isn't. The seven stories in *Winterwood and other hauntings* (Morrigan 182pp £13.95) mostly radiate the magic of his best stuff: mythic places, evil buildings, homicidal cars and utterly believable people. In addition, Roberts illustrates his own tales well, and appears as a lurking apparition in the jacket photo. Collectors take note.

Ian Williams's *The Lies That Bind* (Frontlines 255pp £2.50) is rebellious 'young adult' sf examining standard wish-fulfilment fantasy in a relentless moral light. Here the main characters are gifted teenagers at a special school, firmly set in Thatcherite Britain, where paranormal talents are machined for State use.

There are dollops of sarcasm about comics superheroes' overblown powers and melodramatic agonies. People in *Lies* have low-budget abilities and tend to enjoy their secluded life without realizing the push to make them dependent on the school, incapable of relationships outside. The hero is a quiet rebel who's prepared to sacrifice everything (far more indeed than logically necessary – the dice are loaded for dramatic effect) to be himself.

Quibbles: a few redolent purple patches and some vagueness about talent limitations ... the psychic weight-lifting record is under 18 pounds, yet some people levitate themselves; the top pyrotic can ignite 'at most' 12 sheets of paper, but how often, and mightn't one corner of one sheet suffice? Acceptable dialogue and interesting people, though, and a strong if excessively Worthy message about keeping your integrity even when the System can't be beaten.

The Gollancz SF Classics series has been beset by the problem that so many 'real' classics are contracted to other publishers (whether in print or not). Recent selections are Brian Aldiss's early and erratically brilliant collection *Galaxies Like Grains of Sand* (VGSF 188pp £2.99) and – the first genuine surprise for some while – William Tenn's 1968 *Of Men and Monsters* (VGSF 251pp £2.99).

Tenn has a refreshingly cynical view of our place in the universe. Here, invading aliens have offhandedly swatted down human civilization, leaving its remnants scurrying like mice in the wainscot. Traditional sf solutions would see the invaders bluffed into retreat, won over as allies, or resoundingly defeated by *deus ex machina*. Without being gloomy, Tenn is infinitely more realistic; and as humanity's glorious new future opens out, you can imagine his nasty smile.

(Erudition Dept: I suspect the short 1963 version of this one was heavily influenced by Pohl's and Kornbluth's *Wolfbane*, and in turn influenced John Brunner's inferior *Day of the Star Cities* alias *Age of Miracles*.)

The King in Yellow by Robert W. Chambers (Dedalus 253pp £4.95) is a reputed classic from 1895, praised and pillaged by H.P. Lovecraft, and the source of certain Cthulhu Mythos catchwords. Four portentous stories are linked by the sinister playscript *The King in Yellow*, no healthier for bedtime reading than the abhorred *Necronomicon* itself: 'The author shot himself after bringing forth this monstrosity, didn't he?' Few horror pundits mention that the other six tales are unrelated, non-supernatural romances.

'What a beautiful night ... If only we didn't have to worry about giant crabs!' 'Every so often he felt the striking claws missing him by inches.' 'There's a colossal crab which leads them. I've named him King Crab.' 'The big crab shambled forward ... His revolting features appeared to crease into a lusting grin.' 'The giant crabs had grossly mistimed their attack on the Blue Ocean Holiday Camp.' 'The crabs were spoiling everybody's holiday ...'

Guy N. Smith's *Night of the Crabs* and *Crabs' Moon* (both Grafton £2.99) are, it says here, classic horror bestsellers. Maybe it's a misprint for humour. Next issue, I promise lashings of even worse quotations from worse writers. Cancel your subscription now.

January 1990

84 While I'm Away

The *Bloom County* strip features one of my favourite reviews: Opus the penguin tackling a film which 'has brought the word "bad" to new levels of badness.' He continues: 'Bad acting. Bad effects. Bad everything. This bad film just oozed rottenness from every bad scene.... Simply bad beyond all infinite dimensions of possible badness.'

Long pause. 'Well maybe not that bad, but Lord, it wasn't good.'

Quite. This month we travel back through time, through ultimate dimensions of possible badness in sf, more bad even than L. Ron Hubbard, if such is feasible....

(In case you're wondering, this lapse from reviewing new stuff is to cover my month's absence as guest at an American sf convention. Better, I hope, than just a line saying 'Langford is on holiday'.)

Some say the acme of badness appears in *The Troglodytes* (Digit 19??) by Nal Rafcam, whose very name looks vaguely backwards. 'Rafcam' was evidently *(a)* uneasy with the English language, but *(b)* in possession of an extensive thesaurus. Hence these examples of sf as she is spoke:

'If we are underground at any depth the rock up there must be as hard as carbon.'

'On earth the ecumenical collapse of world cities drew the attention of the public eye to terra firma. The period of strife and universal privation was malingering.'

'Kurt Semen had repeatedly been jailed for disturbing the peace and inciting unnecessary pathos.' (A vile offence, agreed, which *should* be indictable.)

'The echoing of the lesser explosion left the commandos effete.'

'You can probably see that they have to wear camouflage against the strong daylight.'

'No human could have endured the intense heat, let alone super-humans.'

'Everything was cinerated. Every living person was killed the moment the deadly emissions from the tribe's machinery pierced through the camp's superficial structure. So instantaneous and final were these lethal rays that the destructive act was over in but a few minutes.'

Alexander Thynn (Lord Weymouth) failed to electrify the sf field with his privately published *The King is Dead* (1976), promising a 'new concept for religion' explained by super-evolved intelligences whom it's unusually difficult to take seriously:

'I suppose you might liken us to huge steaming lumps of purple jelly, anchored to metallic plates which are embedded within rubberized constructions of great architectural beauty.... And we emit a soft, musical blurping sound for the purposes of communication.'

Some classic pulp lines have such panache as to be almost good: a favourite appears in David Duncan's *Occam's Razor* (1957). 'Gentlemen, we are about to short-circuit the universe!'

'The gripping grab of its gravity waves tugged at our guts,' adds the euphonious Frederik Pohl (*Gateway*, 1977).

Robert Heinlein, after a distinguished sf career, went ape in his final years and produced some thrill-a-second feminist material, as in *'The Number of the Beast'*:

'I'd be an idiot to risk competing with Deety's teats.'

'Our teeth grated and my nipples went *spung!*'

'Her face remained calm but the light went out - and her nipples went down.'

'My darling keeps her feelings out of her face, mostly, but those pretty pink spigots are barometers of her morale.'

In *The Shores of Space* (1957), Richard Matheson of *I Am Legend* fame manages to create an inadvertently furry lady: 'Across her face, the hot wind fanned bluntly, ruffling the short blond hair.'

Not to mention the most versatile eyebrows in fiction: 'He blinked away the waves of blackness lapping at his ankles.'

The happily forgotten *Starship Through Space* by Lee Correy (1954) is an awful warning to writers who proudly quote their own poetry. 'We who have tasted alien stream / And done what others only dream; / We who with earth-dirt on our shoes / Have walked the paths the sunbeams use; / We will trod the Milky Way.'

Silas Waters's *The Man with Absolute Motion* (1955) took a crack at scientists' fuddy-duddy ideas about absolute zero at -273 degrees: 'We can produce temperatures of minus 900 degrees Kelvin.'

And the same book's aliens have a rare command of invective. '"You make me ill!" Volmik said harshly and uttered the most insulting statement known to Alphirkians: "You make my guts tired."'

Characters in *Whirlpool of Stars* by 'Tully Zetford' (Kenneth Bulmer; 1974), besides moving 'with the speed of a striking sex-crazed strooka', are more outspoken still ...

'You great gonil!'

'Goddamned terrestrial plug-ugly curd of a bastard!'

'Blasted womb-regurgitant Lerdun government!'

'What a gang of Charlies!'

'I've said you're a chancroid, Hook, and a burst ulcer, and a candidate for advanced pustular syphiloderma, and I'll go on telling you you're a Pasteurella pestis - '

(This basic vocabulary is rearranged into many further interesting remarks and ejaculations.)

How do voluminous writers keep it up for book after remorseless book? John Norman demonstrates in *Time Slave* (1975), as a subtly characterized woman first meets a *GM* editor:

'She looked upon him. Never before in her life had she seen such a male. He made even Gunther seem a lesser man. Her imagination had not even dreamed that such a man could exist. The men she had known earlier, even Gunther, had been no intimation that there might be males such as these. Such men, she thought, could not exist in her time. In her time there was no place; there could be no place, for such men as these.'

Robert Lionel Fanthorpe, man of a thousand pseudonyms, cheerily admits the awfulness of his countless sf potboilers for the long-departed (and long unmourned) Badger Books. These are now cult novels, since Fanthorpe was bright enough for his pittance-crazed free association into the dictaphone to be awful in startling ways.

Here he flaunts his greatest talent, padding (*Neuron World*, 1965): 'Never, not even in the deepest natural darkness that she had ever experienced, had she encountered an absence of light as total as this. It was unutterably dark, this was the Stygian darkness of which poets wrote. This was the pit of Acheron of which the creators of classic prose made mention. This was a kind of darkness that made thick, black velvet seem like chiffon by contrast. This was the kind of darkness that turned pitch into translucent polythene, when the two were placed side by side. This was the kind of darkness that made the wings of the raven resemble the pinions of the dove ...'

Here are the prose rhythms which compel audiences to chant along (*March of the Robots*, 1961): 'The city slept. Men slept. Women slept. Children slept. Dogs and cats slept.'

Here, plagiarizing *The Tempest*, he adapts Gonzalo's 'born to be hanged, not drowned' speech (*Beyond The Void*, 1965): 'I still think he'll make the devitalizing chamber, though every cubic foot of space tends to argue otherwise, and the whole of the void opens its great maw to swallow him.'

And here's his thesaurus at full throttle (*Galaxy 666*, 1963): 'Our universe is straightforward; this one is whimsical, fanciful and fantastic. This is a temperamental galaxy, an hysterical galaxy, a mad galaxy. This is an insane, freakish, wanton, erratic, inconsistent galaxy; it's a completely unreasonable galaxy. It's undisciplined, refractory, uncertain and unpredictable. It's a volatile galaxy, a mercurial galaxy ... It's a frivolous galaxy; it's inconsistent and inconstant; it's variable; it's unstable; it's irresponsible and unreliable.' (At which point, and not before time, the speaker falls over.)

For further coruscating drivel, seek out Neil Gaiman's and Kim Newman's quotebook *Ghastly Beyond Belief* (Arrow, 1985). A final, extremely posthumous credit goes to poet William McGonagall for his celebration of the print technology which makes *GM* possible: 'And when Life's prospects may at times appear dreary to ye, / Remember Alois Senefelder, the discoverer of lithography.'

That's all, folks....

February 1990

85 Cults & Oddments

Out of the void and the darkness that is peopled by Mimir's brood, from the ultimate silent fastness of the desolate deep-sea gloom (small prize offered to the first reader identifying the quote), I'm back from my American convention trip. One day the world may be ready to learn why at the end of my speech about sf excesses, Greg Bear stalked up and hissed, 'I'll talk to you later....'

Belatedly, my 1989 Naff Award goes to the publications of Barry R. Levin, Californian purveyor of very expensive sf 'collectables'. In November, Levin was gloating over, and asking $6500 for, a special first edition of *The Satanic Verses* signed by Salmon Rushdie, bound in goatskin, printed on vellum - and with the tipped-in autograph of the Ayatollah Khomeini. One can only retch.

Then Levin announced his 1989 'Collectors Awards'. Rushdie was honoured as 'Most Collectable Author of the Year', which I'm sure consoled him no end. 'Most Collectable Book' was Stephen King's *My Pretty Pony*: I remember this as a $2000 limited-edition short story bound into a brushed metal case with, mounted on the front, a small, cheap-looking digital clock. Funny people, collectors.

Onward, hastily, to some real books. Gollancz steams ahead despite its takeover by the American outfit Houghton Mifflin, and as always there's another Terry Pratchett or six: the latest is *Guards! Guards!* (Gollancz 288pp £12.95), of which I'll only say that it's very funny indeed despite - no, in part *because of* the contrast between high daftness and several characters' deserved annihilation in the white-hot flame of the least cute dragon seen for many a trilogy. It is also a Discworld police procedural novel, a send-up of secret cults ('The Door of Knowledge Through Which the Untutored May Not Pass sticks something wicked in the damp'), and generally irresistible.

Speaking of secret cults, Umberto Eco followed up *The Name of the Rose* with the equally erudite though less gripping *Foucault's Pendulum* (Secker & Warburg 641pp £14.95), a novel about modern perversions and distortions of 'occult' matters from mediaeval times onward.

This is crammed with bizarre factoids and makes it amusingly clear that you can lash up a explanation of everything from any material whatever. At one point someone feeds his computer a random set of inputs - starting with, of course, 'The Templars have something to do with everything' - and gets out a persuasive and totally rubbishy theory which to his disgust turns out to have already been published, as *The Holy Blood and the Holy Grail.*

Even false theories, though, can bring disaster. Eco's nasty climax set me thinking back to a key insight in John Crowley's rather better book *Aegypt*: 'secret societies have *not* had power in history, but the *notion* that secret societies had power in history *has* had power in history.' *Pendulum* has its esoteric fascination but moves sluggishly, bloated with too much pseudo-arcane lore.

In *The Fugitive Worlds* (Gollancz 254pp £12.95), Bob Shaw closes his trilogy about the double planets Land and Overland by telling a fourth independent story (the middle book had two). Unifying the sequence by its setting and partial overlap of characters, Shaw avoids the dread and all too common pitfall of an overstretched plot with a central plateau of padding.

This time it's a rattling yarn of (more) visiting aliens, who need the Land/Overland system as a shipyard for a bizarre thingy based on – and desperately needed because of – the unimaginable violence of this alien universe's physics. Will anyone escape the galaxy-wide cataclysm? Will Land be destroyed? Or Overland? Or both? Will the hero find true love, and will the value of *pi* ever become a sensible 3.14159? You'll enjoy finding out: it's not deep but (even if, in Roz Kaveney's words, the yarn rattles because it isn't too well screwed together) it's fun. The final twist might or might not herald a fourth book.

Harry Harrison's 1965 *Bill, the Galactic Hero* was sharp, satirical and funny. I report this with relief, having just reread it ... owing to a sudden ghastly feeling that it might have been a dull, shambolic mass of flabby slapstick, blunt-edged parody and general embarrassment, like his new *Bill, the Galactic Hero on the Planet of Robot Slaves* (Gollancz 236pp £11.95). This features much-repeated jokes such as a planet's being innovatively called Usa so that alien artefacts can be hilariously labelled, in English, MADE IN USA. Which is about as side-splitting as it ever gets. No wonder Harrison is now subletting the series to other writers.

Proteus Unbound by Charles Sheffield (NEL 267pp £2.99) is in the 'hard sf' tradition, complete with Ph.D and rivets. I liked the engineering and kept raising sceptical eyebrows at the psychology. Would you fancy living in space 30 metres from a lethally radiating black hole, merely for the convenience of its tiny gravity? Myself, I'd prefer the relative safety of a penthouse atop Sellafield, but this book's characters don't seem bothered.

They have other worries, like the biosoftware flaws that keep turning people into giant newts (worse, giant *dead* newts), or the arch-villain's unsociable habit of driving his potential enemies insane by beaming them pictures of himself dancing backwards in red tights. It takes all sorts. Read this for a modicum of suspense and ingeniously worked-out technology, not for actual narrative conviction.

Introducing his collection *Tales from Planet Earth* (Legend 313pp £12.95), Arthur C. Clarke confirms that he's retired from writing short fiction. Apart from one bit of piffle and two solid stories in his best manner, all dated 1987, this is a ragbag of items from his other collections, superseded drafts (like the short version of *The Deep Range*) and oddments not previously thought substantial enough for an anthology.

Nevertheless, I suppose it's good to have the material gathered here - a capstone for completists, an introduction for lucky new readers, and a gentle reminder of the haunting effects which, when not collaborating with the awful Gentry Lee, Clarke can still achieve.

Michael Moorcock's *Casablanca* (Gollancz 267pp £13.95) is an even odder mix, with strong stories, evocative stories, and elegantly opaque stories with bloody Jerry Cornelius cavorting with everyone from Ladbroke Grove to the end of time. One of these is a heavy revision of 'The Great Rock'n'Roll Swindle' (allegedly about the Sex Pistols), which became a rarity when the original tabloid-newspaper publication fell inexorably to dust.

Some bits of journalism are included, but not really enough: unless colossally brilliant, brief book reviews and political comments are best served in some bulk, not laid out like *nouvelle cuisine* in big print with wide margins. Worth reading, though: Moorcock's heart is usually in the right place.

But I'm uneasy about his keenness on anti-porn legislation, and not only because he rather blurs the distinction between soft and hard stuff. Historically, every legal weapon forged to attack exploitative filth has before long been misused against writing which merely offends the self-appointed guardians of our sexual and political purity.

It's a dilemma for a wishy-wishy liberal like myself. Good old Moorcock warns us in the name of feminism that porn is responsible for all manner of evils done to women. Yet many informed feminists disagree, like Gayle Rubin: 'Gender inequality and contemptuous attitudes toward women are endemic to this society and are consequently reflected in virtually all our media, including advertising and pornography. They do not originate in pornography and migrate from there into the rest of popular culture.'

So, do appalling sexist covers appear on magazines (no names, now) because the editors want to corrupt you, or because public buying tastes have corrupted those who have to choose a 'selling' cover? Think about it.

March 1990

86 Me, Whitley & My UFO

Regular readers may already be able to deduce what I think of Whitley Strieber's UFO abduction claims in his *Communion* and *Transformation*. Since one serious UFO researcher in this country was threatened with a massive lawsuit for expressing opinions strangely similar to mine, I have no intention of putting my head on the block next to Salman Rushdie's by recording my views here. You'll just have to guess.

Strieber's new work of fiction is a novel called *Majestic* (Macdonald 318pp £12.95), dramatizing the hoary old tale of alien corpses from a crashed UFO in 1947, which every US Government is supposed to have covered up ever since – you know, just as they so successfully covered up Watergate. Imagine my delight at reading that this is firmly 'based on fact', and that the quoted facts include a detailed synopsis of a story which I know, incontrovertibly, to be pure fiction. I know this because I wrote it myself in 1978.

My spoof UFO book *An Account of a Meeting with Denizens of Another World, 1871* (David & Charles, 1979) has for some years been shamefully out of print. It centres on a most implausibly detailed, articulate and scientifically boggling first-person record of a Victorian 'close encounter', which I understand numerous UFO researchers have enjoyed as merely a pleasant frolic, but which in condensed form now occupies pages 46-47 of *Majestic*.

What can I say? You might well wonder how this author's 'years of research' (blurb) missed the coverage in *New Scientist* and *Skeptical Inquirer* which confirmed my story as fictional ... and you might even speculate on how many other 'true incidents' rehashed in *Majestic* are equally solidly based on fact.

(There was also a lively correspondence about *An Account* in *Private Eye*, during which Paul Barnett – the editor who commissioned my Victorian extravaganza in the first place – proved to his own satisfaction that not only was the UFO fictional but so was David Langford.)

In the literary world, as you might imagine, it is considered a bit off for a writer to make free with others' original creations in his own fiction, without asking permission or including a printed acknowledgement. I have begun an enjoyable correspondence with Whitley Strieber's British and American publishers. This one will run and run.

As for *Majestic* ... struggling against mere prejudice, I can heartily recommend pages 46 and 47 but retain a sneaking preference for my original version.

The Arthurian myth is one of the great originals, dominating what used to be called the Matter of Britain; but its lofty romantic tone, heavy Christianization, and downplaying of women can sometimes get up your nose. This is where Fay Sampson scores, continuing her chronicle of the murky flipside in *White Nun's Telling* (Headline 245pp £3.50).

The infant Arthur stays offstage while his half-sister Morgan grows up in the Dark Ages equivalent of women's prison, a convent at Tintagel. This Christian cult is barely established, though; and the narrator, Morgan's new guardian Luned, is a flawed nun who can't keep her precocious pupil from the Old Religion. Blood, betrayal and damnation follow in rapid sequence. Arthur isn't going to know what hit him. Watch for *Black Smith's Telling* in July.

Some authors rework myths; some produce their own, new-minted. After a series of narrative delaying actions (as though he himself were intimidated by his own creation, and felt it better to travel hopefully than to arrive), Robert Holdstock takes us to the hollow heart of myth in *Lavondyss* (Grafton 475pp £3.99). The fulfilment of this quest doesn't leave the usual saccharine aftertaste of rigged success, but the ache of reality. Holdstock writes the Real Stuff.

So, when you've unravelled his cunning little webs, does Gene Wolfe. *Endangered Species* (Orbit 506pp £4.99) collects three *dozen* of his short stories, the title being no doubt an ironic comment on today's short story market. I've been keeping this as a treat and rationing myself, which is just as well, as a full review would need several thousand words. Even minor Wolfe, of which there's a sufficiency here, requires one to think at least twice. If you don't run to the bookshop when I mention that two of these are pendants to the **Book of the New Sun**, you have no taste and deserve to be force-fed Piers Anthony for the rest of your life.

(I cannot even contemplate *opening* the new Anthony, *Pornucopia*, in which this author's legendary subtlety and finesse are applied to a story of bionic groin attachments, with the hero questing for the Ultimate Dildo of the Cosmos. No, I promise I'm not joking.)

A wave of nostalgia came over me at sight of Barrington Bayley's double bill *The Fall of Chronopolis/Collision with Chronos* (Pan 399pp £3.99). Back in the 70s these novels blew my little undergraduate mind and assured me that there was life after Isaac Asimov. Their actual writing may not be too brilliant (he tactfully understated), but the games with time and infinity still dazzle. Bayley scatters bizarre ideas the way other writers use full stops. There are more in *The Pillars of Eternity/The Garments of Caean* (Pan 414pp £3.99). Feel that heady sensation of your brain splattering against the ceiling.

Speaking of reissues, the Gollancz SF classic series has come full circle with a new edition of its first selection, Kurt Vonnegut's *The Sirens of Titan* (VGSF 224pp £3.50). This nastily funny book, in which the whole of human history becomes a shaggy dog story, is a far cry from the self-indulgent slop like *Breakfast of Champions* with which Vonnegut alienated his sf audience. It really is a classic.

So in a small way is *Downward to the Earth* (VGSF 190pp £3.50), from Robert Silverberg's best period in the 70s: a lush and mystical rite-of-passage story which infuses sf with the exotic flavours of Joseph Conrad.

Owing to misgivings, I've delayed dipping into Games Workshop's books based on, or set in the world of, or generally tainted by, their **Warhammer** games. Long ago I was invited to contribute, but after reading the sourcebooks I just couldn't. Perhaps the game plays brilliantly, but its literary background is basic junkfood fantasy and desperately derivative. GW made a great fuss about protecting their original, copyrighted settings of Albion, Nippon, Araby, and Cathay, peopled with innovative and no doubt trademarked creatures like orcs, trolls, dwarves, elves, vampires and the Norse....

'Well,' said one author who signed up, 'sod all that. I did a straight adventure novel and scattered a few Warhammer references to keep 'em happy.'

That wasn't 'Jack Yeovil' (Kim Newman), whose *Drachenfels* (GW 247pp £4.99) leads the list, but the technique here is vaguely similar. The book opens with a routine sequence of adventurers being picked off one by one as they penetrate the ultimate evil heart of (etc., etc.) ... and then becomes a story about recreating all this twenty years on, as a play.

It's competently enough told, mixing light comedy with the Warhammer staples of chaos, death, popping eyeballs and nasty fluids: inoffensive, literate, and – thanks to heavy foreshadowing – predictable. Which sounds like faint praise, but puts it well ahead of the leadenly stereotyped **Dragonlance** series. Don't be deterred by the appearance.

This last was a surprise. *White Dwarf* covers have long been extremely eye-catching, but these books from the same stable look dim and messy, with the big 'Warhammer' motif invisible at any distance. Besides some neat Ian Miller vignettes, *Drachenfels* is illustrated with many dismal full-page drawings showing consistently shaky anatomy and lousy perspective. Better stuff appears monthly in *Dwarf*. Strange.

Small press plug: try *Back Brain Recluse*, a nicely packaged sf/fantasy magazine at £1.25 post free from Chris Reed, 16 Somersall Lane, Chesterfield, S40 3LA.

Well, I must go and stick some more pins in my waxen image of Whitley Strieber....

[*GM* went under after publishing column 85, with the result that column 86 appeared as above only in *SF Commentary*. After a brief interregnum, *GMI* (*GamesMaster International*) rose from the ashes of *GM* and ran a rewritten column 86 with added bits as below. The title reverted to 'Critical Mass' for no very good reason.]

Recently I overcame my trilogy-phobia enough to read through Octavia Butler's **Xenogenesis** sf trio: *Dawn*, *Adulthood Rites* and *Imago*, all now out in paperback (VGSF 264pp £3.99). In this understated sf horror story, aliens bail out humanity after our nuclear war, but at a high price: their driving urge is to trade genetic material, and future generations on Earth will therefore be human/alien hybrids. 'We must love one another or die.'

The first book paints the big picture; the second shows the growing-up of a sympathetic hybrid in the reconstructed world; the third introduces a few complications which weren't really necessary but fill out the trilogy. This is good, restrained sf, which never overstresses its points but leaves you pondering on the attractions and nastiness of Butler's utopia. In the new regime, the last human couples can have wonderful sex via a tentacled alien intermediary ... but are biologically compelled to shun one another's touch. A sneaky dig at religious notions about physical love after Judgement Day?

But the more I think about it, the more profoundly immoral and rape-like the aliens' approach seems. 'We've saved you from extinction and that gives us the right to have you bear *our* children alone.' On the face of it Butler seems icily neutral on the issue, but her choice of viewpoints does tend to imply a tacit endorsement of the visitors' actions.

The latest from the Games Workshop **Warhammer** stable is *Zaragoz* (GW 245pp £4.99) by Brian 'Craig' (Stableford), a fantasy which once again belies the Warhammer ambience by being solidly literate – though, dare I say it, not desperately compelling or original, and lacking the quirkiness of Jack Yeovil's contribution *Drachenfels*. Train-journey fodder. My award for the Book I Would Least Like To Be Seen Reading On A Train goes to Craig's *Plague Daemon* (GW 235pp £4.99), with the least appealing cover of even this uninviting lot. No, I haven't yet read it: I'm awaiting delivery of the ten-foot pole with which I plan not to touch the jacket.

[Brian Stableford claimed to be Very Hurt Indeed.]

August 1990

87 Jug Jug Jug Jug Jug Jug

Faced with a five-hour train journey to what turned out to be the most dismal sf event I've ever attended (details omitted to protect the innocent - me - from the lawyers of the guilty), I bravely selected the fattest blockbuster from the pile. The title alone is about as portentous as you can get: *Earth* by David Brin (Macdonald 601pp £13.95).

Fifty years hence, lots of today's gloomier predictions have been fulfilled: solar ultraviolet is burning through the depleted ozone layer, many more species are extinct, the weather pattern is a mess, etc. There are compensations. This future is as full of mixed blessings as the present, and has the right sort of convincing quirkiness - there's a mad logic in the idea of a bloody war for information freedom, waged against Switzerland and its secret numbered accounts. Meanwhile, within Earth's core, an orbiting singularity is gobbling mass, and the planet could cease to exist in perhaps two years....

This makes for an exciting read. The imaginary physics is particularly good fun - would you believe gravity lasers? - yet it's another mixed blessing. We're promised an 'epic that transcends every genre in its scope and importance', but this ambition doesn't really come off, precisely because the pseudo-science (which in effect can do anything the author wants) overshadows the extrapolations of real, intractable problems.

Brin is an optimist and I like him for it, but in order to keep smiling (and avoid some depressingly plausible future as in George Turner's *The Sea and Summer*) he's forced to pull this technological wild-card from his sleeve and lose in serious impact what he gains in entertainment value. It all gets a bit much, especially when piled on the secondary and more interesting improbability of the 'Gaia' or living-Earth hypothesis achieving literal truth through information technology. Recommended, all the same - more for the incidentals than the climaxes.

One little joke on readers who turn first to the back page and check there's a happy ending: *Earth* finishes with a separate short story. The joke backfires on Brin, because this story's finale is an sf cliché of stupefying off-puttingness.

My new-magazine resolution, besides tackling the occasional blockbuster, is to tackle some new author each month. James Patrick Kelly's *Look into the Sun* (Mandarin 280pp £3.99) is a good, unpretentious sf novel with a rich individual flavour. The technoglitter is kept in its place, as a backdrop to the people:

when the architect hero's new wonder of the world is unveiled, it's seen through a haze of personal problems, and his free ride on an alien ship to create the wonder of another world is dominated by what's done to him so he can survive there, and, indeed, eventually enjoy kinky sex there. Perhaps the aliens are slightly shallow, but Kelly avoids the soft option of making them tiresomely enigmatic ('You know not our ways, Earthman,' etc.), and after hinting at vast Secrets of the Universe is wise enough not to reveal them.

The short stories in Bruce 'Postmodern' Sterling's *Crystal Express* (Legend 317pp £12.99) are less freaked and far-out than you'd expect from the one-time major prophet of cyberpunk. A good example is 'Swarm', which sprays a new coat of glitter on the traditional sf device of taking some cherished assumption – here, that intelligence has ultimate survival value – and saying, 'Oh yeah?' An adapted genetic superman, bristling with smartness and built-in bioweapons, moves in to exploit dumb alien hive-creatures. Too late he learns that the Swarm has merely discarded intelligence as being, like tactical nuclear weaponry, too dangerous a tool to keep lying around....

Philip K. Dick's *Beyond Lies the Wub* (Grafton 510pp £5.99) is the first of five books collecting all his short fiction, emerging at last in paperback with his own afterwords. These 25 early works are surprisingly good value, but Dick's patented derangement really begins to flower in the 27 stories of book two, *Second Variety* (ditto, 493pp). Few 'important' sf volumes are such readable fun.

Castle in the Air (Methuen 208pp £8.95) is Diana Wynne Jones's sequel to the very funny *Howl's Moving Castle*. If there were rules for children's (or rather, all-ages) fantasy, this author would constantly be breaking them all: she seems to babble artlessly and hilariously along, carried away by the flood of her own invention, until suddenly every last plot thread is gathered and tied in a double reverse Gordian knot. This story is slightly swamped by the inrush of characters from *Howl* when the sequel connection emerges near the end, but still scores highly for anarchic misuse of Arabian Nights props: djinns, bottled genies, magic carpets, bazaars, polygamy, the lot.

To show Diana Wynne Jones in different vein, Mandarin have reissued three more (all £2.99). Her complex and allusive *Fire and Hemlock* points up the arbitrary nastiness of faerie ways by echoing the tales of Tam Lin and Thomas the Rhymer in modern dress; it helps if you know the ballads. *The Homeward Bounders* is another powerful one with the humour slightly subdued: it pictures the world and indeed the multiverse as a gameboard where unfortunates who get caught in the wrong hex can become 'discards', like the Flying Dutchman, the Wandering Jew, and our hero. *Hidden Turnings*, edited by Jones, is a collection of original sf/fantasy which will doubtless sell a million thanks to Terry Pratchett's story of a VERY SINISTER DISCO DANCER, but has much other good stuff.

Also reissued in heaping handfuls is Stanislaw Lem, Poland's Mr Science Fiction and self-confessed Master of Intellect (all Mandarin, £4.99). *Tales of Pirx the Pilot* is a wildly uneven collection of clanking, nuts-and-bolts space stories, half of them good. *The Chain of Chance*, a fiendish near-future whodunnit or whatdunnit about seemingly pointless but weirdly linked deaths, has a horrifyingly plausible solution – an unliving serial killer so convincing that you begin to suspect that random, inexplicable deaths must already be happening for closely similar reasons. And *His Master's Voice* shows Lem the intellectual at full stretch, confronting scientists with an intricate message from space which can be decoded and used to create marvels never before seen on Earth, but which still doesn't make sense. Some of the speculations here will make your brain squirt in twin streams from both ears.

Fred Saberhagen presides over *Berserker Base* (VGSF 316pp £3.99), billed as a collaborative novel but really a collection of shorts by six other authors, bodged together in an incredibly lame and clunky narrative framework by Saberhagen himself. His berserkers, spacegoing robot enemies of all life, have become an sf myth which has somehow acquired greater stature than any of the actual stories about them.... Of the contributors, Stephen Donaldson is quite surprisingly bad, Connie Willis scores for writing the first funny story in this saga - and Poul Anderson, Larry Niven and Roger Zelazny all develop the idea, long and carefully avoided by Saberhagen, that it would nice to have a few implacable killer machines on *our* side. It passes the time.

The obligatory graphic novel mention should be of Alan Moore's and David Lloyd's *V for Vendetta* (Titan, £9.95), an early, very odd combination of extravagant and often powerful effects with questionable logic - rather like a sombre version of the old TV *Avengers*, set in a blackly dystopian 1997-8. I had more graphic fantasy fun with *The Waste Land* (Harper & Row US import), cartoonist Martin Rowson's weirdly brilliant pastiche of the T.S. Eliot poem seen as a private-eye movie. The Holy Grail, for example, equals the Maltese Falcon. This makes no sense at all unless you remember a bit about both Eliot and classic *noir* films like *The Big Sleep*.... It's said that Penguin's forthcoming edition will be severely edited after legal complaints from the Eliot estate (deeply ironic, considering how Eliot himself used to swipe material from all over the place). Grab the import while you can.

[Later: the Penguin edition was indeed savaged. 'You can't use Phlebas the Phoenician,' insisted the Eliot estate: Rowson had to rename the character Mike the Minoan. Likewise, a row of vessels in the British Museum had to be relabelled 'vase', 'amphora' and so on, as the lawyers refused to permit the original 'Jug jug jug jug jug jug' ... taken by Eliot from the standard Elizabethan representation of a nightingale's call, 'Jug jug' (cf. Thomas Nashe, 1567-1601).]

September 1990

88 Words Words Fail Fail Me Me

I write this at the height of our heatwave. In my office, word processors are melting and keyboards dripping sluggishly groundwards. I've lugged a computer down to the cellar of our collapsing Victorian home in order to type this in dank coolness ... but woodlice keep creeping into the works. Any obscenities or mentions of Piers Anthony should be ascribed to insect infestation of my disk drives. You have been warned.

Lyonesse III: Madouc (Grafton 358pp £12.95) is the third book of a leisurely pre-Arthurian fantasy sequence which shows Jack Vance's strengths and weaknesses in high relief. He can do you a nicely exotic landscape; his pictures of magical doings are fascinating and menacing; his whimsical names are lovely (e.g. a fairy retreat called Thripsey Shee); and in close-up scenes, the politely ironic dialogue is always a treat. Vance does less well on the wide screen: his picaresque approach is geared to jewelled incidents and elegant chat, not the epic sweep of war.

Thus the world-shaking battles here fall pretty flat, with even the prose losing its usual fizz. Vance's descriptions of food are more heartfelt; here's a man who dreams not of glory but of seven-course oyster breakfasts. The changeling Princess Madouc's rebellion against stuffy court tradition and search for her parents are enjoyable - but in the best Vance plots (*The Blue World*, *Emphyrio*, *The Anome*) the rebellious youth goes on to change the world, and Madouc never has the power or opportunity for that.

Every page of *Madouc* is smoothly readable, but in the end there are too many words to be sustained by the limp plot. You finish it feeling not so much replete as vaguely tired.

Sequels and series and trilogies ... the saga continues. Fay Sampson's *Black Smith's Telling* (Headline 275pp £3.50) offers another dose of her alternative Arthuriad. Familiar characters come to new and sinister life when seen from half-sister Morgan's side. There are no swords in stones, but Modred is duly born. This one is told by a smith who's a warlock of the Old Religion; as the magical rites described consist chiefly of having it off at Sabbat orgies, I was never quite convinced that this easily suborned chap actually wielded all the dark power Morgan was supposed to be coveting. Nice one, though.

A non-review: *Hyperion* by Dan Simmons (Headline 346pp £13.95) has been hugely praised, but it's only half of a fat sf novel. To avoid terminal dissatisfaction, I'm told, you must read straight on to the resolution in part two, *The Fall of Hyperion* – a work not even hinted at in this edition. Naughty, naughty. I'll tackle the complete story when Headline send the rest.

Tales from the Saragossa Manuscript by Jan Potocki (Dedalus European Classics 159pp £5.99) is also incomplete, but for good reason. There's actually a sequel to this 1814 oddity, but one that resolves nothing, as explained in the learned introduction by fantasy knowledge master Brian Stableford. These suave, witty *Tales* of probable ghosts and possible demons suggest a dream-labyrinth which the narrator might never escape. Going to sleep in carnal bliss usually leads to a nasty awakening amid decayed corpses under a gallows. Could this have been one inspiration for the entanglements of Robert Irwin's *The Arabian Nightmare*?

A jaded reader recently said my reviews had become repetitious. It's a fair cop, guv. Er, of course this reflects the repetitiousness of the blasted books. The repetitiousness of the books. Of the books. Such as Piers Piers Anthony Anthony's truly dreadful *For Love of Evil* (Grafton Grafton 318pp £3.99), in which he not only soggily rehashes the entire threadbare sequence of tawdry plots comprising four previous **Incarnations of Immortality** books (five, actually; the first is readable), but congratulates himself in an afterword on how cleverly he's regurgitated his own appalling drivel. Words words fail fail me me.

I'm always interested in weird stuff on the outskirts of science. (Plug: *The Skeptical Inquirer*, the famous US mag which lambasts paranormal loonies, now has a promising British counterpart in *The Skeptic* – details from PO Box 475, Manchester, M60 2TH.) Those wonderfully eclectic people of the 'Whole Earth Catalog' have published a compendium of strangeness in *The Fringes of Reason* (Harmony Books 224pp $14.95).

It's all here. The jacket lists 'channelling, psychic powers, crystals, Bigfoot, shamanism, UFOs, perpetual motion, conspiracies, cults, flat Earth, reincarnation, spontaneous human combustion, dowsing, prophecy, weird phenomena, astral projection, brain machines, living dinosaurs, hollow Earth, Atlantis, alien abductions' ... and there's more, much more, very much more, calculated to make both True Believers and Nasty Rationalist Scientists froth at every orifice.

The great thing about Whole Earth publications is that they don't merely summarize but give addresses and steer you to source material, be it never so daft. Read how to get *Flat Earth News* ('NO PROOF OF ANY KIND EXISTS TODAY 1988 for a Greese [sic] Ball whirling in space!'), join the Church of the SubGenius (the ultimate cult, a hilarious spoof ... *or is it?*), or even 'Learn to project your astral body *while driving!!*'. There's good coverage of sceptical counterattacks, too.

Besides being a book to pillage for oddball inspirations, it's enormous fun to read. Incredibly, I actually bought this – by sending credit card details to Fringes, Whole Earth Catalog, 27 Gate Five Road, Sausalito, CA 94965, U.S.A.

In Dougal Dixon's *Man After Man: an Anthropology of the Future* (Blandford 128pp £14.95), the author of *Life After Man* turns his warped imagination from the 'lower orders' to what *Hom.sap.*, the lords of creation, might become in a few million years. With illustrations. It's uneasy stuff: natural selection is OK for voles but is not supposed to happen to people like you and me. Certain premises are debatable; still, this is good nightmare material. Editor Wayne insists that several appalling examples of speculative human evolution look just like famous games person Marcus L. Rowland, but perhaps he's being a little unfair. See for yourself.

October 1990

89 Seven Languages at Once

If there's anything more brain-numbing than several hundred sf fans at a British convention, it's several thousand of them at the annual world event. I'm writing in the groan-laden aftermath of ConFiction, the 48th World SF Convention and the first in the Netherlands.

This was hugely enjoyable despite shambolic programming. The 'Worldcon' once resembled baseball's 'World Series', in that 'World' is a delicate euphemism for 'USA'. Now, with the Iron Curtain in tatters, it's gone cosmopolitan - pulling the crowds from Eastern Europe and further-flung places. At the all-night parties, you could hear seven languages at once.

Loneliest moment of ConFiction: Brian Stableford realizing that every other member of a 'hard sf' panel had defected, leaving him all alone (until his wife hauled in an unwilling Langford). Most mysterious: the 'Pissed Fly' panel, whose members (including Bob Shaw) never found what the title meant - the organizer who knew the secret went missing. Best bit for me: winning the only Hugo Award which didn't go to the USA, and being congratulated by vast USSR fans glowing with *glasnost* and Heineken. Rather than fill my space with Hugos, I've passed the winners to *GMI*'s news pages.

Coming Worldcons will be Chicago 1991, Florida 1992 and San Francisco 1993. The last venue was voted in Holland, beating the Hawaii counterbid which filled ConFiction with eldritch shirts and helium-filled parrots... all very surreal. Glasgow is bidding for 1995, but so is Australia and only time will tell.

[1992: Glasgow won. 2000: The event is now history.]

One nice thing about these jamborees is the free booze from the book industry. During ConFiction, the SF Writers of America hospitality room was sponsored by many publishers including Gollancz and Games Workshop. In London just beforehand, Grafton threw a birthday party for 70-year-old (and *much* bulkier than his publicity pictures) Ray Bradbury - launching his new book *A Graveyard for Lunatics*. After the Worldcon, Orbit Books organized a bash in the incredibly non-air-conditioned crypt of St Martin-in-the-Fields... a DIY sauna. All this helped me research the many brands of paracetamol which I'll be reviewing soon.

Which reminds me of Brian Aldiss's umpteenth official birthday party of 1990 (he's 65), thrown by his wife Margaret in what seemed the poshest hotel in

Holland. This makes it hard to be nasty to *Bury My Heart at W.H. Smith's* (Hodder 221pp £13.95), a gentle autobiography which gives the effect of sitting in a bar listening to ebullient Aldiss anecdotes - though not, alas, the *really* scurrilous ones. It's been nastily and unfairly reviewed by newspaper critics who seem incensed by his taking pride in a lifetime of writing sf. Few British authors in any field have as much to be proud of.

Greg Bear made it to ConFiction from distant Seattle, neatly in time for the British publication of *Queen of Angels* (Gollancz 385pp £14.95). This new Bear blockbuster is more thoughtful and, I think, successful than the recent *Eternity*. Instead of gigantic, impossible technologies, he concentrates on a rigorously plausible Los Angeles of 2047... 'The City of Our Lady the Queen of the Angels', as its full name translates.

Nanotechnology now allows expensive designer bodies and a believable approximation to psychiatric telepathy. The new vigilantes sentence their victims to computer-induced emotional torments which can burn you out in minutes. Artificial intelligences, sexless and abstract as angels, fumble hopelessly towards their programmed goal of self-awareness, with the breakthrough coming from the cruellest and least expected angle. Messages crawl back from the robot probe out at Centauri. The heroine, another angel of a sort, is conducting a hopeless multiple-murder investigation....

Angels is a book full of doomed hopes which, by serendipity, lead to new breakthroughs and tiny victories. Unfortunately it's rather hard to get into, thanks to dense exposition and determined futurespeak (internal monologues of 2047 are desperately short on commas, and several items of slang take too long to make sense). It's so easy to slip across that fine line between hiding information in the narrative context and hiding it too well. But here there are many rewards. Nice one, Greg.

Eric (Gollancz 126pp £7.99) is not so much another Discworld novel as a brief Terry Pratchett romp - a Faustian travelogue which gives his regular cover artist Josh Kirby a chance to run very slowly amok. I've liked Kirby's sf covers for more years than I, or probably he, would care to admit: twisted, organic shapes and strange lines of force, adorning long-forgotten book imprints like Four Square. Here are fourteen large-format, double-page pictures in his sumptuous Discworld style (sixteen, counting title page and cover). Here in their perverse Pratchett incarnations are Death, Inca sacrifice, Odysseus, Helen of Troy, Creation, Hell, the wizard Rincewind, and the dread Luggage. The mixture as before, with exuberant visual aids.

Langford's Maxim for 1990 has been: 'In an increasingly science-fictional world, sanity can be preserved only by reading the odd non-sf book.' If you're worried about fundamentalism, the Rushdie affair and the idea of getting prosecuted for rudeness about God, Allah or L. Ron Hubbard, read *Blasphemy Ancient and Modern* by Nicolas Walter (Rationalist Press Association 96pp £3.95).

This offers a racy historical overview of past persecutions for heresy, blasphemy and profanity (the Spanish Inquisition was still offing people last century and wasn't actually abolished until 1834), and examines the chaos of British law today. What's worse than merely having an absurd and divisive blasphemy law is enforcing it unequally. Technical blasphemies crowd the history of sf, fantasy and literature at large. If the law were uniformly applied, we'd plunge into a State control of literature more rigid than South Africa's. Instead, blasphemies that don't annoy Mary Whitehouse go unscathed but *Gay News* is prosecuted.

Walter presents the case for repealment and reminds us of many unsung heroes of free thought. One chap last century was jugged for plunging a courtroom into uproar with appalling obscenities and indeed blasphemies quoted from murky corners of... the Bible. Fundamentalists who believe the literal truth of its every word are surprisingly good at skipping awkward pages.

OK, you can stop skipping now....

November 1990

90 Successful Sequels?

The world of publishing is a constant source of surprises, most of them roughly akin to having a masked psychopath erupt into your bathroom with a whirring chainsaw; once in a while, though, something pleasant happens. I wouldn't dream of plugging my 1988 parody collection *The Dragonhiker's Guide to Battlefield Covenant at Dune's Edge: Odyssey Two* (Drunken Dragon Press), but can't resist revealing that its Spanish edition just arrived and is called... *Guia del Dragonstopista Galactico al Campo de Batalla Estelar de Covenant en el Limite de Dune: Odisea Dos.* Scribble that one in the phrasebook before your next trip to Benidorm.

A much more typical surprise was receiving an unexpected copy of my UFO spoof book, plus a gloomy rejection note, from a publisher who'd been sitting on it for more than *five years* and had better remain nameless (seven letters, starts with G). What a whirlwind, go-ahead industry.

Further personal good cheer comes from two absolutely spiffy anthologies which I nervously can't bring myself to review, or even as yet read all the way through, because I'm in them: *More Tales from the Forbidden Planet* ed. Roz Kaveney (Titan, large illustrated paperback 268pp £7.95), and *Digital Dreams* ed. David V. Barrett (NEL 347pp £4.50). Buy them, buy them.

The Kaveney anthology is nicely packaged, with a cover by Moebius and all 15 featured authors and artists given fair and equal billing on the back. The Barrett collection is good value (20 new stories by Brits about computers), but comparatively irritating for contributors: only six 'famous' ones are credited on the back, and only Terry Pratchett on the front, in huge dominating letters, to Terry's and the editor's vast displeasure....

[John Gribbin went bonkers about this, demanding that Barrett – who had no control over the cover – should be ostracized by sf readers for allowing it.]

Can you go back to a world whose story seems rounded and finished? Terrible disappointments may follow when authors return to add another sequel, especially after some time: Asimov, Heinlein, Niven, Pohl, even Wolfe, all failed to recapture the original spark. I was therefore nervous about Ursula Le Guin's *Tehanu: the Last Book of Earthsea* (Gollancz 219pp £9.95). I needn't have been.

The story follows the now middle-aged Tenar (once Arha) from *The Tombs of Atuan*, and continues beyond the deeps of *The Farthest Shore.* There's relatively little action, little magic: this book works in the areas left unlit by the trilogy, such as how magicians and kings look to subsistence farmers at the bottom of the heap, and why women seem to be excluded from high magic. ('Weak/ wicked as women's magic,' people say.) Le Guin weaves some rich explanatory images, and cannily puts many of them into the mouth of an unreliably articulate witch-aunt: there are no straight answers to the biggest questions, only parables.

When, in the end, some magical action does happen, it's shockingly different from the previous books' tales of great deeds seen from a mage's viewpoint. The day is saved by a sort of *deus ex machina* (prefigured earlier) which also suggests a final, burning metaphor about women and men and the sources of power.

Deceptively simple, quiet and passive, *Tehanu* leaves Earthsea richer and darker than before. 'There is no safety. There is no end. The word must be heard in silence. There must be darkness to see the stars....'

Bob Shaw also more or less pulls it off in *Orbitsville Judgement* (Gollancz, hardback 281pp £13.95), rounding up this sequence to a trilogy. Orbitsville, a vast hollow habitat with some 650 million times the living space of boring old Earth, was discovered in Book One and threatened to soak up human expansion forever. At the climax of Book Two it vanished from the universe, perhaps carrying its innumerable settlers to colonize another. Book three tells us where it went.

Any attempt to outdo Book Two would, I feared, result in a story so sprawling and cosmic as to lose interest for ordinary mortals. To avoid this, Shaw hooks you with human drama. Cruelly and humiliatingly fleeced by religious fanatics, the hero turns from a pleasant wimp with Billy Liar tendencies into a nastily driven instrument of revenge ... which traps him into following the cult. What the fanatics want is transport to get off Orbitsville, which to their leader is clearly a Manichaean trap laid by the devil. He is, in a way, right.

Everybody, in fact, is both right and wrong. The major trap is a benevolent but (we learn) misguided alien attempt at ecological conservation – involving, for starters, twin universes and a timespan of forty billion years. The attempted escape proves less wise than staying trapped. After meeting something far bigger than Orbitsville, the saner religious folk are confirmed in their beliefs, and the atheist hero in his. And finally, every thread is tied up more neatly than you'd believe possible.

What drags you along and counterpoints the large-scale action is the painful sight of the hero dehumanizing himself and heading for a sort of secular damnation. It's people and not big numbers that make wide-screen sf work. That said, I remain unhappy that the sunny but disturbing finale of the original *Orbitsville* is so thoroughly invalidated by these sequels. It's a hell of a thing when the best ending in your trilogy is in volume one.

Dedalus, my favourite small publisher, continues to unearth eccentric classics, or at any rate old books. Is there anyone alive today who could contemplate reading the endless tiny print of Eugene Sue's monumental *The Wandering Jew* (847pp £9.99)? Evidently Brian Stableford could, since he provides a meaty introduction - not included in that page count! - explaining that it was serialized in French newspapers from 1844-5, contains 'the most spectacular example of an aborted climax in the entire history of popular fiction' (it was too popular to be let finish), and runs to over 500,000 words. Rather him than me.

[Later: the long sentence in that paragraph was too much for the *GMI* subeditors, who broke it into tiny little pieces and left me saying, quite unambiguously, that the *introduction* was half a million words long. No, no, Brian wouldn't waste a whole week on such ill-paid work....]

Here too is the somewhat more classic *The Phantom of the Opera* by Gaston Leroux (1910 385pp £6.99), issued in competition with a hardback now clogging the remainder shops - 'I *told* them not to do it,' confided Mr Stableford in the usual exclusive interview. And also, in the new series 'Decadence from Dedalus', Octave Mirbeau's *The Torture Garden* (1898 284pp £6.99) is about what its title says, has some actual literary distinction, and should by no means be read before, during or after meals. Not nice at all.

More when my tummy settles down....

December 1990

91 Horror and Ultimate Evil

As I write, Hallowe'en approaches and a terrible, surging, loathsome spawn of the damned is erupting from nightmarish sewers and tombs all around.... In other words, a lot of timely horror-related books are coming out.

Perhaps the oddest is the nonfiction *Fear Itself: The Horror Fiction of Stephen King (1976-1982)* (Pan 255pp £4.99). Without personally being much of a horror buff, I can see that King is a masterly technician who deserves most of his success. The mixed essays in *Fear Itself* shower obligatory praise on him; canny old Fritz Leiber provides needed astringency by hurling buckets of ordure all over Stanley Kubrick's adaptation of *The Shining*.

Beneath the surface of this book lies a story of real-life dread and humiliation - of three horror fans whose co-authored King bibliography is (like everything else here) reprinted untouched from the 1982 US edition, along with a contact address so that millions of people can write and inform them about careless omissions like every single King novel and story for the last eight years.

Surely Pan should have updated this list, or at least done a minute's scissors-and-paste work to spare its compilers the incredible embarrassment of saying in print, in 1990, *after* thanking King for his extensive information and help: 'It has been stated that Richard Bachman is a pseudonym of Stephen King. This is not the case.... Stephen King has never used this name as a pseudonym.' Poor sods, standing there with faces covered in egg.

Here's another King celebration (what is this, his centenary?) with an exhaustive and exhausting bibliography right up to 1990: *The Stephen King Companion* ed. George Beahm (Macdonald 365pp £13.95). Far less dignified and 'literary' than the 1982 collection, this is largely a book of trivia: blurbs and synopses, reviews and interviews, fan club data, fan mail, and so on down to utter barrel-scrapings... self-promotion from the blacksmith who made wrought iron bats for King's house, a potted biography of some book dealer, an inane 'Rating Yourself As A King Fan' quiz, etc.

More substantial pieces include the bibliography, *Playboy*'s King interview, and Harlan Ellison gleefully hurling buckets of ordure over just about every movie version of a King novel. This apart, the tone is pretty adulatory. King's great virtues could stand up to some criticism which goes beyond calling an occasional minor story 'lightweight'.

I personally reckon, for example, that *The Stand* is far too long, that its biological-Armageddon plot and its post-holocaust fantasy quest belong in separate books, and that the climax plunges into ludicrous bathos with the idea of God *nuking* the forces of evil. Reissuing it in a version 75,000 words longer seems a deeply weird notion. But the *Companion* retorts that *The Stand* is the fans' number-one favourite (which is an eye-opener), and manages in the same section to imply a comparison of King with Mozart (which is dribble).

SF fans are likely to approach the new Arthur C. Clarke novel warily, feeling that too many of his books have for too long been needless sequels, wonky collaborations, strained attempts at Even Huger Concepts... or all three at once. In fact much of *The Ghost from the Grand Banks* (Gollancz 249pp £12.95) is a lively, enjoyable performance, crammed with interesting things.

The story centres on plans to raise the *Titanic* one century after it sank in 1912, a vague spirit of competition being provided by two separate and (perhaps implausibly) radically different projects for tackling the two sections of the wreck. Some good, logical surprises emerge, while the narrative churns with Clarke's own thoughts (some half-baked and some undigested) on developments to come in fractals, brothels, computers, glassware, cryonics, even old movies - there's a wonderfully daft industry devoted to the digital editing of filthy old film-scenes which show people ... smoking.

The Clarke world remains strangely bloodless and remote, as though all the drama and emotion were being observed at a chilly distance by his deep-sea probes hovering four kilometres down where the *Titanic* lies on the Grand Banks. Death, melodrama, insanity and sexual oddities are all happening there somewhere, but only a purely intellectual excitement tinged with melancholy gets through to the page. Clarke knows his strengths, and *Ghost* concentrates mainly on things he's good at. It would, however, be hard to imagine an ending that could unify and justify all the speculative loose ends in the book. Clarke merely pulls back his good old temporal zoom-lens for a bit of that familiar perspective-of-eternity which ought to chill but through long custom is really rather cosy.

In one place he's a bit naughty, explaining the fractal ramifications of the Mandelbrot Set with such care to keep it simple - by skating over the 'imaginary' numbers involved - that the explanation just doesn't explain. For enlightenment, turn to the boggling and profound *The Emperor's New Mind* by Roger Penrose (Vintage 602pp £6.99), which will almost painlessly Make You Think about today's real problems in maths, physics and artificial intelligence.

'A video tape is being sent by Evangelists to schools nationwide warning children not to celebrate Hallowe'en because they would be "dabbling with the Devil",' reported *The Independent on Sunday* last October.

I soon heard the inside story from my own mole within Pandaemonium, the Great Parliament of Hell. It seems that Beelzebub started it all with a diabolically awkward enquiry at Question Time: 'What steps does His Infernal Highness propose to take about the shameful levity with which the Great Sabbat of Hallowe'en is now regarded by the general public?'

In his ensuing speech he pointed out with deep sarcasm that the dignity of Hell was seriously harmed by snotty-nosed kids running round in plastic masks trying to cadge sweeties. Recruitment to Satanic worship had fallen off badly thanks to this unfortunate association with giggling cries of 'Trick or treat.' Not to mention bleeding fantasy games, he added.

The massed daemonic ranks - who just like British politicians hate being laughed at - hissed their approval.

Replying on behalf of Ultimate Evil and the Foreign Office, Lord Moloch said that he had been working closely with his opposite number in the Evangelical Alliance to arrange a videotape campaign which would either restore the proper reverent regard for Hallowe'en or at least succeed in making a lot of Evangelists look very silly.

There was a standing ovation in Hell.

Meanwhile, Happy New Year.

January 1991

92 Memory Aids

SF and fantasy authors pinch their ideas from many places. Several have been inspired by Frances Yates's wonderful *The Art of Memory*, which everyone should read (this means you): all about the weird and ancient discipline of using architecture as a memory aid, by imagining vast buildings and filling them with luridly memorable images. Strolling mentally through cluttered corridors, you are supposed to find again the objects you mentally placed there and be reminded of detail after detail by this threatening figure, that cup, those ram's testicles (I don't know either, but that's what it says in the original Latin treatise quoted by Yates).

John Crowley in *Little, Big* has his mage Ariel Hawksquill use the Art for divination, on the believable and practical basis that the mnemonic images will change with time and provide short-cut access to what you know only unconsciously: this is the one aspect of the manipulations of astrology, tarot, and so on which makes perfect sense to me. In *Aegypt*, Crowley showed the Art being used – as it was in real life – by Giordano Bruno, the Renaissance hermetic philosopher.

Gene Wolfe uses it, too: his amnesiac hero Latro struggles to provide himself with an artificial, architectural memory in *Soldier of Arete*, and the idea underlies that deceptively cosy-seeming novel *Peace*, whose secrets unfold when you realize it's an ever-chillier tour through the decaying House of Memory of a hero who's long dead when the book begins.

Now Ian Watson has extrapolated the Art along his own bizarre trajectories, in *The Flies of Memory* (Gollancz 220pp £13.95). The alien 'Flies' don't use writing, but store their knowledge in a group memory based, once again, on architecture. Having run out of places of their own to use as mental information dumps, they visit Earth to upgrade their storage system by memorizing all *our* architecture. Only there are metaphysical complications.

The understructure of the universe, Watson suggests, is memory. If you're in tune with it – well, when humans interfere with the Flies' memory tourism, buildings and cities can be forgotten so thoroughly that they vanish from Earth. Which is merely the beginning.

Predictably unpredictable as ever, Watson proceeds by dizzy leaps to a finale haunted by solidifying memories of Hitler's rise to power in a Munich which has turned up again on Mars. Enough said. Some of the metaphysics is reminiscent of his 1979 *God's World.*

This is fine, far-out stuff, told by several female narrators in a variety of styles from mystical to zappy. Part 2 is the most stylistically uncomfortable, with a buttonholing, second-person narrative giving the feeling that this schizo young lady is talking at you from about three inches' range: you want to back away. I will not mention the puns.

It's vintage Watson and, like all his best work, fills you with bogglement salted by occasional irritation.

(The engraved-looking cover art, by Mike Litherland, is nice – Gollancz are phasing out their ghastly 'standard' jacket design, and not before time.)

Speaking of memory, some of the late great Philip K. Dick's best stories about thought and reality appear in *The Little Black Box* (Gollancz 395pp £14.95). A personal favourite is 'The Electric Ant', whose hero discovers to his dismay that not only is he a machine, but his *entire* perception of the world is arriving not through his senses but from a tape unreeling in his chest (think about that, but not too hard). In 'We Can Remember It For You Wholesale', an impoverished tourist visits Mars by purchasing not a trip but implanted memories of a trip, little knowing that the implant technique will unearth his real, erased memories of a top-secret mission to Mars, whereupon ... Part of this story – though not very much – was used as a peg on which to hang reels of movie action-adventure for *Total Recall.*

All the MPs who voted in our new, restrictive Official Secrets Act should be compelled to read the most utopian story Dick ever wrote, 'The Exit Door Leads In'.

As Thomas Disch indicates in the introduction, PKD was a great primitive writer who handled astonishing material in an undistinguished and sometimes downright clumsy style. The bright side is that he's always accessible and never, except perhaps in *Valis,* intimidating. Someone once told James Thurber that if he could draw any better, he'd be lousy.

This completes the five-volume collection of all Dick's short fiction, a worthy project indeed. The others are *Beyond Lies the Wub, Second Variety, The Father-Thing* and *The Days of Perky Pat.* Grafton are doing the paperbacks.

Arranging the hardbacks on the shelf and looking at their spines, you see that the last two titles are annoyingly out of line and that Dick's name is split over two lines in two different ways. This is a Nearly Matched Set. But Gollancz has just acquired a new art director.

Two more fat anthologies for short story fans: *Best New SF 4* ed. Gardner Dozois (Robinson 598pp £6.99) and *Best New Horror* ed. Stephen Jones and Ramsey Campbell (Robinson 390pp £6.99). The sf collection, covering the best of 1989, is masterfully chosen and excellent value at 1.17 pence per crammed page. I'm sure the horror volume (not so much my kind of thing) is a good selection, but why does it cost over 50% more per page of fewer words? To pay for the foil on the jacket?

Still speaking of memory ...

Boring old reviewers, such as myself, like to go on about how they have Read It All Before. This isn't so much a languid Oscar Wilde pose ('There is only one thing worse than having read it before, and that is ... not having read it before!') as an occupational hazard.

Thus I opened *Enchanted Pilgrimage* by Clifford Simak (Mandarin 218pp £3.99), a routine-looking fantasy quest with sf garnish, and about three-quarters of the way through found it was getting a shade too familiar. Where had I read before about a Lovecraftian 'Chaos Beast' giving posthumous birth to a cute robot? Yes, in Methuen's identical 1985 paperback, not even hinted at on this reprint's copyright page. Tut tut.

So, like most later Simak, *Pilgrimage* is inoffensive and forgettable, just saved from oblivion by a few dotty ideas and a faint whiff of his old Midwestern pastoral charm. To find his best stuff, check original copyright dates for the period 1951 (*Time and Again*) to 1965 (*All Flesh is Grass*). From 1953 there's *Ring Around the Sun* (Mandarin 205pp £3.50), a dated but still nifty tale of magical science and economic attack on poor old Earth. This diabolical assault takes the form of razor blades, light bulbs, cars, etc., that *never wear out*. Tremble in your shoes, Earthling industrialists!

I remember the NFT launch party for Terry Pratchett's *Moving Pictures* (Gollancz 279pp £12.95). I definitely remember there was wine. Lots of wine. No popcorn, but wine. Terry was there somewhere. So was a lot more wine. 'People don't want to listen to speeches at these things,' said hero Gollancz editor Richard Evans: 'We're here to get pissed.' I remember I agreed and had some wine. One flaw in the Art of Memory is that it doesn't seem to help at all with locating bottles of paracetamol.

More, if I remember, next month....

February 1991

93 Fix-ups

One of the seediest terms in sf criticism was invented by A.E. van Vogt: 'fix-up', the result of bolting together vaguely related short stories and calling them a novel. When the stories aren't particularly connected, you get the famous van Vogt effect of thrilling, heady incoherence. But 'fix-up' also covers works of real genius like Keith Roberts's *Pavane*, so it's not mere abuse.

As On a Darkling Plain by Ben Bova (Mandarin 189pp £3.99) is a fix-up of the most irritating kind: an unremarkable sf novelette inflated to book length with unrelated tales of exploration. The frame story is about all these puzzling alien machines on the moon Titan (influence: 'The Sentinel' by Arthur C. Clarke). What is their dark secret? In order not to find out, Earth rushes a futile expedition into the high-pressure depths of Jupiter (embarrassingly strong influence: *The Dragon in the Sea* by Frank Herbert) and another to, of all places, Sirius. As someone nervously explains at this point, 'Nobody expects us to find anything.'

Only near the end does anyone stoop to the obvious by taking a scientific look at the Titan installation. This machinery, based on technology far beyond our own, does indeed have a sinister purpose ... to wipe out the human race! What's more, it's been doing it without pause for several millennia already. Inscrutable, these alien johnnies, but fortunately we saw through their plot just in time.

An awful book. Still, I treasure the scientific insight whereby people who've been modified to breathe water notice that their submarine voices are 'a bit slower and deeper than normal.' Also lower in information content, surely: not so much 'His gill rate is getting critical!' (an actual line) as '*Glub, glub, glub*.'

When is a fix-up not a fix-up? When it reads that way because several collaborators haven't managed to mesh very well, as in *Close Encounters? Science and Science Fiction* by Roger Lambourne, Michael Shallis and Michael Shortland (Adam Hilger 184pp no price visible). This is a feeble book about the science in sf ... no, in the central chapters it's a good essay about how sf movies have presented or caricatured scientists ... with digressions on any movie an author feels like mentioning (sometimes two appear to discuss the same film at length, independently, in different chapters) ... but then there's a random dose of ecology stuff, and a weird chapter on religion which gets quite alarmist about the possibility that Spielberg's *ET* might have the 'effect of undermining traditional religious thought'. Blimey. Why should that be a bad thing, by the way?

This bittiness is not, as nasty reviewers might suspect, a mistake. The introduction says openly that the book is not intended to offer any argument, reach any conclusion, or form a unified whole. 'This diversity ... is one of the qualitites [sic] that distinguishes [sic] this book from others that have dealt with similar subjects.' The result is a mass of inoffensive writing with rambling, patchy sf coverage and a heavy cinematic bias. Perhaps the authors – all university lecturers – were tired of student essays crammed with boring old arguments and conclusions.

Another kind of fix-up is the Art Potboiler, containing heaps of unrelated jacket pictures strung together with tongue-in-cheek narrative. Chris Foss's *Diary of a Spaceperson* (Paper Tiger 143pp £16.95) is the usual travelogue, described as a 'sensual and spiritual odyssey'. 'Sensual' indicates that the heroine enjoys many a tasteful bonk with all sexes and species, 'spiritual' that she has dope-dreams to justify the weirder paintings lying around the Foss studio....

It looks terrific: Paper Tiger's production is always superb, though I wearied of their hard-to-read 'handwritten' typeface (the text is skippable). Chris 'Enormous Machinery With Windows' Foss has a distinctive airbrushed style which gives his big set-pieces an overall unity, no matter how inconsistent their details might be. Meanwhile, Chris 'I Also Illustrated *The Joy Of Sex*' Foss contributes mildly raunchy pencil drawings ... no hard porn, but a nipple count in the mid-eighties.

With its severely technophilic cover, this should do well with frustrated sf fans too embarrassed to be seen reading *Playboy* or *Knave.* Guardians of our morals will not approve.

It's always cheering to find a new British writer. Jenny Jones's *Fly By Night* (Headline 499pp £4.99) is a promising debut, a good gloomy fantasy which builds on an old sf metaphor about immortality and sterility to produce quite a new feel.

It begins conventionally enough, with the traditional importation from our 'real' world of Eleanor, a useless-seeming saviour who isn't initially much of a person (like a Stephen Donaldson protagonist) but is clearly destined to grow and to end the unchanging stasis that freezes the twilit fantasy domain. Jones then conscientiously tangles the often too-simple issues of good and evil. Most people on the 'wrong' side are likeable, perhaps just a little selfish: contrast Western civilization and the suffering Third World. The moon-goddess on the 'right' side destroys an innocent bystander in a shockingly gratuitous way, merely to underline her authority. Few characters are certain that they're doing the right thing, or that it will lead to the right end.

This being a first novel, there are several minor flaws, mainly stylistic – like the overused word 'exigent', a Stephen Donaldson favourite. But it kept me reading and, despite opening a trilogy, came to a satisfying conclusion.

I must admit that Games Workshop have now sorted out some of their books' image problems. *Warhammer 40,000: Inquisitor* by Ian Watson (GW

Books 246pp £4.99) has a bold and legible silver-foil title on the cover. The jacket artwork remains terrible, but less so than on earlier titles.

Ian Watson is a brave man. Not only does he put his own name on this thing [unlike 'Brian Craig', 'David Ferring', 'Jack Yeovil' *et al*], but he's evidently read all the *Warhammer 40K* rules: *Inquisitor* is conscientiously larded with stuff about Genestealers, warps, demons, assassins, kinky deformities ... even a cute dwarf. Weighted down by this, the great innovator of British sf tells a galaxy-spanning but remarkably ordinary tale, reminiscent of the early Moorcock on a bad day. It's the start of a trilogy.

I tactfully asked the author how he regarded *Inquisitor*, and he evasively replied that it was very much the sf book he'd wanted to read when he was fifteen. If you're a doddering 16-year-old or even more senile than that, you have been warned.

In brief ...

Arthur C. Clarke struck dread into my heart with a 'sensational new first chapter' for his little classic *Childhood's End* (Pan 200pp £3.99). I was afraid he'd spoil the bloom, but the update amounts to two rewritten pages at the start ... later in the same chapter, although this is supposed to be the 21st century, the technology is still 'electron tubes' (valves). This remains the one book where Clarke's mysticism really works and leaves no loose ends.

In a anthology not yet released over here, Isaac Asimov is honoured by sf pals and admirers: *Foundation's Friends* (Tor 464pp $4.95). These stories set in Asimov's universes contain a lot of routine pastiche (like Poul Anderson setting up a laws-of-robotics quibble too finicky even for Asimov to have used), but there are gems. In particular there is Orson Scott Card, an author I've never much liked in the past, whose 'The Originist' could well be the best Foundation/Empire story ever written.

Perhaps I've softened towards 'shared world anthologies' since writing some stories for new British ventures. I'll tell you more next time.

[I didn't, though. I forgot.]

March 1991

94 Dream Parks

For role-playing gamers, the affordable edition of *The Barsoom Project* by Larry Niven and Steven Barnes (Pan 340pp £4.50) presumably came as the first major treat of 1991. For mere interested spectators (me) it's still a pretty good read.

The book follows the general pattern of the authors' earlier *Dream Park*, with minor links to their thin little technothriller *The Descent of Anansi*. Dream Park is the ultimate in live-action game environments, with holographic effects and a vast supporting technology like an extrapolated Disneyland. Once again a game is in progress, with twists: the fantasy background is unusual (Eskimo) and the purpose partly 'educational', a lose-weight game for fatties. Once again there's huge intrigue behind the scenes: crimes and machinations and an alternate use of Dream Park for planetarium-style presentation of an ambitious 'real world' Mars program, as per title. You keep turning the pages.

Yes, it's solid and well-researched sf, a nifty read if taken at face value. But when you pause to think, there are niggles. One whole narrative thread lacks tension because, no matter how well told, it's still just people playing a game. Then consider Disneyland, which turns a profit on its *much* cheaper and lower-tech sideshows only by processing umpteen thousand visitors a day: here a party of ten gamers is monopolizing vast resources for days on end, and whatever they paid it wasn't enough. (There's some feeble attempt at justifying this by saying the whole thing will later be packaged for domestic video sales. Pull the other one, chaps, it rings Kent Treble Bob Major.)

It is also irritating that no argument against the authors' much-loved but fantastically expensive space project is even expressed ... and worrying that Dream Park resources are used extra-legally and without visible qualms to give the villain an unpleasant and fatal come-uppance. There would not be that much moral difference if the book's President of the USA favoured policies which would lead to closing down Dream Park and/or the space programme, and the 'good guys' responded by democratically assassinating *him*.

In the main, Niven and Barnes are writing enjoyable wish-fulfilment. Ignore the propaganda, remember the glad fact that Californian sf writers have little if any real political power, and you can't help liking it.

There's always another book about the famous Inklings group (principally Tolkien, C.S. Lewis and Charles Williams): the latest is *The Magical World of the Inklings* by Gareth Knight (Element 258pp £9.99). Knight seems to want to put the creations of these very Christian authors into a broader, vaguer context of occult tradition and ceremonial magic, but he makes so little effort to organize his material that nothing much comes of it.

The book consists chiefly of wearisome plot summaries – of all Lewis's and Williams's fiction, the *Silmarillion*, and the non-fictional works of Owen Barfield (with which I'm not familiar). From time to time Knight waxes enthusiastic about random occult connections. He reels in amazement that the very widely read Lewis should have quoted some snippet of esoteric lore in *That Hideous Strength*. He later suggests that Tolkien, to create his worlds, simply must have had 'imaginative access to the record on the subtle ethers of all that has ever happened'. This sounds deeply patronizing, like Erich von Däniken explaining that our 'primitive' ancestors could never have invented anything without alien assistance.

The low point is a straight-faced transcript of what you might call role-playing or group therapy (Knight calls it High Magic), with punters acting out a visit to Tolkien's western isles and undergoing much dire spiritual uplift: no swordplay or such vulgar stuff, but heavy elvish insights like, 'I get the feeling they think our time oriented existence is pretty weird.' Here Knight drones on about healing and regeneration without addressing the possibility that Tolkien, as a Catholic, would have liked to kick the participants' bottoms and advise them to go to church for that kind of thing.

I must confess a lack of sympathy for writing which can't describe a minor coincidence without adding that it was 'perhaps by a divine or occultly inspired synchronicity', and which remains so consistently foggy about its own philosophical standpoint. (Too occult to be revealed, maybe.) Of all the books about the Inklings, this must be the most dispensable.

Also on the mystical side is *The Bruce Pennington Portfolio* (Paper Tiger, 28 plates, £9.95) ... which might sound expensive, but really it's 28 paintings on individual 42 x 29cm sheets of heavy paper, suitable for framing if you can bear to cut up the book. (Though if you can bear to cut up any book, I do not wish to know you.) There is also a brief introduction which scatters a few biographical details but neglects to say anything about the actual choice of paintings.

Most are sf and fantasy book covers from the 1970s, omitting the famous cover art of *Dune*. 1980s specimens include two – not, alas, all four – of the splendid architectural covers done for **The Book of the New Sun**, and some weirdly evocative pictures from Pennington's recent and more private work. Exotic, fluorescent colours predominate. Heady stuff.

Matching portfolios in the series feature Jim Burns, Chris Foss and Rodney Matthews.

Here by way of light relief is a hard-bitten fantasy police thriller in a series by Simon R. Green, a new British author: *Devil Take the Hindmost* (Headline 201pp £3.50). Hawk (he) and Fisher (she) are tough city cops, I mean Guard Captains. 'People tended to be very law-abiding when Hawk and Fisher were around.' There is a crooked election coming up. And they have to protect the nicest of the candidates from a sticky end. With mercenaries, magic, abominable gods and household traitors to contend with. Often in short sentence fragments. Like this. Sounds like trouble. Pages turn. And fast!

It's fairly routine stuff, but the plot thickens enough to give it interest, and I can guarantee an absence of quests, Dark Lords, cute nonhuman races and (for the most part) archaic syntax. Perhaps, as the series continues, Green will add more colour to the prose and flesh to the characters: his opening in particular has a schematic feel, and the story improves further on. (I could also do with less of the clashing blades and people carving bloody paths through crowds, but that's just me.) Good marks for incidental invention, such as the city's eccentric lesser gods.

[Re-reading the above, it looks as though I liked Green's relatively empty little entertainment more than the Niven/Barnes blockbuster ... which isn't really true. Green simply offers nothing much to quarrel with, while Niven and Barnes offer lots.]

Not many books can really 'change your life', but if you happen to be terrified of numbers and statistics, I do recommend *Innumeracy: Mathematical Illiteracy and its Consequences* by John Allen Paulos (Penguin 135pp £3.99). It's easy reading, with many examples of how shock-horror figures should be taken with a pinch of mathematical salt. One case discussed is the media sensation a few years back about the much-publicized statistic that 28 young D&D players had ... committed suicide!

Alarming? Listen to Paulos: 'There are estimates that up to 3 million teenagers played it. Second, in that age group the annual [US] suicide rate is approximately 12 per 100,000. These two facts together suggest that the number of teenage "Dungeons and Dragons" players who could be expected to commit suicide is about 360!'

I don't remember any fundamentalist/media scare about the statistic implied by these (doubtless incomplete) figures: that teenagers were nearly 12 times more likely to commit suicide if they *didn't* play D&D.

April 1991

95 Overdose?

As I write, Sir Kingsley Amis's *Memoirs* (Hutchinson 346pp £16.99) are causing a stir for their relentless curmudgeonliness and scabrous anecdotes. I myself had hoped for a few appalling stories about the author's pal Brian Aldiss, but perhaps owing to some lingering fondness the sf world gets off lightly. It's thirty years since Amis's *New Maps of Hell* appeared as the first 'respectable' – i.e. non-cult, non-small-press – survey of sf. This remains witty and readable, however outdated ... but the *Memoirs* imply that the sf overdose left Sir K. unable to absorb any more, just as he could no longer enjoy the James Bond books after writing his enthusiastic book on *them*. When you can't even face the fearful task of looking for anything good in a genre, it's perhaps time to shut up about it.

Unlike Sir K., I'm not shutting up yet: worthy stuff still appears. Here for example is John Kessel's *Good News from Outer Space* (Grafton 403pp £5.99), a wonderful example of 'comic inferno' sf (another Amis phrase). It's 1999, with Apocalypse expected at the dawn of the year 2000. North America is falling apart as in a John Sladek novel but with even blacker, even more deadpan humour, and more sympathetic people.

'Trashnews' datanets, electronic *Sunday Sports*, dominate the information services. Fundamentalists plan for the Second Coming's televisual problems such as 'high intensity lumination from the Holy City's descent'. Thanks to modern medicine, the dead rise but have a bad time socially. Backstreet biochemists are fostering new retrovirus plagues like AMPS, Acquired Melanin Production Syndrome, whereby white chauvinists who don't take proper precautions in bed turn black. 'Dadaist punks' might break at any moment into your car and instal an expensive stereo system. UFOs abound. Aliens are seemingly amongst us.

What the 'aliens' are doing (perhaps there's just one, and perhaps *this* is the Second Coming) is messing around with people's heads, playing out personal psychodramas. One example: the ghastly TV preacher is confronted with a horrible though illusory choice between privy amputation and, in his terms, damnation. This is darkly funny, but Kessel doesn't take cheap shots as most writers might: the Reverend actually keeps his integrity – again, in his terms.

Good News is full of goodies, spinoff ideas like on-line politicians programmed to vote unthinkingly as their constituents would wish ('Thought is just resistance in the circuit'), the doctrine of Spiritual Economics, and a quantum theory of morality. And at midnight on December 31st, 1999 ... but that would be telling. Read it yourself.

I haven't seen the Roger Corman film based on Brian Aldiss's 1973 *Frankenstein Unbound*, and find it hard to imagine. That novel is very literary, full of debate, pastiche and cross-references, like the science-fictional 'time shifts' which are also the easy time-transitions of novels themselves: 'Eighteen years later ...' Now comes *Dracula Unbound* (Grafton 199pp £13.99), which despite the smooth Aldiss touch does seem a more clunky and filmic tale, as though the storyline were influenced or even dictated by Corman – who according to the grapevine will indeed be filming this.

So instead of allusive time shifts we get a solid, physical time machine – a time railway, in fact – and a sprinkling of familiar paradoxes. The visionary city at the close of the first book gives way, in the sequel, to an all too unambiguous stronghold of vampires dominating a far-future Earth. One major plot device is a continent-busting superbomb which if detonated in the far, far past could erase the vampires and guess what else?

(Worst line: a young American most implausibly yelling 'I'll save Daddy from that fate!' Please let this be Corman, not Aldiss.)

Aldiss does much better with the real-life Bram Stoker who in 1896 displaces van Helsing as vampire-hunter ... and also with the vampire metaphor itself. Stoker's *Dracula* carries a terrific sexual charge, the bits you couldn't describe in a Victorian novel being transferred to those glamorous night visitors. *Unbound* expands on the ugly side of the glamour: Stoker died of syphilis, and here his vampires become a filthy, self-propagating disease of evolution with similar long-term effects. The new angle gives a new, authentic shudder.

But look. *Frankenstein Unbound* had much to say about science, Shelley's Prometheus, and things you can't put back in the bottle once they're released. In *Dracula Unbound*, despite one routine 'is-this-really-the-end?' hint, evils *are* magically undone and the metaphorical horror *is* rebottled. Yes, and AIDS will go away if we all clap our hands.

It's a good read ... but rather minor Aldiss.

Would you like to learn *How to Write Tales of Horror, Fantasy & Science Fiction* (Robinson 242pp £4.99)? The book is edited by J.N. Williamson; the subject order in the title suggests correctly that horror gets top billing. It contains nearly 30 brief essays, about eight of them worthwhile, and a 60-page wodge of favourite titles in 'Book of Lists' style.

Some of the professional contributors apparently have no idea of how to construct an essay: they open with wincingly formulaic 'narrative hooks' and continue with zappy writing which fatally distracts from what they're trying to teach. Others, desperate for material, pad out one tiny observation to several pages. Some are too brief or too general (couldn't be bothered to provide illustrations), some too personal: Colin Wilson has only to rinse out his mind with Faculty X, while Ray Bradbury says he just jots down a word and it grows into a story ... fine, fine, Ray, but what happens *in between*?

The book dates from 1987 America and, as is now traditional in these days of disk storage and instant electronic publishing, has not been updated. Defunct magazines are cited as markets, the small press listing is a farce, and no British publication (such as *Interzone*, a paying market then and now) appears at all.

Generally, this kind of how-to book is best written by a single author. Try *The Art of Fiction: Notes of Craft for Young Writers* by John Gardner, whose precepts translate into any genre. Brian Stableford's and Chris Evans's how-to books on sf are also well worth a look.

In brief ...

Series continue. Brian Craig (Stableford) still turns out the smoothest and best constructed fantasies in the dread world of the **Warhammer** game, and in a way I rather liked *Storm Warriors* (GW 271pp £4.99), third book of the storyteller Orfeo. Warhammer novels generally get better as they shake loose from the Warhammer gamebook, whose creators had zero originality and less feel for language: consider Nergal, the Babylonian (I think) demon of pestilence and devastation who has featured quite effectively in the *Hellblazer* comic, but who in Warhammer becomes 'Nurgle'. That one inept change of spelling transposes the whole thing into the Goon Show.

In *Taliesin's Telling* (Headline 277pp £3.99), Fay Sampson continues her painful reorganization of the Arthurian myths around the dark centre of Morgan, alias Morgan le Fay. Very personal, very bloody, not at all Christianized, and recommended as ever. This is book four.

GMI's Associate Editorthing Wayne alarmingly tells me that people either love this page (full marks in the current *GMI* reader poll) or don't ('Please bury Langford at once under six feet of radioactive bat droppings.'). He doesn't say which lot is winning on votes. The former might like to know that besides sf/fantasy, I'm now banging on about other genre writing of yesterday and today in each issue of *Interzone*'s sister magazine *Million: the Magazine of Popular Fiction* - subscription enquiries to *Interzone*, 217 Preston Drove, Brighton, BN1 6FL. Worth a look, honest.

[1992: Although the magazine totters bravely on, I don't know how much longer my *Million* connection will survive, as hero editor David Pringle can no longer afford to pay *Million*'s contributors and the incentive has, alas, dwindled a bit. *Interzone*, however, remains healthy, strong, thrusting, vital, immediate, and all that. (Mr Pringle is nervously anxious that I should say this.) 2000: *Million* folded in 1993. A shame.]

May 1991

96 In Search of Anthony's Brain

How many games fans actually know any game theory or probability maths, I wonder? Of course the mathematics doesn't apply to role-playing, whose essentials are naked imagination and ingenuity plus (sometimes) encyclopaedic knowledge of the rulebook. In card games like poker, though, it's vital to know the odds. Lotteries, football pools and fruit machines are easily analysed as sucker games: the prominence of a very few big winners obscures the need for that immense horde of losers who finance the whole operation.

Can a prize be so huge that it makes the gamble mathematically worthwhile for every player? The great Blaise Pascal, of Pascal's Triangle fame, suggested in the 17th century that Christianity was a good bet - since a trifling investment of belief could lead to the colossal payoff of eternal life. (I think there might be a fallacy there.) The twentieth century has its own equivalent of Pascal's wager, with rewards so potentially mindboggling as to make large stakes seem worthwhile ... if you believe the theory. This game is called SETI, the Search for Extraterrestrial Intelligence.

First Contact ed. Ben Bova and Byron Preiss (Headline 438pp £5.99) records the state of the art and is a welcome change from the UFO rubbish which pollutes our bookshops. SETI comes in three parts: informed speculation, hopeful listening and politics. This collection covers all three, with sf writers strongly represented.

Isaac Asimov contributes a worthy but unexciting look at what we mean by intelligence; Hal Clement probes the basics of what chemical environments might support life, and I wish his piece were longer; David Brin offers a 'where are they?' meditation which is a nonfiction complement to his thoughtful story 'Lungfish'; Greg Benford is sensible about possible alien technology and Arthur C. Clarke visionary as ever.

Meanwhile the SETI scientists report on projects, political sufferings and lack of funds. The field remains wide open. Even amateurs have a chance, as often before in astronomy: there are so many possible directions and frequencies for Their hypothetical message that a home outfit (satellite dish, gigahertz-range scanner and off-the-shelf computer) could scoop the billion-to-one jackpot before the major projects. If so, this book also prints the international guidelines for what to do when you pick up that interstellar message. Be prepared.

Are the aliens broadcasting out there somewhere, spilling technological secrets? I don't know. These authors don't either, but their hopes and fears and arguments are worth reading.

Here's Asimov again, in *Frontiers* (Mandarin 390pp £4.99). His science essays are normally reliable if not always frightfully exciting, but this book is definitely substandard. It contains over 120 very short pieces, written as newspaper columns. At this length everything is over-compressed, there's no time to reflect on side issues or develop an analogy or let the Asimov ego bulge entertainingly, and all too often the piece stops abruptly in mid-air because there was no room to engineer a climax.

Coverage? Everything: prehistory, scientists, Earth, the universe. Revelations? Only about a dozen facts or insights new to me, but then I usually read *New Scientist* every week.

Judging by his long-running column in *The Magazine of Fantasy and SF*, Asimov is more comfortable at several thousand words' length (when the *F&SF* pieces are collected, there are usually 17 essays to a volume). Since he likes to recycle material, the book or books in which he expands on the topics of *Frontiers* should be worth a look. Even for those who like the stuff, this one is far too breathless.

More names from *First Contact* reappear in the joint package of Arthur C. Clarke's *Against the Fall of Night*, from 1948, with Greg Benford's new sequel *Beyond the Fall of Night* (Gollancz 239pp £13.99). The Clarke is better known in its expanded version, *The City and the Stars.*

Introducing it, Clarke muses that many people still prefer the 1948 original. *City* improves on *Night* in hundreds of ways: the mechanisms, pastimes and decor of the eternal city Diaspar are lovingly depicted, a routine minor character is replaced by a wonderful polyp-creature, travelogues are made more colourful, and so on. But every moment of high emotion (and for all its youthful literary fumblings this is *the* supreme Sense of Wonder novel) is carried over intact from *Night*: plangent chords, dying falls and cosmic vistas. Clarke had the sense not to tinker with any of this.

Benford's follow-up *Beyond* explores the areas left barren in *Night.* The worldwide deserts have been reseeded from ancient gene banks, the Solar System already teems with spacegoing life (including a living homage to the Clarke space elevator), the Sun itself has been moved during those huge wastes of time evoked by Clarke... and the biggest, nastiest and most implacable loose end of *Night* is on the rampage.

The tone of the sequel is very different, nodding to its original across another expanse of time – forty-odd years of frenetic technological progress, decades over which Clarke's doomy vision of Man and the Universe has become less convincing than Benford's view of solar life as a linked whole. 'Man' is less prominent here. The lead characters are a woman and an evolved quasi-raccoon, and their travels though a wildly revised solar system make for good stuff – though not, perhaps, a good sequel. Surely there should be some continuity of tone?

I think Greg Benford suffered one bout of amnesia when writing this. In both *City* and *Night* it's a historical fact (with a plot turn depending on it) that the Moon has long been destroyed. In *Beyond*, without a word of explanation, it's back again. Naughty!

The Magic Spectacles (Morrigan 181pp £13.95) is James P. Blaylock's first 'children's' novel. He's a quirky, distinctive author, and at first I wondered how he'd adapt to writing for children – who don't need to be written down to and are as quick on the uptake as adults, if not more so, but who would grow impatient with Blaylock's occasional fondness for atmosphere and allusion at the expense of actual plot.

This one moves well enough. American small town ... mysterious magic shop ... fantasy world visible through magic spectacles ... kids climb through ... goblins ... eccentric but friendly characters ... After these moderately familiar stages, the book focuses on one eccentric, Mr Deener, who is more than a figure of fun. His situation is a painstaking allegory of mental illness, retreat from the world, retreat from himself.

If Blaylock were to zoom in any closer on this chap, the book would take on an altogether darker (and more Blaylockian) tone. Instead he keeps his distance. The boy heroes watch as Deener tries to escape himself in an abortive climb to the Moon, hindered by the goblins of his own dark side; they watch his self-fragmenting magic; they finally take action as he lapses into complete delusion. It's his story more than theirs.

Interesting, but from Blaylock I expected something richer and stranger. Maybe next time. Besides the story there are illustrations by Ferret, who doubtless appeals hugely to some, and a copyright page referring (in the maddening way of small presses) to an afterword by Lewis Shiner which you can't actually read without paying £45 for the special edition. Boo, hiss.

Yes, I did sample Piers Anthony's *And Eternity* (Grafton 411pp £4.50), which rounds off the **Incarnations of Immortality** series by having everyone gang up on God. The best moment is another of Anthony's sensitive feminist insights: in turn, two women are turned into chaps and instantly run amok, overcome by dread male hormones, unable to resist raping the nearest female. Yes, they've learned their lesson all right: 'It seems that men have passions that women do not.' Now at last they know that rapists can't help it really. No more, please: I need a month to recover.

June 1991

97 The Foot is a Gland

One supposedly disparaging thing reviewers say is: 'This book is all right for train journeys.' In fact, the timeless aeons of British Rail offer a good chance to settle down in peace and get to grips with a big demanding book. Keep *good* books for trains. Which is what I tried to do on the way to Mexicon.

I thought you'd never ask. Mexicon is a biannual British convention devoted to sf in its original form of words on paper. What makes this so particularly Mexican is shrouded in the mists of time and in-jokes. It's deeply weird to sit around talking professional shop in an old-fashioned hotel while drinking vile imported Mexican beer containing slices of lime. Favourite guest this year was the indescribable Howard Waldrop from Texas, whose highly addictive collection *Strange Things in Close-up* came out a while ago (Legend 363pp £4.50) and will shortly be followed by *Night of the Cooters* (again Legend).

On the way I bit the bullet and tackled Dan Simmons's Hugo-winning *Hyperion* (Headline 346pp £13.95): also, some hours later, its conclusion *The Fall of Hyperion* (Headline 468pp £14.95). Waiting for book two to be on hand was sensible, because you pick up so much momentum by the end of book one that it's painful to stop.

This is cosmic stuff, full of ideas and literary jokes. It opens in *Canterbury Tales* fashion, with pilgrims to the mysterious world Hyperion swapping stories as they travel ... but the stories intertwine, parts of an ambitious whole. Bit by bit you get the picture of galactic civilization: Earth devoured, thousands of new worlds linked by a web of matter-transmission, high-tech barbarians lurking offstage, artificial intelligences about their own incomprehensible affairs, and imminent war. At the same time Hyperion itself grows more enigmatic. Time Tombs moving backwards from a distant future are due to open. The Shrike, an invincible death-machine associated with the Tombs and forming the centre of a new cult, prowls through each story. And that's just a taste of book one.

Book two goes much further. Some later revelations are so brain-boggling that Simmons can't let them emerge with his usual subtlety: they have to be more or less spelt out (albeit by an eccentric AI who obfuscates with a weird mix of Keats and Zen koans – two characters being reconstructions of John Keats himself, whose epic poem also supplies both titles...). For example, what the Shrike actually *does* seems gratuitous sadism but is reasonably if wordily explained as the baiting of a trap for God. Other ironies are left unemphasized, like one memorable spasm of destruction whose perpetrator eventually turns out to have been desecrating his own tomb. In context, the final grand slam of galaxy-wide violence is tragic, triumphant and logically necessary.

These are recommended reading. I could do without certain relentless allusions (humanity's leader is a woman called Gladstone, a minor character is named for Keats's publisher Leigh Hunt, the final confrontation with the Shrike loses force in a groan-making reference to an old Harlan Ellison story, etc), and far too many conveniently enigmatic actions of the Shrike fail to make sense in the light of its actual purpose ... but overall, it's too much fun to pick holes in.

Enigmatic alien artifacts, left by almighty Builders who have not stuck around to answer questions, are an old favourite of hard sf. Charles Sheffield offers an entire trilogy about artifacts and Builders in **The Heritage Universe**. Out so far are *Summertide* (VGSF 257pp £3.99) and *Divergence* (Gollancz 281pp £13.99).

Perhaps it's unfair to come to this unambitious, schematic stuff after the richness of *Hyperion*, but although the characters are pretty good for Sheffield – characteristically for him, the most engaging is a computer – it all seems a bit weary. There are 1,236 mildly mindboggling artifacts dotted round the galaxy. One looks particularly dull but for awkwardly explained reasons is Special: something is going to Happen. Rival factions converge, one as a result of numbing coincidence, and start double-crossing each other. Hellish cataclysms are promised. An anticlimax is delivered, and book one ends.

In *Divergence* we come two stages closer to the Builders, via awesome super-entities who correspond to their doorman and reception clerk. Also on hand are preserved representatives of an 'extinct' race of murderous alien bullies who eat people, breed like flies, and have no tact. What the still absent Builders seem to want emerges with staggering banality: it's time for a spot of serious natural selection, with the major races toughing it out precisely as in *Arena* of Fredric Brown and *Star Trek* fame. On this cliff-hanger, the curtain falls. Book three awaits. God help us, for we knew the worst too young.

It was a long journey back from the merry fun of Mexicon. I was a bit distracted from *Catface* by Clifford Simak (Mandarin 251pp £3.99) owing to the singing drunk who sat behind me, spreading dismay and a thick haze of beer down the railway carriage.... Simak's sf always seems better than his fantasy, perhaps because his personality radiated a sort of gentle Midwestern sanity with no room for the madness of Old Magic or Wild Hunts. This one is sf.

It's the story of a nice academic on rustic vacation, his nice if pushy girlfriend, the village simpleton, and a friendly alien ... which could be any of a dozen Simak tales. This alien makes tunnels in time for its friends; pretty soon a dotty commercial operation is offering safari facilities for those who've always wanted to shoot a tyrannosaurus. Things get more complicated until ...

Wait a minute, I remember thinking during the twenty-minute unscheduled halt while police coaxed the singing drunk away. This book is about tinkering with the past. There's even a plan to ship back the world's starving millions to the lush, unspoilt Miocene. Which raises major questions: are they all foredoomed to die out in prehistory? Or will their presence and consumption of natural resources wipe out the 'future' from which they came? Or is there some sort of alternate-world escape from the looming paradoxes?

None of this is even momentarily considered. The narrative is vaguely enjoyable, but I decided poor old Simak had been way past his sell-by date when he wrote *Catface* (1978). And for my blasphemy I was punished by sf's Elder Gods, who escalated that delay into a series of missed connections that made me five hours late. Don't giggle.

A British Rail-haunted midnight found me gibbering over the occult revelations of *The Book of the SubGenius* (Simon & Schuster £8.95) – the alternative religion (or joke, con trick, insane artform) that makes Scientology look like Secular Humanism.

Astonishing revelations fill this unlikeliest of holy books: 'Yes, the foot is actually a *gland*.' Rival saviours are naturally condemned: 'No matter what their IQs they are all a brick short of a full load (so are we, but *they're* missing the *wrong bricks*).' And psychic mysteries are explained: 'All the rest of the cattle mutilations, as well as 75% of all other paranormal phenomenon of a similarly *hideous* nature, were perpetrated by the Elder Gods' Watchers *for no other reason* than to confuse the living daylights out of us and let us know *in no uncertain terms* that we are UTTERLY HELPLESS.'

The Book contains more unlikely pop-art, CAPITAL LETTERS, excessive *emphasis* and *RANT* than you'd believe possible. (Plus exclamation marks!!!!!) Treat it as a joke *at your peril*. Possibly the least suitable ideas supplement for a *Call of Cthulhu* adventure yet marketed, but don't let me stop you trying.

July 1991

98 Endless Bloody Universes

Do you cringe on reading the words 'Set in the same universe as...', or do your eyes light up with feverish enthusiasm? Of course it depends – on whether it was a good universe to begin with, and whether the writer has something decent to add. The awful temptation is to squeeze one more book out of a once successful background, and then another, and another: it's a long time since Anne McCaffrey's dragon soaps produced the old thrill, or since the Stainless Steel Rat acquired a halfway new plot-device.

I had a different problem with Paul J. McAuley's *Eternal Light* (Gollancz 384pp £14.99). McAuley has for some while been tipped as *the* young British hard-sf writer to watch, and this is billed as his breakthrough novel. Megastardom awaits. Good for him: but I found the opening slightly heavy going (admittedly I had a stinking cold, but the third sentence on page one made me wonder how far the proofreader got). Suddenly the laborious backfill of crowded sentences and technical information tipped me off: this is a sequel to McAuley's *Four Hundred Billion Stars*, in which *Eternal Light*'s lead character obviously goes through many preliminary adventures, and which I'd neglected to read. No time now, not before delivering this column. If only books carried government health warnings about this.

Somebody out there has decided I'm a UFO expert. Here to purge us with pity and terror is *Abduction: the UFO Conspiracy* by David Bischoff (Warner 328pp $4.95). This breaks new ground in being billed not as sf or True Fact but as a thriller.

In fact it's clearly intended as a best-seller. There is much padding: the author even takes time out to tell you about the word processor he uses, and which function key you press to save a document. The characters are all solid, triple-ply cardboard. Venal, coke-snorting *National Intruder* reporter, unwashed and babbling UFO nut, Sagan-like sceptic with drink problem and mind as flexible as a steel trap, sceptic's beautiful daughter who inevitably has an Encounter.... Most of all I enjoyed the psychopathic CIA killer, just barely reminiscent of the Executioner in *From Russia with Love*: they have to keep him doped to stop him running amok, and he gets in the mood for murder by sensually dropping a hamster into his kitchen-sink disposal unit, turning the switch, and savouring the tiny screams. Subtle, eh?

Naturally there's plenty of mayhem, all ludicrously overdone. Victims are tortured or knocked off to the accompaniment of corny remarks intended not for them but for readers: as in a grade Z movie, the baddies are playing to the audience. So before being shot, a broadcaster who has stumbled on the Secret is gloatingly informed: 'It's time for the big sign-off... Your ratings were just terrible.'

The plot concerns another (yawn) conspiracy theory. Stop me if you've heard this one, but it's that desperately villainous and clandestine organization the US Government which is behind flying saucers – using drugs, painful medical examinations and robot aliens to establish the story of UFO abductions which it's simultaneously denying, refusing to believe and struggling to cover up. Conspirators, who can figure 'em? Meanwhile, what about these enigmatic chaps who walk on occasionally and act all enigmatic: could they be *real* aliens? Who are the sinister 'Publishers' who control everything, including most especially the CIA, and arrange routine murders through their diabolical hitmen the 'Editors'? (This post-Le Carré terminology is the best thing in the book.)

Abduction is so awful that I'd have no hesitation in revealing the answers, but Bischoff neglects to provide them. After a false climax which leaves one villain dead and one beautiful daughter abducted, the book stops. The hideous revelation is presumably that there's more to come; meanwhile, you're cheated of the one slender reason for finishing such dross, the catharsis of learning whodunnit and what on earth it was all about. If volume two shows itself on my doormat, it will follow the hamster into oblivion.

You never know what to expect from Ian Watson. *Stalin's Teardrops* (Gollancz 270pp £13.99) collects a dozen of his wildly varied stories, first published in 11 different places. The title story is wonderfully surreal mixture of Orwellian and folklore Russias: in the first, geography as well as history has been rewritten by repeatedly falsified maps – 'the lie of the land' – resulting in dead spaces, unmapped quarters, secret territories where logic doesn't prevail.

Elsewhere in the book, a ghost flits through the insubstantial spires of a holographic cathedral; the Inter-City from Birmingham to London short-cuts through the Cretaceous period; South Africa is mapped on to a single strange household; Sherlock Holmes tackles the Cinderella case; a pharaoh undergoes a strange resurrection (much of this one in eccentric blank verse – blimey); and for an impressive finale the eye of the late Ayatollah lives on to direct Islam's high-tech and low-magic search for an author condemned to die. There is more. Some of the horror tales seem too slight, but the collection has more weird ideas per page than anything since Watson's last.

Can one imagine a humorous collaboration between the raucous slapstick-merchant Harry Harrison and the whimsical, often spaced-out Robert Sheckley? No, not really, and from internal evidence *Bill, the Galactic Hero on the Planet of Bottled Brains* (VGSF 236pp £3.99) is mostly the latter. Alas (and it is a genuine, heartfelt alas), Sheckley's best work was long ago. That hallucinated humour, those disorienting transitions, ornery computers and philosophical asides: this story offers pale echoes of them all but lacks the remembered sparkle.

Certainly I'd never have imagined Sheckley resorting to such emergency life-jokes as yet another *Star Trek* spoof, complete with Captain Dirk, Mr Splock and a full ensemble of pointed-ears gags. Oh, how we all laughed.

[Much later I ran into Harry Harrison himself, who complained that Bob Sheckley's draft hadn't been funny enough and that Harry himself had had to spice it up with lots of really good jokes about pointed ears. H'mm.]

As Bill himself remarks: 'I think I have heard of computers writing novels.... At least I have read lots of them that could have been written by a computer.' This feels like one. Except that a computer would have read the original book, registered the extreme improbability of thicko Bill reading anything but low-grade comic strips, and erased that particular speech.

The next in this appalling series, *Bill, the Galactic Hero on the Planet of Tasteless Pleasure* (Gollancz 213pp £13.99) has guest author David Bischoff... who has already received enough of the heady wine of Langfordian praise for one column.

One semi-famous oldie that I'd never read is *The Boats of the 'Glen Carrig'* (Grafton 188pp £3.50), by William Hope Hodgson of *House on the Borderland* fame. This was a period horror novel even when first published in 1907: it's set in the 18th century, a sort of 'Robinson Crusoe meets Cthulhu' with the authentic creepiness of unknown seas.

Note the page count. There's no padding: Hodgson starts with the ship *Glen Carrig* already five days sunk, and its escaped boats are just coming to an unpleasant estuary. No Lovecraftian adjectival gibber: we get tight-lipped descriptions of the roaming thing that seems to be made of raw beef, and of some vegetation whose nasty habits are not too fully spelt out. After this first episode, the remaining boatload of seamen ends up beached with masses of interesting nautical problem-solving to do ... the contrast of hard slog by day and terrors by night is effective.

Slight but more readable than many an acknowledged 'classic', this one deserves its revival.

The first of the British 'shared world' anthologies I mentioned months ago appears from Penguin in August: *Temps*, a sort of sleazy, low-budget (and not wholly unsatirical) equivalent of the American *Wild Cards* superhero series. Next comes *The Weerde*, with a horror scenario about shapeshifting nasties, and then *Villains*, being genre fantasy from the viewpoint of the bad guys. That nice Mr Crump had better review the first and third, which contain Langford stories, and the second, against which I'm prejudiced because of this here rejection slip. Follow-ups are planned.

[Alan Crump was *GMI*'s other regular book reviewer.]

August 1991

99 Great British Hopes

I'd like to let you into one of the closely guarded secrets of sf: reviewers are not infallible. No, not even Alan Crump. (Half the audience swoons.) In an ideal world each 'Critical Mass' would carry a cigarette-style warning panel, reminding everyone that phrases like 'This book is lousy' need to be prefixed with 'Langford says' and footnoted 'Who does he think he is anyway?' And there'd be a banner headline: MOST DOCTORS DON'T READ THIS COLUMN.

Last issue, medical science was helpless against my foul cold, under the influence of which I confessed total inability to get into Paul McAuley's new book. Perhaps this was unjust ... later research revealed that it helps to have absorbed the complex galactic background from his first novel *Four Hundred Billion Stars*, and even more to have recovered from your cold.

The new *Eternal Light* (Gollancz 384pp £14.99) is a very ambitious blockbuster indeed. Rather like Greg Bear, McAuley tackles cosmological ultimates with great confidence and still keeps interesting characters in motion against his gigantic backdrop. He also does well at the difficult task of blending real and unreal science, where wrong notes are so easy. (In the earlier book I boggled at scientists' calm acceptance of a low-density shield against neutrinos, particles which ghost their way happily through entire planets.) There's some particularly cheeky play with pure mathematical weapons.

The sobering background is a galaxy shaped (literally) by an ancient alien race's family wars, which led to all sorts of minor side effects such as human intelligence. As the characters move in a complex web of plot, via neutron star and spatial wormhole to the galaxy's central black hole, it emerges that the nastiest alien brood of all is working away there on a gigantic *Lebensraum* project which endangers the physical universe. When you add religious fanatics, empathy, telepathy, parasite personalities, time travel and a non-religious view of angels, creation and Heaven, the word 'ambitious' seems a little feeble.

It all works fairly well. There are perhaps a few too many words, some of them arranged into jaw-breakingly awful sentences, and I wasn't wholly convinced either by the late-breaking melodrama of a combat pilot shooting up suns or by the precocious wonder-child born in the final section (we had quite enough of her in *Dune*). But *Eternal Light* is a big provoking book, already exuding that unearthly glow of award shortlists.

If McAuley has a touch of the Greg Bears, Stephen Baxter is trying very hard to be Britain's own answer to Larry Niven. *Raft* (Grafton 264pp £14.99) might seem powerfully reminiscent of Niven's *The Integral Trees*, both featuring free-fall ecology in a vast breathable gas-cloud enfolding a dense core ... but there are notable differences.

The less important one is the wildly audacious setting. One of our spacecraft has gone astray, slipping on an inter-universal banana skin and lurching into this otherspace where the gravitational constant is a billion times greater. Turbulences in the gas nebula routinely collapse into short-lived stars hardly bigger than Ben Nevis; *Raft* opens on and around the iron core of a burnt-out star just fifty yards wide, whose surface gravity is a crippling 5g. Human survival seems impossible. People manage in ingenious ways, but mere generations after their arrival the waste products of dying stars are poisoning the whole ecosystem, and ...

The important difference from Niven's somewhat flabby travelogue is what follows that 'and'. From chapter one there's a certain driving urgency. *Everyone* will die unless something drastic is done. Revolution and war follow. Inevitably our hero passes through the three human habitats - the iron miners orbiting that star core, the flying Raft constructed from the original stranded ship, and a third option of remarkable if not exactly one- hundred-per-cent credible grisliness - and onward in a Wonderful Journey which reveals a solution. Though not an easy one.

This is a solid example of 'traditional' hard sf, simply told, with the heavy physics kept offstage apart from a few excusable pop-science lectures. In keeping with the same tradition, there are distinct traces of 'idiot plotting' and the characterizations are lumpy and unpolished. Likewise much of the writing, although *Raft* makes one fairly witty addition to Samuel Delany's list of phrases which take on new meanings in sf. Meeting a woman and feeling 'the pull of her body' sounds clichéd. But here, even people have a noticeable gravitic field.

[Every single reviewer seems to have picked up on this one neat detail, and interviews show that the author himself is particularly fond of it. In retrospect, we could really have done with a lot more such touches. It is also rather a pity that *Raft*'s biology is so much less convincing than its assured physics.]

Yet another Great British Hope is Storm Constantine, who does not have a lot of time for physics and the hardware of boys' toys. *Hermetech* (Headline 502pp £4.99) is set in another of her ravaged near-future worlds. Above are space habitats and below is an Earth of partial eco-disaster: domed cities, variously barren lands, flesh-eating fog, and 'Naturotech' wanderers vaguely reminiscent of those convoys they won't allow near Stonehenge. Once again the only creative, transforming force in Constantine's lurid landscapes is 'Magick', accessed by Sex.

Two storylines converge. Ari Famber is fourteen and has been genetically rearranged by her vanished father: when she enjoys, er, intimate congress she'll be able to tap into this world-shaking primal force, *if* she can control its awesome might, etc. She joins a passing convoy and goes looking for her destiny. Meanwhile, lowlife city boy Zambia Crevecour is persuaded by evil madame Jahsaxa Penumbra into becoming an intersexual 'SHe' [sic], pronunciation uncertain.

This involves surgery to implant, in the book's most brain-stopping phrase, a 'fleet of sphincters'. Further gaudy names abound: Cabochon, Quincx Roirbak, Tammaz Malamute, Alix Micklemas, and so on.

It's a heady, offbeat story which surges towards, in every sense, a climax. In my rotten sceptical way I doubt that one can achieve much in the real world by abandoning all logic and reason in favour of leaping into bed and tapping that old orgasmic potential ('Drop your pants, Luke, and use the Force!') ... but Constantine's energy and colourful intensity force you to accept it for the time being as an sf/fantasy premise as valid as McAuley's or Baxter's variant physics, which is what counts. Gripping stuff. I need a cold shower.

Flying Dutch (Orbit 252pp £12.95) is Tom Holt's third funny fantasy about ancient and/or legendary characters loose in today's Britain, and he still makes me chuckle. As in *Expecting Someone Taller*, he draws on Wagner's operas ... the Flying Dutchman, of course. The trouble for Captain Vanderdecker and his crew isn't a curse but immortality plus a serious personal problem which isolates them almost entirely from civilization. The trouble for civilization is that a tatty piece of vellum the Captain has been carrying since the sixteenth century could wreck the world economy.

Like Terry Pratchett, Holt is a very *practical* joker with a shrewd eye for the humour in how things would actually have to work ... the real-world complications of alchemical immortality, and what to do about repairing a vessel doomed to sail forever. He also explains who truly runs the world, why the Spanish Armada failed, when computers were actually invented (1694), the real reason for nuclear power stations, and the terrible secrets of Radio 3 and the Milk Marketing Board.

Vanderdecker gets plenty of good lines: 'I remember when you could have bought all the beer in Bavaria, plus sales tax and carriage, for the price of half a pint of this. I even remember flared trousers. That dates me.' But there's an undertow of seriousness, even gloom, which makes it quite difficult for Holt to engineer the happy-ever-after ending he wants. The result is pleasant enough but has an odd fuzziness, as though it needed one final twist or punchline. Intermittently good fun nevertheless.

September 1991

100 Party Time

I've just been helping unveil Penguin's new fantasy and sf imprint, 'Roc'. Unexpectedly in these times of recession, they threw a huge launch party which had sf pundits groaning and taking aspirin for days after....

This happened in one of those subterranean London nightclubs with black decor and an invisible entrance ... fervent thanks to Kate Stableford, daughter of the more famous Brian, for brilliantly spotting the Roc logo on a bunch of balloons outside. Appalling scenes of scheming, boozing and group photography duly took place, and countless notables were reduced to the level of the beasts as they struggled to eat (without cutlery) chicken legs engulfed in a barbecue sauce cooked in accordance with H.P. Lovecraft's own recipe for blasphemous ichor.

The 'Midnight Rose' editorial collective (Neil Gaiman, Mary Gentle, Roz Kaveney and Alex Stewart) gloated over the appearance of their first sf anthology, *Temps* (Roc 354pp £4.50) - or perhaps not its *appearance* exactly, since it looks decidedly odd and unbooklike. 'Precisely *why* do you want a cover picture of a flying Swiss Army knife?' Roz had reputedly asked the Penguin art department, sarcastically adding, 'I suppose it's the cutting edge of sf....' Penguin liked this phrase so much that they added it to the cover. Anyway, *Temps* seemed popular at the party: vast stacks of display copies were nicked within about an hour, while no one showed much interest in stealing the three fantasies by Americans which formed the rest of the Roc launch.

Next day's event was more typical, an evening session at Waterstone's in Bath where six *Temps* people and the aforementioned three Americans faced an eager audience of (I calculated, subtracting Penguin and bookshop staff) seven actual members of the public. Two of these later proved to be lady companions of the US contingent. It was an uproarious occasion, you bet. Neil and Alex attempted a rather shifty-sounding explanation that, far from being an imitation of *Wild Cards*, the *Temps* idea had actually predated it: controversy was defused when the audience proved never to have heard of *Wild Cards* either. We signed all the books in the shop and ran for it.

Orson Scott Card has added a third book to the *Ender's Game / Speaker for the Dead* series which has won implausibly many awards. *Xenocide* (Legend 463pp hc £14.99 pb £8.99) is the most determinedly ambitious yet. It's well written, it has a lot going for it, and I was sorry to feel let down by the climax.

We're back on Lusitania, the world of *Speaker*, where a highly resourceful and unpleasant virus has reshaped native life and threatens the human colonists. Despite not understanding its full menace, humanity's devious leaders have already despatched a spacefleet with world-wrecking weapons. Luckily the continuing hero Ender has a artificial-intelligence friend who can cut off this armada's communications. But on another human world is this special breed of geniuses (who pay a nasty genetic price for their talent), one of whom is on the case and could at any moment sniff out the AI and loose the slaughter. Meanwhile, the surviving queen of the insect race exterminated in *Game* has spawned a new horde of workers, redeveloped space technology, and offered the native Lusitanians the chance to spread across the stars, *with* their appalling virus....

There's much more: in lesser hands the book would be a jumbled mess, but Card works long, hard and quite successfully to make it harrowingly convincing. It seems that the fearsome moral burden of xenocide – the wiping out of an entire alien race – must fall on someone. Even the quasi-intelligent virus might not deserve extinction, though *this* speculation is in the end quietly dropped. I promise that you'll be biting your nails.

Then, having constructed his enormous moral and technological problems, Card proceeds to solve them. Two minor characters die en route, and the tragedy of a third provides a strong final chapter ... but in between, alas, there's a ghastly old sf cop-out. Resolving their differences, the best brains of two worlds rapidly fudge up this brand-new physics which out of a single hat produces: *(a)* faster-than-light travel; *(b)* a means of synthesizing an 'impossible' counter-virus merely by thinking about it; *(c)* a quick cure for genetically inherited obsessive-compulsive disorder; *(d)* the healing of an incurable cripple; and *(e)* the resurrection of the dead.

It is all too much of a good thing, and it is a shame.

There is usually rejoicing when a new Barbara Hambly novel appears. She has a real gift for dusting off old fantasy props and showing them in a fresh, appealing light, against grittily realistic backgrounds (the sleaze and grime of *Dark Hand of Magic* were so effective that one wanted a hot bath after each chapter). Something of this quality appears in *The Rainbow Abyss* (Grafton 256pp £14.99), an enjoyable yarn of an aged magician and his cheery young apprentice, with interesting new slants on magic.

They bumble around, getting run out of towns for various reasons and barely escaping with their lives. There are several exciting adventures and a strong romantic subplot. But clearly the real plot has to centre on the magical 'Dark Well' which the old wizard opened near the beginning and through which he heard a cry for help from another universe. Then it's destroyed and they're on the run. On and on and bloody on ...

A terrible suspicion gripped me at the two-thirds mark, and I peeped at the last page, which reveals the secret Grafton have carefully neglected to mention anywhere else. *Abyss* is merely part one of a sequence called 'Sun-Cross', presumably a trilogy. Hambly writes as well as ever, but there's something frustrating about an entire book devoted to elaborate games of procrastination (one maddening plot device is that Dark Wells only work at a solstice or equinox!), deftly avoiding its own promised theme until the final pages. [This was actually a two-book sequence, which concluded strongly with *The Magicians of Night.*]

Albion by John Grant (Headline 311pp £14.95) stands alone as a complete fantasy, and a very strange one. Albion is a different sort of magic island, whose geography rearranges itself capriciously from day to day and whose inhabitants suffer complete tyranny without even knowing that they suffer, because they have no memories. Dimly, instinctively, they till the land, unable to resent it more than briefly when the oppressors come to loot the harvest and enjoy a little rape....

This is a hideously effective metaphor, the background for a grim, bloody and powerful book. Every so many generations, someone from the World outside is shipwrecked on Albion; immune to the clogging amnesia, he gives people names and a past and a future; and in due course there's an insurrection which always, ultimately, fails. Until the last one.

(Er, since resistance to Albion's disease of amnesia seems to be hereditary and since the non-amnesiac oppressors go in for so much enthusiastic rape, I'd have expected a whole crowd of new revolutionaries each generation, without need for castaways.)

[Later: 'Oh bugger,' said John Grant to me, 'the sodding copyeditor cut out the explanation that only the pure-bred oppressor *aristocracy* are immune.' As practised organization men, they delegate the rape to proles.]

It's an adult story, featuring tortuous personal relationships and less-than-nice good guys while rejecting too-easy answers like 'Hey, let's just slaughter all the baddies now.' It also offers some inventive magical twists, like the Dreamers whose sleeping nightmares take all too tangible shape for everyone awake around them. One snag is that by starting with all the gory details of what happens to the leader of the book's first, failed revolution, and then going into a long, long flashback, Grant replaces the potential tension of half the narrative with mere gloom. Another is that the author seems so infected with the hopelessness of the situation he's set up that a more or less literal *deus ex machina* has to be introduced.

Grant is perhaps best known to *GMI* readers for his co-authorship of the 'Lone Wolf' novels (loosely based on Joe Dever's gamebooks), and his eccentric goddess Alyss has strayed across from these to *Albion*. She's fun, though a shade too cheerful for this dark tale.

Another lawsuit. Psychic investigator and fraud-detector James Randi is being expensively sued 'in every state and in every country' by the infamous Uri Geller. A defence fund exists. SAE for details: [long-obsolete address omitted]. Randi can sometimes be – nay, usually is – irritating but free speech remains important....

October 1991

101 The Unpublished Column

Is world recession set to continue? According to doom-laden pronouncements by all publishers (suspiciously similar to what they've been saying without pause for as long as any living author can remember), the industry is dying and next year there will be approximately 2.4 books published in Britain, by 1.7 remaining publishers. We'll have to make them last somehow ... but meanwhile, the autumn splurge of books seems as huge as ever.

Hugest on my current pile is R.A. MacAvoy's *Lens of the World* (Headline 286pp £14.95), perhaps the most interesting thing she's done since her first novel *Tea with the Black Dragon*.

MacAvoy writes well, but we knew that already. Her fantasy world is just different enough from the 'generic' consensus to come up fresh and new. Here an industrial revolution is beginning, with fine metals, lenses, telescopes. There's apparently no magic, although we meet strange creatures and ambiguous visions ... the narrator Nazhuret makes a special point of the ambiguity.

Nazhuret, regarded as small and ugly, spends his early years in a military school and is then taken in hand by the very strange Powl, who trains him on eccentric lines reminiscent of the Zen samurai 'way'. The descriptions of mental and physical discipline are fascinating, full of good bits like the pupil's gradual and ingenious (but wrong) deductions about the purpose of Powl's astronomical observatory. Eventually, superbly trained but with absolutely no quest or objective, Nazhuret goes out into this violent world....

This is his autobiography, begun some twenty years later. There will be sequels, yet the book stands perfectly well alone. Will certain obscure points about werewolves and visions be clarified in future volumes, or does this text hold even more than I noticed on a first reading? It's possible, and I'll be glad to read it again.

Roger Zelazny's new fantasy isn't called *Forever Amber*, but it might as well be. *Knight of Shadows* (Orbit 251pp £4.50) continues the story of young Merlin (no relation to King Arthur's chap) from *Trumps of Doom*, *Blood of Amber* and *Sign of Chaos*, themselves built on the seething complications of his father Corwin's adventures through five previous Amber books, and clearly set to chunter on forever.

There's little left of the descriptive dazzle and inventiveness of Zelazny's heyday. Innovation is choked in a dusty clutter of plot devices and superpowers. Where were we? Merlin is a lord of Amber (good guys) who has walked its Pattern (gaining various powers like walking between worlds), and is also a lord of Chaos (formerly bad guys, now not so certain) with powers of shapeshifting and magic ('My Concerto for Cuisinart and Microwave spell would have minced him and parboiled him in an instant'), who has traversed the Logrus (resembling the Pattern but conferring powers of apportation useful and indeed much used for summoning pizza) and additionally possesses Amber's inevitable Trumps (occult teleportation and cellphone service), a sentient and self-propelled strangling wire, the magical computer complex 'Ghostwheel' (which can do almost anything for him when not sulking), and ... I forget the rest, but he collects further goodies here, including a magic ring controlling hordes of exciting new powers. Just what he needed!

It is fairly difficult to provide this guy with credible opposition, especially since he also has sorcerous pals to help him out of tight spots. My lack of interest in Merlin's perils was fanned into a blaze of apathy by this book. Avoid at all costs.

From the 'younger readers' side of the tracks, here's *The Drowners* by Garry Kilworth (Methuen 153pp £8.99).

This is a straightforward tale of rustic melodrama with ghostly trimmings, set early last century in the Winchester area. It comes alive through Kilworth's evident love for the river-country, and for farm technologies so nearly forgotten that (in an almost sf way) they seem new again. Drowners manipulate the river to flood and thaw water-meadows after the terrible winters of those years. The complex skills involved lead to a market advantage (early grass, fatter cows) and the enmity of the traditional Evil Baronet whose farm is in competition. Then comes tragedy.

Add the old belief that the dead can return if called three times, and the plot works itself out with a neat inevitability. A nice little story with nothing ponderous or 'major' about it. Methuen's copyeditors can presumably take credit for the jarring anachronism of 19th-century measurements in metres and litres.

[Later: Garry Kilworth explained that the copyeditor insisted on metric measures because children 'wouldn't be able to understand' yards or gallons. Suddenly the generation gap seemed a whole lot wider. I had this fantasy of all mentions of half-sovereigns becoming an easy-to-understand '53 pence', and all references to playing halma or diabolo turning into Nintendo.]

Never thought I'd receive a new Robert Heinlein book again, but the dead can return if called by huge enough advances.... *Grumbles from the Grave* (Orbit 336pp £4.99), ed. Virginia Heinlein, is an annotated selection of Heinlein's correspondence.

If interested in his work (and despite later excesses he wrote an awful lot of solid and influential sf), you'll enjoy these peeps behind the scenes ... but the curtain is never lifted far. His wife Virginia has been careful to blue-pencil personal revelations. There's still a fair bit of vigorous stuff on safe topics, tooth-gnashing insights into editorial horrors, and some bibliographically important information on certain cuts and changes in his books.

Some quibbles. Arranging the letters not chronologically but under topics (e.g. 'Fan Mail and Other Time Wasters') makes for tiresome reading – you keep being jerked back in time from Heinlein's final years to start again in the 40s or 50s. One two-page credo ('Our nation has had the most decent and kindly internal practices and foreign policies to be found anywhere in history') appears twice in full. And since anyone who buys this will be a Heinlein fan, the gormless plot summaries of his books are a further waste of space.

Another author from whom I hadn't expected anything fresh is Lewis Carroll. *The Dedalus Book of British Fantasy: The 19th Century* (Dedalus 416pp £8.99), ed. Brian Stableford, has several surprises including an absurdist (or just immature?) story not found in any of my twenty-odd Carroll books, which include two different 'Complete Works' volumes.

The 21 pieces here carry other familiar literary names – Coleridge, Keats, Dickens, Tennyson, Lear, Wilde, Christina Rossetti – and fantasy ditto: William Morris, George MacDonald, F. Anstey. All give good value. But some of the best items will be unfamiliar to most, like the story from Richard Garnett's splendidly satirical *Twilight of the Gods* collection, or Andrew Lang's moral fable about finding oneself in the wrong Paradise (like his token paleface retained in the Ojibway Happy Hunting Ground for regular scalping purposes).

This fine collection saves many good things from oblivion. It is conscientiously edited, with a sensible introduction and informative notes on every author present plus several more. Can we hope for companion volumes?

In brief ... Terry Pratchett's slim but appropriately priced *Eric* (VGSF 155pp £2.99) is a minor romp which to many fans feels somehow out of sequence in the increasingly elaborate and complex Discworld series. Probably because it was written specifically to be illustrated by Josh Kirby for 1990's lavish edition, and because Kirby took a long, long time to deliver. Without the central showpiece of this artwork it now looks undernourished, though there's still plenty to raise a smile.

Robert Thurston's *Way of the Clans* (Roc 284pp £3.99) is labelled as a **Battletech** novel. Thus it's built around the daft-sounding premise of gigantic battle machines on legs, which may produce a good game but doesn't convince as fiction. (Bits of the introduction read more like rehashed game rules than sf.) Wouldn't tracked vehicles be more stable? With the given space technology, wouldn't these monsters be instantly taken out from orbit? One can swallow a certain amount of implausibility, but not when combined with the ludicrous military posturing of the opening chapters. Unreadable.

L. Ron Hubbard ... oh goody, I've run out of space.

Written December 1991

Afterword

And there, at no particularly good stopping-place (is there ever one?), *GMI*'s parent company went bust and the magazine folded – before column 101 could appear, in fact. My pen halts, though I do not. Reader, you will walk no more with me. It is time we both take up our lives.

I confess that I've committed some recycling, eager to foist the better wise-cracks from these columns on to an sf fan audience which claimed never to buy *White Dwarf*. The *Critical Mass*-based item which has most haunted me in later years is the speech 'The Dragonhiker's Guide to Battlefield Covenant at Dune's Edge: Odyssey Two', delivered at the 1984 British Easter SF Convention and reprinted in all sorts of places since (including the UK men's magazine *Knave*). This is not to be confused with my identically named 1988 book of sf parodies.... The 1987 World SF Convention suffered my speech 'Trillion Year Sneer', similarly compiled from favourite bits of polemic and several times reprinted. Other sf talks drawing to some extent on *Critical Mass* and its successors were 'Fun with Senseless Violence' (Orycon 11: Portland, Oregon, 1989) and 'Tell Me the Old, Old Story' (Boskone 29: Springfield, Massachusetts, 1992). All these, plus much other stuff, are included in the New England SF Association Press's hefty 1996 collection of Langfordiana, *The Silence of the Langford*. Which cheered me up no end by first being shortlisted for the Best Nonfiction Hugo Award and then needing to be reprinted in 1997.

David Langford

Acknowledgements

My thanks to the successive *White Dwarf* editors Ian Livingstone, Jamie Thomson, Ian March, Paul Cockburn, Mike Brunton, Sean Masterson and Phil Gallagher, and *GM/GMI* editors Wayne Paul Boughton and Tim Metcalfe - for publishing the original columns, for leaving several sentences almost unaltered, and for censoring only the *really dirty* bits. Thanks to Bruce Gillespie for not only reprinting many columns in his *SF Commentary* but for giving the unnamed ones titles, several of these shamelessly pinched or adapted here. (Individual columns first appeared with titles in *White Dwarf* but not thereafter.) *The Complete Critical Assembly* is dedicated to all of them.

A tip of the hat to the great and erudite Patrick Nielsen Hayden, who said nice things about the first edition and pointed out a few errors which I couldn't blame as usual on *Dwarf* typesetting - how can I ever recover from the ignominy of misdating *The Shaving of Shagpat* in the original column 44?

All credit too to Christopher Priest, photocopier slave (and pointer-out of major flaws in the layout, some even corrected when I could face it) for both the original printed *Critical Assembly* volumes.

My fond memories of the deceased publishing companies Croftward Ltd of *GM* (liquidated 1990) and Newsfield Ltd of *GMI* (liquidated 1991) may be summed up in the simple, touching epitaph, 'The bastards still owe me money.'

Original appearances ... Columns 1 to 68 first appeared as monthly 'Critical Mass' review pages in *White Dwarf* magazine, issues 39 (March 1983) to 106 (October 1988). 'A Critical Alphabet', as noted in the text, was an extension of column 50. Columns 69 to 85 appeared as 'Critical Hits' in *GM* (*GamesMaster*) magazine, volume 1 issue 3 (November 1988) to volume 2 issue 7 (March 1990). Columns 86 to 100 appeared as 'Critical Mass' in *GMI* (*GamesMaster International*), issues 1 (August 1990) to 15 (October 1991). Column 101 appeared for the first time in *Critical Assembly II*.

Micro-Glossary

A few words on arcane games terms for those puzzled by this stuff: *Call of Cthulhu*, *Diplomacy*, *Dungeons and Dragons* (D&D), *Advanced Dungeons & Dragons* (AD&D), *Paranoia*, *Starweb*, *Traveller* and *Warhammer* all get a mention in these columns. Most are role-playing games (RPGs) played by 'gamers' (ugh) and run by a referee or 'game master' (GM). The game backgrounds vary: Lovecraftian (*Cthulhu*), fantasy (D&D, AD&D, *Warhammer*) or SF (*Paranoia*, *Starweb*, *Traveller*). Games Workshop (often abbreviated as GW), founded by awesome Ian Livingstone and Steve Jackson, flogs the things and produces *White Dwarf*. (Actually *Dwarf* no longer acknowledges the existence of any games but GW's own – *Warhammer* etc – which has made the magazine substantially more boring in later years.) A rival magazine *Imagine*™ (edited by Paul Cockburn) was run by the local division of the huge US games outfit TSR, but perished: its addiction to TM and ® marks was notorious. Lew Pulsipher, Marcus Rowland and Pete Tamlyn are or were at the time roving columnists, game designers and general Huge Name Pundits in this twilight world, while E. Gary Gygax apparently invented D&D in the first place – with, I gather, a little help from friends whose names later tended to be expunged from the histories. *Noughts and Crosses*™ is a registered trade mark of ... look, I can't keep this up any longer.

Index

Printed in the United Kingdom
by Lightning Source UK Ltd.
101802UKS00001B/194